Landscape and Settlement in the Vale of York

This project was funded by the University of York, as site developers, with additional funding provided by the Heritage Lottery Fund to facilitate community engagement with the work. The authors and publisher are grateful to the following organisations for their generous financial support.

The University of York
Heritage Lottery Fund

UNIVERSITY *of York*

HERITAGE FUND

Landscape and Settlement in the Vale of York

Archaeological investigations at Heslington East, York, 2003–13

Steve Roskams and Cath Neal

Research Report of the Society of Antiquaries of London No. 82

SOCIETY OF
ANTIQUARIES
OF LONDON

First published 2020 by
The Society of Antiquaries of London
Burlington House
Piccadilly
London W1J 0BE

www.sal.org.uk

ISBN: 978-0-85431-302-0

British Cataloguing in Publication Data
A CIP catalogue record for this book is available from the
British Library.

Project management: Lavinia Porter
Copy-editing: Mary Hobbins
Proofreading: Lavinia Porter
Index: Sue Vaughan
Original series design: Tracy Wellman and Sue Cawood
Design and layout: Sue Cawood
Printed and bound by Lavenham Press, Lavenham, Suffolk

Front cover figure: Base of good-quality stone kiln. © DoA

Back cover figure: Head pot fragment from ditch G12. © DoA

Contents

List of figures

List of tables

Preface

This publication considers the results of the complex, long-term fieldwork project at Heslington East. This site is situated in the Vale of York and on the fringes of York, a major historic town since its Roman foundation up to the present day (fig 0.1). The decision of the University of York to expand onto a new area of greenbelt adjacent to the original 1960s campus generated a need for archaeological evaluation work from 2003 to define a strategic response to such proposed development. The resulting fieldwork represents the largest exposure of prehistoric and Roman activity to be subjected to detailed archaeological investigation in the immediate hinterland of York. Running from 2007 to 2013, it used a combination of commercial organisations, student training and local community inputs to generate a wide range of assemblages and associated written, spatial and stratigraphic records. Post-excavation analysis of this material then generated the current publication.

The Heslington site is situated at the centre of The Vale of York, a low-lying zone running up the middle of Yorkshire that has both shaped, and been shaped by, communities living there since the end of the last Ice Age (fig 2.1). A glacial moraine bounds the site in the north and mobile groups passing along this 'hardstanding' across The Vale first utilised its landscape resources. Such interactions are certainly evident on the site from the Neolithic period, if not before, and took place on an increasingly regular basis into the Bronze Age. From c 800 BC, itinerant engagement gave way to more sedentary occupation involving the creation of landscape divisions. By the end of the Iron Age, this had culminated in the definition of recognisable field systems. These landholding systems were later transformed as a result of monumental reorganisation in the late Roman period, followed by traces of Anglo-Saxon activity. Various forms of medieval and modern agricultural land use mark the end of the sequence of occupation here.

Throughout all periods, diverse types of activity were

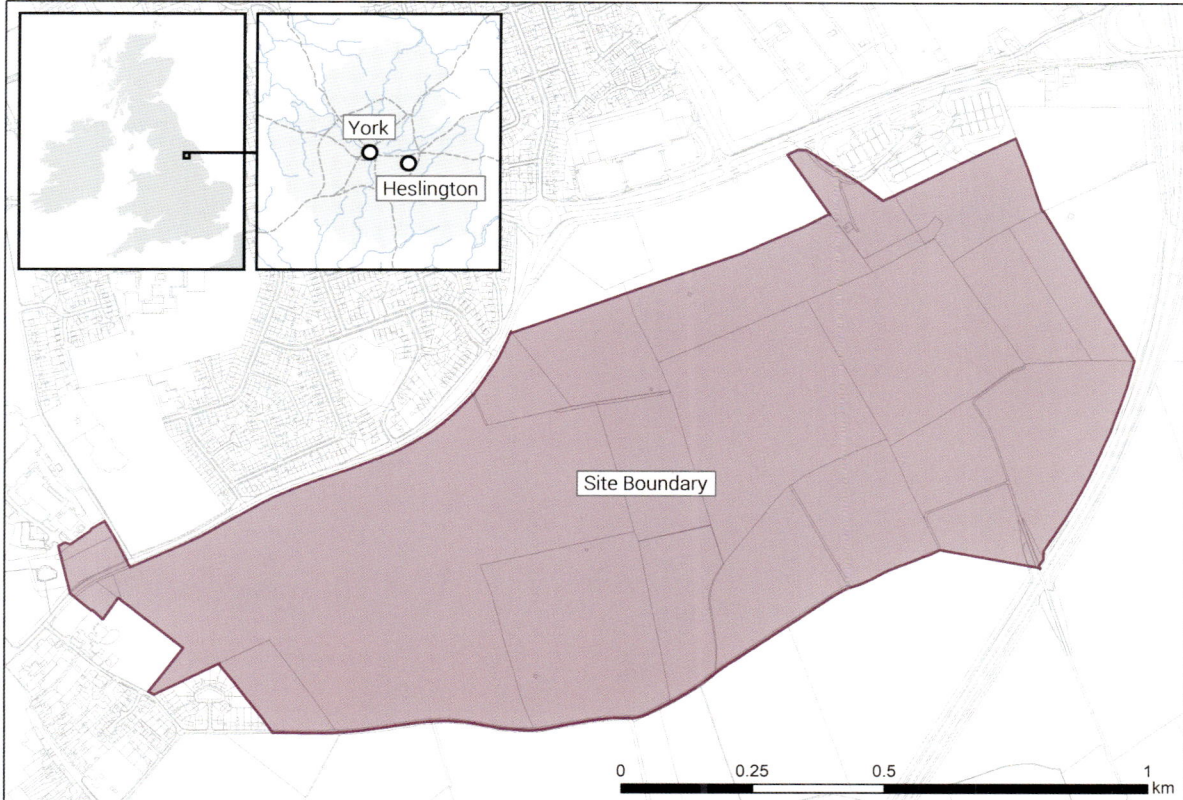

Fig 0.1 Site location plan. *Drawing*: Helen Goodchild (contains OS MasterMap® Topography Layer [FileGeoDatabase geospatial data], Scale 1:1250, Tiles: GB, Updated: 1 November 2017, Ordnance Survey (GB), Using: EDINA Digimap Ordnance Survey Service, <http://digimap.edina.ac.uk>, Downloaded: 2018-05-29 11:49:34.438)

evident in this landscape, taking significantly different forms at different points. Many such processes of development crossed conventional period boundaries. For this reason, rather than discuss each facet within a simple chronological framework, this account adopts a thematic approach to describe evidence for matters such as managing water, growing crops, building structures or acting out rituals. Thus, whilst Chapter 1 evaluates the process of site evaluation, both as a methodological reflection and to flag up the limitations and potentials of the evidence recovered here, subsequent chapters consider landscape resources (Chapter 2), boundaries (Chapter 3), food production (Chapter 4) and manufacture (Chapter 5). We then turn to structures and household activities (Chapter 6), before considering consumption practices (Chapter 7) and ideological facets such as human burial, monumentality and other specialised deposition (Chapter 8). This specific order of presentation is based on the materialist principle that we must first understand the fundamental relationships between people and their immediate environment and its resources (Chapters 2–5), before we can explore domestic organisation, trade and exchange, or ritual activities (Chapters 6–8).

Finally, as noted above, we recognise that pivotal landscape changes here do not fit easily into the period-based divisions commonly used to describe prehistoric, Roman, medieval and modern developments; yet we still acknowledge that a sequence of development is evident at the Heslington site. Thus, within each landscape theme there is an element of chronological presentation. Further, our concluding Chapter 9 is structured in relation to what we see as key points of transition in landscape activity here: from mobility and sedentism (section 9.1); between the Iron Age and Roman periods (section 9.2: in our case, a 'non-transition'); within the Roman period (section 9.3); between the late Roman and the sub-Roman/Anglian periods (section 9.4); and between the medieval and modern periods (section 9.5). Our justification for this atypical approach is that, if newly emerging evidence is always described in terms of pre-existing frameworks, it may seem to give them support that they do not really deserve. In contrast, we believe that the role of any new site should be to question and sometimes pull apart the categories used by archaeologists to divide up the past that we study. In this way, new sets of data will either be shown to reinforce existing frameworks or, where they do not, will facilitate the emergence of more convincing alternatives.

Steve Roskams
Cath Neal

Acknowledgements

A project of this scale and time length has necessarily employed numerous people from several organisations. The University of York, as developer, resourced the main fieldwork under the direction of Jon Meacock, initially as Heslington East Project Director, latterly as Head of Estates Development. He benefited from archaeological advice initially from archaeological consultant Dr Dominic Perring (who produced an initial desktop study in 1999) and latterly, for the majority of the project, from Dr Patrick Ottaway. Claire McNamara ably dealt with financial administration within the Department of Archaeology.

Initial reconnaissance and evaluation work was undertaken by the York Archaeological Trust, various elements being reported on by Dave Evans (desktop study); Martin Bartlett and Mark Noel (geophysics); Toby Kendal and Isobel Mason (fieldwalking); Isobel Mason, Jane McComish and Neil McNab (trial trenching); Mark Johnson (site evaluation); and Bryan Antoni, Dave Evans, Jane McComish and Sarah Whittaker (various watching briefs in the vicinity of the site).

The main excavations undertaken by the York Archaeological Trust were overseen by Bryan Antoni, Mark Johnson and Jane McComish. Corresponding work by On-Site Archaeology was directed by Graham Bruce. Finally, excavations by the Department of Archaeology, prefaced with geophysical survey directed by Steve Dobson and Ben Gourley and fieldwalking overseen by Cath Neal, led to the excavation directed by the current authors, during which York and District Metal Detecting Club helped with the recovery of metal finds from spoil heaps and excavated areas. Cath Neal also organised the community work and negotiated support for it from the Heritage Lottery Fund, with booklet and site information board outputs facilitated by Gavin Ward (design) and Eva Fairnell (copy editing).

Work on assemblages involved a variety of specialists, as follows:

- Post-excavation assessment of assemblages and conservation: Mags Felter (conservation), Allan Hall and Harry Kenward (environmental samples) and Nicky Rodgers (finds assemblages of York Archaeological Trust).
- Prehistoric material: Anne Bird (axe thin-sectioning), Chantal Conneller (Mesolithic flint), Peter Didsbury (pottery), Don Henson (synthesis of flint evidence), Gareth Perry (pottery fabric characterisation), Peter Makey (flint) and Terry Manby (Bronze Age burial and axe).
- Roman material: Steve Allen (wooden items), Craig Barclay (coins), Hilary Cool (non-ceramic finds), David Griffiths (oil lamp), Kay Hartley (mortaria), Nick Hodgson (stonework), Ruth Leary (pottery), Jane McComish (ceramic building materials), Gladys Monteil (samian ware), Jenny Price (glass), Ian Tyers (dendrochronology) and David Williams (amphorae).
- Miscellaneous/multi-period studies: Chris Carey (geoarchaeological analysis), John Cruse and Dave Heslop (quern stones), Rachel Cubitt (hammerscale identification), Malin Holst and Anne Fotaki (human osteology), Ailsa Mainman (Anglian pottery), Cath Mortimer (lead), Sonia O'Connor (human brain, assisted by the wide range of specialists listed in O'Connor et al 2011), Stuart Ogilvy (geological samples), Jane Richardson (animal bones) and Ellie Simmons and Kim Vickers (environmental samples).

Helen Goodchild was essential in facilitating the storage and analysis of spatial data from the site. She was also responsible for the plans and maps used in this report, alongside tables and charts prepared by Neil Gevaux.

The above list ignores the myriad individuals whose combination of physical and mental labour in the field and in post-excavation processing was a vital prerequisite in generating the site data and assemblages that those listed above then subjected to analysis and interpretation. These fieldworkers deserve the main credit for the success of the project.

Finally, a note on division of responsibilities and authorship between Cath Neal (CN) and Steve Roskams (SR). The original idea to combine commercial excavation with community work and student training at the site came from SR, who then negotiated the process. SR subsequently oversaw the main fieldwork phase, alongside detailed direction by CN, who also ran the community project. SR undertook stratigraphic analysis of the Department's work and correlated that sequence with those generated by On-Site Archaeology and the York Archaeological Trust. CN assessed the

Department's assemblages and organised the resulting specialist work, as well as checking, then synthesising, their outputs. Both SR and CN were pivotal to planning the form and content of this publication and, although it is in the words of one (SR, who therefore takes responsibility for the final interpretations it reaches), its production is a result of SR and CN's integrated efforts. Indeed, but for the vagaries of university employment contracts, CN would have written a significant proportion of these chapters.

Summary

This volume describes the results of a long-term rescue project in the Vale of York, North Yorkshire, which took place ahead of university expansion at Heslington East, in the south-eastern part of the city of York. The project constitutes the largest exposure of prehistoric and Roman activity investigated archaeologically in York's immediate hinterland. By combining work of commercial organisations, student training and local community volunteers, we illustrate the complex development of landscape here from at least the Neolithic period, but most intensively in Iron Age, Roman and modern periods. This development is discussed using a series of types of human engagement, rather than via a period-based format.

The methods employed here, derived from the thrust of PPG16, demonstrate the advantages of the process of site reconnaissance and evaluation, deposit modelling and data gathering, then assemblage assessment and analysis. Yet they also expose the iterative nature of post-excavation analyses in MoRPHE-compliant contexts and the need to confront challenges concerning archiving and publication, notably the notion of a 'final' report.

Landscape resources were influenced by the site's geological setting, situated just downslope of the York moraine. This setting shaped site formation processes on the hillside and the timber and stone sources available for human exploitation. Access to water, however, had by far the greatest impact on the location and character of such activities, with a variety of wells being dug into the springline along the hillside.

Boundaries to control animal, and later human, movement were established here as mobile communities gave way to greater sedentism. In the west, these initially comprised an isolated funnel channelling livestock but, by the end of the Iron Age, formal droveways integrated with adjacent fields and water sources had been set out, whilst further east, individual enclosures containing roundhouses were established along the springline. These arrangements remained in place into the second century AD, i.e. well within the 'Roman' period. By the third century, however, the focus of activity had moved over 500m to the east, where a new road was laid out along the springline. Successive large enclosures to its north related initially to livestock management, but then gave way to a ritual enclosure in the fourth century AD. At the tail end of the latter century, the northern site margins were re-organised by local terracing, before the whole of this landscape fell under the plough in the medieval and modern periods.

Food production at Heslington was, from the start, part of a mixed farming economy. Pastoral elements, as noted, concerned the watering and movement of stock, faunal evidence suggesting that domestic fowl, goat and wild resources were always of marginal relevance here from the Iron Age onwards. The common domesticates demonstrate a clear shift from sheep to cattle in the Roman period. Yet the gene-pool of these animals expanded only from the third century AD, whilst animal stature remained unchanged, and the vast majority of stock was culled only after surplus to traction, manuring and other requirements of the rural economy. Thus, if Roman central authority was trying to impose its will on these producers, that process was long delayed and then only partially successful. Evidence for cropping regimes suggest a similar story, with a gradual change from hulled barley to greater proportions of oats and various types of wheat. The Roman period saw a particular emphasis on bread wheat, a winter hardy crop producing higher yields, yet more vulnerable to pests and disease and needing greater soil fertility. The extra investment implied by this change is perhaps reflected in evidence for crop drying and mechanical milling here in the late Roman period.

Manufacturing is suggested circumstantially from the Neolithic period onwards, in the form of finishing flint roughouts from sources on Yorkshire's east coast, and perhaps from charcoal-rich fills containing a profusion of burnt pebbles from early Iron Age pits. More direct evidence comes from later Iron Age horizons, with indications of iron smithing, and perhaps smelting, on some scale, the latter presumably utilising local iron pans. These strata also indicated the processing of jet, copper and perhaps silver in carefully enclosed spatial contexts. Very early in the Roman period, a dedicated industrial zone was inserted just north of the easternmost well, adjacent to a roundhouse alongside a rectangular, sunken building. Finally, unconnected with any of the above, the newly created terraced area on the northern extremities of the site (above) saw intensive production of iron and other manufacturing activities at the very end of the Roman period in the form of a stone kiln alongside hearths and working hollows.

Concerning *domestic structures*, flint processing (above) might suggest Neolithic household activities, whilst the increased incidence of worked wood and nails from the start of the Iron Age could derive from buildings. But structures are provably present here only towards the end of the first millennium BC, when a considerable number of roundhouses, ranging in size from 3.5m–10m, were inserted into this landscape. The larger, earlier houses were set up in dedicated enclosures, probably for purely domestic use, and this continued to be the case into later decades towards the centre of the site. Smaller structures in the west, however, suggest a range of other uses later on, including the metal production/working and the manufacture of jet noted previously. Many of these activities continued into the formal Roman period, in the course of which more monumental structures are suggested hereabouts by the recycling of worked stone in well linings, including blocks indicating the use of the *opus quadratum* construction technique and a roof finial. It is only in the fourth century AD, however, that two definite buildings were identified on the northern margins of the site. The first comprised a rectangular, timber-framed building, with stone tile roof, set on rough masonry foundations. The second, laid out above the first but after a gap in time, was constructed of posts inserted above clay and cobble pads. Its use may take us into the fifth century AD.

Consumption practices are at their clearest in the period *c* 200 BC to *c* 450 AD, but those occupying this landscape had drawn on widespread sources from an early date, notably in their use of flint but also in stone for grinding corn and, latterly, in ceramics. Pottery, first used in Bronze Age cremations, turned towards domestic usages in the course of the Iron Age, almost entirely in the form of storage jars. When Rome moved up to the Humber estuary, these communities were able to obtain pots that, although made locally, incorporated Roman techniques. After formal conquest, tablewares imported from outside Britain were quickly evident, replaced in the course of the second century AD by vessels made in York. Food preparation took a little longer to change than its serving, mortaria only being evident in significant numbers later in the second century. Most of this early Roman material seems likely to have arrived via York but, from the third century onwards, supply mechanisms seem to be orientated increasingly on diverse regional and local sources. This was followed by a move back to a jar emphasis before the end of the fourth century, by which point ceramic functional signatures closely resembled their Iron Age counterparts.

Ideological practices (in particular, human burial – but also monumental building and structured deposition) seem to have played a significant role in the Heslington landscape from the outset. Thus, particular items were placed in Neolithic pits to create 'ancestral geographies' and barrows were inserted beside the moraine on the northern margins of the site in the Bronze Age to mark the passage of mobile communities along that route. By the end of the latter period, however, cremations were being used to make more local landscape claims and, by the middle of the Iron Age, formal boundaries began to appear in this landscape, a decapitation being placed in an early ditch terminal to reinforce that feature's significance. When the western part of this landscape was abandoned, this zone saw the insertion of a Roman cremation, together with closure deposits in its main well: this form of landscape organisation was gone but not forgotten. As settlement shifted to the centre of the Heslington landscape in the third century AD, and new enclosures were created to demarcate agricultural functions, neonatal burials were carefully placed at the margins of these activities. Later, when landholdings expanded across this zone, adult inhumations were used to reinforce the sanctity of the new boundaries, a role that they seem to have enjoyed for an extended period of time. In the fourth century, a new enclosure was set up here on an extensive terrace. Access into this zone from east was controlled by a gateway, that to its west by a masonry tower and two associated burials, their heads seemingly nailed in place. Within the area thus defined, a prestigious, hypocausted building was inserted, accompanied by carefully placed pots in the south and, to its west, the crouched burial of a disabled man. Finally, a substantial masonry well later dug north of this ritual zone was itself closed using a combination of young and old, wild and tame, animals.

In sum, the transition from mobility to sedentism involved a move from activities marking re-visitation in the Neolithic and nearby movement in the Bronze Age, to making more local landscape claims towards the end of the latter period and the development of field systems and settlements by the end of the Iron Age. The latter households, involved with both the rural economy and prestigious artefact production, continued vibrantly into the formal Roman period, although now able to access ceramic imports via York. Later, however, settlement shifted eastwards to the centre of this landscape and agricultural production intensified. This may have included supplying demands from beyond the immediate landscape, though did not seem to involve expanding the productive base of that economy, whilst ceramic consumption now increasingly by-passed York. Before the end of the fourth century AD, a 'ritual enclosure' with associated monumental buildings was inserted here. In later decades, a timber-framed building, masonry well, and evidence for manufacturing on the northern margins of the site suggest vibrant activity in this zone into the fifth century AD, yet evidence for social tensions beyond. These activities were eventually covered by naturally formed hillside deposits, before ploughing of medieval and modern date occurred. The character and spatial organisation of the university buildings which now occupy the Heslington East site express the marketised nature of higher education today, in marked contrast to their counterparts established in the 1960s to the west.

Steve Roskams
Cath Neal

Résumé

Ce volume décrit les résultats d'un long projet de secours qui a eu lieu dans la vallée de York, North Yorkshire, juste avant un agrandissement d'une université située à Heslington East, au sud-est de la ville de York. Ce projet constitue la plus grande exposition d'activité préhistorique et romaine, examiné d'une façon archéologique, dans l'arrière-pays immédiat de York. En unifiant le travail des organisations commerciales, des étudiants en formation, et des bénévoles de la communauté locale, on illustre le développement complexe de ce paysage, au moins depuis la période néolithique, mais surtout de l'âge de fer, la période romaine et moderne. Ce développement est décrit par rapport à une série de genres d'engagement humain, plutôt qu'un format chronologique.

Les méthodes utilisées ici, dérivées des idées de PPG16 (Planning and Policy Guide 16) (guide de planification et politique 16), démontrent les avantages du processus de l'étude de terrain et de son évaluation, le modèle de gisement et la collection des données, puis l'évaluation et l'analyse de l'assemblage. Pourtant, elles exposent aussi le genre itératif de ces analyses d'après-excavation dans le contexte conforme à MoRPHE (Management of Research Projects in the Historic Environment) (gestion de projets de recherches dans l'environnement historique) et le besoin de confronter les défis concernant l'archivage et la publication, notamment le concept d'un rapport "définitif".

Les ressources du paysage furent influencées par la situation géologique du site, qui était situé juste en dessous de la moraine de York. Cet environnement a façonné les processus de la formation du site sur le flanc de coteau, ainsi que le bois et les pierres disponibles à l'exploitation humaine. Cependant, l'accès à l'eau eut de loin l'impact le plus important sur l'emplacement et la nature de ces activités, avec une variété de puits creusés sur la ligne de sources le long du flanc de coteau.

Des limites pour contrôler le mouvement des animaux, et, plus tard, ceux des humains, furent établies ici, à mesure que les communautés itinérantes cédaient la place à une plus grande sédentarité. À l'ouest, ceux-ci se composèrent initialement d'un entonnoir isolé canalisant le bétail, mais, à la fin de l'âge du fer, des chemins formels intégrés aux champs adjacents et aux sources d'eau furent établis, tandis que plus à l'est, des enclos individuels contenant des rotondes étaient établis le long de la ligne de sources. Ces dispositions restèrent en place au deuxième siècle après JC, c'est-à-dire effectivement au cours de la période "romaine". Cependant, au troisième siècle le centre d'activité s'était déplacé de plus de 500 mètres vers l'est, où une nouvelle route fut tracée le long de la ligne de sources. Les grandes enceintes successives au nord furent initialement liées à la gestion du bétail, mais ont ensuite cédé la place à une enceinte rituelle au quatrième siècle après JC. À la fin du siècle, les marges du site nord furent réorganisées par des terrasses locales, avant que l'ensemble de ce paysage ne tombe sous la charrue à l'époque médiévale et moderne.

La production alimentaire à Heslington fut partie, dès le début, d'une économie agricole mixte. Les éléments pastoraux, comme indiqué, se concernaient à faire boire et à déplacer le troupeau, des preuves fauniques suggérant que la volaille domestique, la chèvre, et les ressources sauvages étaient toujours d'une pertinence marginale ici à partir de l'âge du fer. Les domestiques communs démontrent une transition claire des moutons aux bovins à l'époque romaine. Pourtant le patrimoine génétique de ces animaux ne fut élargi qu'à partir du troisième siècle après JC, tandis que la stature animale restait inchangée, et la grande majorité du troupeau était abattu qu'après excédant à la traction, au fumier et d'autres besoins de l'économie rurale. Par conséquent, si l'autorité centrale romaine tentait d'imposer sa volonté à ces producteurs, ce processus fut retardé à longue durée, et n'avait ensuite qu'une réussite partielle. Des données disponibles sur les régimes de culture suggérèrent la même histoire, avec une transition progressive de l'orge décortiquée à de plus grandes proportions d'avoine et de variétés de blé divers.

La période romaine a mis un accent particulier sur le blé tendre, une culture résistante au froid produisant des rendements plus élevées, pourtant plus vulnérable aux ravageurs et aux maladies et nécessitant une plus grande fertilité de la terre. L'investissement supplémentaire impliqué par ce changement se reflète peut-être dans les preuves du séchage des cultures et du broyage mécanique ici à la fin de la période romaine.

L'industrie est suggérée de manière indirecte à partir de la période néolithique, en forme de l'achèvement de bifaces de silex sortant des lieux sur la côte est de Yorkshire, et peut-être des remplissages riches en charbon de bois contenant une profusion de cailloux brûlés datant des premières fosses de l'âge du fer. Des preuves plus concrètes provinrent d'horizons ultérieurs de l'âge de fer, avec des indications de forge et, peut-être de fusion de fer, à un certain niveau, ce dernier en utilisant probablement des plats en fer locaux. Ces strates indiquaient également le traitement du jais, du cuivre et peut-être de l'argent dans des contextes spatiaux soigneusement clos. Très tôt dans la période romaine, une zone industrielle dédiée fut introduite un peu au nord du puit situé le plus à l'est, adjacent à une rotonde à côté d'un édifice rectangulaire et enfoncé dans le sol. Enfin, sans aucun lien avec ce qui précède, la zone en terrasses récemment créé sur les extrémités nord du site (ci-dessus) a connu une production intensive de fer et d'autres activités de fabrication à la toute fin de la période romaine, en forme d'un four à pierre à côté des foyers et des creux de travail.

En ce qui concerne les *structures domestiques*, le traitement de silex (ci-dessus), pourrait suggérer des activités ménagères néolithiques, tandis que l'augmentation de l'incidence du bois travaillé et des clous, dès le début de l'âge de fer, pourrait provenir des bâtiments. Mais les structures sont ici présentes de manière prouvée uniquement vers la fin du premier millénaire avant JC, lorsqu'un nombre considérable de rotondes, d'une taille entre 3,5 et 10 mètres furent insérées dans ce paysage. Les maisons plus grandes et plus anciennes furent bâties à l'intérieur des enceintes dédiées, probablement pour un usage uniquement domestique, et cela se perpétua dans les décennies suivantes vers le centre du site. Cependant, des édifices plus petits à l'ouest suggèrent une variété d'autre fonctions plus tard, y compris la production/le travail des métaux, et la fabrication de jais, noté ci-dessus. Beaucoup de ces activités continuèrent dans la période romaine formelle, au cours de laquelle des structures plus monumentales sont suggérées aux environs par le recyclage de la pierre travaillée dans les revêtements des puits y compris des blocs indiquant l'utilisation de la technique de construction de l'*opus quadratum* et un fleuron de toit.

Pourtant, ce n'est qu'à partir du quatrième siècle après JC que deux édifices définis furent identifiés sur les marges nord du site. Le premier comprenait un bâtiment rectangulaire à pans de bois avec un toit en tuiles de pierre, posé sur des fondations de maçonnerie grossières. Le deuxième, disposé au-dessus du premier, mais après un intervalle de temps, fut construit de poteaux insérés sur de supports d'argile et de pavés. Son utilisation pourrait nous amener au cinquième siècle après JC.

Les pratiques de consommation furent les plus clair au cours de la période d'environ 200 avant JC à 400 après JC, pourtant ceux qui occupèrent ce paysage avaient puisé depuis longtemps des sources répandues, notamment dans leur utilisation de silex, mais aussi de la pierre pour moudre le maïs, et plus tard de la céramique. La céramique, d'abord utilisée dans les crémations de l'âge de bronze, se tourna vers des usages domestiques au cours de l'âge de fer, presque entièrement sous forme de pots de stockage. Lorsque Rome se déplaça vers l'estuaire de Humber, ces communautés avaient pu obtenir des pots incorporant des techniques de fabrication romaines, bien qu'ils fussent fabriqués localement. Après la conquête officielle, la vaisselle importée de l'extérieur de la Grande-Bretagne apparut rapidement, remplacé au cours du deuxième siècle après JC par des récipients fabriqués à York. La préparation des aliments prit un peu plus de temps à changer que son service, *mortaria* n'étant qu'en évidence en quantités importantes plus tard durant le deuxième siècle. La plupart de ces premiers matériaux romains semblent probablement être arrivés via York, pourtant, mais à partir du troisième siècle, les mécanismes d'approvisionnement semblent être de plus en plus orientés vers des sources régionales et locales. Cela fut suivi d'un retour à un accent sur les pots avant la fin du quatrième siècle, par lequel les signatures fonctionnelles de la céramique ressemblaient étroitement à leurs homologues de l'âge du fer.

Les pratiques idéologiques (en particulier, l'enterrement des humains – mais aussi la construction monumentale et les 'dépôts structurés') semblent avoir joué un rôle important dans le paysage de Heslington dès le début. Par conséquent, des objets spécifiques furent placés dans les fosses néolithiques afin de créer des 'géographies ancestrales' et des tumulus furent insérée à côté de la moraine sur les marges nord du site a l'âge de bronze pour marquer le passage des communautés itinérantes le long de cette route. Cependant, à la fin de cette dernière période, les crémations furent utilisées pour faire des revendications paysagères plus locales et, au milieu de l'âge du fer, des limites formelles ont commencé à apparaître dans ce paysage, une décapitation étant placée dans un premier terminal de fossé pour renforcer l'importance de cette caractéristique. Lorsque la partie ouest de ce paysage fut abandonnée, cette zone a vu l'insertion d'une crémation romaine, ainsi que des dépôts de fermeture dans son puit principal : cette forme d'organisation paysagère avait disparu mais pas oubliée. Pendant que la colonisation se déplaçait au centre du paysage de Heslington durant le troisième siècle après JC, et de nouvelles enceintes furent créées pour délimiter les fonctions agricoles, des sépultures néonatale furent placées soigneusement aux marges de ces activités. Plus tard, lorsque les propriétés terriennes se sont étendues à travers cette zone, des inhumations d'adultes étaient utilisées pour renforcer le caractère sacré de ces nouvelles enceintes, un rôle qu'ils semblent avoir joué durant une période étendue. Au quatrième siècle, une nouvelle enceinte fut établie ici sur une vaste terrasse. L'accès à cette zone par l'est fut contrôlée par une entrée, celle à l'ouest par une tour en maçonnerie et deux sépultures associées, leurs têtes apparemment clouées en place. A l'intérieur de la zone ainsi définie, un bâtiment prestigieux avec hypocauste fut inséré, accompagné de pots soigneusement placés au sud, et, à l'ouest, l'enterrement d'un homme handicapé accroupi. Finalement, un puit important en maçonnerie creusée plus tard au nord de cette zone rituelle fut fermé en utilisant un mélange d'animaux jeunes et vieux, sauvages et apprivoisés.

En résumé, la transition d'une vie itinérante au sédentarisme a impliqué un passage des activités marquant l'acte de revisiter dans la période néolithique et du mouvement voisin dans l'âge du bronze, à des revendications paysagères plus locales vers la fin de cette dernière période et le développement de parcellaires et de colonies à la fin de l'âge de fer. Ces derniers foyers,

impliquaient ainsi dans l'économie rurale et la fabrication des objets anciens prestigieux, continuèrent avec dynamisme jusqu'à la période romaine officielle, bien que ils soient désormais en mesure d'accéder aux importations de céramique via York. Ultérieurement, pourtant, la colonisation se déplaça vers l'est, et donc plus au centre de ce paysage, et la production agricole s'est intensifiée. Cela aurait pu incorporer la fourniture de demandes au-delà du paysage immédiat, bien que ceci n'ait pas impliqué un agrandissement de la base de production de cette économie, et tandis que la consommation de céramique contourna de plus en plus York. Avant la fin du quatrième siècle après JC, une 'enceinte rituelle' avec des bâtiments monumentaux associés, fut insérée ici. Au cours des décennies suivantes, un bâtiment à pans de bois, un puit de maçonnerie et les preuves de la production sur les marges nord du site suggèrent de l'activité dynamique dans cette zone jusqu'au cinquième siècle après JC, bien qu'il existe des preuves de tensions sociales au-delà de cette période. Toutes ces activités furent éventuellement recouvertes par des dépôts à flanc de colline formés naturellement, avant le labour de l'époque médiévale et moderne. Le caractère et l'organisation spatiale des bâtiments universitaires qui occupent désormais le site de Heslington East expriment aujourd'hui la nature commercialisée de l'enseignement supérieur, contrairement à leurs homologues établis dans les années 1960 à l'ouest.

Steve Roskams
Cath Neal

Translation par Bianca Knights

Zusammenfassung

Dieser Band beschreibt die Ergebnisse eines langfristigen Rettungsprojekts im Vale of York, Grafschaft North Yorkshire, das vor der Erweiterung der Universität in Heslington East im Südosten der Stadt York stattfand. Bei dem Projekt handelt es sich um die größte Freilegung prähistorischer und römischer Aktivitäten, die bislang im unmittelbaren Hinterland von York archäologisch unter- sucht wurden. Durch die Kombination der Arbeitsergebnisse kommerzieller Organisationen, der Ausbildung von Studenten und Freiwilligen aus den umliegenden Gemeinden können wir die komplexe

Entwicklung der Landschaft vor Ort zumindest seit der Jungsteinzeit, am intensivsten jedoch in der Vorrömischen Eisenzeit, der Römischen Kaiserzeit und der Neuzeit auf- zeigen. Anstelle einer Zeitperioden-basierten Gliederung wird diese Entwicklung anhand einer Reihe von Kategorien menschlicher Tätigkeiten diskutiert.

Die hier angewandten *Methoden*, die sich aus der Stoßrichtung der PPG16 (Ausführungsanweisung zur Planungsrichtlinie 16) ableiten, zeigen die Vorteile des Prozesses der Fundorterkundung und -bewertung, der Boden- und Reliefmodellierung und der Datenerfassung sowie der anschließenden Auswertung und Analyse des Fundmaterials. Sie verdeutlichen aber auch den iterativen Charakter der Grabungsauswertung in MoRPHE (Management von Denkmalschutzprojekten)-konformen Zusammenhängen und die Notwendigkeit, sich den Herausforderungen bezüglich der Archivierung und Veröffentlichung zu stellen, insbesondere dem Konzept eines „Abschlussberichts".

Die *landschaftlichen Ressourcen* wurden durch die geologischen Gegebenheiten des Standorts beeinflusst, der sich in unmittelbarer Nähe hangabwärts der Yorker Moräne befindet. Diese Umgebung prägte die Entstehungsprozesse am Hang sowie die Rohstoffquellen für Holz und Stein, die für die menschliche Nutzung zur Verfügung standen. Der Zugang zu Wasser hatte jedoch bei Weitem den größten Einfluss auf die Lage und den Charakter solcher Aktivitäten, wobei eine Vielzahl von Brunnen in den Quellbereich entlang des Hangs abgeteuft wurden.

Einfriedungen zur Kontrolle der Bewegung von Tieren, und später auch von Menschen, wurden hier errichtet, als mobile Gemeinschaften einer größeren Sesshaftigkeit Platz machten. Im Westen bestanden diese zunächst aus einem einzelnen Trichterpferch, der das Vieh kanalisierte, aber zum Ende der Vorrömischen Eisenzeit wurden dezidierte Viehtriebpfade angelegt, die in das System der angrenzenden Felder und Wasserquellen integriert waren, während weiter östlich entlang der Quelllinie einzelne Einfriedungen mit Rundhäusern errichtet wurden. Diese Anlagen blieben bis ins 2. Jahrhundert n. Chr., d. h. bis weit in die „römische" Zeit hinein, bestehen. Im 3. Jahrhundert verlagerte sich der Schwerpunkt der Aktivitäten jedoch um mehr als 500m nach Osten, wo eine neue Straße entlang der Quelllinie angelegt wurde. Die aufeinander folgenden großen Gehege im Norden dienten zunächst der Viehzucht, wurden dann aber im 4. Jahrhundert durch eine Einfriedung mit rituellem Charakter ersetzt. Ganz am Ende dieses Jahrhunderts wurden die nördlichen Randbereiche des Areals durch Terrassierung neu geordnet, bevor die gesamte Landschaft im Mittelalter und in der Neuzeit unter den Pflug fiel.

Die *Nahrungsmittelproduktion* in Heslington war von Anfang an Teil einer gemischten Agrarwirtschaft. Pastorale Elemente betrafen, wie erwähnt, die Bewässerung und die Bewegung des Viehs, wobei die Auswertung der Tierknochenfunde darauf hindeutet, dass Hausgeflügel, Ziegen und Wildressourcen hier seit der Vorrömischen Eisenzeit immer nur marginale Bedeutung zukam. Im üblichen domestizierten Viehbestand zeigt sich während der Römischen Kaiserzeit eine klare Verlagerung von Schafen zu Rindern. Allerdings erwei-

terte sich der Genpool dieser Tiere erst ab dem 3. Jahrhundert n. Chr., während die Tiergröße unverändert blieb und der Großteil der Bestände erst gekeult wurde nach dem der Bedarf an Zugtieren, Düngung und anderen Erfordernissen der ländlichen Wirtschaft gedeckt war. Wenn also die römische Zentralverwaltung versuchte, diesen Erzeugern ihren Willen aufzuzwingen, so fand dieser Prozess nur nach langer Verzögerung statt und war auch dann nur teilweise erfolgreich. Die Belege für die Ackerbaupraktiken legen einen ähnlichen Ablauf nahe, mit einem allmählichen Wechsel von Spelzgerste zu größeren Anteilen von Hafer und verschiedenen Weizensorten. In der Römischen Kaiserzeit lag ein besonderer Schwerpunkt auf Brotweizen, einer winterharten Kulturpflanze, die höhere Erträge liefert, jedoch anfälliger für Schädlinge und Krankheiten war und einer größeren Bodenfruchtbarkeit bedurfte. Die zusätzlichen Investitionen, die diese Veränderung mit sich brachte, spiegeln sich hier vielleicht in den Hinweisen auf Getreidetrocknung und eine Mechanisierung des Mahlvorgangs in der spätrömischen Periode wider.

Hinweise auf *handwerkliche Tätigkeiten* lassen sich seit der Jungsteinzeit nachweisen, und zwar in Form der Fertigstellung von Feuerstein-Planken aus Quellen an der Ostküste von Yorkshire sowie möglicherweise auch anhand von holzekohlereichen Verfüllungen früheisenzeitlicher Gruben, die große Mengen verbrannter Kiesel enthielten. Unmittelbarere Belege stammen aus Fundhorizonten der späteren Vorrömischen Eisenzeit, u. a. durch Hinweise auf Eisenschmieden und vielleicht auf Verhüttung in gewissem Umfang, wobei für Letztere als Rohmaterial vermutlich lokale Eisenpfannen verwendet wurden. Diese Schichten deuteten auch auf die Verarbeitung von Gagat, Kupfer und vielleicht Silber in sorgfältig begrenzten räumlichen Befunden hin. Sehr früh in der Römischen Kaiserzeit wurde nördlich des östlichsten Brunnens eine dedizierte Industriezone eingerichtet, die an ein Rundhaus neben einem rechteckigen Grubenhaus angrenzt. Ohne mit den oben genannten Bereichen in Verbindung zu stehen, wurde schließlich ganz am Ende der Römischen Kaiserzeit in dem neu geschaffenen, terrassenförmig angelegten Bereich an der nördlichen Randzone des Geländes (siehe oben) intensiv Eisen produziert und andere handwerkliche Aktivitäten durchgeführt, was sich anhand eines Steinofens sowie von Herden und Werkgruben belegen lässt.

Mit Hinblick auf *häusliche Strukturen* könnte die Verarbeitung von Feuerstein (siehe oben) auf neolithisches Hauswerk hindeuten, während das vermehrte Auftreten von bearbeitetem Holz und Nägeln seit Beginn der Vorrömischen Eisenzeit von Gebäuden stammen könnte. Bauliche Strukturen sind hier nachweislich aber erst gegen Ende des 1. Jahrtausends v. Chr. vorhanden, als eine beträchtliche Anzahl von Rundhäusern mit Durchmessern von 3,5 m bis 10 m in dieser Landschaft errichtet wurden. Die größeren, früheren Häuser wurden in eigens dafür bestimmten Einfriedungen erbaut, wahrscheinlich für rein häuslichen Gebrauch, und dies war in Richtung des Fundplatz-Zentrums auch in späteren Jahrzehnten der Fall. Kleinere Strukturen im Westen lassen für einen späteren Zeitraum jedoch auf eine Reihe anderer Nutzungen schließen, darunter die zuvor erwähnte Metallproduktion/-verarbeitung und die Verarbeitung von Gagat. Viele dieser Aktivitäten wurden bis in die Römische Kaiserzeit fortgeführt, in deren Verlauf das Vorhandensein monumentalerer Strukturen durch wiederverwendete, bearbeitete Steine in Brunnenauskleidungen angedeutet wird; so fanden sich u. a. Blöcke, die die Nutzung der *opus-quadratum*-Bauweise andeuten, sowie ein Giebelzier-Ziegel. Erst für das 4. Jahrhundert n. Chr. lassen sich jedoch zwei definitive Gebäude im nördlichen Randbereich des Fundplatzes nachweisen. Bei dem ersten handelt es sich um einen rechteckigen Fachwerkbau mit Steinziegeldach, der auf einem groben Mauerwerksfundament stand. Das zweite, das über dem Fachwerkbau aber erst nach einer Zeitlücke errichtet wurde, bestand aus Pfosten, die auf individuellen Lehm- und Kopfsteinfundamenten standen. Seine Nutzung könnte bis in das 5. Jahrhundert n. Chr. reichen.

Das *Konsumverhalten* ist für die Zeit von ca. 200 v. Chr. bis ca. 450 n. Chr. am deutlichsten zu erfassen, jedoch nutzten die Bewohner dieser Landschaft schon früh weitverbreitete Bezugsquellen, vor allem bei der Versorgung mit Feuerstein, aber auch Mahlsteinen und später Keramik. Die Gefäßkeramik, die zuerst für bronzezeitliche Brandbestattungen genutzt wurde, fand im Laufe der Eisenzeit Verwendungen im häuslichen Bereich, und zwar fast ausschließlich in Form von Vorratsgefäßen. Als der römische Machtbereich sich zur Humbermündung hin ausdehnte, konnten diese Gemeinschaften Gefäße beschaffen, die zwar lokal aber unter Einbeziehung römischer Techniken hergestellt wurden. Schon kurz nach der römischen Eroberung ist von außerhalb Britanniens importiertes Tafelgeschirr nachweisbar, das im Laufe des 2. Jahrhunderts n. Chr. durch in York hergestellte Gefäße verdrängt wurde. Veränderungen bei der Zubereitung von Speisen ließen etwas länger auf sich warten als beim Servieren, wobei ein nennenswerter Umfang an Mortaria erst später im 2. Jahrhundert festzustellen ist. Der Großteil dieses frühen römischen Materials ist wahrscheinlich über York verhandelt worden, aber ab dem 3. Jahrhundert scheinen sich die Versorgungsmechanismen zunehmend auf verschiedene regionale und lokale

Quellen zu konzentrieren. In der Folge verlagerte sich vor Ende des 4. Jahrhunderts der Schwerpunkt der Gefäßformen wieder auf den Krug, wodurch die keramischen Funktionssignaturen ihren eisenzeitlichen Gegenstücken sehr ähnlich waren.

Ideologische Praktiken (insbesondere menschliche Bestattungen – aber auch monumentale Gebäude und strukturierte Deponierungen) scheinen von Anfang an eine wesentliche Rolle in der Landschaft von Heslington gespielt zu haben. So wurden bestimmte Gegenstände in neolithischen Gruben niedergelegt, um „Ahnengeografien" zu schaffen, und am nördlichen Rand der Fundstätte wurden in der Bronzezeit neben der Moräne Hügelgräber errichtet, um den Durchgang mobiler Gemeinschaften entlang dieser Route zu markieren. Gegen Ende der letztgenannten Periode wurden jedoch Brandbestattungen eingesetzt, um mehr lokale Landschaftsansprüche zu erheben. Seit Mitte der Vorrömischen Eisenzeit sind formale Parzellierungen in dieser Landschaft nachweisbar, wobei eine enthauptete Bestattung in einem früh-datierten Grabenende niedergelegt wurde, um die Bedeutung dieses Befunds zu verstärken. Nach Aufgabe des westlichen Teils der Landschaft wurde in dieser Zone ein römisches Brandgrab angelegt, zusammen mit Schlussdeponierungen in ihrem Hauptbrunnen: Parzellierung als Form der Landschaftsorganisation war verschwunden, aber nicht vergessen. Als sich die Besiedlung im 3 Jahrhundert n. Chr. in das Zentrum der Landschaft von Heslington verlagerte und neue Einfriedungen zur Abgrenzung der landwirtschaftlichen Funktionen entstanden, wurden Neugeborenenbestattungen sorgfältig in den Randbereichen dieser Aktivitäten platziert. Später, als sich der Landbesitz in dieser Zone ausweitete, wurden Bestattungen von Erwachsenen genutzt, um die Unverletzlichkeit der neuen Grenzen zu verdeutlichen; eine Rolle, die sie anscheinend über einen längeren Zeitraum hinweg gespielt haben. Im 4. Jahrhundert wurde hier auf einer ausgedehnten Terrasse eine neue Einfriedung errichtet. Der Zugang zu dieser Zone von Osten her wurde durch ein Tor kontrolliert, jener im Westen durch einen gemauerten Turm und zwei dazugehörige Bestattungen, deren Köpfe anscheinend festgenagelt waren In diesem so abgegrenzten Bereich wurde ein repräsentatives, hypokaustiertes Gebäude errichtet, das im Süden von sorgfältig platzierten Töpfen und im Westen von einem in gehockter Lage bestatteten, behinderten Mann flankiert wurde. Zum Abschluss wurde ein später nördlich dieser rituellen Zone abgeteufter, massiv gemauerter Brunnen mit einer Kombination aus jungen und alten, wilden und zahmen Tieren verschlossen. Zusammenfassend lässt sich sagen, dass der Übergang von mobiler zu sesshafter Lebensweise durch eine Verlagerung von Aktivitäten markiert wird, die sich durch ein wiederholtes Aufsuchen in der Jungsteinzeit und Bewegung in der näheren Umgebung während der Bronzezeit kennzeichnet; gegen Ende Bronzezeit geht die Entwicklung hin zu mehr lokalen Landschaftsansprüchen und gegen Ende der Vorrömischen Eisenzeit zur Ausformung von Flursystemen und Siedlungen. Die Haushalte der letztgenannten Periode, die sowohl in die ländliche Wirtschaft als auch die Produktion von Prestigegegenständen eingebunden waren, setzten ihre dynamische Entwicklung bis in die Römisch Kaiserzeit fort, obwohl sie nun über York Zugang zu Keramikimporten hatten. Später verlagerte sich die Besiedlung jedoch nach Osten in das Zentrum dieser Landschaft, und die landwirtschaftliche Produktion intensivierte sich. Dazu gehörte vielleicht auch die Versorgung der Nachfrage von außerhalb der unmittelbaren Landschaft, was jedoch nicht mit einer Ausweitung der Produktionsgrundlagen dieser Wirtschaft verbunden schien wohingegen der Keramikkonsum nun zunehmend unter Umgehung von York befriedigt wurde. Vor dem Ende des 4. Jahrhunderts n. Chr. wurde hier eine „rituelle Einfriedung" mit zugehörigen monumentalen Gebäuden errichtet. In späteren Jahrzehnten lassen ein Fachwerkgebäude, ein gemauerter Brunnen und Hinweise auf handwerkliche Produktion am nördlichen Rand des Bereichs eine lebhafte Aktivität in dieser Zone bis ins 5. Jahrhundert n. Chr. hinein vermuten, aber auch Hinweise auf darüber hinaus anhaltende soziale Spannungen. Diese Aktivitäten wurden schließlich von natürlich entstandenen Hangablagerungen überdeckt, bevor der Bereich im Mittelalter und der Neuzeit überpflügt wurde. Der Charakter und die räumliche Anordnung der Universitätsgebäude, die sich heute auf dem Gelände von Heslington Ost befinden, sind Ausdruck des marktorientierten Charakters der Hochschulbildung von heute, im deutlichen Gegensatz zu ihren in den 1960er Jahren im Westen errichteten Pendants.

Steve Roskams
Cath Neal

Übersetzung: Jörn Schuster

strategies mitigating development impacts: assessment became the first resort in archaeological fieldwork, full excavation its last resort, as embedded in Planning Policy Guidance Note 16: Archaeology and Planning (PPG16).[4]

Finally, the developer, as 'polluter', was to pay for creating these mitigation strategies. Working in consultation with an archaeological curator, they were responsible for carrying through a sequence of activities, starting with reconnaissance using desk-based assessment, aerial photography, geophysics and fieldwalking, then evaluation deploying more destructive techniques such as machine-dug trenches and hand-dug test pits. Ideally, all of this information would be brought together in a model defining the extent, depth, legibility and finds repertoire of deposits within the development footprint,[5] a model which could be set beside research objectives to define a strategic way forward in relation to any proposed development.

In the UK today, reconnaissance and evaluation exercises, together with any subsequent, larger-scale fieldwork, are carried out by commercial fieldwork organisations competing for the work on the basis of price, with the result that professional excavators, often on short-term contracts, move to different places as the work requires. Equally, specialists concerned with assemblage analysis now operate mostly at arm's length from the site, usually as separate businesses. Thus, although all members of any project are working to a common end, communication between them may be minimal. Finally, if initial professionalisation divorced fieldworkers somewhat from the public they served, later commercialisation and workforce mobility has further extended this distance. All of these factors have had a huge impact on how fieldwork happens, and how its data is analysed and then published.[6]

All the above trends were evident in the Heslington project. Thus, the initial desktop study was carried out by a consultant employed directly by the University of York as developer.[7] At a later stage another archaeological consultant, Patrick Ottaway, was chosen to act as an adviser to the developer. The York Archaeological Trust (henceforth YAT) undertook fieldwalking and trial trenching on the site, subcontracting geophysical survey to a specialist third party. In the post-PPG16 environment, YAT, originally set up in 1972 as a rescue unit with overall responsibility for all of York's archaeology, now competes with other organisations for such work. Indeed, when further commercial fieldwork was required at a late stage of this project, one such competitor, On-Site Archaeology (henceforth OSA), was contracted to carry it out. The majority of specialists employed to analyse material generated by our fieldwork

were self-employed individuals or very small businesses, few of whom had a base in the locality of York.

It is worth noting, in passing, that the UK fully deregulated model is not an inevitable consequence of developer funding.[8] In France, for example, a development tax is used to resource INRAP (*Institut national de recherches archéologiques préventives*),[9] which then funds a limited number of major research projects in the field. Where this system of competitive tendering has been adopted in full however, most obviously in Britain and the Netherlands, its influence has been marked. General trends in economic development now impact profoundly on fieldwork,[10] particularly when an economy moves from boom to bust.[11]

Today, in part as a reaction to some of these trends, the historic environment is increasingly acknowledged as a shared resource incorporating the significance of place and sustainability.[12] When PPG16 was replaced in the UK by the National Planning Policy Framework,[13] for example, a much greater emphasis was placed on community engagement. Such principles are central to the Faro Convention,[14] which came into force from 2011, but has yet to be ratified by the biggest European 'players'. It argues for an inclusive heritage in which the everyday is seen to have merit alongside the iconic. Promoting democratic engagement will need to deal first with the previously noted rift between fieldworkers and 'their' public. If it adopts the current UK approach of creating deposit models to set beside research potential and thus define a fieldwork strategy, the critical question will become: who should set that research agenda?

Although the driving force behind our work at Heslington was to find out about the past, it was equally an attempt to engage with these debates, and to remake the links between fieldwork and local communities. To the latter end, and facilitated by an Heritage Lottery Fund grant of £27,000, we tried to connect with various groups.[15] This involved regular site tours for local working people; the production of a booklet, distributed to all nearby households, and the setting up of information boards on the site; opportunities for people, whether living on a local housing estate or beyond, to take part in the site work, from geophysical survey to excavation and post-excavation processing; attempts to engage homeless people; and giving local schoolchildren transitioning between primary and secondary education a chance to carry out fieldwork in a controlled and safe environment (fig 1.1). The overall results of such endeavours have been presented in a dedicated publication, along with their limitations.[16] Their implications for this specific project are considered at the end of this publication (see section 9.5).

Landscape assessment – evaluating archaeological site evaluation

This section acts as a source criticism, clarifying the potentials, yet limitations, of the evidence gathered by the project as a prelude to what is presented in later chapters. It starts by sketching in the background to the project (section 1.1), before assessing the archaeological reconnaissance techniques adopted on the site in relation to differential visibility, seasonality and spatial resolution (section 1.2). We then examine the effectiveness of the evaluation methods required by the archaeological curator based on (then) PPG16 principles, including aerial and geophysical survey, fieldwalking, machine-dug trenches, hand-dug test pits, augering and deposit modelling (section 1.3). This allowed the survival characteristics of both deposits and artefactual/ecofactual assemblages to be estimated, in turn influencing the excavation strategy and associated data gathering (section 1.4). We finally consider the programmatic, yet iterative, nature of post-excavation assessment and analysis (section 1.5), finishing with a discussion of archiving, publication policy and future access/further research (section 1.6).

1.1 Project background

The work undertaken at the Heslington East site (henceforth referred to as Heslington, for convenience) is, in many ways, a direct expression of how archaeological fieldwork is carried out in the twenty-first century, so it is first useful to contextualise where we are today. The UK fieldwork profession was created in the 1960s and 1970s as a reaction to the long economic boom post-World War II and the impact it was having on archaeological remains in both rural contexts (notably the extraction of aggregates, road building, re-afforestation and ploughing) and their urban counterparts (in particular, settlement expansion, high-rise buildings and ring roads). The 'rescue movement'[1] argued at the time that these large-scale threats required large-scale interventions, thus promoting a strategy of excavating ahead of development to create an 'archival record' in place of the site itself. The multi-period, complex sites that had to be dealt with, and

the various difficult, and sometimes dangerous, working conditions that diggers encountered, required new specialist methods and technologies, plus full-time professional fieldwork 'experts' to deploy them.[2]

The existence of a professional element within the discipline became increasingly recognised in the UK through the 1980s. At a European level, it was formalised with the Valletta Convention,[3] which argued that fieldwork should be undertaken only by qualified, specially authorised archaeologists. As a result, archaeological endeavours became part of structure plans, and thus of environmental impact legislation. If the 1970s saw fieldwork as rescuing a resource with the potential to inform and educate people, the 1990s saw it as being employed to solve a development 'problem'. Further, as this heritage was fragile and irreplaceable, it required, where possible, preservation *in situ* rather than destructive, if informative, intervention. Reconnaissance and evaluation were therefore needed to define

Fig 1.1 Local schoolchildren enjoying the hands-on experience of learning to make a Roman kiln and then using it to fire pots. The completed pots were later put on display at their schools. © DoA

1.2 Reconnaissance

Initial reconnaissance for this project comprised a series of industry-standard desk-based assessments. Perring's report surveyed and synthesised documentary, especially newspaper, and cartographic sources.[17] It also incorporated the limited amount of controlled archaeological work undertaken in the vicinity of the development (for example, landscape survey ahead of the University of York Science Park development), plus topographic and geophysical survey near one of its Computing blocks.

Sporadic finds – for example, a flint scraper and flint-working debitage (albeit mixed with post-medieval pottery) and a looped Bronze Age spearhead, said to have been found in Heslington Field in 1889 – were held to indicate prehistoric occupation hereabouts, perhaps on the higher ground of Heslington Hill. Such archaeological encounters, although infrequent, were deemed significant, as there had been few opportunities to investigate prehistoric levels within or near the historic core of York.

It seems likely that any such activity, from whatever period of prehistory, would concentrate along the glacial moraine across the Vale of York, cut hereabouts by the River Ouse (see section 2.1). Further afield, Neolithic axes, a beaker burial and possible Iron Age burials were found during nineteenth-century railway works just outside York's historic core together with flints recovered at The Mount and a Bronze Age burial under Clifford's Tower.[18] Developer-funded work in the last decade has recovered another Bronze Age burial at Lawrence Street[19] and also generated increased numbers of lithics, especially at the confluence of the Ouse and Foss, yet the nature of the landscapes associated with these finds is entirely unclear.

Roman findings are more numerous, unsurprising at a site located only 3km south-east of the Roman fortress and civilian town of Eboracum. Two Roman roads are thought to exist in the area. One lay to the north of the site, running from York to Brough-on-Humber,[20] largely followed by the present-day A1079. A second, 1.5km to the west of the site, had been thought to be preserved in the straight parish boundary between Pool Bridge and Germany Beck, Fulford[21] (but see section 9.3 for questions on its existence). Burials in stone coffins had been recorded between these two proposed thoroughfares, some accompanied by prestigious glass and metal grave goods, which suggest important activity but not necessarily a cemetery. Two Roman coin hoards, which came to light with initial university development, may be of a similar, late Roman, date (see section 8.3). Finally, investigations taking place in 2002 ahead of other campus development revealed evidence for agricultural activity of Roman date in the area.[22]

Anglo-Saxon burials found at Lamel Hill in the mid-nineteenth century show that human burial in the vicinity was not confined to the Roman period.[23] Evidence for activity after this date is restricted to indications of medieval ridge and furrow in the vicinity of

Siward's Howe, the one scheduled monument in the vicinity (SM26623).[24] Heslington Hall, now a listed building, constructed 1565–8 for Thomas Eynns, enlarged by Yarburgh in 1854 and sold to the university in 1963, lies partly within the Heslington Conservation Area (see section 9.5). Few modern features beyond agriculture and modern field boundaries are apparent here, but this landscape remains, for some, a contested arena (see further, below).

Perring drew out various implications from the above,[25] arguing the need for more detailed archaeological evaluation, initially facilitated by further desk-based work.[26] Despite repeated overflights, aerial photography gave little indication of what might lie beneath the ground in the immediate vicinity, although an undated rectilinear enclosure, a trackway and a possible Bronze Age ring ditch have been recorded to the east around Grimston village, further along the glacial moraine.[27] Further developments in data analysis, for example the calculation of vegetation indices and multivariate analysis as deployed along the Trent Valley,[28] might have better success in finding archaeological features in these unpromising landscapes. In this case, however, Perring thought that fieldwalking was unlikely to be productive, but that trial trenches and selective test pits might help in evaluating the extent and quality of archaeological remains.

This evaluation phase, agreed following planning advice from City Principal Archaeological Officer John Oxley and monitored by consultant Patrick Ottaway, comprised: a campaign of fieldwalking; a series of geophysical surveys; and machine-dug trenches across the development area.

1.3 Evaluation

Commercial fieldwalking, undertaken by YAT, took the form of experienced fieldworkers line-walking the southern and western edges of 20m squares set up across the whole development area, picking up material from 1.5m either side of that line (four 100m × 100m squares were walked in their entirety to act as a control).[29] This work, undertaken over the winter, had to contend with mixed visibility, standing water, frost and a burst sewage pipe. Little clear patterning emerged, although prehistoric flint and Roman pottery were found, seemingly thinly, across the whole zone. The flint, which included a fragment of polished stone axe, was thought to range in date from the late Neolithic to the Early Bronze Age (fig 1.2). It had a slightly higher density towards the north-east of the area, with Roman pottery concentrated in the

east (albeit comprising only sixteen sherds) and Roman ceramic building material (CBM) in the west (just twenty-five fragments).

Large areas were then subjected to geophysical survey in the form of 40m wide strips down the hillside, with 40m wide gaps in between.[30] This allowed more and less 'busy' areas to be defined, but, given the nature of the coverage, had difficulty in recognising individual linear features, let alone defining any more focused activity. The most interventionist aspect of evaluation, covering a c 1.58 per cent sample of the development area, consisted of 115 machine-dug trenches of varying sizes and orientations (fig 1.3).[31] These were positioned to intercept the busy areas identified by geophysics and, by way of a control, to also investigate areas lacking such anomalies.

Based on the above information it became possible to define some priority areas (A1–3) and subsidiary areas (B1–7) on the site, plus an outline set of period-based research objectives set beneath four research topics (landscape and environment in early prehistory; prehistoric/Roman transitions; cult and ritual; and late-/Post-Roman changes). Other topics added later, concerning early landforms, Iron Age metal-working and, later still, waterlogged organics,[32] allowed research interests to extend to the examination of significant palaeoenvironmental sequences, the profile of natural deposits across the site, waterlogged or arid deposits and their depth, and whether a meaningful archaeological deposit model could be constructed. More detailed questions were also listed, notably whether the site might yield any evidence for Roman burials, for Anglian or Anglo-Scandinavian occupation or for a medieval graveyard or tithe barn. Finally, the issue of its use during World War II was also raised but, in the event, this period played a very limited role in our investigations.

At this stage it was agreed that Areas A1 and A2 had to be excavated quickly to allow development to proceed. Yet A3, where timetables were not so pressing, could be investigated as a separate project concerned with student training and local community participation. This was carried out by the Department of Archaeology, University of York (DoA) under the direction of the current authors. The DoA also agreed to collate the results from all fieldwork, and thus deliver a research dividend from both the commercial and non-commercial elements of the project. In the event, a later change in the planned development programme required a zone to the south of A3 to be excavated more speedily than student and community inputs would allow. This work was therefore allocated to OSA. Thus, the present report incorporates information generated by two competing commercial

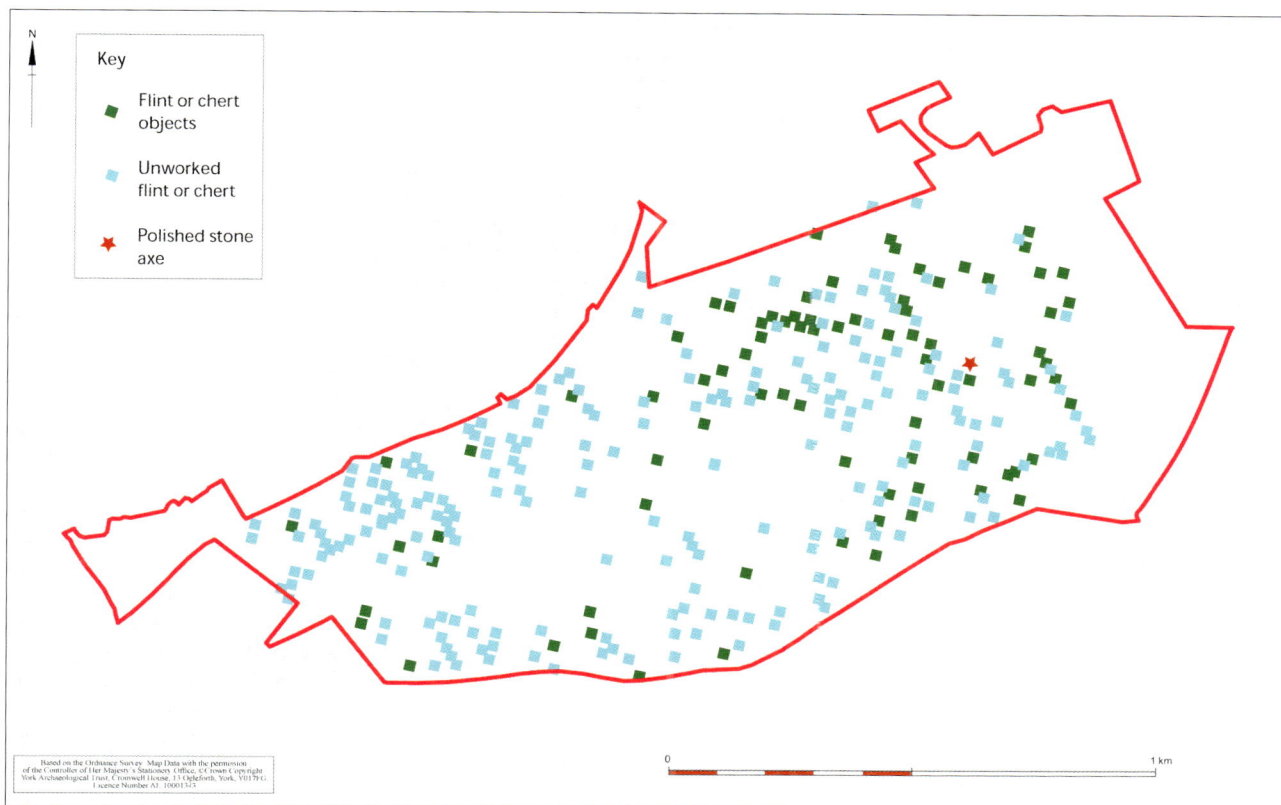

Fig 1.2 Distribution of flint from YAT fieldwalking undertaken during site evaluation. *Drawing:* YAT/Neil Gevaux

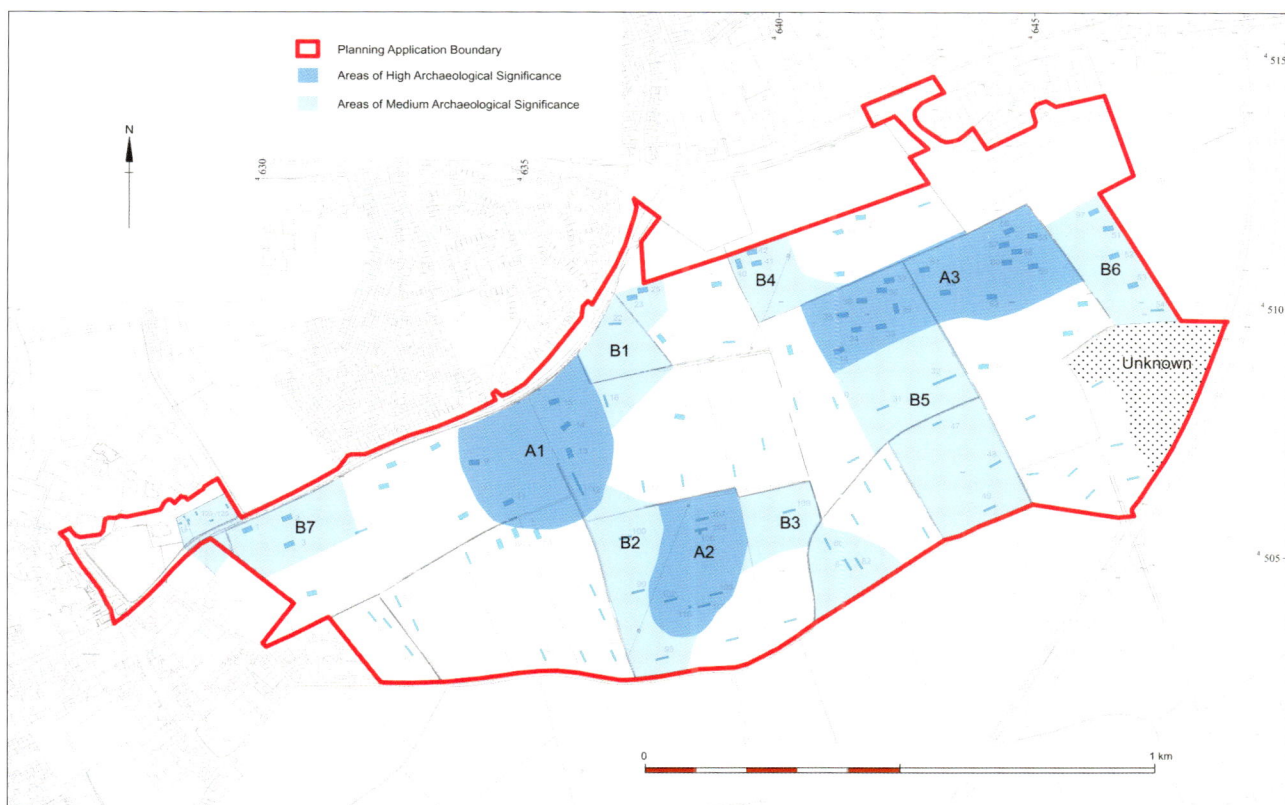

Fig 1.3 Positions of machine-dug trenches (dark blue) dug by YAT early in the reconnaissance process. This work, together with geophysical survey (see fig 1.4), allowed the definition of three priority areas A1–3 (mid blue) and seven areas of subsidiary interest B1–7 (light blue). *Drawing:* YAT

organisations using full-time professional excavators and an academic institution using, mostly, less experienced fieldworkers.

The extended timetable available for A3, in turn, allowed a second phase of more focused evaluation to take place within a single, large area towards the centre of the development (Fields 8 and 9 in Area A3: these had already been surveyed in the initial evaluation, but only at the broad-brush level described above). This secondary work comprised: fieldwalking of the total area using students, and with plotting of metal finds from local detectorists; geophysical survey in a single, connected area as part of student training over two years; and further, dedicated test pitting, boreholes and deposit modelling. One objective of this extra work was to evaluate the foregoing commercial procedures. It then led to the excavation of selected larger areas using both students and local community volunteers.

In contrast to the initial fieldwalking, the more intensive reconnaissance and evaluation work by DoA, unsurprisingly, generated a lot more material. The proportionate change is, however, significant: ninety-seven worked flints were gathered from the whole site, in contrast to forty-eight from the latter, much smaller, area plus sixteen Roman sherds across the site in contrast to forty-six from just the additional area, both representing a huge increase in density. More importantly, this new material showed distinct patterning: worked flint concentrated towards the west, with an even clearer profusion of Roman pottery to the east. This spatial information was then deployed in planning trench positions for DoA excavations.

In terms of the two sets of geophysical survey, simple comparisons are problematic due to the very different circumstances in which data was gathered: commercial work was undertaken by a single individual in one campaign, whilst its later counterpart, carried out at a different resolution, was directed by different personnel over two seasons. The latter also used inexperienced labour, some of whom did not fully recognise the need to be 'magnetically hygienic' in the field (although the latter issues could mostly be solved by extra processing to tidy up data, for example de-staggering to correct for walking errors). To some extent, these negative elements in the latter work were compensated by undertaking these surveys after topsoil stripping and by surveying a single connected area, rather than areas with 40m wide strips missing, and using a combination of magnetometry and resistivity. The former technique showed up pre-medieval linear features, the latter medieval ridge and furrow and, of most significance in strategic planning, different levels of water retention (fig 1.4).

These results led, in turn, to a campaign of limited, hand-dug trial trenches that aimed to ground-truth geophysical interpretations by concentrating on feature alignments to characterise deposits and, particularly, to test indications of waterlogging (fig 1.5). We also endeavoured to see whether horizontal stratigraphy survived anywhere on the site. Finally, borehole transects were used to enhance understanding of the depth and character of deposits. As with the test trenches, these transects were positioned to cross interfaces implying differential preservation, as suggested by geophysics.

Having assimilated the results of this second phase of evaluation activity, it became possible to develop a more focused set of Roman research aims for Area A3. These concerned: the timing of Roman arrival and the speed of development thereafter; the form of landscape exploitation and changes in land holding/agricultural practice at this time; and whether such changes were best explained in terms of the functional or ideological needs of that society.

Various lessons can be drawn from comparing the two evaluation processes, most of which are not unexpected. In making these points, we would wish to emphasise that curatorial requirements here were much in line with current general practices (with the implication that, if extra resources to do more work had been demanded for just this project, these might have generated a legal challenge as being unreasonable). Also, the commercial work was carried out exactly as required by the curator and completed professionally.

The initial broad-brush fieldwalking was successful in showing that a range of prehistoric and Roman activity was likely to have existed across the area. Yet it was unable to clearly define its character, for example by distinguishing occupation areas from other landscape usage, or to identify any specific concentrations. Subsequent work in Area A3 approached both these objectives more effectively, providing answers to questions that subsequent excavation showed to be essentially accurate. In part this is much as expected, due to the greater spatial resolution adopted in the second phase of work (and despite the relative inexperience of those carrying it out). Yet it is also due to being able to choose when the work should be done in terms of current cropping regimes, weather and so forth – factors which purely commercial exercises can rarely control.

Second, to move beyond identification of hotspots of activity, as per the initial survey, and define linear features and differential waterlogging, geophysical prospection must cover large, continuous areas. Furthermore, different geophysical techniques need to be deployed in unison to generate such strategically useful information. Finally,

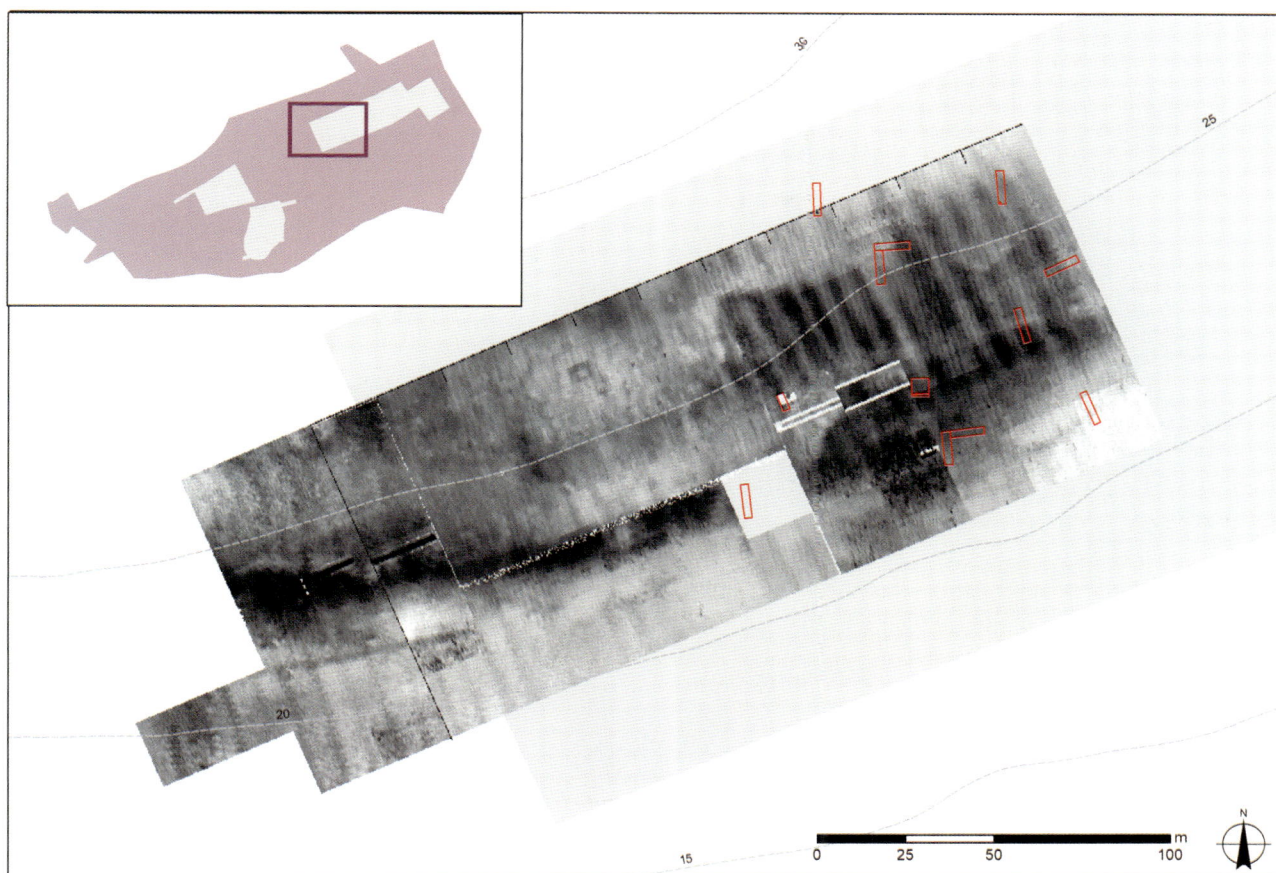

Fig 1.4 The results of geophysical prospection in the central part of the site undertaken by DoA students under the direction of Ben Gourley. Areas with higher water retention, and thus perhaps enhanced preservation, are indicated in black, cut by medieval ploughing. The clear dark rectangular feature (towards centre at top) revealed, on excavation, the foundations of a tower structure (G16/G17; see section 8.5). The rectangular areas in red represent evaluation trenches dug in response to patterning in the geophysical survey. *Drawing*: Helen Goodchild

additional data-processing of geophysical data sets can recognise more patterning than first meets the eye. The case of medieval furrows is especially interesting here. These were picked up in excavation where resistivity had predicted and securely dated as medieval. Yet not all furrows seen 'geophysically' could be identified physically as intrusions into the surviving subsoil, especially towards the north of the hillside, which were subject to greater modern disturbance. The obvious explanation is that medieval deposits remain 'locked' within the modern plough soil: the furrow's distinctive signature is sufficiently articulated to remain visible geophysically, yet it cannot be recorded by conventional excavation techniques.

Third, with this greater geophysical resolution, it became possible to plan a much more detailed, if less extensive, campaign of trial trenching to enhance deposit modelling. In fact, it is only with this greater level of resolution that we can legitimately talk of 'modelling' in a way that allows meaningful development of an excavation strategy.

A penultimate lesson concerns the need to use data sets interactively and iteratively. Fieldwalking and geophysics guided the position, orientation and dimensions of test pits/trenches in a way that maximised information yield for expenditure of effort. Yet, with some initial results from trenching, it became possible to return to the earlier data sets and notice new patterns. Our test trenches, for example, confirmed the position of most linear features suspected in geophysics, but also discovered other components of potential importance. With this knowledge, these newly exposed elements, especially non-linear features, could be recognised in the original geophysical data. It is widely acknowledged, when using aerial photography at the reconnaissance stage, that current land use and seasonality will impact on site visibility, and thus that repeated data gathering may be needed to obtain meaningful results. Clearly, similar considerations apply to the use of geophysics in later, more detailed site evaluation.

A final matter concerns the spatial resolution of differential preservation across the site, a key component

Fig 1.5 Trial trenching from the site confirming the existence of a linear feature (top left: running perpendicular to trench at its centre); showing increased organic survival (top right: dark area in foreground); and suggesting the possible survival of horizontal surfaces (bottom: stony stratum in section). © DoA

of deposit modelling. Once patterning in geophysical data had been tested against test pit observations ('ground-truthed'), we were able to chart broad zones where waterlogging could be expected: essentially on the springline along the hillside in the east, though less exactly defined in the west (see fig.1.4 and section 2.1). This knowledge in turn influenced our choice of excavation areas and sampling strategies. However, serendipity also sometimes intervened and had to be accommodated, most obviously with the survival of brain matter in an Early Iron Age ditch in the west of the site (see section 8.2).

More difficult to chart, and thus deal with strategically, was the survival of bone. Thus, two adjacent Roman inhumations, 613 and 726 (Group 24 – all such cross-referencing is shortened to G24 etc in what follows) are interpreted below as reinforcing a single field boundary (see section 8.4: fig 8.4). They were buried at much the same time in similar subsoil; however, the former's survival was very poor, the latter much better (though still not good). It would be difficult for any model of bone survival to define meaningful sampling strategies when research potential varies over such short distances. Beyond these specific features, general soil conditions impacted on both metal finds and the survival of worked wood. Taking account of differential survival in interpreting assemblage is no easy matter. Iron tools and blades, for example, are less easy to identify when fragmented than some other objects, hence are probably under-represented in our catalogues.

1.4 Data gathering

Data gathering took a fairly conventional form in all three parts of the project (YAT, OSA and DoA): removal of topsoil by machine; definition and recording of the physical, spatial and stratigraphic characteristics of underlying features (mainly intrusions into subsoil, although horizontal strata were encountered fortuitously in one or two limited zones); and gathering of assemblages, either by hand or as environmental samples. These aspects are considered in turn below for the way in which they facilitate, or, more often, constrain, interpretation of the archaeological record.

Topsoil clearance in the fraught, time-limited conditions of commercial work differed from that in the student/community operation. The latter part of the work not only gathered *more* finds from topsoil (about 40 per cent of samian sherds came from such contexts, for example, although such red, glossy pottery is more visible under machining than darker fabrics). These artefacts

could also be plotted by rough topsoil zones and thus later correlated circumstantially with underlying, excavated features: ninety unstratified samian sherds lie roughly above their 209 stratified counterparts, so remained useful analytically. Topsoil finds from commercial zones were not collected in this way and, given time pressures, any surviving horizontal stratigraphy might have been less easily recognised.

That said, where testable, spatial patterning in finds derived from overlying topsoil were broadly similar to those recovered from stratified layers, hence little real information seems to have been lost. Flint provides a good illustration. Both topsoil and stratified material had the same mixed character and rough date, running mainly from the Neolithic to Bronze Age periods, with a few tools perhaps belonging to the Mesolithic (see section 2.2). Breakage was equally low in both contexts and any spatial concentrations of flint recognised in post-excavation analysis were found to be merely a function of the extent of the areas exposed and the volume of soil excavated.

Because fieldwork took place over an extended period, additional modern features were dug into the site during its period of investigation. YAT evaluation trenches were inserted in Area A3, for example, some years before DoA work took place there. In addition, late in the DoA part of the project, geotechnical pits were excavated across the whole area to search for clay sources for use elsewhere in the modern development. This was something, unfortunately, that we were not able to observe archaeologically. When encountered in formal DoA excavations, both YAT trenches and geotechnical pits were simply recorded in the same way as any other archaeological intrusion (although their stratigraphic relationship with modern topsoil was problematic, as they both cut, and were sealed by, this horizon).

The recording systems used by the three organisations were applied consistently within each sphere. Although different in detail, in essence they had much in common in the descriptive and stratigraphic information that they generated. The only exception concerned the nature and level of resolution, in the spatial record, which was obtained in different ways by each organisation. Thus, in order to allow consistent analysis, these data sets had to be reconciled retrospectively and joined together.

Both sampling strategies and assemblage recovery methods were explicitly defined in relation to the character of any given assemblage and how it matched designated research objectives, and so are reasonably comparable between them. In places, finds recovery processes became more convoluted; small glass beads, flint fragments and small bones were recovered only when processing environmental samples, for example, and so had to be fed back into assemblage records retrospectively. Such problems existed within each part of the overall project, however, and are anyway commonplace in most archaeological fieldwork today.

1.5 Post-excavation assessment and analysis

As a MoRPHE-compliant project (Management of Research Projects in the Historic Environment),[33] all material generated in the field was subject to subsequent assessment to define options for fuller examination. This took the form of spatial and stratigraphic analysis by YAT, OSA and DoA and, alongside this, assemblage assessment by external specialists. The results of these work programmes then informed later analytical strategies.

The need to reconcile different spatial records to allow all such information to be viewable in a single database has been noted previously (in our case, the ArcGIS geographical information system, henceforth GIS). The stratigraphic component of this work was challenging for several reasons. First, the complex process of stratigraphic grouping was approached quite differently by each organisation, particularly in how and at what stage each of them incorporated preliminary finds dating. Thus, DoA records were placed in 134 groups solely on the basis of stratigraphic and spatial criteria (G1–134 incl.); YAT, using the structure of their Integrated Archaeological Base (see further below), used a combination of stratigraphy, deposit types and spatial matters, plus initial spot dating, to put 3,697 contexts into 887 sets, making 267 groups subsumed under eighty-nine phases; and OSA defined sixty-seven groups based on sequence, trench position and rather fuller Roman pottery dating.

Rather than redo all this analysis, we took the practical decision to take the work of each organisation at face value. We re-ordered the YAT work at their group level to form higher-order entities that matched the DoA concept and were numbered where we left off (thus turning their g1–g267 into G135–185). We also did something similar with OSA groupings (numbered G186–238). In what follows, this has the value of there being a fairly consistent way of referring to all stratigraphic units from the site using a single, consecutive group numbering system. The downside is that, where excavated features physically coincide (as OSA and DoA do at certain points in the landscape), there may not be a one-to-one correspondence of feature numbers. This is unfortunate at the group level, but easily

understandable if one 'drills down' to the feature concerned. Such correlations were also checked to ensure that stratigraphic inconsistency was minimised.

That said, it is important to emphasise the complexities that this process of amalgamation can generate. By way of example, this can be gauged by a brief consideration of elements in what was finally defined as Group 167 (G167). This encompasses several YAT groups, including g528 (comprising set 601), g529 (sets 597 and 598), g530 (set 602) and g531 (sets 599 and 600), all originally linked together under Phase 515. In fact, g528 is earlier than g530 and interpreted as a corn dryer. It is, essentially, undated: g529 is earlier than g531 and interpreted as a waterhole. Its earliest, organic fills, presumably evidencing its initial use, are seemingly of early Roman date (although mixed with some prehistoric material, probably disturbed from the ditch that it cut). Its latest, non-organic, fills are clearly late Roman in date. It is unclear whether the latter finds date its final use, implying that it functioned over an extended period of time, or comprise material dumped sometime after its demise to prepare the area for future usage. Interpretation is further clouded by the fact that all these features lie directly below topsoil and are therefore subject to modern truncation. Thus, the single, seemingly simple, entity G167 covers a multitude of intricate arguments. This is always the case when amalgamating stratigraphy into higher-order groupings (see sections 2.3 and 4.2, respectively, for wider interpretations of the waterhole (Well 3) and the corn dryer that make up G167).

Finally, having decided groupings on the basis of spatial and stratigraphic information, we also endeavoured to allocate all excavated features on any one part of the project to one of several different feature types. These comprised 'open cuts' (boundary, linear ditch, curvilinear ditch, gully, furrow, land drain, beam slot and miscellaneous); 'closed cuts' (pit, posthole/ stakehole, grave and miscellaneous); 'deposits' (ploughsoil, natural strata, spread, fill, skeleton and weathering); and 'structures' (kiln, hearth, structural slot, corn dryer, pad, wall, waterhole, cobbles, post-built structure and hypocaust). The objective here was to allow such feature types to be analysed spatially in a single GIS and to assess them in relation to assemblage evidence ('Is a specific pottery type discarded differentially into boundary ditches, or found particularly in association with structures?' and so on; see section 7.4 for some results).

Of course, it must be noted again that the imposition of such classifications is itself problematic. Any scheme needs to be sufficiently diverse to cater for the variety of evidence but not so complex as to preclude meaningful analysis. There is also the issue of grey areas; for example, when distinguishing between a boundary and another type of linear ditch, or deciding whether a truncated feature that survives as a mere scoop is to be designated as a posthole or a pit. Re-cut features associated with water extraction (see section 2.3) might be interpreted as springs, waterholes or wells; sometimes distinctions were clear, sometimes opaque. As with the process of creating stratigraphic groups, a simple label conceals a multitude of complex, and sometimes questionable, arguments. The only solution is to make the underlying, more primary, evidence accessible to check allocations.

Turning next to assemblage assessment, some on-site 'errors' had to be rectified: jet and shale of Iron Age date were only distinguished at a late point in our work programme, for example, and so had to be accommodated retrospectively in post-excavation strategies. Similarly, Argonne ware, initially identified as samian, had to move between specialists (in the process, fortuitously solving a stratigraphic conundrum). Such complications are commonplace and will become more so with finds specialists increasingly divorced from the fieldwork process (see section 1.1). This stage of work resulted in a series of recommendations for further analytical work, as per the MoRPHE requirements noted previously. Decisions on what material should be taken forward, and in what detail, are always difficult, and not just because they involve tricky financial negotiations with the site developer. Relevant criteria for this project included the volume of material (certain questions can be answered only with a large assemblage size, for example in animal bones); level of survival (notably the organic vs inorganic nature of environmental samples); site context (formation process and their primary or secondary nature – an initial pit fill, for example, may tell us about the feature's specific function, whereas later deposits only about general rubbish disposal); date (our proposed 'Anglo-Saxon' pottery might be considered more worthy of further resources than our better-known Roman material – although the converse could also be argued); and broader significance beyond Heslington (our millstones constituted the largest collection yet recorded from the region, for example, and were thus examined in some detail).

This process was made more difficult in our case by the fact that assessment of material from the YAT excavation of Areas A1 and A2 took place some years before work was completed in A3; hence, strategic assemblages selected for 'full' analysis were not always consistent across the project or recommended to take place at the same level of resolution. This issue is most obvious in the case of environmental samples. Not only did different organisations carry out each assessment

(Palaeoecological Research Services for YAT, Hall and Kenward for DoA, Sheffield Archaeobotanical Consultancy for OSA), but also some researchers took a much more selective approach in making their recommendations than others.

To add to this diversity, researchers from other projects also contributed their expertise to our fieldwork where objectives fortuitously coincided. The two most significant here concern the input of the InterArChive project[34] to our understanding of human burials (see section 8.3) and coring work by the British Geological Survey on Badger Hill, with implications for our understanding of the moraine here in prehistory (see section 2.1). None of these factors is especially problematic or that unusual, although the byzantine interaction of timescales here may be less common (in effect, fieldwork for the project ended up taking place over almost a decade).

Finally, the notion embedded in MoRPHE of data collection, leading to assessment, leading to (selective) analysis belies the iterative nature of much post-excavation work. Items selected for conservation, for example, yielded further information in the process, which then required extra specialist input. These problems, minor when teams work together, are exacerbated when such activity is sub-contracted. More complicated is the interaction between decisions on stratigraphic grouping, resting ultimately on interpretation of site formation processes, and interpretations derived from assemblage analyses, which might question (often quite rightly) those earlier decisions. Recognition of Roman finger rings from a spread-out midden, for example, led to a reconsideration of site stratigraphy to decide between whether these items were a product of fortuitous survival or meaningfully positioned. Elsewhere, work on other Roman finds showed that items found from metal detecting topsoil were less fragmented than finds derived from stratigraphic excavation, with important implications for future collection strategies.

Perhaps inevitably, the most complex discussions here revolved around dating, in particular when finds did not match decisions based on sequence alone. Independent dating of our sequences was supplied by a number of methods, notably optically stimulated luminescence (OSL) dates for its earliest parts and, due to fortuitous survival, dendrochronological dates at the start of the Roman period (giving the first such dates from the Vale outside York itself; see section 5.3). C14 dates were used to understand early site development and could sometimes be linked to specific stratigraphic events, for example, G153 (although this can also be problematic: see above discussion of G167). C14 determinations, although each contains varying degrees of latitude, provide the most secure form of dating on the site and are thus stated explicitly in the text and listed as a whole here (see table 1.1). Further information on calculation details, laboratory methods, how δ13C values were measured and calibration data used are available in the site archives.[35]

That said, it is not C14 but artefact dates, notably coins and pottery, that lie at the heart of most dating of sequences. Coins, as directly datable finds, give absolute *terminus post quem* dates to specific contexts in a fairly straightforward way, yet are far less common than ceramics. Also, concentrating on this dating role can obscure other numismatic potentials; for example, comparing our coin profile with those from other site

types to define numismatic signatures. Coins can also be used to chart formation processes where horizontal stratigraphy survived. The period over which G102 may have formed, for example, and the sequence of later development between G103/G106 and G113, can be explored by plotting coins in relation to sequence as a way to try to understand coin re-deposition and trajectories into the post-Roman period (G114, see discussion in section 6.4: the numbers of coins in the latest levels here may, however, be indicative of a disturbed hoard).

Coinage also allows comparison across this landscape. Thus, in the west of the site, coins from initial evaluation exercises were all of early Roman date, confirming that this zone was in use at that time. The paucity of late

Table 1.1 Critical C14 dates generated by the site

Laboratory number	Group number	Material & site context	δ13C (‰)	Radiocarbon Age (BP)	Calibrated Date cal BC/AD (95% confidence)
Wk 4114	N/A	Peat from fill of kettle hole (no designated group)	-	10719 ±28	10780–10680BC
Wk 4115	N/A	Peat from fill of kettle hole (no designated group)	-	10613 ±29	10740–10590BC
Beta 292064	G193	Peat in Well 1	-28.7	3630 ±40	2020–1870BC
Beta 321670	G191	Timber lining of Well 1	-26.6	3350 ±30	1680–1520BC
Wk 42498	G98	Calcined bone from unnumbered cremation	-22.2	3554 ±20	1960–1870BC, 1850–1810BC, 1800–1770BC
Wk 34412	G98	Calcined bone from cremation 1439	-25.6	3489 ±27	1891–1741BC
Wk 34411	G98	Calcined bone from cremation 1276	-25.4	3437 ±28	1786–1667BC (73%)
	G135	Branch wood from fill of palaeochannel		3400 ±40	
Beta 246849	G135	Branch wood from fill of palaeochannel	-27.5	3160 ±40	1460–1310BC
Beta 246851	G135	Root wood from fill of palaeochannel	-28.5	3010 ±40	1300–1020BC
Wk 39333	G230	Organic accumulation between Wells 4 and 5	-	2733 ±30	970–960BC, 940–810BC
Beta 248712	G138	Wooden cylinder, possible water channel	-28.2	2730 ±60	930–780BC
OxA 20677	G138	Skull of decapitated inhumation	-20.5	2469 ±34	673–482BC (58%), 763–681BC (28%), 468–415BC (10%)
Wk 39536	G199	Round wood from fill of Well 1	-	1981 ±28	50BC–80AD
Wk 39535	G199	Alder charcoal from fill of Well 1	-	1957 ±25	40BC–90AD, 100–120AD
Wk 34415	G104	Bone from perinatal inhumation 1757	-	1730 ±25	245–385AD
Wk 34416	G104	Bone from perinatal inhumation 2139	-	1736 ±25	242–383AD
Wk 26402	G24	Skull from extended, adult inhumation	-19.6	1707 ±30	250–410AD
Wk 24022	G4	Skull from flexed, adult inhumation	-19.9	1648 ±39	260–290AD (4%), 320–540AD (91%)

Roman equivalents was corrected, to some extent, in later, more extensive excavations, which generated coins of mid-third century date onwards from the final accumulations above its main well, G170 (Well 2, see section 2.3). Some of these coins may have been from a hoard deposited into a wet zone long out of use but still remembered (see section 8.3). A clear majority of late Roman coins came, however, from the centre of the site to the east, showing a marked change of focus in the course of the Roman period.

Ceramic studies formed a major part of the project's post-excavation programme, most of it focused on Roman material. Analytical techniques for ceramics are well known, as are its systems of classification (even if details of the latter can change; for example, over 'problematic' grey burnished wares). For pre- and post-Roman ceramics, however, further problems arise. In part, this is because the material is less diagnostic and less well studied. At its most severe, some pottery was claimed by both Iron Age and Anglian specialists, and other sherds were not wanted by either. This is difficult to solve without either carrying out further fabric analysis, for example thin-sectioning, or recovering stratified material from other sites rather than our dissociated features (the fact that these fabrics are presently indistinguishable is, of course, telling us something quite significant about both the Iron Age and post-Roman periods, and by implication the intervening 'Roman' centuries).

The more straightforward research on Roman ceramics allows a broad-brush understanding of what was deposited on the site and when: low activity until mid-second century (3 per cent), rising between the mid-second to early-third centuries (9 per cent), further mid-third to mid-fourth centuries (23 per cent), with a main focus in the mid- to late-fourth century (over 60 per cent). Of course, this generalised picture charts only ceramic deposition, in turn raising further questions: does general under-representation of ceramics dated c 150–225 AD really indicate less occupation or differential ceramic disposal? General samian distribution shows low sherd weight in Areas A1 and A2, where pre- and early-Roman occupation is soundly evidenced, and less disturbed material in Area A3, with no such pre-existing activity. Why was this tableware being dumped, and then remaining relatively undisturbed, in the latter zone? See sections 6.2 and 8.5 for possible explanations.

Such general trends, inevitably, conceal some complexity when one links assemblage with specific contexts. Challenges here derive from various factors: the difficulty of defining the exact extent of layers and features during excavation; the different formation processes involved (spreads of materials vs fills of cut features); and the assemblage size and context type not being evenly distributed through the sequence. Divergent interpretations can also be the result of an undue reliance on spot dating. Thus, for example, deposit 1911 (G153), containing a third century AD coin, fills a ditch that is clearly cut by ditches G150 and G142 of proposed Iron Age date. Based on wider considerations of alignment and pottery dating, the stratigraphy is almost certainly correct: the Roman find is either intrusive or, more likely, something that drifted into a hollow created above an underlying, long-disused pre-Roman feature.

At other times, however, the problems stem from levels of uncertainty in both stratigraphic and assemblage analyses: initial phasing is only a 'best guess' and, equally, although certain finds are diagnostic and well-dated, others have much more latitude and may only be tied down more accurately when encountered in large assemblages. Compare, for example, the (rather exact) arrival of early Roman Ebor wares or late Roman Crambeck wares on this site to the extended use of coarse ware jars: dating accuracy varies not only between periods, but between find types within such.

Sometimes interpretations must remain open, even after detailed re-reading of the evidence. Thus, on the basis of ceramic spot dates, OSA records several 'second/3rd century linear features' that co-align exactly with ditches seen as being fourth century in DoA work. These ditches might be interpreted variously as: early Roman features with a long life; truly late Roman features with a little residual material in their base; or short-lived, early Roman intrusions with late Roman deposits accumulating much later on top of them (see above on a Roman coin in an Iron Age ditch). The varied approach to topsoil removal, noted earlier, has implications for the differential truncation of these uppermost 'fills, making comparisons still more problematic. Lacking any surviving, datable horizontal stratigraphy to associate with these cuts, this is ultimately a question of comparing fill types and their position in each feature, and the size and character of associated ceramic assemblages. Where there is any doubt, we have erred on the side of believing stratigraphic relationships if clearly established on site. This does not, however, solve all such conundrums.

Beneath the above discussion lurk the twin problems of intrusive and residual finds. Certain ceramics are certainly intrusive, for example small amounts of late material in 'early' groups G73, G98, G143, G142, G141. Elsewhere, it is clear that Roman material concentrates in the same zones, sometimes in significant quantities. It may even be evident in the same stratigraphic group, as with the content of G69, which yielded handmade pottery of Late Iron Age date and Dressel 20 oil amphora and samian bowls, dishes and a cup. This implies something more than simple intrusion, with important implications for the transition between Iron Age and Roman periods (see section 6.2, Roundhouse 15).

The opposite phenomenon, residuality, can be difficult to quantify in single contexts. The extensive series of spreads G103, for example, has more second and third century AD ceramics than any other group, but, stratigraphically, all should be residual compared to the fills of adjacent intrusive features. The patterning would be explained if these deposits formed over an extended period of time (cf also coins in these accumulations, noted above).

In the very latest Roman levels, from the second half of the fourth century AD, only 4 per cent of the whole are residual, all in small groups or derived from intrusions cutting earlier levels. Here, comparative residuality is not just a problem, but telling us something quite significant about reduced disturbance at the very end of the Roman sequence. The fact that this signature also matches the implications of the numismatic profiles adds some weight to its being a 'real' pattern, not a misleading product of an assemblage derived from grouping together a number of deposits with mixed formation processes for the purpose of analysis. Sometimes Roman ceramic assemblages are even large enough to show a correlation with a feature type. Thus, our category of 'structural intrusions' was dominated by medium-mouthed jars, but, within this, walls had an over-representation of narrow-necked jars, perhaps an indicator of liquid containers concentrating in better 'domesticated' contexts (see section 7.4, discussion of discard practices, and section 6.4, discussion of building G112).

Beyond the intricacies of dating sequences, another interpretative issue concerns the nature and size of the sample derived from the site work. Setting deposit models against stated research designs, our recommended approach discussed above necessarily involves ignoring some objectives when prioritising others. Our own decisions generated a considerable volume of finds, notably animal bones, worked building stone and CBM, and quern stones, plus myriad groups of smaller material. Assessing the analytical viability of each group brought out further limitations. Two of the main bulk finds groups, bone and CBM, provide some insights here, as do querns.

We recovered a large group of bones, with 24,153 fragments recorded on the database. Despite this volume, this faunal assemblage has considerable interpretative limitations, especially as most bones were hand-collected.

More representative assemblages were generated by wet-sieving soil samples with set volumes. Unfortunately, however, these tended to yield only tiny, often unidentifiable, bone fragments (although they did generate evidence for vole, shrew and other small mammals, plus three fish bones). Just 14 per cent of the total faunal assemblage was identifiable and, whilst this still allowed some patterning to be recognised, only those assemblages from the latest Roman horizons were large enough for metrical data to be significant (and, even then, had to be combined into a single large group to generate meaningful interpretations; see section 4.1).

The methods deployed in faunal analysis are well-known and mainly unproblematic.[36] Yet, challenges remain in distinguishing sheep from goat, within equids (horse is assumed by most analysts, with implications for how traction and load-bearing might be understood) and chicken from pheasant (the former assumed, thus limiting our ability to discuss wild vs domestic food sources). Age at death was recorded, alongside condition, erosion and size, each with implications for site formation processes, plus examples of articulation ('associated bone groups': ABGs). Data on gnawing, burning, butchery marks, pathology and biometrical matters (eg to calculate animal stature) were gathered where possible. Sex data via metrics were, however, rarely of sufficient volume to allow meaningful interpretation, limiting our understanding of exact male/female proportions and any consideration of animal castration in relation to herd control. A fundamental tension here is that sizeable groups are needed to elucidate many questions. Yet, even with large-scale excavations, these can only be obtained by amalgamating groups of material and thus merging broadly contemporary, but often very different, site formation processes (primary middens combined with secondary dumps and tertiary ditch fills, etc).

Secondly, more than 650kg of CBM and stone tile was gathered in the fieldwork, dominated by Roman material (97 per cent of the total, hence medieval and post-medieval material was not considered further post-assessment). This constitutes one of the largest collections from York's hinterland and is thus of considerable significance. Plotting of this material showed significant patterning, therefore suggesting that it derived from nearby primary structures recycled into local spreads/cut features (unlike, for example, small metallic finds, which may have moved considerably down the hillside). This more spatially secure CBM, which was also less fragmented than contemporary York assemblages, was therefore subject to full scale, albeit macroscopic, analysis.

Almost the opposite applies to a third class of evidence subjected to specialist study: quern stones. All the Heslington examples were re-used: discarded in wells, employed in well linings or for other construction purposes, exploited as a convenient platform for artisan activities, and so forth. Most are so large, however, that they are unlikely to have moved far. In addition, they form the second largest group from York's hinterland (after those from Shiptonthorpe, some 30km distant[37]), including unique examples among some more common forms, and lie immediately adjacent to the city. This all suggests that they can provide meaningful information about agricultural processing as well as possible trading links to the site. They were therefore subject to detailed specialist analysis.

On a related, more general, strategic note, when defining post-assessment priorities for analysis, there is a tendency to downplay provably re-deposited assemblages; yet, calculating residuality can be useful in its own right in understanding site formation processes. In ceramics, for example, the size of specific assemblages often limits estimates of brokenness, yet the tail of residuality can still be clear with well-dated wares. Thus, as noted above, the relative completeness of our very latest Roman groups implies reduced disturbance in these final levels. Similarly, sherd links between samian pottery suggest connections between features and perhaps contemporaneity (links are, of course, much more difficult to recognise in less diagnostic wares, at least without a huge expenditure of resources). ABGs and bone fragmentation indices, plus flint patination and condition (here showing plough damage in topsoil contexts and upper pit fills), can all be fed into interpretations of site formation processes. Finally, proven re-use of querns and other worked stones can be diagnostic of recycling. There can be dangers, therefore, in trying to define residual assemblages simply in order to write them off analytically.

Another type of challenge derives from making post-assessment decisions on the basis of deposit spacing, status and, especially, preservation.[38] Evidence for worked wood, for example, will only be available where ground conditions facilitate survival. Particular species are preferentially disposed to flourish in damp contexts and, if we prioritise the investigation of such places on the basis of their better preservation, the results generated would provide a misleading view of overall woodland exploitation (although this might be corrected for using pollen evidence or charcoal and other plant macrofossils).

When one considers environmental samples, it is understandable that those with the best preservation conditions were collected most readily and were then later recommended as needing the greatest scrutiny and post-excavation resources. The first tendency was corrected by our more general sampling policy of taking

20l soil samples from all stratified deposits (although, within this, we still endeavoured to respond to particular opportunities or fortuitous survivals, for example by sieving basal fills of human burials in line with the protocols of the InterArChive project mentioned above, or by taking extra samples in waterlogged contexts). These post-assessment strategic decisions mean that we have a good understanding of the past environment around specific, damp contact springs of different periods, allowing environmental change at such points to be discussed; yet, comparisons along the whole springline, or with landscape zones beyond this, are restricted as a result. Finally, by concentrating so much on the 'preservation' criterion in resource allocation, we *de facto* constrain our understanding of the very earliest, Mesolithic and Neolithic, parts of our sequence and of the post-Roman elements.

This consideration of how post-excavation assessment and analysis were undertaken on the site has been presented in some detail since, at every turn, it influences how the interpretations set out below have been reached and the limitations/problems in doing so. Even when evidence has been studied with as much care as possible, of course, certainty can still fall beyond our grasp (see, for example, the discussion in section 6.4 of whether the latest levels in one part of the site were forming at the end of the fourth century AD or in the decades, or even centuries, beyond this).

1.6 Archiving, future access and publication policy

The physical finds and site records generated by the project are held by the Yorkshire Museum and will thus be available for consultation at any point into the future (stored under the accession code YORYM: 2011.1129). In general, all the material gathered on-site has been retained, the one exception being Roman and medieval CBM, a sample of which has been kept using the museum-specific guidelines developed by our own specialist, Jane McComish.

All other documentation generated by the work is held either by the Archaeology Data Service (ADS),[39] or, for the basic YAT information, in their Integrated Archaeological Data Base.[40] The ADS holdings include specialist finds and environmental reports on various classes of assemblage and detailed discussion of stratigraphic and spatial development of different parts of the site. They also incorporate higher-order summaries of the former and commentaries on the sequences derived from YAT and OSA work, part of the attempt to create a single grouping structure across the project (see section 1.5).

This publication does not claim to be the last word on the interpretation of the site – a 'final publication' – and this is for two reasons. First, we hope that access to its primary archive will allow others to undertake further analysis on particular topics and thus to reach other, perhaps different, conclusions on what this site 'means' (a recent, open access article has been produced specifically to facilitate this process of engagement with this complex, underlying documentation[41]). Second, we have been deliberately selective, both in what we have examined in detail (a combination of what the resources allocated to us allowed and what was thought likely to be most important: see above), and in what we have then chosen to disseminate in this volume (what we believed to be most interesting). Because of what was found in excavation, this publication necessarily concentrates on the Bronze Age to Roman periods.

As is apparent from the contents page of this volume, these thoughts are not organised into a simple chronological discussion, rather a description of different forms of human engagement with the Heslington landscape that cross period boundaries. Their order of presentation below is based on a belief that it is only by first understanding the fundamental relationship between people and their immediate environment and its resources (see chapters 2–5) that we can then explore other activities such as domestic organisation or trade and exchange (see chapters 6 and 7). Furthermore, matters such as ritual activity must find their context in material circumstances, not *vice versa* (hence the material in chapter 8 comes near the end). Naturally, such principles are contested; Whittle, for example, believes that 'where and how people chose to settle, and for how long, is at least as interesting as the variety of crop they cultivated or the age at which they slaughtered cattle'[42] and so might give priority to our chapter 6. Other authors, particularly those influenced by post-modernist social theory and its 'linguistic turn',[43] would want a greater role for ideological structures in driving, rather than reflecting, social change, and so might place our chapter 8 near the start.

Finally, although wishing to think about landscapes thematically, we still acknowledge the existence of a sequence of site development at Heslington. Thus, within each theme there is an element of chronological presentation; yet we also feel that the pivotal points of change here do not fit easily into the period-based divisions conventionally used to describe prehistoric and Roman developments. For this reason, our closing chapter discussing overall changes and their contexts is structured around periods of significant transition (see sections 9.1 and 9.3–9.5) or lack thereof (see section 9.2). To us, this site calls into question the way in which the past is divided up and presented. We hope to play a small part in developing new chronological frameworks, rather than reinforcing those existing structures.

Landscape resources – nature and culture

2

In this chapter we consider the site location, geological setting and associated deposit formation processes, particularly in relation to the York moraine (section 2.1). Attention then turns to the natural resources available in this landscape, where we use a variety of data sets to describe timber and stone sources (section 2.2). We finish with a discussion of access to water (section 2.3), which has had, by far the greatest impact on the location and character of human activity here.

2.1 Drift geology and formation processes

The Vale of York, in which the site is situated (fig 2.1), comprises a relatively flat and open landscape surrounded by higher land to the north (the Howardian Hills), east (the Yorkshire Wolds) and west (the Pennines, here in the form of a Magnesian Limestone ridge). The rivers that drain those surrounding landscapes run south towards the Humber basin, helping form the distinctive character of the Vale. The City of York itself, an important focus of settlement since at least the Roman period, is centrally located within the Vale at a transitional point between the varied topography and the mixed farming landscapes of the Vale of Mowbray to the north and the more open landscapes of the Humberhead Levels to the south. The soils of the Vale, largely deep permeable sandy loams of the Blackwood association,[1] are formed from glacial till, sand and gravel, making them generally fertile and suitable for arable use. Today, large fields enclosed by intermittent hedges and occasional trees give the landscape a generally open character.[2]

Two glacial moraines ran across the Vale of York composed of materials deposited by retreating glaciers:

the York moraine and, 13km to its south, the Escrick moraine. They rose above the plain to their south to define the limit of what constituted Lake Humber in the preceding period, a basin that now forms the present southern Vale of York landscape. A buried soil near Doncaster deposited at the final stage of the lake's existence yielded a date of 11,400–11,000 cal BC.[3] These two moraines have been interpreted as significant prehistoric routeways crossing the Vale (but see further discussion in section 9.1). This is because of the flint implements that have been found along their length and their alignment with proposed long-distance trackways evident on the Yorkshire Wolds to the east, thought to date back to at least the Bronze Age (notably, Towthorpe Ridgeway and Sledmere Green Lane[4]).

The York moraine formed the hillside at the northern part of the Heslington site, here comprising a series of ridges of sand, silt, clay and gravel, known locally as Kimberlow Hill (fig 2.2). This landscape does not lie within the catchment of any significant streams or rivers, water simply draining into Germany Beck and Stillingfleet Beck, the latter via the Tillmire Drain. It is, however, situated above a minor aquifer that feeds into watercourses in the area. Springs rose on the lower slopes of Heslington Hill to the west of the site (hence the

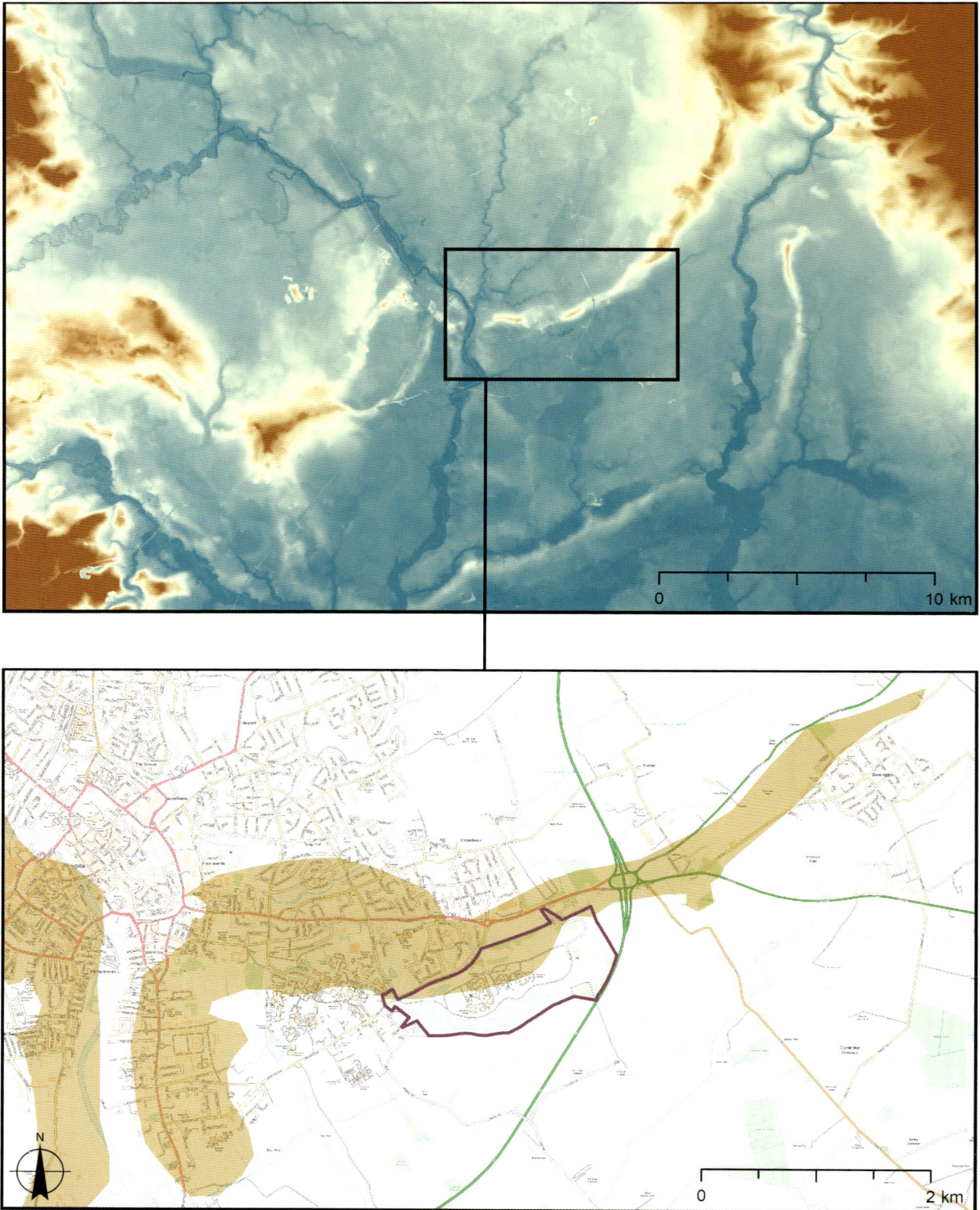

Fig 2.1 Top: general plan of the Vale of York (blue central area, relict river channels in darker blue) with higher ground of York moraine crossing the Vale (brown), the Dales to the west and the Yorkshire Wolds to the east (both dark brown). OS Terrain 5 DTM (© Crown copyright and database rights 2018 Ordnance Survey). Bottom: position of Heslington East site (red outline) on the southern edge of glacial moraine (brown shading: from Brit ce Glacial Map V2.0, Clark *et al* 2004). *Drawing*: Helen Goodchild

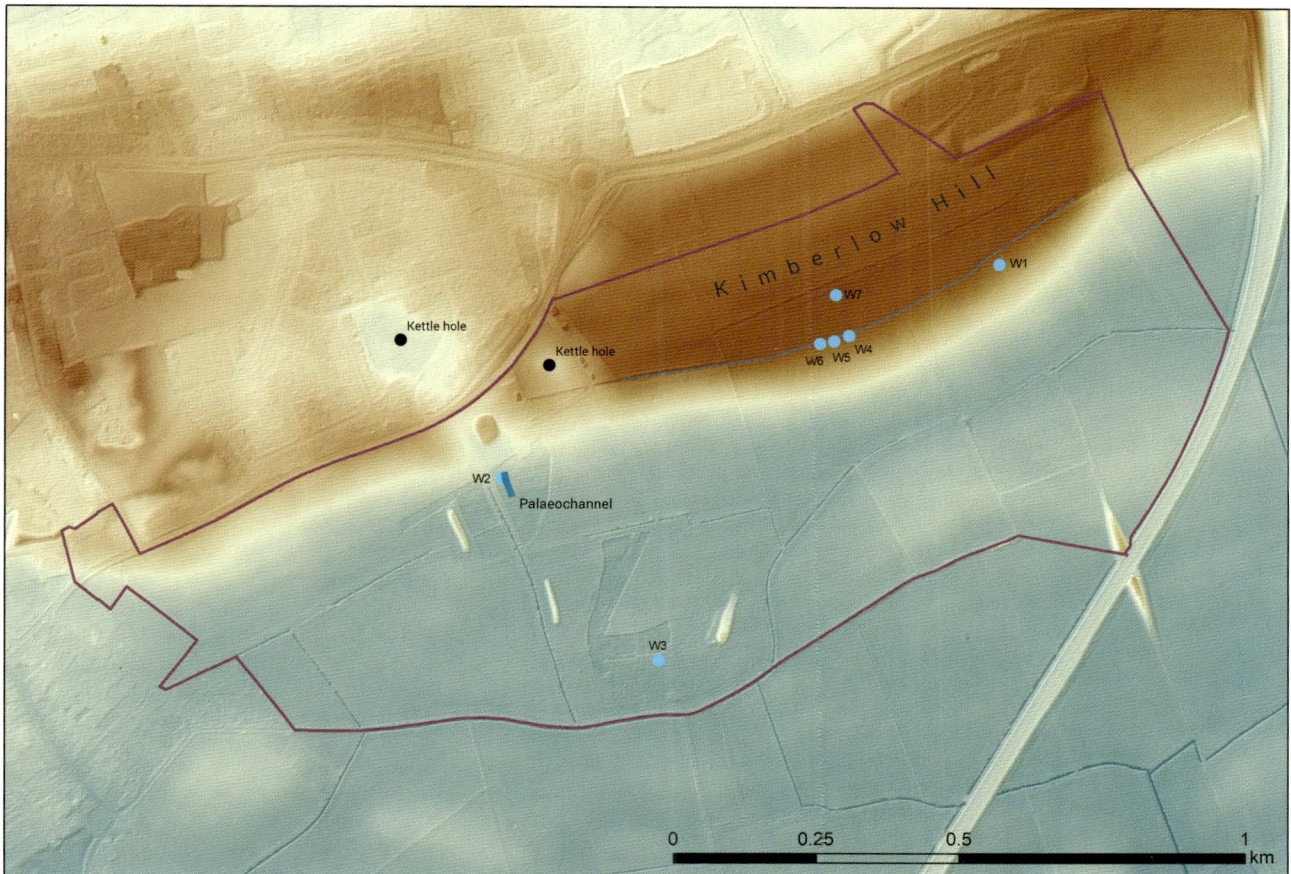

Fig 2.2 Site features showing Kimberlow Hill, kettle holes, palaeochannel, springline at 22m OD (blue dashed line) and position of Wells 1–7 (blue). *Drawing*: Helen Goodchild

name of Spring Lane) forming a distinct line that influenced human activity in general, and well-digging in particular, on the site, notably along the springline at 22m OD (see further below). A small stream, later used for provisioning fishponds at Heslington Hall in the seventeenth century,[5] still flows behind St Paul's Church in Heslington village and may be linked to such springs.

A borehole survey, undertaken to a depth of around 20m for structural engineering purposes, illustrates the nature of the geology at the site. Solid geology, only seen in small areas, comprised Sherwood and Keuper Sandstones. This is overlain in the north by sands, gravels and boulder clays and in the south by silts and blown sands ('the 25 drift'[6]). These boreholes paint a simple picture of what is quite a dynamic landscape at the detailed scale, such sedimentary processes having a complex relationship with human activity on the site.

Two significant kettle holes (that is, depressions, mostly under 10m in depth, which form at the edge of glaciers as wedges of ice melt and then gradually fill with sediment[7]) lay in the vicinity of the site. The first, situated within the development area of the nearby residential

estate of Badger Hill, was identified on Ordnance Survey maps as a boggy zone from the 1930s onwards and so not then built on due to the unstable ground. It measures approximately 100m × 150m and was investigated by the British Geological Survey when mapping the Vale of York in 2005. This work identified the peat-filled depression as a possible ice-marginal deposit with associated kettle hole.[8]

The second, another peat-filled depression on the northern margins of the development area, measured c 30m east–west by c 60m north–south and cut natural boulder clay and silts/sands. Defining its extent and character in the field created some challenges, waterlogging limiting our understanding of its detailed nature. Samples from its base, however, date to the early Holocene period (10,719 ±28 BP and 10,613 ±29 BP: see table 1.1). The surrounding area was hummocky in character, the localised floodplain of old river channels flowing down the slope to provide continual drainage. This kettle hole had no clear relationship with human activities on the site, with the possible exception of a Bronze Age burial in its vicinity (see section 8.1); yet it was undoubtedly a water source from an early date,

19

thus attracting wild food resources to the area and helping to support a distinct ecosystem.

A series of extensive palaeochannels were identified running down from Kimberlow Hill and from these two kettle holes in the west of the site. Although these features are spatially discrete from any clear occupation of the landscape, a specialist programme of geoarchaeological work in one such channel (G135: fig 2.3) allows us to explore in detail the relationship between human activity and the potential resources of this landscape. This showed that the channel cut down in successive phases and contained articulated animal bone, perhaps deliberately placed, and charcoal. Its successive fills dated to 3400 ±40 BP, 3160 ±40 BP and 3010 ±40 BP (G135: see table 1.1), so it seems to have been filling up over several centuries during the Bronze Age, perhaps in a wooded landscape. The headless body of a red deer (*Cervus elaphus*) was deposited in this feature during this process.

Field systems were set out above this palaeochannel in the course of the Iron Age (see section 3.2) and seemed to continue in use into the Roman period. From *c* 200 AD onwards, however, there was a dramatic change here, with areas of intensive activity replaced by erosion channels, followed by a more general, concluding phase of hill wash

(G175). Thus, natural agencies first played a role in site formation processes within the Roman period, then completely sealed the area in the late fourth century or just afterwards. The removal of the lining of Well 2 (see below) allowed wind-blown sands to accumulate on its site (G170). The dating of these events is complex, with Iron Age and early Roman finds, probably disturbed from lower levels, occurring alongside third- and fourth-century artefacts. The latter include two coin hoards, which suggest the area was still significant (see section 8.3).

Elsewhere, at the eastern edge of the site, early deposits encountered towards the base of the hillslope suggest wetland environments, along with silts, sands and gravels (G186). This whole landscape was later covered beneath sandy clay deposits (G187) interpreted as hill wash and forming at a time when there was little human activity here. The layer accumulating above this horizon in the centre of the site shows this process occurring before the second century AD, but there was no directly associated artefactual material to allow formal dating of its formation. It seems likely, therefore, that, although woodland clearance may have taken place in certain sectors, natural processes dominated this landscape for much of prehistory.

This general picture also applied in later centuries,

Fig 2.3 Strata filling the palaeochannel, here being prepared for geoarchaeological sampling. © YAT

with certain human interludes. In particular, towards the base of the hillside at the centre of the site, an Iron Age enclosure containing roundhouses (see section 6.2, Roundhouses 12 and 13) and with an adjacent well (see section 3.2, fig 3.5) was later sealed by an extensive series of clay, silts and sands (G79, G195), accumulations probably derived from higher up the slope. These also built up more generally along the springline contour noted previously, here together with more localised wind-blown sands and silts. Finally, a nearby sequence of fine, discontinuous deposits seems to represent episodes of trampling at a time when discrete pits, some provably of Roman date, were being dug and perhaps trees removed (G206). Later ditches here containing ceramics dating to the second and third centuries AD appear, however, to respect the position of the enclosure and adjacent well, showing that the latter may not have been entirely obscured. In short, after a distinct episode of Iron Age activity, deposits were being washed down the hillside and wind-blown materials deposited in depressions, yet partially sealed earlier features continued to affect later landscape divisions: the relationship between human activity and natural deposition was clearly a complex one.

At the top of the hillside at its centre, a second zone containing only irregular features of various dates in the Roman period alongside evidence for processes of weathering, tree growth and the remnants of natural water channels (G93) suggest that natural processes predominated here at that time. Just to the east of this, however, intensive human activities dating to the second to fourth centuries were evident, before further accumulations formed towards the end of the latter sequence (G109, G113), again overlain by a concluding phase of hill wash.

Overall, therefore, initial natural features related to glaciation and water flows in the west of the site were replaced by intensive Iron Age activity, but returned to the creation of erosion channels and wind-blown accumulations by the late Roman period. At the eastern margins, a prehistoric wetland landscape remained largely devoid of human intervention. In the central area, however, Iron Age activities along the springline at the base of the hillside later gave way to a combination of hill wash and localised wind-blown accumulations before the third century AD, the latter processes having a complex relationship with human activity here. Further up the hillside, colluvium forming in prehistory was overlain in one zone by intensive late Roman occupation. The decline of the latter activity allowed spreads and accumulations to develop again, then general hill wash in post-Roman centuries. This last process was evident across the whole site and later cut by a range of medieval

furrows (see section 4.2). Some of the latter seemed to align with the position of underlying Roman ditches, but this is assumed to be a common product of the general slope of the hillside, rather than an indication of continuity between the periods. This evidence for medieval ploughing was succeeded by its modern equivalent following enclosure in the nineteenth century AD (see section 9.5).

Concerning the general character of this landscape, a paucity of pre-Iron Age data means that early contexts are difficult to define. By the end of that period, however, evidence suggests a variety of habitat types, including muddy banks, meadow and woodland (part of this last element may be due to hedge lines, rather than distinctive woods *per se*), with some features indicating the burning of turves at this time. Evidence from around the centre of the site suggests a mainly open agricultural landscape, but with pollen and other data implying the existence of woodland along the course of the springline crossing this area. The latter zone was then cut by a high energy event in a wetland edge environment. A later reduction in waterflow, associated with the accumulation of organic material, indicates localised soil erosion around that springline in the Late Iron Age to Roman transition.

The Roman period profile also suggests an open landscape containing pasture and some arable land, whilst the (tentative) evidence of beetles implies grazed grasslands and disturbed ground, with a smaller element of species indicating a woodland habitat. Invertebrates which live in dry hay residues came from these horizons and may originate inside a nearby structure or within dry litter in grassland, whilst a more unusual group living on rotting wood and bark likely relates to a decomposing timber structure, for example the lining of Well 1 (see below). Later deposits from this feature further indicate low-energy, episodic flow along the wooded springline in a landscape otherwise of open pasture, with some associated animal dung. The abundant alder charcoal and other round wood from here seem to date to the first century AD (1981 ±28 BP and 1957 ±25 BP respectively, both G199: see table 1.1), a point at which willow pollen indicates that the waterhole was drying out. Overall, the picture during the Roman period is one of waterholes for livestock, open grassland and some disturbed cultivated landscapes, but a lack of 'imported' species.

By the end of that period, there is general evidence for charred barley/wheat (predominantly spelt with a small proportion of emmer, the latter likely a contaminant of other crops) and chaff and some wild/weed plant seeds, including a range of segetal taxa commonly associated with fertile disturbed soils and cultivation. This, together with physical evidence for crop driers (see section 4.2), suggests crop processing. Some zones also saw dung accumulating in trampled areas at this time, perhaps associated with detritus-rich water and muddy banks. Ditch fills of this date accumulating beside the timber lining of Well 1, for example, generated assemblages indicating wet and muddy conditions, together with evidence for watercress and some scrub plants including bramble, raspberry and elder (all are edible, but their presence here probably relates to highly humic local conditions). Corresponding evidence for post-Roman periods was not recovered.

2.2 Exploitation of wood and stone sources

Woodland resources in the vicinity of the site can be understood using a number of sources of evidence. Some was derived from analysing environmental samples (such analyses aimed to take place on a scale to allow comparison between different parts of the site: see section 1.5). Elsewhere, geoarchaeological work investigated sediment samples and, in a few cases, information was derived from preserved wooden artefacts or well linings (dendrochronological information was generated for a structure inserted above Well 1, thus giving unparalleled accuracy for the felling date of this timber: see section 5.3).

Oak was being accessed from the beginning of our sequences in the Bronze Age, with hazel and alder root common at this point (fig 2.4), whilst a yew stump in an early pit indicates prehistoric ground clearance in one location. Unworked round wood included maple, alder, hazel, ash, oak and willow, with the last also used in wattle construction. Deliberately hollowed logs made of alder (*Alnus* spp), traditionally associated with water resistant properties, suggest that trees of a significant diameter were growing locally, as well as the smaller alder material used as stakes and rods. Parts of five separate log

linings were recovered, with the earliest, poorly preserved pair dating to the Early Bronze Age, the two better-preserved examples, over 1m long, to the Late Bronze Age (see section 5.2, fig 5.3) and a final example from the Late Iron Age. None were found *in situ* or complete, but some can be linked circumstantially to the use of nearby wells, perhaps being discarded when these features were decommissioned. The logs had been finished using adzes, with gouges for the inner faces and a combination of axes and adzes to shape the inner bevel, whereas tooling marks on material from general prehistoric contexts show that axes were employed to form stakes, posts and rods.

General timber usage appears to be relatively stable in prehistoric levels, although some proportions changed over time and specific features used particular species; for example, the Iron Age well lined almost entirely with alder rods using either maple or alder stakes (see further below). Less maple was apparent in the mid-Iron Age and by the Late Iron Age a considerable range of species was being exploited (fig 2.5), notably alder and hazel. The recovery of Scot's Pine (*Pinus sylvestris*) from a prehistoric horizon at the site is noteworthy. This species is rarely recovered from archaeological contexts before the late medieval period, the assumption being that stands of *Pinus* and other conifers were only exploited on a significant level after the sixteenth century (finds of most softwoods from before this date are generally thought to be imported from the continent or the Baltic[9]). By the late Roman period, wood sources may have become more restricted, with the use of alder, hazel and willow in association with structures, presumably as wattles, but rarely oak or elder.

When surviving wattle structures are considered in detail, interesting results emerge. Part of an early lining of Iron Age Well 2 (see below for details) was made almost entirely from 12–28mm alder rods, held in place with alder and acer stakes, whilst another part of this feature utilised smaller ash and hazel rods supported by radially faced oak stakes: each element was the outcome of careful

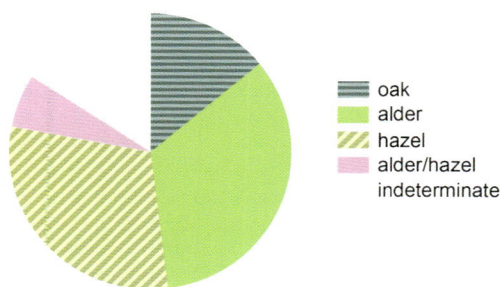

Fig 2.4 Charcoal assemblage composition by total number of fragments from earliest levels on the site. *Drawing*: Neil Gevaux

- oak
- alder
- hazel
- alder/hazel
- indeterminate

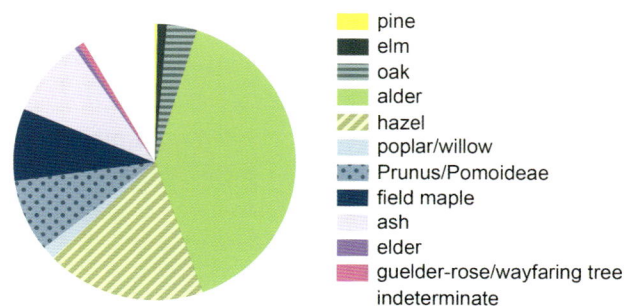

Fig 2.5 Charcoal assemblage composition by total number of fragments from late Iron Age levels on the site. *Drawing*: Neil Gevaux

- pine
- elm
- oak
- alder
- hazel
- poplar/willow
- Prunus/Pomoideae
- field maple
- ash
- elder
- guelder-rose/wayfaring tree
- indeterminate

planning, involving the acquisition of particular wood species and sizes for specific purposes. Such plans changed between episodes of construction, either because of different structural requirements or, more likely, different timber availability or artisanal expertise/ preference.

A range of *stone sources* are evident on the site, some relatively local and others that have travelled a greater distance. These stone objects are discussed here in general, but appear in more detail in subsequent chapters where relevant (for example, a Bronze Age battleaxe made of dolerite, probably from the Whin Sill on Hadrian's Wall, some 150km north of York (see section 8.1), and jet from the Whitby area used to manufacture artefacts in Iron Age contexts (see sections 5.2 and 6.2)).

Flint implements mainly represent periods from the Mesolithic to Bronze Age (see section 6.1 for details). Occasionally, however, evidence (unfortunately unstratified) for earlier activity turned up, for example a possible Late Upper Palaeolithic artefact, and also for more recent pursuits, for example a modern gun flint. Spatially, material came from all parts of the site, but the small number of Mesolithic artefacts recovered concentrate in the west, as do most Neolithic finds. By the Bronze Age, material seems more evenly distributed. The majority comprised regular till flint from the glacial contexts nearer the east coast. Most of these items arrived as roughed-out nodules, but some were worked more fully at Heslington, as indicated by hammerstones, cores, flakes and waste from knapping (see section 5.1). Most artefacts represent domestic activities on the site, but two objects were associated directly with a Bronze Age cremation and a Roman inhumation (see sections 8.1 and 8.4 respectively).

Quern stones arrived at the Heslington site from a variety of sources to its north and west (see section 4.2), starting with a saddle quern from an Early Iron Age context indicating mixed farming from that date (Well 4, see below), and at least six further saddle querns from Iron Age contexts. The single Beehive quern from the site, of poor quality and very worn, came from the fill of Well 6, whilst six disc hand querns were also recovered, three made from Mayen lava and three derived from regional sources (see section 7.2 for trading implications). Finally, the site yielded evidence for six much larger millstones, probably powered by animals, all from late Roman contexts. These suggest an increased investment in milling practices at that time (see section 4.2).

Building stones included siliceous sandstone from a Pennine source and oolitic limestone used in Roman buildings, alongside occasional examples of Corrallian limestone from the Malton area, a Jurassic formation.

Much of this stone was recovered from ditch fills adjacent to the footprint of a known building, or from places where such buildings can be assumed to exist nearby. Pink-coloured bioclastic limestone from an unknown source, decalcified to some extent, was recovered, whilst corroded fossils from reddish sandstones suggest a source in Swaledale or Wensleydale.

A number of dressed stones were incorporated within the uppermost levels of wells, including a re-used roof finial (Well 7, below) and two groups recycled from demolished structures (Well 5). The latter material comprised three crude gritstone voussoirs of differing size derived from an arch with a span of *c* 1.75m, perhaps the round-headed doorway of an agricultural building, and a second group suggest the dismantling of a building using an *opus quadratum* technique (see fig 6.4). The collapsed roof of building G106 employed tiles made of pale brown, fine-grained, well-cemented micaceous (muscovite) sandstone, probably from a source in the Pennine Coal Measures Group to the west (see sections 6.4 and 8.5 for further details of all such structures), whilst some pink sandstone containing iron oxide, most likely from a Pennine source, was found.

Overall, therefore, it can be seen that a variety of stone sources was utilised on the site, but, with the possible exception of prehistoric flints, most of those sources used for specialist agricultural or structural functions were brought in from elsewhere in the region. Indeed, even the flint items found here derived initially from the glacial contexts on the east coast, mostly arriving as pre-processed roughed-out nodules.

2.3 Exploitation of water sources

By far the most significant local resource to influence human activity on the site was water. This was true of the earliest period in prehistory, and continued until the most recent landscape development: the newly created, ten-hectare lake at the Heslington East campus (see section 1.1) is intended to have amenity and habitat value, but was also created to manage water on the site. Having such a large water surface there today belies the earlier landscape development of this zone. As noted previously (see section 2.1), much of this flows from springs on the hillside in the northern part of the site, where a series of ridges of sand, silt, clay and gravel was deposited when retreating Ice Age glaciers created the York moraine. Given the absence of a fully flowing watercourse, there is a marked variety of water exploitation methods and access points at Heslington: water is clearly a resource offering significant benefits both to people visiting it initially, whether occasionally or seasonally, and to those later staying there on a more permanent basis. Spring water could be drawn using patches of land surrounding the springs themselves or, later, was accessed from specially laid gravelled or cobbled areas.

Investment is most evident in those waterholes where the consolidation of surrounding land took place over an extended period of time, and this often included the construction of wells and other access mechanisms. Whilst many of these wells were unlined, necessitating re-cutting to allow extended use, some were lined with timber, such as wattles, from the start, and others augmented with cobbles and re-used masonry. The ubiquity and variety of water access points can be seen as significant in making such springs a locale for complex social action, embodying a cultural/natural dynamic not commonly recognised or appreciated: water, being a more basic and immediate human need than either food or shelter, necessarily involves a fusion of symbolic and functional imperatives. The use of wells at Heslington East was certainly on a par with the influence of more substantial water flows such as rivers and streams.[10] Wells, after all, are points where subterranean, hidden water can be 'captured' and, seemingly, then ceases to flow; their construction required technical knowledge and investment. Further, for that investment to be worthwhile, it necessitated a regularity of access, sometimes involving control of the adjacent landscape.[11]

All of these elements are evident in the numerous water-related features known from Heslington East. Seven of the most significant examples have been chosen to illustrate such factors. This sample is designed to represent the full date range and the best preserved/most thoroughly investigated features, together with those that had a significant impact on landholding in their vicinity. Well 1 lay on the springline towards the east of the site, and Wells 2 and 3 at its western edge in the area of a former palaeochannel (see section 2.1). Wells 4, 5 and 6 were situated along the springline at its centre, whilst Well 7 lay in an atypical position high on the hillside above the latter (see fig 2.2). Information about each is summarised in table 2.1.

Towards the east of the site, the natural glacial deposits noted above, dated to *c* 10,000 BC, were cut by a complex of features labelled *Well 1* (the constant inflow of groundwater made distinguishing between each intrusion problematic). In its earliest form (fig 2.6), this comprised a number of broadly contemporary shallow, sub-circular or oval pits (G191) containing organic fills, bands of cobbles and two phases of hollowed-out log linings made of alder (neither exhibited tool marks, but then both are poorly preserved). These intrusions ranged in size from

0.50m up to 4m in diameter, although the largest examples may have comprised several cuts eroded into one. They were typically between 0.30m and 0.50m deep, and none in excess of 0.75m. Analysis of their fills generated evidence for insects from shallow and stagnant water with damp decaying vegetation and some beetles from meadow or grassland habitats. A contemporary cobble-filled cut nearby contained wood charcoal from alder, hazel and oak, a 50 per cent frequency of fungal hyphae in the charcoal indicating rotting wood. The sediment below the logs was dated by OSL to *c* 1900 BC and by C14 to 3630 ±40 BP, and the log lining itself to 3350 ±30 BP (G193 and G191 respectively; see table 1.1), placing both within the Bronze Age. The number of successive features around the contact spring suggest that they are waterholes, some lined and others not, associated with cobbled areas of hardstanding.

A spread of organic material containing a concentration of wooden fragments (G192) overlay the initial pits, perhaps marking a hiatus in the exploitation of this contact spring. This was cut, in turn, by further pits (G193) containing only Iron Age and early Roman pottery, thus adding weight to the idea of a gap in use. At some point the area here was enclosed with ditches (G77/G194; see section 3.2 and fig 3.6), some of which had been re-cut on successive occasions (G199), perhaps at the same time as a large, sub-circular pit (G197), another water-extraction feature, was inserted just to the north east. This was lined with oak offcuts from boards or planking, rather than the usual wattle and roundwood, timber perhaps recycled from nearby structures. Environmental analysis of the fills of this last element indicate stagnant water and terrestrial decomposers that live in detritus and dung (the presence of some invertebrate aquatic taxa but no aquatic plant taxa might suggest only temporary standing water). Pottery from the final fills of the adjacent ditches imply that they were part of a Late Iron Age/early Roman re-use of this spring. A complex timber structure comprising two squared oak uprights cut from the same, long-lived tree, with a felling date between AD 53 and 89, was set out above the latest fills, perhaps the base for a framed structure (see figs 5.6 and 5.7; see section 5.3 for wider interpretations of this feature and how the changing waterflows in the well's upper fills may link to adjacent artisanal activities).

The most reasonable interpretation of this evidence is that the water source was employed from shortly after 2000 BC for some centuries, then fell into decay before being put into use a second time from *c* 200 BC or a little later. The alder linings used in its first lining suggest a considerable investment in maintaining access to water in an apparently open landscape. By the Late Iron Age,

Table 2.1 Seven selected wells, giving information on related stratigraphic groups, summary description and date of use. The latter categories comprise Neolithic (Neo), Early Bronze Age (EBA), Early or Late Iron Age (EIA/LIA), early, mid or late Roman (ER/MR/LR) or combinations of such.

Well Number	Group number(s)	Summary Interpretation	Period(s) of use
1	77/191/192/193/194/197/199	Alder-lined pits in an open landscape, sealed by organic accumulation supplying a lacuna in use. Later, a replacement oak-lined feature was inserted here in a now-enclosed landscape, finally overlain by a timber-framed structure after silting up	EBA, gap, LIA/ER
2	137/138/139/140/141	Alder-lined waterhole, associated with the first boundaries in the vicinity. Its later, stone-lined access favoured human over animal use, perhaps at a time of greater cereal cultivation in the vicinity. Structured deposition of distinct items into late Roman period, some long after the demise of the feature	EIA to ER
3	167	Wattle-lined, with cobbled access, influencing initial (undated) features controlling stock movement here and later Iron Age field systems	?EIA to ER
4	212	Two large pits, the first showing clean running water, with its replacement evidencing dung deposition and a saddle quern: a mixed farming economy from at least the start of the Iron Age	?Neo or EBA to EIA
5	227	Wattle-lined pit, employing recycled stonework from dismantled buildings to reinforce access. Unusual finds may represent special deposition and/or ritualised closure.	MR to LR
6	229	Wattle-lined well, probably linked to nearby artisanal activities and perhaps replacing Well 5. It influenced the laying out of a 'ritual enclosure', occupying the latter's SW corner.	LR
7	111	Masonry-built well incorporating symbolism in both its construction (new stonework and re-used finial) and its demise (dumping of water raising kit before ending access, followed by separate closure evidenced by the deposition of young and old animals and heirloom ceramics).	LR

ditches enclosed the waterhole, with its fills generating a number of grazed grassland beetle taxa and rather fewer aquatic beetles. These can be set beside, respectively, invertebrates from a grass meadow habitat and dry hay residues from the general area, and those indicating a range of rotting wood in its immediate vicinity.

Well 2 was inserted at the western edge of the excavated area, in a zone previously occupied by a palaeochannel that had been gradually filling up in the course of the Bronze Age (see above). Near the start of the Iron Age, material was dumped here (G137) to level the ground for the insertion of a series of pits, channels and a possible boundary ditch (G138). The southern terminal of the latter feature contained a decapitated skull, presumably commemorating the creation of the first such boundary on the site (see section 8.2). The function of these early pits is not entirely clear, but some were lined with hollowed cylinders carved from alder

roundwood dated to 2730 ±60 BP (G138; see table 1.1), with their associated channels lined with wickerwork. Their position matches that of a definite well of later date (see below) and this, together with the channels, suggests that the preceding features were also used for water extraction. They contained organic silt and sand, alongside evidence for foul conditions and dung deposition. The surrounding landscape at this time appears to be mainly open, but with some woodland in defined corridors along the springline.

This spring was later re-dug and lined to create another feature, more certainly a well (G139). Its wicker lining incorporated the remains of a small wooden shovel, in addition to a single fragment of red deer bone, interpreted on the site as an animal trapped in the feature (see section 8.1 for wider interpretation of the shovel, and section 9.1 for the implications of its association with the deer bone). The use of this re-lined feature was accompanied by

Fig 2.6 Early Bronze Age cobbling associated with Well 1 in its initial phase (visible partially in plan, partially in section), with a later Iron Age or early Roman oak lining inserted into it after a gap during which the primary feature had silted up. © OSA

nearby digging of pits with various functions (see section 5.2) and the laying of cobbled surfaces. The latter may have formed a north–south routeway above the backfilled palaeochannel noted previously but were interleaved with waterborne sediments, implying that this earlier channel may still have been active at this time or, minimally, had created a lower zone that encouraged water accumulation. The new well was later re-lined, with pits and ditched boundaries then dug nearby (G140), the latter features suggesting that the well was now enclosed. The laying of the final surface was accompanied by the creation of a stone-lined well head, a small sub-circular tank and three blocks of millstone grit forming steps leading down to the water level (G141). These more formalised features, dated to c 200 BC, suggest an emphasis on human over animal access at this time.

This increased investment in access late in the life of Well 2 goes alongside changes in the local environment. Here, the deposition of sands and organic materials was seemingly in decline, accompanied by cycles of soil erosion and silting. Indications of increased wet woodland species along the springline, and of cereal grains more generally here, were then followed by evidence for an open landscape with grasses and sedges.

The final well fills here yielded Iron Age ceramics and Roman brick, the latter presumed to be intrusive. Long after it had been fully sealed, atypical finds continued to be inserted into the site of the former water source, some implying structured deposition in a boggy area of former significance (see section 8.3).

In summary, Well 2 was created near the start of the Iron Age, at first as a series of informal pits and as part of the first landscape boundaries here (see section 3.2). It seems to have a significant role in watering stock at this point, with perhaps a local wooded area surrounded by open countryside. By the end of the Iron Age, and perhaps into the Roman period, that landscape still shows damp woodland nearby but perhaps cereal cultivation beyond. The well had become enclosed by this stage and invested with stone lining, tank and steps. It now favoured human access over that of animals.

Well 3 lay more than 400m to the south east of Well 2 and comprised two roughly circular pits (their inter-relationship is unclear) with a total length of more than 10m and up to c 5m across (G167). Associated gullies ran north and south from this feature for a distance of more than 17m, and its sloping base was sealed by five successive cobble surfaces up to 0.22m thick. Clearly, this cut was designed to give access to water, as its base lay at the level of the water table and the cobbles created a ramp down to it. The waterhole had an alder wattle lining (and a single willow – perhaps a repair) held in place by roundwood stakes that may have also consolidated the edges of the cobbling.

The earliest landscape boundaries here focused on this point, the first ditches forming a funnel leading towards it, replaced by a curvilinear enclosure with an adjacent entrance (both are interpreted as relating to stock control; see section 3.2). There seems little doubt, therefore, that Well 3 functioned as a waterhole in the Iron Age and indeed dictated the initial spatial organisation of this zone. Its position further influenced the laying out of the first proper field systems later in the Iron Age, and even the line of a much later Roman corn dryer (see section 4.2). This last phase of activity was no doubt the source of intrusive finds in the top fills of the feature (see section 1.5 for a discussion of the complexities of grouping and dating stratigraphy on the site).

The next three wells to be described lay close together along the main springline at the centre of the site, but are of considerably different date. They are described below in proposed chronological order. *Well 4* comprised two large, stratigraphically early, pits (G212). One, with a maximum diameter of 7m, had primary fills of yellow sand and organic matter containing abundant water scavenger beetles indicating aquatic deposition. Its final grey sand fill, derived from the collapse of surrounding strata, represents its demise. Rare finds in the initial fills include a single, probably intrusive, Iron Age sherd and a flint of possible Early Bronze Age date. The latter seemingly represents the date when this feature fell out of use, so it may have been inserted as early as the Neolithic period. The second pit, just 5m to the west, and a possible replacement in the Early Iron Age, generated environmental samples from its (undated) basal deposits showing foul water/dung assemblages and indicating livestock watering, whilst a saddle quern from the same feature suggests that a mixed economy operated from that early period (see section 4.2).

Well 5 comprised a large sub-oval construction cut *c* 2.5m across and 1m deep, lined with carefully constructed wattle to form a cylindrical shaft 0.90m in diameter (fig 2.7); clearly a substantial well (G227). Frequent cobbles, timber posts, planks and clay alongside the wattle may be packing in the cut or an earlier form of lining, whilst re-used squared masonry blocks set at the top of the feature may have formed a low wall around the

Fig 2.7 Wickerwork lining of Well 5, with capping/wall of re-used masonry. © OSA

well. Datable finds from the well were scarce, but did include an unusual Ebor Ware flagon, deposited long after its date of manufacture (see below on dating and also section 8.3), and a tile in an atypical fabric plus the radius of an adult human (see section 8.5). These must be residual, as they date at least a century before the well was dug into part of a ditch of the late fourth century AD. Artisanal activities to the west of this well (G230) may be associated with its use, a zone already associated with working hollows (G223) in the late Roman period.

Well 6, inserted 25m west of Well 5 and set in a construction cut 1.65m across (fig 2.8), comprised a shallow, wattle-lined feature, 1m in diameter (G229). Its use may be associated with a larger, adjacent feature consolidated with driven stakes, posts, horizontal timbers and large cobbles including a substantial fragment of beehive quern, possibly a second well. Difficult ground conditions make it impossible to ascertain the precise stratigraphic relationships here, but Well 6, even if in use from an earlier period, seems to have influenced the positioning of a late Roman enclosure in whose south-west corner it lay (see sections 3.4 and 8.5).

Well 7, dug in the second half of the fourth century AD, was inserted in a seemingly anomalous position 75m north of the main springline in the centre of the site (fig 2.2). It comprised a substantial, masonry-lined feature (fig 2.9) dug down to a depth of over 4.5m to access the water table on the hillside in a construction cut 3m across to allow a 1m diameter well to be built at it centre (G111). Its carefully laid lining incorporated a strangely positioned roof finial (see fig 6.5 and wider

discussion in section 6.3) and was extended above ground to include a masonry superstructure. Overall, this represents a major monumentalisation of the hillside, perhaps in use with building G112 to its west (see section 6.4).

The use and demise of this well are described in detail elsewhere (see section 8.6), as is the combination of ritual and routine practices that these processes may have encompassed.[12] In summary, its lowest fills suggest regular cleaning, then an episode during which the deposition of two adult pig skulls fouled the water source, discarded at a time when scrub and heathland were evident in the vicinity and insects and frogs/toads were falling into the well. A wooden bucket and virtually complete jar (see section 7.3), best interpreted as the discard of water-raising equipment, also came from this horizon.

The next fills formed at a time when environmental evidence implies a wasteland setting in the immediate vicinity and contained pitfall insects and frogs/toads. A very large cobblestone now dumped into the feature clearly precluded access to water from this point, whilst bones emphasise the deposition of a distinct combination of young and old animals and pottery the selected deposition of old items: the deliberate closure of the well. Post-closure deposits then formed in near-stagnant water, interleaved with the gradual collapse of the well's

Fig 2.8 Wickerwork lining of Well 6. © OSA

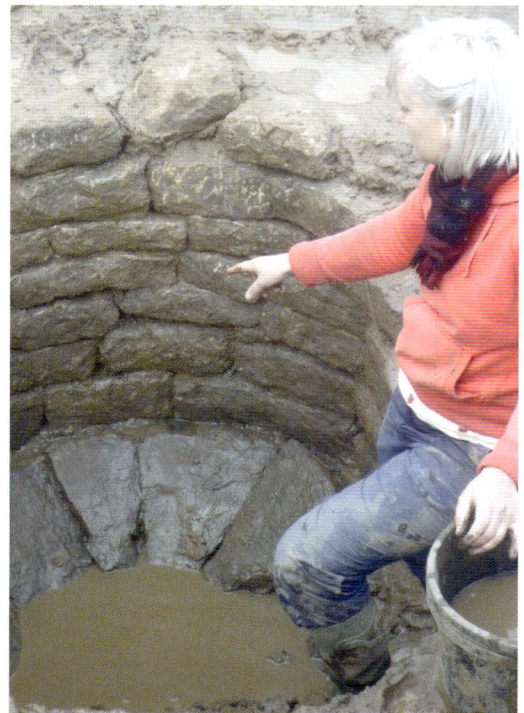

Fig 2.9 Well-laid masonry lining of Well 7, with triangular base slabs partially exposed. © OSA

lining before its complete demise. Layers of a much later date then accumulated in the hollow formed above the well.

The wells selected above for detailed description show that accessing water was of major importance from the start of the Bronze Age, if not before (Wells 1 and 4) until well into the Roman period (Wells 5, 6 and 7). No springs were used continuously across all these periods, however, although some places could be re-used after a gap (Well 1, in use from at least the Early Bronze Age, was covered with colluvial deposits, but its site was still evident enough to allow new water-related features to be inserted here at the end of the Iron Age). The form of wells ranged from unlined scoops, often early in the sequence, to a variety of wickerwork linings (Well 6) planks (Well 1) and stonework, whether recycled (Well 5) or specifically quarried for this purpose (Well 7). Early wells seem dedicated to watering stock, with cobbled areas to enhance access (Wells 1 and 3), but others appear to have been converted for human use later on (Well 2), whilst Well 7 could have been entirely for human consumption.

These features also serve to elucidate surrounding activities, whether from evidence from their fills (for example, dung assemblages and the saddle quern from Well 4 showing a mixed farming economy in existence by the start of the Iron Age; see section 4.2), or from adjacent features (for example, pits with burnt pebbles

south of Well 2 in the Iron Age (see section 5.3) or the working areas between of Wells 5 and 6 in the Late Roman period). The environmental samples derived from these features provide information on local landscape setting; for example, the woodland that seems to develop around these points in most periods (Well 2) or the waste end that became evident immediately beside Well 7 as the latter fell into decay. Such sources also chart general trends in landscape development, as with the early indications of mixed farming in Well 4 mentioned above, or the greater incidence of cereal cultivation evident in their vicinity (Well 2).

Finally, wells also had fundamental impacts on how this landscape was organised; for example, when setting out early boundaries to control stock movement (Wells 2 and 3), thereby enclosing the landscape – the (unnumbered) well incorporated into the western boundary of the first Iron Age enclosure at the centre of the site (see section 3.3), or the late Roman 'ritual' enclosure set up to include Well 6 at its southwest corner (see section 3.4). Further, in their construction, use and demise, wells clearly embodied a complex combination of functional and ritualistic activities, from the red deer (*Cervus elaphus*) bone and the shovel incorporated into Well 2 early in the Iron Age, to Well 7 and the roof finial in its construction, plus the young and old animals and distinctive pottery selected to mark its closure.[13]

Bounded landscapes – enclosure, delineation and movement

3

Next we explore the modification of the landscape to control/facilitate the movement of livestock and human populations within or through it. This includes descriptions of processes such as ditch digging to enclose certain areas or to define larger tracts of land, and more major modifications such as terracing to facilitate the construction of buildings. In addition, we consider the creation of axes of movement (for example, tracks and various forms of routeway). This sequence of activity starts with ditch systems evidencing the control of livestock in the west of the site (section 3.1), followed by the setting up of more formal Iron Age field systems both here and on its eastern margins (section 3.2). Roman landscape boundaries focused at the centre of the site are then dealt with (section 3.3), including the creation of a major new enclosure (section 3.4) in the third or fourth centuries AD and, very late in the Roman period, modifications to landholding on the northern margins of the site (section 3.5). The whole of this landscape appears to have been under the plough in the medieval and modern periods (section 3.6).

3.1 Early control of livestock

As noted in section 2.2, the site had been visited from the Neolithic period, if not before, with such visitations being clearly influenced by the needs of water access along the springline from the early Bronze Age onwards. This, however, was not a continuous process of occupation, as dates vary across the site and at least one contact spring that included the deposition of an organic horizon implies a hiatus in its exploitation (see section 2.3, Well 1). Beyond these nodal points, wetland deposits overlain by a sequence of silts, sands, gravels and clays had formed by the Neolithic period, overlain by colluvial sandy clay (G186 and G187 respectively).

From the Late Bronze Age onwards, human activity becomes more common and more concerted. This included, in the west, the setting out of a fence line running south from Well 2 (G138). This alignment was later reinforced by digging a ditch (fig 3.1), but which now extended further south (a pit inserted at the latter's southern terminal contained a decapitated skull with surviving brain: see section 8.2). The creation of this alignment may be associated with the construction of a possible early rectilinear, post-built structure (see section 6.1) and, more certainly, with the creation of a metalled routeway across a now-silted up palaeochannel (see section 2.1, G139). These features represent the first proven point at which occupation proper, rather than visitations to access water, are evident on the site. Pottery related to the fence line is dated to *c* 900–600 BC and this group is associated with wooden cylinders with a C14 date of 2730 ±60 BP (see section 2.3, G138; table 1.1). The character of these developments suggests that, by the Early Iron Age, access to Well 2 was now being controlled, perhaps to keep groups of animals separate when being watered, yet no complete enclosures were

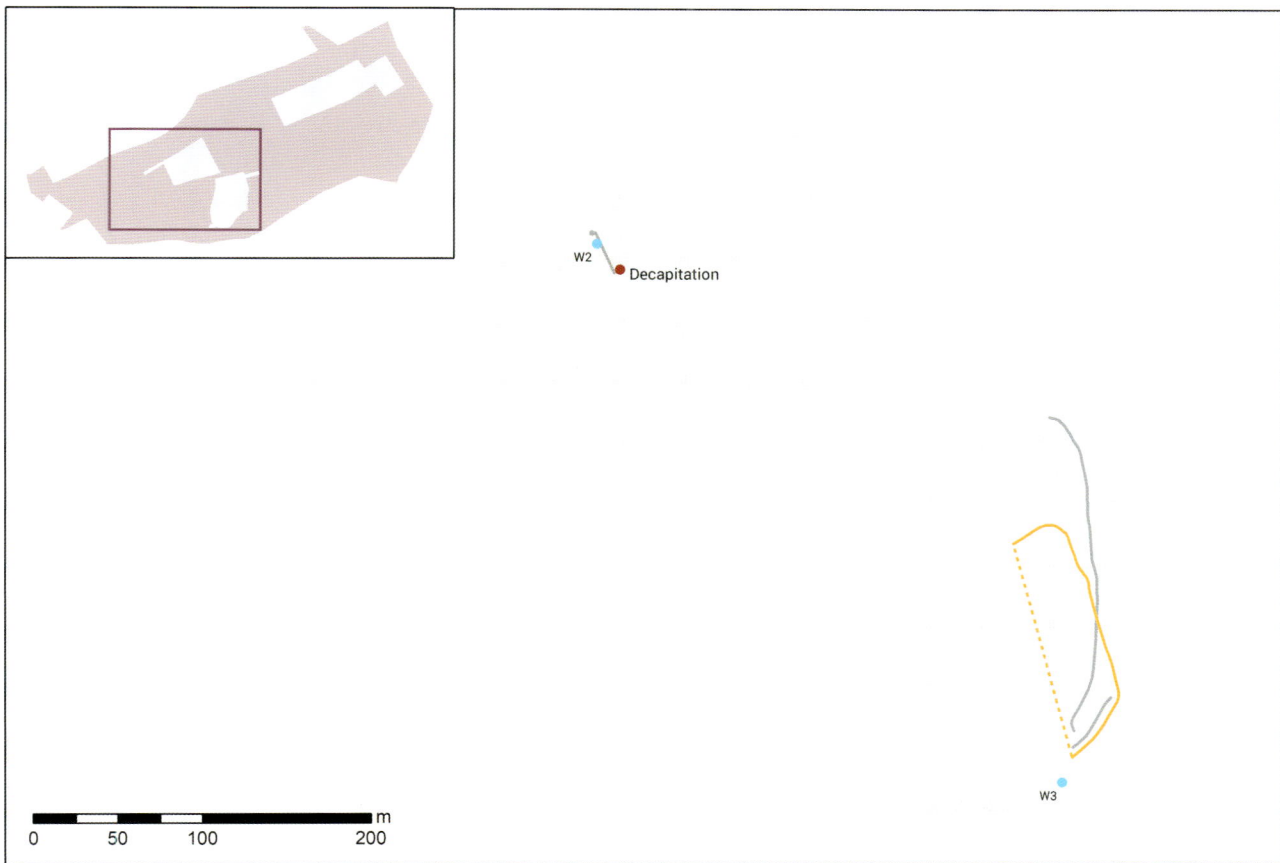

Fig 3.1 Plan of early landscape divisions in the west of the site: early funnel (grey), replacement enclosure (yellow), Wells 2 and 3 (blue) and decapitation (red) with first ditched boundary (grey) running between Well 2 and this burial. The funnel and later enclosure, both thought to relate to early stock control, lie just to the north east of Well 3, their articulation implying that its role as a water source continued overtime. *Drawing*: Helen Goodchild

discovered on the site at this time.

To the south east, the earliest development of the landscape comprised the insertion of ditches forming a funnel shape (G143) leading towards a contact spring, Well 3. The latter waterhole was only partially investigated and is only provably in use in the Roman period; yet, given the nature and position of this funnel, this spring appears to have been exploited before this, the ditches channelling stock to a watering point.

The funnel was replaced by a curvilinear ditch, which appears to have been bounded by trees in the west to form an enclosed space (G144). Various pits and ditches dotted around its vicinity are loosely related to such developments (G145), as was a second curvilinear ditch to the south west (G173). For the most part, the new enclosure completely ignored the pre-existing funnel arrangement. Its south-west corner did, however, coincide with the end of that funnel, implying that water access remained significant in this later phase: stock corralled in this newly enclosed zone still used Well 3. The date of these new arrangements is not entirely

certain, but both original funnel and later enclosure were replaced by elements provably of Late Iron Age date, even though the ceramic material from them is not significantly earlier than that in those replacements. Thus, some time before the end of the Iron Age, stock was occupying this part of the landscape with sufficient frequency to make it worthwhile investing in increasingly detailed mechanisms to control its movement, first by funnelling it towards a water source, then setting up an enclosure that allowed continuing access to that spring in one corner. This probably happened some centuries after the landscape near Well 2 had been divided off.

It is unclear, however, whether farming communities lived in these landscapes at the time and, if so, where. The site was, it seems, being visited with greater regularity in the course of the Neolithic and Bronze Ages (see section 7.1) and that process may have taken a more focused form within the latter period, based on changes to burial practices (see section 8.1). At what point this first involved continuous settlement could not be determined, still less the degree to which this might have been self-contained or linked into wider networks. This situation clearly changed, however, during the course of the first millennium BC.

3.2 Iron Age field systems at the western margin and enclosures to the east

Later in that same period, this process was taken one stage further. The northern contact spring, Well 2, had been fully enclosed by this point, before being reinforced with a considerable new investment of surfaces, a stone well head, tank and steps for access (see section 2.3). A further series of ditches was then dug to its south and east, thus creating large rectilinear enclosures (G142 and G146). They covered most of the area exposed in excavation (fig 3.2), the largest measuring 150m east–west by 100m north–south. There were at least five such distinct compounds, but perhaps six in all, set up in three pairs either side of the long-term boundary running south of the now-enhanced well head. The new system was accompanied by a square enclosure to its south east

measuring 100m by 100m (G147). This contained a subsidiary area at the north-west corner, roughly 50m square, with a 2.5m wide entrance to its south giving access into the larger enclosure. This was flanked by further 6m long ditches in the south, implying sophisticated access arrangements (fig 3.2).

These new configurations completely transcended all pre-existing features in this zone, apart from a continued focus on Well 2 to the north and perhaps Well 3 in the south. It thus created the first known *system* of landholding in this landscape. A large roundhouse (Roundhouse 1: see section 6.2) set up in the south-eastern enclosure represents the first point at which structures were evident anywhere on the site; visiting this landscape to obtain water or whatever in the Neolithic and Bronze Ages, and then investing in features in the Iron Age to hold stock or move them towards the long-used watering points, must now have given way to more permanent occupation.

By the end of the Iron Age, a second entirely new field system had been laid out (G150), although still focused on long-used Well 2. These new arrangements comprised three, smaller but more regularly defined rectangular fields running east from that waterhole, with

Fig 3.2 Plan of the first landholding system in the west of the site, clearly articulating with Well 2. *Drawing*: Helen Goodchild

Fig 3.3 First enclosure on the site, of Iron Age date, in the course of excavation (see also fig 3.2). © YAT

indications of a corresponding set of enclosures to their north, on the other side of a ditch running east from the well. Where exposed completely, these new components each measured *c* 60m north–south by 50m east–west (fig 3.4).

The system continued south from the easternmost field, but survived later truncation less well here. It seems to comprise one long paddock and, in fragmented form to the south, several other enclosed zones. To the east of this, although the subsidiary enclosure with roundhouse was retained in this new arrangement, the larger enclosed area beyond it was swept away. There are hints, at the eastern limit of excavation, that the further fields may have been defined on this side too: various ditches seen only in outlying evaluation trenches to the north, mostly undated, imply that the landscape here was being divided up at some point, probably in the Iron Age (G165).

Two elements emerge clearly from such configurations. First, a large zone to the south and west of the new, small fields, measuring as much as 250m north–south by 100m east–west, seems to have remained unenclosed. Second, two linear elements, best described as droveways, now existed either side of these fields. That in the west was 40m wide and at least 150m long (south limit unclear) and seems to have led up to Well 2 at its north-east corner, with access beyond this point restricted by a newly inserted ditch. That in the east was 60m wide (a dimension probably dictated by the size of the retained subsidiary enclosure at its northern end) and at least 190m long (southern limit again unclear), its western side aligning with the position of Well 3, which was also probably retained in use at this point.

This system of landholding, in place by the Late Iron Age, seem to have continued without substantial modification into the first millennium AD. Yet, there is only minimal evidence of activity in this western zone into the Roman period proper. This comprises several parallel gullies on a different alignment from their prehistoric counterparts (G168). Some of these contained second century AD pottery, implying local reorganisation of the landscape early in the Roman period. In smaller trenches beyond the main excavation area, north–south and east–west ditches, plus several pits, also included some features dating to the second century AD (G174). Exposure of these zones is very limited; hence, it is impossible to suggest interpretations or draw out their wider implications. Finally, and perhaps most diagnostically, this was also the point when Well 2, a major water source from the Bronze Age, finally fell out of use: it was sealed by accumulations and erosion deposits containing two sherds of third century AD date, overlain by levelling and aeolian accumulations (G169 and G170 respectively).

In the centre of the site contact springs had been exploited for some time in the course of prehistory (see section 2.3), yet there is limited evidence for landscape development until the Late Iron Age. Although truncation in Roman and later periods is more prevalent here than elsewhere, this lacuna seems to be a true reflection of zonal differences, rather than a simple function of survival. In this area, a sub-square enclosure, with entrance to the east, was set out, symmetrically straddling the springline (G205) (fig 3.5). It measured 35m across, thus being comparable with the sub-enclosure to the west (45m), and contained two, probably successive, roundhouses. The enclosure ditches were re-cut on the south and west sides, also implying that the whole was in use for an extended period of time.

Pottery from the primary fills of the main ditches contained Late Iron Age into early Roman material,

Fig 3.4 Plan of the field systems in the west of the site (grey) as developed by the end of the Iron Age, set out in relation to Wells 2 and 3. The early Roman period saw only minor modifications to this system in the form of two short ditches in the south and a cremation in the west (red). *Drawing*: Helen Goodchild

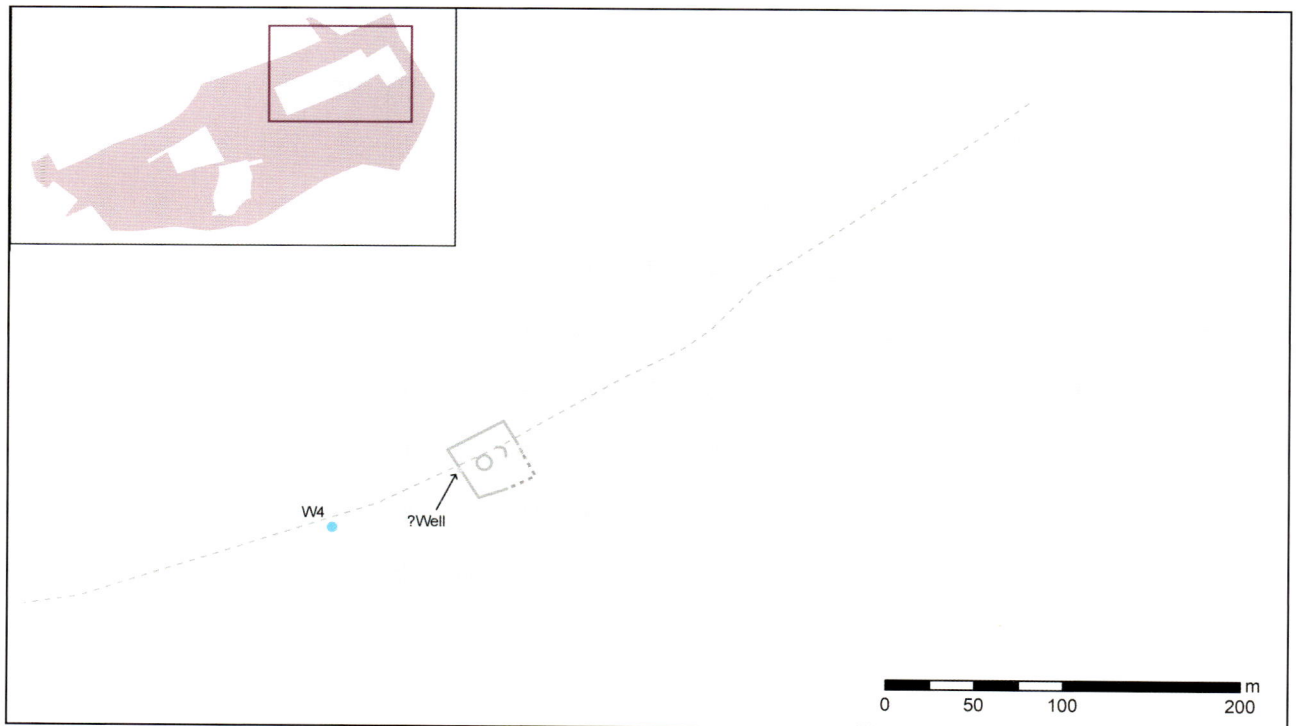

Fig 3.5 Iron Age enclosure in the centre of the site, straddling the springline along the 22m OD contour (dashed). Well 4 (blue) may have been in retained use at this point, as may a second possible well, evident at the western edge of the enclosure. *Drawing*: Helen Goodchild

suggesting that its use spanned the transition between these periods (although the latest backfills may have been deposited to level the area for subsequent development). The positioning of this enclosure, its western limit lying immediately above an earlier water source that had now been sealed by colluvium, seems to have been coincidental (G204). Being set up symmetrically along the springline must be intentional, however, as some of the water sources to the west (Wells 4, 5 and 6, positioned at a distance of between 75m and 135m: see section 2.3) seem to have continued in use at this time.

Finally, in the far east of the site, in an area much disturbed by modern ploughing, lay a series of roundhouses (Roundhouses 14–16, described in detail in section 6.2) (fig 3.6). Well 1 (see section 2.3) just to their south had Iron Age pottery in its upper fills and may have been in use with these structures. At a certain point, a large north–south ditch was inserted running south from this waterhole (G194), whilst a second ditch was set out to its west, then turning northwards to form an L-shape

(G199, G77). Material from the latter's upper fills shows that material continued to accrue within it up to the mid-third century AD. Taken together, these ditches show that water supply here now took place in a bounded landscape, and that the roundhouses themselves were enclosed. Thus, despite the limited exposure of this zone and later disturbance, it can be suggested that initial structural development here was accompanied by attempts to enclose the landscape, restricting access to a contact spring that had been used for many centuries but, seemingly, in a more open setting.

Forty metres to the south of Well 1, a substantial north–south ditch containing a profusion of Iron Age/early Roman pottery was set out (G194). It implies that space was being divided up around the waterhole at this point, as do two co-aligned ditches even further south (G203). An early ditch was also inserted in the area 50m to the north-east of the well (G61), with parallel and perpendicular shallow counterparts to the east (G62), also suggesting some attempt to formalise landholding here. This was happening at a time when cobble-filled

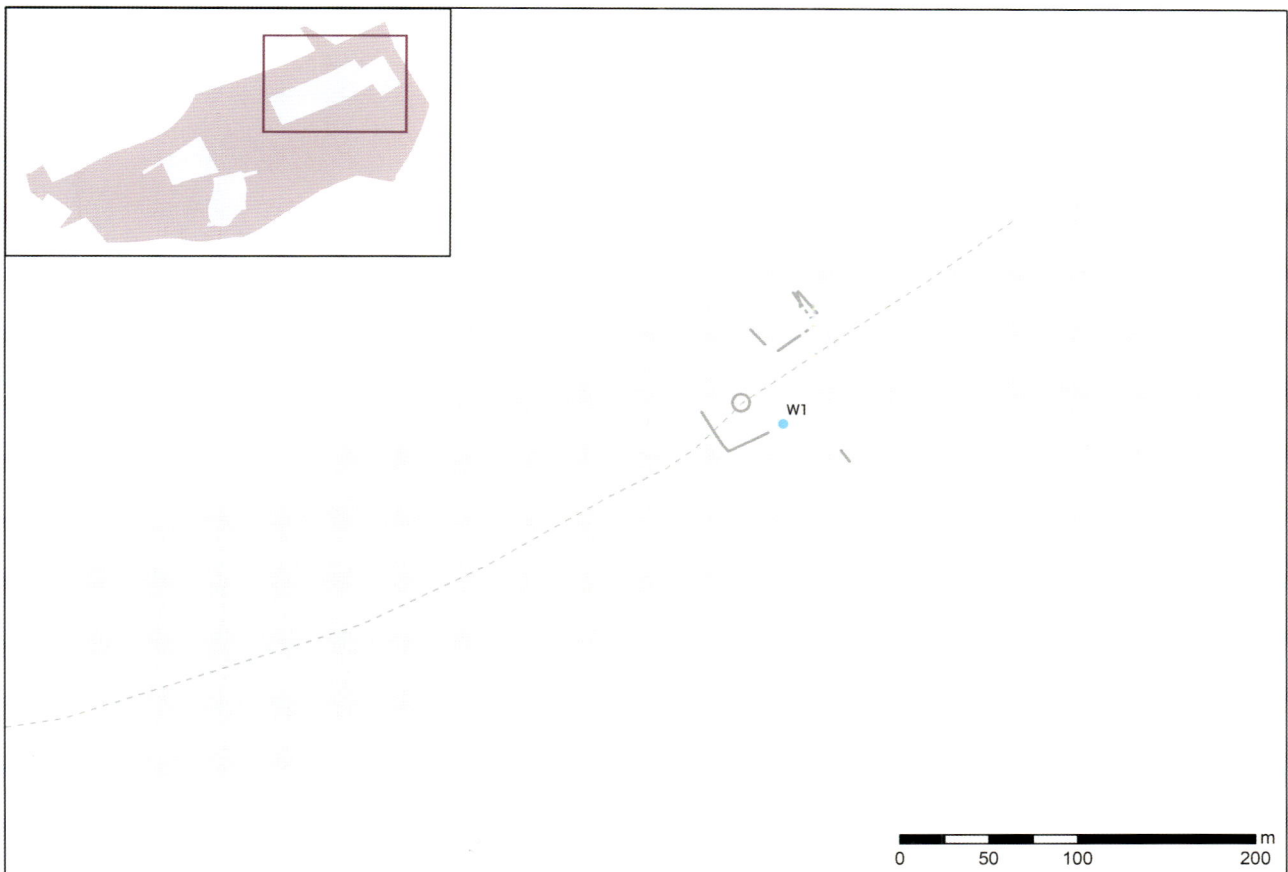

Fig 3.6 Enclosures of various dates in the Roman period in east of site. The southern enclosed zone included a roundhouse, possibly newly constructed, north-west of Well 1, which straddled the springline along the 22m OD contour (dashed). The enclosure to its north and east seems to have been dedicated to some form of artisanal activity. *Drawing*: Helen Goodchild

cuts and possible hearths were in use nearby, overlain by sinuous features, some of which are dated to the second century AD (G63).

Taken together, this evidence shows that the vicinity of Well 1 was being intensively exploited in the Late Iron Age/early Roman periods, if not before. The features concerned, at least in their surviving form, may have been less substantial than those seen at the western end of the site. In the latter zone, vibrant activities of Late Bronze Age date were augmented by setting out field boundaries of increasing intensity during the Iron Age: prehistoric landscape enclosure was not only extensive, but increasingly intensive over time, with all such divisions influenced by the need to use Wells 2 and 3 (see fig 3.4). In the east, water access was still critical, but organisation less concentrated and, arguably, limited to later in the Iron Age; yet the point at which both zones fell into decay, by the start of the third century AD, is the same. The demise of such long-used areas to the west and east, henceforth becoming relative backwaters (with the possible exception noted above: G168), contrasts markedly with greatly increased investment in boundaries at the centre of the site in the late Roman period (see section 3.3). This comprises a real shift in emphasis, rather than an accident of survival or a product of the extent of archaeological investigation.

The second half of the first millennium BC, therefore, sees the development of a highly complex, increasingly sub-divided settlement in the west of the site, in contrast to discrete, seemingly more simple, enclosures to the east along the springline. All of these zones engaged in agricultural activities (see section 4.2), whilst the former may have included manufacturing in its outputs (see section 5.2). The wider implications of this essentially prehistoric development, plus the vexed question of its relationship with Roman activities, is discussed elsewhere (see section 9.2).

3.3 Roman landscape boundaries in the centre of the site

The central landscape saw significant development throughout the Roman period. A double-ditched, east–west road was inserted above the Late Iron Age enclosure G205 noted above, thus representing its demise and formalising hillside access along the springline (G221, G52: henceforth Road 1) (fig 3.7). This thoroughfare, at least 115m long, formed the southern limit for the majority of archaeological features in the area and clearly represents a fundamentally new element in the landscape. It seems to have been laid out in the

second or third centuries AD and then continued in use throughout most, if not all, of the Roman period.

A large enclosure was created north of Road 1, bounded by ditches in the west and north (G234 and G123, respectively). This measured almost 70m north–south by at least 100m east–west (east end beyond the limit of excavation) and was then sub-divided by a series of parallel ditches defining further landscape divisions within it (G210, G34, G35, G36, G46, G29 and G123). These sub-divisions would have channelled movement the full length of the enclosure, down a track that was less than 3m wide in the north, broadening to almost 4.5m where it approached Road 1 to the south, to which it allowed access.

The new enclosure also contained three east–west elements. The northernmost feature formed a boundary ditch offset 40m from the road, which avoided crossing the north–south track. The other two linear features comprised side ditches for a routeway just over 20m to its north. Once again, where this met the north–south element, a gap was retained, thus creating 'crossroads' at this point. When first encountered in excavation, a mound of cobbles between these ditches was interpreted as a metalling (G45, G37). Wider exposure, however, showed it to be a more extensive natural collection of stones derived from geological, probably glacial, activity. It could still, however, have played a role here as a hardstanding or as an east–west route through the landscape.

Clearly, this whole zone was being more intensively developed than hitherto. Some of the above components provably cut the Iron Age enclosure G205 described previously – although its northern limit seems to have been respected by these later additions. Presumably, as the rest of the enclosure had been completely superseded by the new roadway, this was either coincidental or done for the practical reason that it was easier to dig a ditch along an old alignment than into virgin ground. Other features in this new development are dated to the Roman period by the ceramics contained in their lower fills. Taken together, this evidence implies that this system was in place by c AD 250, thus soon after Road 1 was set out to the south and perhaps part of a single process of development.

Macrofossils derived from one of the northern ditches demonstrate that damp ground taxa were growing in their vicinity (G123). Wild or weed taxa commonly associated with grassland habitats (ribwort plantain, hawkweed and ox tongue) were also sporadically represented, perhaps derived from grassy field margins or plants collected from grassland or meadows as hay for fodder (or used as tinder, roofing or flooring material).

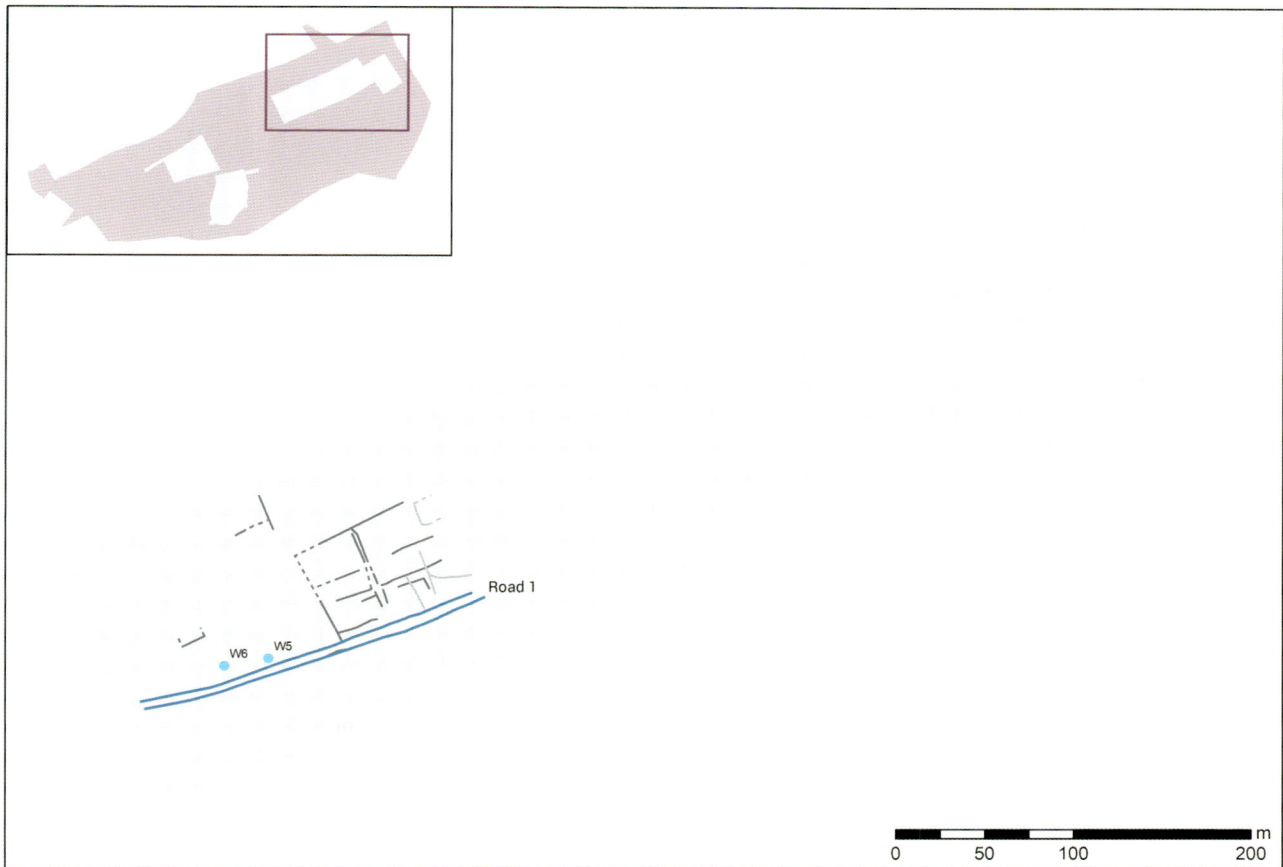

Fig 3.7 Road 1 (blue) and associated Roman enclosures, with central 'crossroads' (grey). Later ditches and enclosures (lighter grey) modified landholding to the east, but retained the pre-existing crossroads. *Drawing*: Helen Goodchild

This environmental evidence and the ditch configurations suggest that stock may have been moved south here to gain access to Road 1 and/or to water along the springline which that road followed.

At a later point, substantial changes took place in the eastern part of this new large enclosure. A small enclosure, only the western end of which fell within the excavation area, was inserted in its north, respecting its internal divisions (G43). To the south and west of this lay a symmetrically placed curvilinear ditch (G211) with an associated north–south ditch (G220) running south from its curving corner and with further east–west ditches nearby (parts of G231). All of these additions seem to completely ignore the ditches running from the 'crossroads' to their west, although not that intersection itself.

Thus, after the large enclosure was created, either its internal divisions were over-ridden after only a limited period of time or, more likely, they were retained in their original form, including the 'crossroads' to the west but augmented and elaborated – the east with greater emphasis on a 'holding' enclosure. Most of this new arrangement lay beyond the eastern limit of

excavation. Hence, it is impossible to decide whether these final modifications were extensive, with only the crossroads retained, or localised, with just a small zone in the south-east modified and the rest of the original enclosed space kept intact. These developments of the second and third centuries AD imply that a mixed farming economy continued at this point (see section 4.2) but that stock movement may now have involved driving some animals off-site (see section 9.3). Where these farmers were living at the time is not entirely clear (see section 6.3).

Other signs of activity in the central area during or before the mid-third century AD are quite limited. To the north lay a shallow north–south ditch, following the natural slope of the hillside here, and an east–west counterpart (G101). Both were subsequently sealed by naturally formed hillside deposits, suggesting a gap in the occupation sequence before activity of a provably later Roman date commenced (G102). To the south west, a fragment of curving, east–west ditch set out immediately north of Well 6 seemingly formed the southern end of an enclosure (G86). It was also cut by ditches more securely dated to later Roman period development.

3.4 A new late Roman enclosure at the centre of the site

At some point, the above arrangements were entirely superseded by the creation of a new enclosed area in the west (fig 3.8). This started with the setting out of another east–west routeway, Road 2, along the hillside 70m north of Road 1 (G2). In places, metallings surviving later truncation comprised a good-quality, pebble surface. Accumulations along its northern edge dating to the second half of the fourth century AD (G122) were later cut by a dump of cobbles and tiles to form a new road surface, with various installations then set into this latest surfacing (G124). Clearly, Road 2 was in active use for an extended period.

In the west, the new thoroughfare was flanked by ditches, both sides seemingly continuing in use throughout its existence (G3, G53, G29, G21 and G22 in the south, G96 in the north). Its northern ditch further east was also in use at a very late date (G126), here being

associated with features that might represent building frontages (G123: see section 6.4). The earlier thoroughfare to the south, Road 1, was retained in the new arrangement and perhaps extended westwards (G225) to create a thoroughfare of at least 200m long.

Two major north–south ditches, set c 90m apart, ran north from retained Road 1 up to the limit of excavation (G30/G38 in the east and G91/G96 in the west). Where they crossed the line of new Road 2, however, this meeting point was deliberately marked out. Western access was denoted by constructing a tower-like structure and associated burials (see section 8.5). Interestingly, the ditch seems to have originally been set out along its entire length before the tower was inserted. All are nonetheless argued to be part of a single process of development. This boundary was further reinforced by subsidiary ditches offset c 5m to both sides, with another east–west ditch set out to its west (G218). The gap between it and the main boundary ditch perhaps formed a north–south access point here, outside the enclosed area.

Where the boundary ditch was interrupted by Road 2

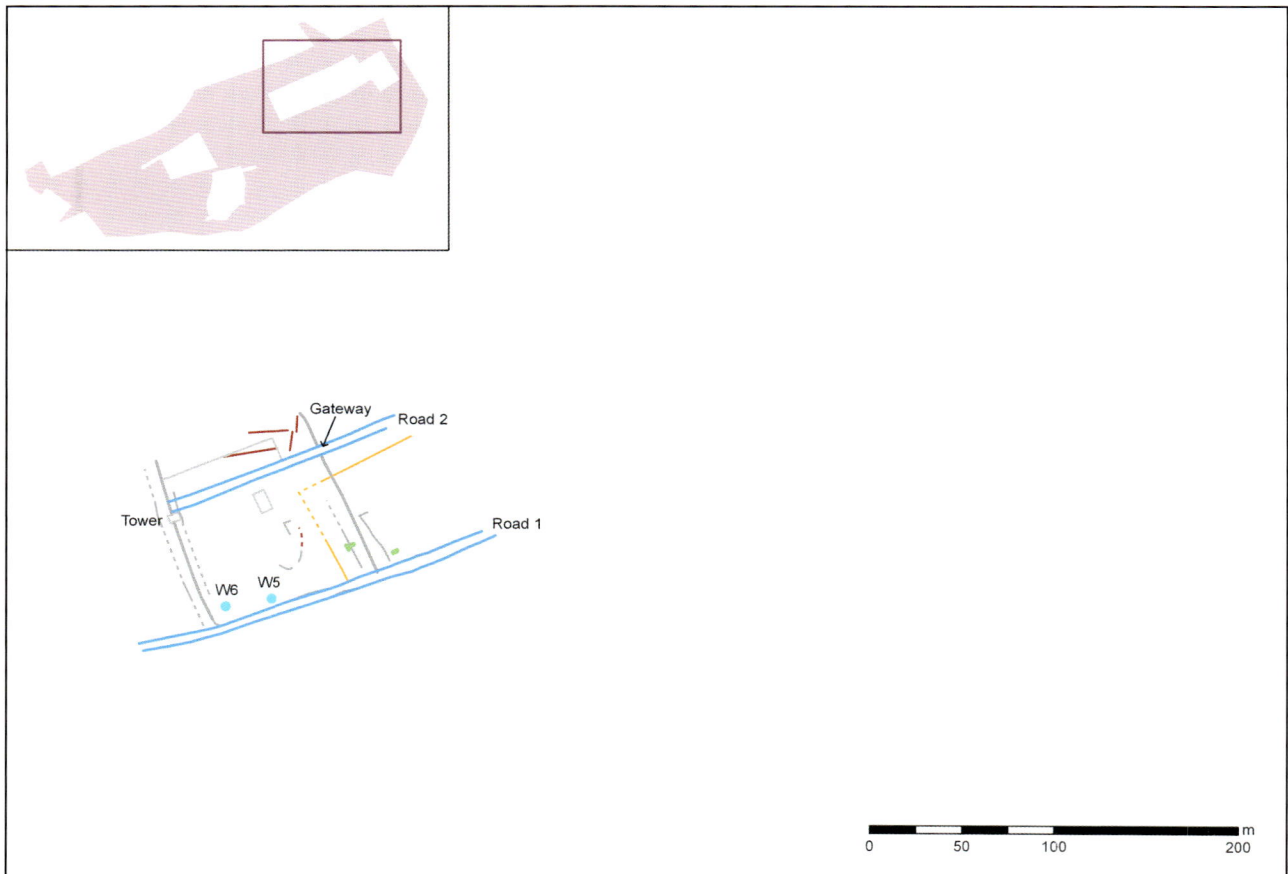

Fig 3.8 Road 2 and associated late Roman enclosure laid out north of Road 1 (with positions of corn driers delineated (green) and late change of alignments at the end of the fourth century AD (red). The main pre-existing enclosure to the east (yellow) was now superseded. *Drawing*: Helen Goodchild

in the east, two large postholes were inserted flanking a 2.5m gap between the ditch termini. This suggests the position of a gateway controlling movement along the thoroughfare. Patchy pebble surfaces show that it was metalled at the gated entrance, either the fortuitous survival of a once-extensive surfacing or just a reinforcing of an entry point. Special forms of deposition were evident in the ditch terminals immediately either side of this proposed gateway (see section 8.5).

Within this new enclosure proper, an L-shaped ditch ran up to, but not beyond, the subsidiary ditches flanking the main (western) boundary, suggesting that the two landscape divisions were in use together (G224). This ditch defined a 10m-wide zone north of Road 1 within which the majority of contact springs (see section 2.3) were situated. Water may, therefore, have remained accessible from that roadway even after the enclosing of the area to its north. Indeed, it could be argued that the main, western boundary of the system was set out to deliberately incorporate the position of long-used Well 6 at its south-west corner.

Similar features flanked its eastern boundary, but, critically, these subsidiary elements entirely ignored ditches related to the earlier 'crossroads' noted above. This implies that the creation of Road 2 and adjacent enclosure meant the demise of the initial enclosure set out north of Road 1. Deciding the exact point at which this development occurred is problematic for reasons concerning dating rehearsed elsewhere (see section 1.5). Our estimate, however, is that this replacement enclosure was in place by c 300 AD, and then continued in use throughout the remainder of the fourth century and perhaps beyond (see further, below).

In sum, the laying out of Road 2 and extending of Road 1 defined a new scheme of landholding on the central hillside, comprising the creation of an enclosure measuring c 90m east–west by 70m north–south. It was flanked by the retained Road 1 in the south and new Road 2 in the north, with water access at its south-west corner (and perhaps elsewhere within it) and, at its centre in the north, a terraced space for the construction of a hypocausted building and associated burial (see section 8.5). The earlier spatial organisation of this landscape has been interpreted as controlling the movement of stock and/or agricultural production. These new monumental features, in contrast, are different in kind: the western section of this newly defined area, to which access was restricted by the tower in the west and a gate in the east, now emphasised non-agricultural practices. In short, this part of the landscape could be seen as taking on monumental and ritual airs.

Elsewhere in this central area it is not so clear that landscape functions changed so radically. In the east, an enclosure – of which only the western end fell within the excavated area – was inserted within boundaries belonging to earlier third century AD organisation of this landscape (G50); finds from within its ditches match the date of assemblages from the latest Roman features in the vicinity, implying their contemporaneous use. This resembles stock enclosures seen elsewhere in earlier periods and, taken at face value, suggests that farming practices still held sway here. A stone floor tile from this area, a rare find on the site and situated at a considerable distance from any other examples, could suggest more substantial structural investment, but need not be out of place with animal management.

To the north of the ritual enclosure, c 20m beyond of Road 2, two L-shaped ditches were set out on that thoroughfare's alignment (G103), accompanied by parallel features 10m to their north (G12). Further north–south elements created a boundary to this layout in the east, with other parallel ditches to either side. This suggests that, on the opposite side of the road from the monumentalised zone, landscape divisions were now inserted more intensively than hitherto (perhaps now extending over a zone once used for perinatal burial: see section 8.4). Structures occupied this area at the time (G106: see section 6.4) and this zone then seems to have been dedicated to artisanal production (G103: see section 5.4). Thus, it functioned very differently from that on the south side of Road 2.

Finally, west of the ritual zone, activity at all periods was much less concerted. One east–west ditch might suggest limited division of space on the hillside c 20m north of Road 2 (part of G96), but the rest of this zone was occupied only with amorphous, sinuous intrusions, all largely devoid of artefactual content (G93). At least some of these features seem to be a product of natural agencies such as weathering, water erosion or tree growth. This was clearly an area of only marginal interest throughout the Roman period.

In sum, the area to the north of the monumentalised enclosure had a focus on artisan production (see section 5.4) and that to the east continued with agricultural activities. The area to its west was of more marginal interest throughout this period. These arrangements seem to have continued mostly unaltered through much of the fourth century AD (with the exception of the zone to the north of the enclosure, discussed next). This enclosure contained prestigious architecture and atypical mortuary practices (see section 8.5) and seems to represent the first point at which this landscape was used for something other than purely 'functional' activities (see section 9.3).

3.5 Modifications to landholding in the northern central zone in the late fourth century AD

On the hillside immediately north of Road 2 there is clear evidence of a substantial change of use late in the fourth century AD (see fig 3.8). This zone was terraced, and a new boundary set out running north-east to south-west, aligned with some earlier burials (G20: see section 8.4). Further elements ran west from this, including a roughly perpendicular, L-shaped component in the north (G11), plus a not-so-carefully aligned counterpart further south (G105). The terrace and ditches ran at an oblique angle to their third-century forerunners and to the natural slope of the hillside, suggesting an entirely new organisation of space.

The ditch flanking Road 2 to on its north side was modified where this new alignment met that thoroughfare, implying that the latter remained in use at this stage (G56 and G57). Equally, to the east, the fills of the main gated ditch line contained material from deep in its fills dating to after AD 350. In addition, ditches alongside Road 2 in the east continued to be re-cut well into the fourth century AD, and arguably beyond. Finally, to the south, the western limit of this new system ran up to, but did not cross, Building G106, which seems to have remained in use into the fourth century AD (see section 6.4). All of this suggests that the new terraces altered landholding in only one, restricted part of the landscape, with existing divisions retained beyond this.

The subsequent history of boundaries in this central, northern area takes us into the sub/post-Roman period. A well-defined east–west ditch was cut into the southern edge of Road 2, running parallel with the underlying thoroughfare (G3). It contained material of late fourth century date, but also a small amount of Anglian ceramics. The digging of this feature suggests that the thoroughfare remained in use, but perhaps in a substantially narrowed form: either it now represented a less formal route along the hillside or had simply become a boundary.

Further east, cobble spreads above possible structures flanking Road 2 (see section 6.3) seem to mark the demise of that route (G125), perhaps deposited at the time when a midden containing bone, ceramics and CBM sealed the terminal of the eastern, gated enclosure ditch (G31). Finally, at the south-west corner of the same enclosure, an east–west ditch cut across internal divisions within the latter but stopped just beyond its main

western limit (G88). This new ditch contained material belonging to the closing decades of the fourth century AD and, being noticeably less substantial than its forerunners, would not have constituted a real barrier to movement. It suggests that spatial organisation within the main enclosure had changed, but that the external bank defining its overall limits still exerted an influence on the organisation of the landscape here (for wider discussion and for the implications of any 'post-Roman' gap, see section 9.4).

3.6 Medieval and later activity across the site

There is very little evidence for human occupation of this site between the fourth century AD and the point where medieval ploughing took place. One major exception concerns part of a central zone, which is therefore discussed in detail elsewhere (see section 6.4; see also section 9.4 for the broader implications). A minor exception concerns the zone beside Well 1 in the east, where a narrow ditch containing three sherds of Anglian pottery crossed the entire excavation area (G198). It lay on the same line as the underlying, early Roman ditches here, but, given the absence of intervening late Roman activity, this seems likely to be a common product of the hillside slope at this point and an interest in water access, rather than an indicator of institutional continuity. A curving ditch to the west may also be broadly contemporary with this late phase of use (G203), if the single Anglian sherd in its uppermost fill is securely stratified, as may a nearby slot, which also yielded Anglian material (G206). These features, especially the first, narrow ditch, suggest that the springline may have been brought back into use at this late date, but also show that access to its water was now only controlled at a local level, not as part of a wider landscape development.

For most of the period after the fourth century AD, strata accumulated here through natural processes (hill wash, as described in section 2.1), later cut by ploughing (see section 4.2). For the medieval period proper, however, only a few boundaries survived modern activity (fig 3.9). One exception is medieval ditch G176, which cut Roman and pre-Roman stratigraphy at the eastern end of the site. At its eastern extremity, two parallel ditches running north-west–south-east intruded into prehistoric colluviation, forming a 7m wide trackway with evidence of trample at its surface (G188) and maybe associated with tree-boles to either side (G189, although these may be of very different dates and none had associated artefacts). The fills of the ditches either side of

Fig 3.9 Medieval furrows across site (black) and possible contemporary droveway near its eastern limit (blue). Modern field boundaries are represented in grey. *Drawing*: Helen Goodchild

the proposed trackway yielded a small quantity of abraded brick of proposed Roman date, plus two medieval sherds. These features may therefore date to the latter period.

Elsewhere, other fields comprised modern land divisions such as field boundaries (G90, G179 and G237) and subsidiary fence lines (G180, G181), some associated with field drains (see section 4.2). Certain recent drains seem to directly overlie their medieval counterparts, the latter presumably related to Heslington village, established by Domesday (Baggs *et al* 1976). Neither the building of Heslington Hall in 1568 nor the creation of the university in the 1960s made any significant

alterations to this landscape, although the insertion of Heslington Road by 1771 may have done so.

It is only during the most recent years, with the construction of the new university campus, that this landscape moved away definitively from its agricultural setting, evidenced by the modern plough soil that initially covered all excavated areas (G185). Preparation for this structural development disturbed several areas (G184) (with a mostly negative impact on archaeological understanding: see section 1.1), and the modern development that then took place marked the first point in time at which this landscape has been taken up completely with non-farming activity (see section 9.5).

Productive landscapes – food production

4

This chapter considers food production at Heslington, split between the pastoral and agricultural economy (Chapter 5 considers manufacturing in the landscape separately). The first section (4.1) describes evidence for the watering and movement of stock, focused on the creation of ditched fields and paddocks, and the use of land drains. It also deploys faunal evidence to describe the animals that were farmed here and artefacts representing mechanisms to control stock. The second section, on agricultural development (4.2), uses botanical evidence, mainly carbonised seeds, to look at the plants grown, and at ploughing, mainly furrows, and processing as indicated by site features and artefacts, notably quern stones.

4.1 The pastoral economy

Maintaining livestock seems to have been a significant component of this landscape almost from its earliest use, notably in the evidence derived from the contact springs discussed previously (see section 2.1) or from their vicinity. Thus, environmental samples from the (undated) basal deposits of Well 4 yielded foul water/dung assemblages, indicating livestock watering (a saddle quern from this same feature suggests a mixed economy from an early period too – see below). This feature is clearly in use early in the Iron Age, perhaps replacing an adjacent well of Bronze Age or earlier date. By the first century AD another contact spring between Wells 4 and 5 generated evidence for silting up and low-energy water extraction, plus watering of livestock, which an overlying deposit shows to have continued over time (G230). Equally, approximately a quarter of the beetle remains from Iron Age and Roman pits associated with the management of Well 1 suggests dung and decay, implying grazed/fertilised ground in its vicinity. Finally, there is the evidence for nitrogen-enriched and trampled soils in the

well sequences themselves (see section 2.3): animals were visiting watering holes on a regular basis from the Bronze Age, if not before, into the Roman period.

In the west of the site, features for the control of livestock were also being dug at an early stage of human activity (see section 3.1). These features initially comprised Iron Age ditches to funnel movement, then a curvilinear enclosure bounded in the west by trees. Later, these were replaced by a new system of large fields or paddocks, accompanied by the first enclosure with a roundhouse, then a second, more extensive, system of landholding system comprising smaller fields set out east of Well 2 and a second set turning south at their eastern end (see section 3.2). The final components were still articulated around the positions of Wells 2 and 3 and thus created two droveways, one 40m wide running south from the former well and a second 50m across running between the latter well and the retained roundhouse enclosure.

On chronology, these successive systems were clearly Iron Age in origin and while some may have continued in use into the Roman period, they seem to have been swept away by the end of the second century AD. Only one component does not fit with this picture of demise within the Roman period. This comprised two parallel, north-west–south-east gullies near the south-west limit of the earlier system, which contained material of late second century AD date or later (G168). These intrusions only just survived later ploughing and so may have once been more extensive. Taken at face value, however, they imply merely local reorganisation of this landscape sometime near the start of the Roman period. For these systems of landholding, of whatever date, access to regular water supplies by means of long-established contact springs was critical.

It is difficult to be sure that these fields, at least in their final, most sub-divided, form, had a single function rather than multiple uses. In their inception, and arguably until the end, however, one of their main roles appears to have involved bringing livestock under greater control. Yet, despite such movement being increasingly constrained, there is no evidence that these boundaries played a role in moving animals off the site entirely. Boggy areas to the south, beyond the limit of excavation, would have limited animal movement in that direction, and, in any case, the ditches here seem to run out indeterminately. If livestock was being regularly taken out of local circulation on any scale, it would have been logical to drive it towards drier, higher ground to the east, west or north. Yet, there was no surviving evidence for major routes going off in these directions: the pastoral economy seems mainly self-contained.

In sum, this western zone comprised a landscape with unbroken use of early water sources in association, from c 800 BC, with the movement of stock, and increasingly sub-divided and controlled from perhaps 200 BC. The Roman conquest had little immediate impact on these fields, notwithstanding the creation of a full legionary fortress at York less than five kilometres away in the closing decades of the first century AD. Yet, nearly all of this system, in its most developed form, had fallen out of use by the start of the third century AD (see sections 9.2 and 9.3).

In the course of the Roman period, concerted activity moved to the centre of the landscape 500m to the east. Double-ditched Road 1 was set out and a large enclosure created to its north containing a north–south access route leading down to the road, with subsidiary ditches creating a crossroads just 20m north of the main thoroughfare, part of which seems to have used a natural exposure of cobbles as a hardstanding (see section 3.3). Ceramic evidence implies that this system was in place by c AD 250, whilst macrofossil assemblages from one of its ditches indicate damp ground and grassland habitats,

perhaps taxa derived from field margins or plants collected for fodder. This suggests that livestock was moved south out of this enclosure to gain access to water along the springline, but also onto Road 1, which ran beyond the limits of the site. The investment implied by the creation of this major routeway suggests that exporting animals on the hoof had taken on far greater importance in the late Roman period.

What happened to these pastoral systems after the end of the Roman period is unclear, but still more extensive and systematic movement of animals is evident nearby in much later centuries. By 1484, Green Dykes Lane, to the west, is recorded as being used as a droveway; Perring's early evaluation suggested that this might have had Roman origins,[1] but this can now be discounted.[2] By the end of the fifteenth century AD, therefore, it had become the norm in the vicinity of the site to transfer livestock for processing and consumption elsewhere on considerable scale and over long distances. What this meant for the particular organisation of medieval landholding at Heslington could not be explored here archaeologically.

The successive systems of landholding on the site would have taken a considerable investment to produce, and were clearly maintained over time, as seen with ditches being re-cut on successive occasions. The flat blade and handle of a broken wooden shovel, usable single-handed and found within the lining of Well 2 (see section 2.3), hints at the labour needed to maintain the system. The Late Bronze Age date of that lining shows that digging the soil was important from that early point. Such objects would, no doubt, have played an even more important role as the field systems were sub-divided and intensified in later centuries. Indeed, if the Heslington example was deliberately (and perhaps 'ritually': see section 8.1) incorporated into that lining, this would suggest that the significance of the labour needed to create boundaries was explicitly understood at that time (see further in section 9.1).

Finds of two bridle bits show what would have been needed to control animals in this landscape. These were discarded in a mid- and a late-Roman ditch set some distance from each other, attesting their long-term importance and widespread use over the Roman period (G210 and G30 respectively). In similar vein, an ox goad was discarded in a late fourth century ditch (G22). Animal management strategies are also seen in evidence for penning elbow in goats, a condition evident in lipping or exostosis on humeri and radii thought to indicate confinement ('penning') of the animal in question. Finally, a large crescent-shaped shale pendant from a late fourth-century AD context (G110), whose size might imply its use with a horse rather than a human, suggests that animals were valued enough to be decorated, not just viewed in purely functional terms.

The livestock that once inhabited this landscape is hinted at in the above landscape features, and in environmental samples containing dung beetles. Inevitably, however, the most direct evidence for animals comes from faunal assemblages. Due to the vagaries of depositional practices and survival in different soil conditions (much less favourable in the west than east, and thus with limited assemblages of prehistoric date to draw on), our information on wild vs domestic matters, age, sex, metrics and pathology is at its most secure for the Roman period, and then more for the last two centuries than before AD 200 (see section 1.5).

Although different site recovery methods impact considerably on relevant material, study of taxa from sieved samples suggests that domestic fowl was a minor component of food consumption throughout the Roman period, whilst little goat and fish appear in such levels (assemblages are too small for them to have registered in earlier horizons). Red deer was used for its antler at various times, but only provably as food in the latest Roman levels (the absence of roe deer after the Iron Age may be due to forest clearance and/or over-hunting: see section 2.2).

With the more common taxa of cattle, sheep, pig and horse, it becomes possible to discuss broad-brush patterning. Even here, however, there are limitations. Most bone groups are too small to generate meaningful measurements in terms of minimum number of individuals, and so we are forced to employ fragment counts. In addition, not all are identifiable: the figures tabulated in table 4.1 amalgamate proven numbers of sheep/goat, pig and cattle/horse with counts based on bone size (small, middle and large respectively, the latter divided between cattle and horse in proportion to those which could be securely identified as one or the other). Next, this is the material discarded on the site, which may

not be an exact representation of what was raised there. Finally, most groups come from broad chronological categories and probably embody re-deposition of earlier material into later levels (hence the very broad categories employed in table 4.1, where *Prehistoric* comprises an amalgamation of all pre-Roman material; *early Roman* dates roughly from the late first to early third century AD; *late Roman* from mid-third to mid-fourth century; and *very late Roman* to the second half of the fourth century).

All that said, the general patterns are so clear that it probably provides a reasonable picture of change over time. Although assemblages from pre-Iron Age contexts are vanishingly small, the picture that has emerged by the start of the Roman period is of a landscape in which sheep dominated, alongside a significant presence of cattle and some pig. In the course of the Roman period, cattle increase significantly – although how immediately this occurs is difficult to calculate, due to the small size of early Roman assemblages. By the third and fourth centuries AD it is clear that cattle dominate sheep, a trend which continues into the second half of the fourth century, by which point Heslington profiles resemble contemporary sites in York itself, for example Coppergate and Tanner Row.[3]

Congenital problems for cattle can be suggested by the reduced/absent third cusp of the third molar. This anomaly is much more evident in our early Roman assemblage (36 per cent) than later in that period (6–7 per cent; it is fairly rare in cattle as a whole, typically 1–2 per cent in modern cattle, and 3–5 per cent in medieval samples). This profile suggests a small founder population and a high degree of inbreeding in the early Roman period and, conversely, larger gene-pools and more movement or exchange of breeding stock later. The closer correspondence between York and Heslington cattle profiles and lower proportions of this tooth anomaly imply that, if a new meat market was emerging, this only came to full fruition in the course of the late Roman period, also the point at which, as noted above,

Table 4.1 Summary of faunal data for main domesticates by fragment count (basis for calculating actual figures explained in text)

	Prehistoric (%)	Early Roman (%)	Late Roman (%)	V Late Roman (%)
Cattle	20.80	88.10	78.30	83.80
Horse	8.30	0.90	3.90	3.60
Sheep/Goat	70.10	10.00	10.60	9.50
Pig	0.80	0.90	7.20	3.20

the first thoroughfares for moving animals systematically off-site became evident. The burgeoning citizenry of Eboracum would have needed to be supplied with food immediately after the fortress was built there, yet their requirements only dominated meat production to a degree which necessitated landscape reorganisation and new forms of herd management in the last two centuries of Roman occupation (and even then 'market forces' may not have been able to dictate culling patterns: see general discussion in section 9.3).

Age data augment this picture, but mostly for late Roman levels when numbers are sufficient to make realistic interpretations. Roman period pigs, as expected, were killed at an optimal point for consumption, although with higher numbers of sub-adults in closing decades (note the aged sows thrown into Well 7: see section 8.6). Cattle suggest the production of some prime livestock for meat, a trajectory increasingly evident through the fourth century AD (even at its close, however, very old animals still comprise 30 per cent of that total). It is clear that beef was being cured on the site, either through smoking or salting, both in pre-Roman and Roman periods. Yet, the culling of a large animal does not, in itself, show that it was destined to be eaten elsewhere: it could either be processed to be kept over a more extended period of time or, sometimes, consumed quickly through large-scale, presumably collective, feasting.

It seems safe to assume that sheep were reared at Heslington more for their wool yield and perhaps manuring role than to fulfil dietary needs. Yet, it is the latter, meat supply, that most readily affects culling practices. Sheep from early Roman levels show sub-adult slaughter, in apparent contrast to Iron Age adults (though cf above on sample biases), whilst late Roman sheep were allowed to live beyond 30–42 months, with sub-adult animals being more evident at the end of that period. Prime livestock was available for consumption on-site throughout, whilst general sex data, where available, suggests a breeding population, as do occasional neonates. Lambs are generally absent, perhaps the counterpoint of their presence in Roman York. It is not clear, however, whether these were supplied to fulfil York's demand for young meat or simply despatched from Heslington to avoid over-wintering large herds there. Either way, a breeding stock was maintained until the very end of the Roman period, even if livestock was being killed at a slightly younger age in its closing decades.

One intriguing pattern of note is the consistent increase in proportions of sub-adult pigs, sheep and even horses in the very latest Roman levels. The latter group lacks evidence for foals and that for pigs is unsurprising,

given that they are essentially kept for meat production, plus a small number as breeding stock. The late increase might suggest an unsustainable approach to this animal, although such pressures can be quickly compensated for, as shown by documented famines in which almost an entire pig herd can be slaughtered but bred back up again in just a few years. Sheep are a different matter. The culling of younger animals implies smaller breeding flocks, presumably because meat was now being valued as the primary product over secondary wool or milk. Whether this trend was being led by external demand or due to the internal dynamics of the pastoral economy is unclear.

Finally, metrical data indicate that the mean height of cattle varied little across the late Roman period (1.15m–1.12m) or with respect to figures from contemporary animals in York (1.11m[4]). The same is true of sheep (0.58m at Heslington, 0.59m in York). Hence there is no sign here that animal size was boosted as a result of the Roman presence.

Overall, animals from the Roman period imply a focus on manure production and traction, the former process backed up by artefactual evidence (see section 7.4), the latter indicated faunally by degeneration due to osteoarthritis caused by work stress. Prime meat from pig (pork) and sheep (mutton), and probably from cattle (beef), was consumed here. Ceramic cheese presses, mostly from late Roman levels but widely distributed on the site, suggest that processing of milk products took place at this point, whether related to sheep, goats or cattle. Pigs, at least, suggest local reproduction. More widely, these changes might be reflected in a greater emphasis on moving animals off-site (see section 3.3) and in other developments visible in the course of the Roman period (see section 9.3).

4.2 The agricultural economy

Developments in crop husbandry are best charted, albeit circumstantially, in environmental samples. Some methodological limitations must be remembered when considering some of the trends outlined below, however, especially transitions into the Roman period. Thus, although oats may represent a significant crop at later points, the lack of chaff makes it difficult to distinguish between a weed and a cultivated plant.[5] Similarly, bread/club wheat (henceforth 'bread wheat'), as a free-threshing cereal may be under-represented in the smaller samples from pre-Roman periods.[6] Also, although the proportions of species may change over time, crop production at any one point would have involved different species, either because they were destined for different forms of consumption, given that animals needed to be catered for alongside humans (and so changing pastoral regimes impacted on cropping decisions), or because crop rotation would be required to ensure long-term soil productivity. We therefore comment first on broad trends within such changing demands.

The earliest parts of the crop record, some of which goes back into the Late Bronze Age, is dominated by hulled barley, alongside a very small proportion of spelt wheat, bread wheat and oats. Limited amounts of small wild/weed plant seeds are evident here, and any charring is presumed to be accidental, either during processing or food preparation. Hulled barley dominance continues into the Iron Age, whilst asymmetrical grains indicate that the six-row barley was present in both Early Iron Age and late Roman phases (its absence in intervening periods is almost certainly a recovery/sampling bias). Two-row barley rachis internodes in one Roman sample indicate its cultivation then, whilst spelt wheat is evident in increased proportions from the end of the Iron Age.

Bread wheat appears mainly in Roman phases (although see above on its possible under-representation in small, pre-Roman samples), but then in increasing proportions throughout that period. This is a type that produces higher yields and is winter hardy, yet more vulnerable to pests and disease. It also requires a greater degree of soil fertility than other wheats.[7] The extra investment required for bread wheat may explain why it only becomes a significant cereal well into the Roman period. Emmer wheat may have been cultivated still later (tentatively identified grains and glume bases could equally represent contaminants). The notion of an increasing adoption of bread wheat in the Roman period is further supported on circumstantial grounds. Waterlogged plant macrofossils from later Roman phases comprise mostly taxa associated with fertile disturbed ecotypes, especially in the vicinity of damp springs and ditches (note in section 4.1 the use of animals for manuring and their regularly accessing waterholes). This increased fertility may have provided the conditions in which bread wheat cultivation could flourish.

Moving beyond these main crops, wild/weed plant seeds are evident from diverse environments from the start of the Roman period, for example in G205, with later Roman ditch G210 yielding the first evidence of cultivated fruit, plus charred wild/weeds associated with cultivated, disturbed and damp ground. The latter types are then seen throughout the remaining Roman period, along with charred heather stems, culm bases and rhizomes. Overall, the fertile ecotypes evident in Roman

ditch fills are paralleled in taxa represented in much earlier pits and gullies beside Iron Age roundhouses. Hence, appropriate ground conditions would have been equally evident then, at a time when there is no evidence for a bread wheat emphasis: the latter change was not simply determined by increased fertility.

The above evidence demonstrates that much of the Heslington landscape was used to produce crops from at least the start of the Iron Age. Direct evidence of production is, however, far from common. An ard made of alder was found in an early Roman ditch in the east of the site (G199), matched by a second in the west (G167). Both had fractured in the same place, perhaps the product of a structural weakness at this point (or perhaps deliberately broken off: see section 8.3). The fact that both come from early Roman contexts, which are few and far between on the site, is assumed to be coincidence rather than implying a greater emphasis on agriculture over pastoral exploitation then. In fact, geoarchaeological information from broadly contemporary contexts in G199 indicates mainly open pasture at this time, albeit with some cereal cultivation.

In a similar vein, a rectangular-sectioned bar tapering to a square tip, cautiously interpreted as part of a broken rake, was discarded in a late Roman ditch (G103). If correctly identified, it would be an example of a tool that would have been common in such landscapes, originally featuring a wooden beam and stepped individual prongs.[8] Beyond these chance survivals, the only clear evidence for preparing the ground for cultivation comes from evidence of ploughing in recent centuries. This aspect, based on both map and archaeological sources, is discussed first, followed by archaeological evidence for processing, in terms of drying and grinding, in earlier periods.

Evidence for ploughing was noted in the initial aerial photographic reconnaissance (see section 1.2) and via the 1857 Enclosure Map. Its straight-sided form suggested to Perring a fairly late date, perhaps a sixteenth century improvement following medieval 'strip farming'.[9] Furrows were recorded archaeologically across much of the development area (see section 3.6). In the east these comprised only north–south features (G5, G14, G54, G81, G89, G97, G115, G127, G207, G208 and G236). In one area to the west, corresponding north–south medieval features had also survived modern ploughing (G177), together with a single, more limited, east–west group (G178). Where the two alignments coincided, the east–west furrows were provably later than their north–south counterparts. A Y-shaped configuration of ditches in one area towards the west of these surviving furrows (G164), although not well stratified, did yield two medieval sherds, so may also be of this date, as may other pre-modern field boundaries to their east (G176).

As well as indications of medieval and post-medieval ploughing, this landscape had been prepared for use by drainage schemes in these late periods. A single stone land drain (G80) found towards the centre of the site is likely to be of late medieval date, as it was cut by differently aligned modern ceramic drains, themselves on various alignments, some of which were demonstrably successive constructions (G182, G190 and G238). These were in turn sealed by modern plough soil covering all excavated areas (G10, G15, G19, G28, G33, G41, G51, G55, G58, G60, G92, G100, G117, G128, G134 and G185). Even accepting differential survival, modern drainage schemes were clearly quite unlike their medieval counterparts in scale, conception and consistency of materials employed: modern farming was qualitatively different from anything that had happened in this landscape before, with consequent disjuncture between culture and nature (see section 9.5).

Although no ploughing was identified in pre-medieval periods on the site, there is direct evidence of crop processing from three driers of probable Roman date and, more circumstantially, from quern stones either discarded or re-used on the site at various points in both prehistoric and Roman periods. The first such crop processing feature lay in the west of the site (G167). It was set into the top of the ditch that formed the western boundary of a droveway running up to an Iron Age enclosure lying 180m to the north (see above and section 3.2). The intrusion was c 0.50m deep and comprised a central gully 1.6m long and 0.60m wide, with two square intrusions 1.4m across at either end. It was interpreted on site as a corn-drying oven. There is no direct dating evidence associated with this feature, although it cuts the Iron Age ditch in such a way that the latter must have fallen out of use at this point. Thus, a Roman date seems likely.

To the east lay two further crop driers (because both features have been grouped in G233, they are distinguished below in terms of actual context numbers – 6254 for that in the west and 10071 for its eastern counterpart: see fig 3.8 for positions in relation to broadly contemporary landscape boundaries). Their use is probably linked with intercutting pits (G234) and a more isolated feature (G235) in their vicinity. 6254 comprised a T-shaped feature 3.80m long by 3.5m wide (fig 4.1). Its western end survived as a single course of poor stonework bonded with clay, with flue extending to the east, where the location of its firebox and stokehole is suggested by *in situ* burning. It contained a single sherd of third-century pottery, presumably residual as the ditch it cut (part of G231: see section 3.3) clearly belongs to the late fourth century (given the feature's form and underlying relationships, the single sherd of medieval pottery also recovered from it, dated eleventh to thirteenth century, is assumed to be intrusive). It was directly associated with a small pit containing charred grain.

Another crop drier, 10071, was located c 20m to the south-east of 6254. This was roughly rectangular, 4.80m in length, with an eastern element up to 1.30m wide and a western counterpart extending for just over 2m. Parts of the outside of the cut had been lined with clay and tile (fig 4.2), some of which had clearly been burnt *in situ*, and the fills contained considerable quantities of ash. Later disturbance makes its original form hard to

Fig 4.1 Crop drier 6254 in the course of excavation. © OSA

Fig 4.2 Tile lining of crop drier 10171. © OSA

determine, similarly its date: the feature appears to truncate the southern end of a ditch dated to no later than the early fourth century AD, although this relationship is compromised by a later plough furrow and modern land drain. More significantly, several fragments of Romano-British brick and flue tile were re-used in its lining, so a fourth century AD date seems most likely.

These last two driers yielded a rich assemblage of charred cereal grains, along with moderate proportions of chaff and wild or weed plant seeds, including both small and large seeded taxa. That in 6254 comprised mainly bread wheat, with a small proportion of hulled barley and spelt wheat. In contrast, a greater proportion of the cereal grain in 10171 was composed of hulled barley and spelt wheat, followed by bread wheat. It is tempting, if the two features are contemporaneous, to see this diversity as evidence for specialisation of processing across the site (although see this section's opening comments on crop rotation being a necessary part of agricultural regimes, implying that species overlap is only to be expected). Alternatively, based on the above notion of an increased emphasis on bread wheat over time, it might be that 6254 was in use after 10071. The former was clearly inserted in the landscape after c AD 350, whereas the latter can only be suggested to be in use after AD 300. However, these are just the dates after which these features must have been in use.

When considering the supposed differences between the two assemblages, however, it must be remembered that spelt wheat comprised the predominant cereal chaff type in both features, and that these carbonised assemblages represent each feature's final usage: both may have been used for a variety of types of crop beforehand, then cleaned out systematically afterwards. Finally, the

survival of these carbonised components is due only to accidental charring and such samples are unlikely to be representative of either drier in its more successful, earlier usage (such accidents may have been common; ethnographic studies indicate[10] that crops were spread beforehand to dry on nearby platforms of straw or similar, which could easily have been ignited by sparks from the flue).

Waste material found in association with the features from processing (for example, glume wheat) was probably used as fuel, along with wood or peat if available.[11] The presence of wild/bird cherry in our own case might suggest more dedicated fuel supply. Beyond this, it is presently impossible to define what wood species were used to heat the crop, how consistently such choices were made and how they changed over time. Other charred materials in these assemblages include weeds such as ruderal, segetal and marsh species, presumably contaminants. There is a relatively high presence of brome grass seeds in several samples, such seeds being of similar size to cereal grain and so difficult to identify and discard. This may be an accidental impurity, although brome grass can be utilised for food.[12]

Whatever the differences between the two features and their implications, it seems clear that parching of bread wheat, hulled barley and spelt wheat was being carried out here. Free-threshing wheat does not generally require parching to assist in chaff removal,[13] but this can greatly assist milling,[14] and may also prevent spoilage or help to prepare grain for storage.[15]

Even given the vagaries of survival, the two features seem to represent different types of investment, the one, 6254, a fairly conventional T-shape and the second, 10071, resembling a badly preserved version of the large, rectangular 'oven' seen at Wharram Percy on the Wolds.[16] In the Wharram example, this feature, set in a hole at least 2.5m wide by 3.5m across, was a re-designed version of a T-shaped forerunner. This would be the reverse of the sequence at Heslington tentatively suggested above in which T-shaped 6254 might have been in use after rectangular 10071.

This picture of intensification of woodland exploitation might also be hinted at in the general wood charcoal assemblage (fig 4.3). This shows an increased proportion of oak in the course of the Roman period: oak is an excellent fuel wood, producing a good heat and a long-burning fire, properties particularly consistent with the function of a dryer (a Roman crop drier at Nostell Priory was also found to have low taxa diversity, here with hazel, also an excellent fuel wood, as the dominant fuel type[17]).

Whether the oakwood used at Heslington was derived from the local area or collected from further afield (see

section 2.2) is unclear. Either way, if supplied on a regular basis for vital agricultural processing, it implies the management of such sources. In the very latest Roman levels, however, the proportion and frequency of oak were again low, perhaps indicating its reduced availability in the vicinity of the site. It is possible, then, that the intensified production which the driers allowed could not be sustained by local woodland. Charred plant macrofossils suggesting the possible use of turves as fuel at this late stage could be a strategy to get around this problem.

Elsewhere on the site there are also hints at late Roman specialisation in the disposal of burnt debris. Thus, a rich assemblage of charred cereal grains was derived from the fills of a ditch of probable third-century AD date, part of a system of stock control north of Road 1 (G210: see section 3.3). This was dominated by cereal grains, including a high proportion of various wheats and some barley, whilst chaff, mostly wheat glume bases and wild or weed plant seeds, was also present. A similar charred plant assemblage was derived from an even later Roman ditch fill, part of the terracing and reorganisation of boundaries in the central north of the site in the fourth century AD (G105: see section 3.5). Both assemblages suggest discard from nearby drying activity, the former being fairly close to the two driers described above.

The latter assemblage, however, has no such association with a feature, at least within the excavated area (it is quite close to the northern limit of excavation here, the zone beyond being subject to considerable truncation anyway). This second, very late, assemblage implies that, if there was pressure on fuel supplies at the very end of the Roman period, it was clearly a problem for which solutions were found. (A third dump of field maple in a pit (G6) is the likely product of a fire using this type of fuel. In this case, rather than crop processing, it probably relates to the specialised use of this 'ritual enclosure': see section 8.5.)

Processing of crops is also suggested, if less directly, by several quern stones discarded or re-used on the site. The excavation yielded recognisable fragments from at least twenty-five examples, comprising the second largest published assemblage west of the Ouse (forty-five stones were reported from the settlement at Shiptonthorpe[18]). The earliest comprised a saddle quern from an Early Iron Age context in Well 4, a feature already argued to evidence livestock watering (see section 4.1). This indication of early processing is matched by a notable increase in cereal grains from this point: from the start of human settlement in the landscape, a mixed farming regime seems to have been employed. Charred wheat chaff and pollen evidence for cereal growth were derived from Iron Age and Roman pits (G199). As noted above,

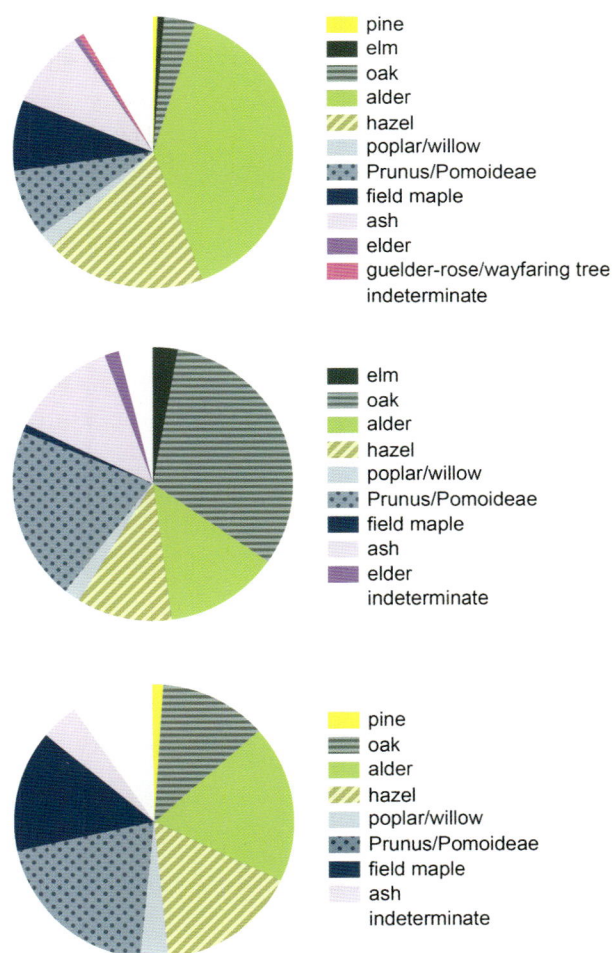

Fig 4.3 Charcoal assemblage composition by total number of fragments: at end of the Iron Age (top graph, as per fig 2.5); by the middle of the Roman period (centre); and at the end of the Roman period. *Drawing*: Neil Gevaux

these samples also generated coleopteran evidence indicating dung and decay, thus implying grazed and fertilised ground. Mixed farming remained the dominant mode of landscape exploitation into later centuries.

At least six further saddle querns, used in a back-and-forth motion, came from Heslington, an unusually high proportion for sites in the region. The majority derived from Iron Age contexts, perhaps accounted for by the scale of exposure of that period. The dimensions of relatively intact examples are broadly consistent with Neolithic examples, however, which may imply limited development over the course of prehistory. The grinding surfaces tended to be concave across both length and, to a lesser extent, width, implying an upper stone whose length was less than the width of the lower. The single beehive quern from the site came from the fill of Well 6 and was of poor quality, but unusual for its asymmetrical wear and repositioned spindle, the latter perhaps suggesting extended usage.

Six disc hand querns were recovered, three of Mayen lava and three from fairly local sources (one each millstone grit, sandstone and crinoid grit: see section 7.2; the first two derived from late Roman layers, but in re-used contexts). The Mayen lava is light and good for efficient milling, but fragile and prone to shattering, making them less susceptible to archaeological recovery. Such fragmentation is suggested by the occasional concentration of lava crumbs encountered in excavation, and might mean that such imported querns are under-represented in this assemblage.

The site has yielded evidence for six millstones, all from late Roman contexts running to the very end of the fourth century. One of these had been very little used before discard, but others were worn, sometimes to excess. One of the latter had its inner face roughened by random pecking, with the outer portions finished by a mixture of misaligned grooves along with an off-centre, D-shaped perforation (fig 4.4). Its four cavities are interpreted as representing a pair of opposed feed-pipes on top of the stone. This is supported by wear patterns, implying rubbing by a conical hopper, fixed to the stone, feeding grain into the two pipes (note examples at Wanborough[19] and at Mesclans in Gaul[20]). Insufficient material of its central 'eye' survived to confirm how power was transferred to this stone and, generally, none of this group were of sufficient size to prove definitively that they were powered by animals or humans.

The surface of a roughly worked millstone grit block found in topsoil towards the centre of the site evidenced a square socket 70mm across and 70mm deep in its surface and hints of circular vertical member 0.24m diameter surrounding this. The socket is too shallow to locate a free-standing upright, implying its use within a framed superstructure.

Taken together, these stones imply an increased investment in processing which, where datable, belongs to the third and fourth centuries AD. It is tempting to relate this to greater involvement of the state in agricultural management, something, presumably, linked to York. Such millstones are rare at that settlement and, except where re-used in structures or re-deposited in post-Roman horizons, entirely lacking from the fortress proper. This suggests that, if York-based authorities were indeed interested in controlling milling in the surrounding landscapes, they received the end product as flour or bread (see section 9.3 for a wider discussion of the relationship between Heslington and Roman state authority).

Indications of control of milling in the later Roman period recalls how pivotal the position of the miller became later, in medieval society. Equally, a tithe barn near St Paul's church in Heslington village, a settlement established by Domesday and with a church by 1299,[21]

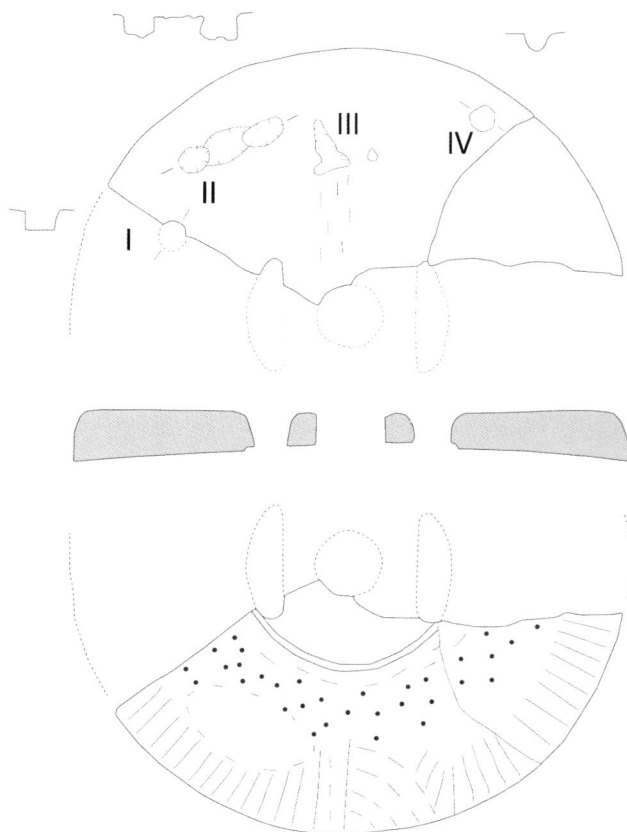

Fig 4.4 Millstone with off-centre, D-shaped perforation, plus evidence of random pecking (dotted zone) misaligned grooves at edges. Four cavities (I–IV) are interpreted as evidence for a pair of opposed feed-pipes set on top of the stone. *Drawing*: Neil Gevaux

suggests that grain storage took place here on some scale in the medieval period, in this case legitimated by association with religious authority. By the late eighteenth century AD, a windmill set on Siward's How shows that processing in this landscape had become still more controlled.[22] Equally, the ability to store surplus meat over winter on a considerable scale is suggested by the ice-house north of Heslington Road, seen on the 1853 OS map alongside out-houses and farm buildings. The bleach works set up nearby in 1804 similarly imply flax retting on a new scale: post-medieval processing and storage facilities on this scale usher in the type of systematised approach to agricultural production and processing in operation today (see above on modern ploughing). Paradoxically, this greater specialisation led finally to this landscape being removed entirely from agricultural production and occupied by university buildings (see section 9.5).

Productive landscapes – specialist manufacture

5

There is a range of evidence for non-agricultural production at Heslington, falling into one of three categories: artefacts, limited in number, that are directly indicative of production but have been derived from re-deposited contexts, and hence have no direct implications for the function of the zone from which they were recorded; features such as hearths or other areas of in situ burning that seem to indicate artisanal activity, but do not tell us its nature; and finds directly associated with the features or buildings in their vicinity, thus having both functional and spatial indications for the use of the site at that point.

The first type of circumstantial evidence includes a variety of flint objects, plus bone working, iron working and a pottery waster (section 5.1). Prehistoric production involving the working of ferrous and non-ferrous metal and of jet is evident on both margins of the site (section 5.2), together with a dedicated focus of early Roman artisanal activity in one zone towards the east (section 5.3). The most concerted production, however, takes place at its centre in the late Roman period and involves a kiln and a range of hearths and working hollows (section 5.4).

5.1 Artefacts circumstantially indicating production

In terms of surviving materials, flint assemblages provide the earliest evidence for production at Heslington. Some of this material includes cores consistent with Grooved Ware associations, thus belonging to the late Neolithic period,[1] perhaps 500 years or more before other evidence for activity is directly visible on the site. Retouching and knapping of various forms are evident in the flint assemblage from all periods. The latter, sometimes using anvil but mostly by hammering, is of high quality throughout. It is worth noting here that there are five flint hammers derived from the site. Unfortunately, all are from ploughsoil so the implications of their distribution are unclear. Some knapping generated a mixture of flakes and blades/bladelets whose size and form suggest a Neolithic,

rather than Bronze Age, emphasis, thus reinforcing the idea of early human presence in the landscape.

A key question, of course, is how much of this processing happened at Heslington itself. As only 6 per cent of this flint comes from primary core reduction, it would appear that, in all periods, fist-sized nodules were prepared beforehand and supplied to the site, with most cores then worked to exhaustion. This might imply pressure on such external sources, as could evidence of core rejuvenation flakes (although these focus on blades, so may be from other cores). In terms of sources, some of the flint from every period came from glacial gravel deposits that would have been available from the diverse geological contexts at the head of the moraine here. Yet, the vast majority used regular till flint from the glacial contexts nearer the east coast. Overall, flint working occurred here from the Neolithic period onwards, sometimes in its entirety but more often using roughed-out nodules brought in from sources to the north and east.

Later indicators of production include a bone rough-out from mixed spread of very late Roman date, simply discarded at this spot (G113). A rectangular, square-sectioned iron bar with broken end, which may be a smith's punch or a chisel, was deposited in a late Roman context (G224). Neither object seems likely to have been moved very far from its point of use, thus implying that bone-working and either iron- or wood-working were practised on the site in the third or fourth centuries AD. The first is interesting, the other hardly surprising, and both are backed up by other evidence to be described below.

More intriguingly, Well 5 yielded sherds of an Ebor Ware waster flagon of late-second/third century AD date. This came from a late Roman context, so must be residual. It seems very unlikely that such a vessel was produced on-site: kilns elsewhere are known to manufacture this pottery type.[2] The flagon was, therefore, probably being used here as a second (see section 7.3). However, lead alloy repairs of Roman pottery, one discarded in Well 7 and three others concentrated in a zone south of the hypocaust building (G6 and G8: see section 8.5), imply that pottery was being mended on site, and perhaps especially in the latter area.

5.2 Prehistoric production at the margins of the site

Direct evidence for production in the form of known, securely located features comes from various parts of the site. The earliest, located in the east of the site (fig 5.1),

comprised two cobble-filled cuts that may represent hearths (G201: see fig 9.2 for exact position). The paucity of finds in these features itself suggests an early date. One did, however, contain a fine, heavily burnt, needle-like point, most likely a fragment of leaf-shaped arrowhead of non-standard form. There are somewhat similar pieces in some Late Upper Palaeolithic sites in southern England, such as Hengistbury Head, Dorset,[3] but no published parallels in later Neolithic and Early Bronze Age assemblages from the Yorkshire region. This has therefore been interpreted as an artefact of early Neolithic or earlier date, implying the use of the associated hearths before the Bronze Age.

In the west of the site lay a circular pit (G136), positioned some 70m north east of Well 3. Measuring 1.3m in diameter but only 0.5m deep, its fill generated the blade end of a polished stone axe, butt end broken off, made of a fine-grained mineral, most likely a Greywacke from the southern uplands of Scotland (fig 5.2). The lack of chips on its smooth cutting edge, which would have worn very quickly, might suggest that it was used more for show than as a practical tool. This pit also contained a jet offcut fragment. This may be intrusive, as other jet fragments were found in the vicinity (see further below), but it did derive from the same fill as the axe. The pit suggests the use of this zone in the Neolithic period, but, if true, this was not accompanied by any other signs of contemporary human activity (it lay just to the east of funnel-shaped ditches G143 (see section 3.1) but these are of much later, Iron Age, date, so this seems likely to be mere coincidence).

The only hint at production at such an early date comes from undated features (G136), some in the vicinity of Well 2 cutting the early palaeochannel (see section

Fig 5.1 Possible early hearth in the east of the site.
© OSA

Fig 5.2 The blade end of a polished stone axe, made of a Greywacke from a probable Scottish source, from a Neolithic pit. © YAT

2.1), others more widespread. Analysis of slags from certain features suggests the presence of haematite. This might be naturally occurring here but, if so, is not evident in subsequent intrusions in the vicinity (except in a much later Roman feature, G170, which probably simply

disturbed such material from these earlier levels). Haematite is known to be used as a pigment on Late Neolithic Orkney[4] and in Early Iron Age finewares from All Cannings Cross in Wiltshire.[5] Given this and their stratigraphic position, these pits might also date to one of those periods.

From the end of the Bronze Age, production processes can be much more securely charted in the western area, where fills from various cut features south of Well 2 suggest diverse functions (G138). The earliest seem to be associated with the use of a hollowed wooden cylinder carved from a section of roundwood alder trunk (fig 5.3). Two quarters of the same object were found side by side and dated to 2730 ±60 BP (see section 2.3, G138, and table 1.1). This was not a trough, as the surviving end is shaped and hollowed. Part of a second cylinder of similar size and form was found nearby, implying their non-random discard and perhaps a link to activities taking place in the vicinity. Thus, both items may be related to the functioning of the nearby well, perhaps a container for liquid or for channelling such.

A group of later pits inserted here were sometimes filled entirely with charcoal-rich soils, some animal bones and heat-shattered pebbles, whilst others had unburnt pebbles at their base but were then sealed by such fire-

Fig 5.3 Two quarters of a hollowed wooden cylinder carved from a roundwood alder trunk, dated to 930–780 cal BC. © YAT

cracked materials (G139). It is unclear whether the latter represent closure deposits or the straightforward functioning for the pits. Either way, the non-fired elements at the base of some suggest a specialist function. Elsewhere, burnt mounds of stone of Bronze Age date have been interpreted as a product of heating water for cooking, bathing or artisan production.[6] Given the C14 date of the underlying horizon, any such activities at Heslington would have run into the Iron Age.

Iron working provides most of the evidence for metal production on the site, whether circumstantial via the general distribution of diagnostic materials or, more rarely, where particular features are associated with such residues (fig 5.4). The former type of evidence is considered first. General concentrations of hammerscale, although not in the huge amounts seen in the Roman period, were derived from a range of different pre-Roman features here (G153, G156, G157 and G158), whilst slags clearly cluster around Well 2 and in the drip gullies of Late Iron Age roundhouses in enclosures to its south (see section 6.2). This evidence implies a background noise of smithing in particular parts of the site in the Late Iron Age, a point when this landscape was becoming increasingly controlled with field boundaries (see section 3.2).

Within this general distribution, some specific zones and features mark themselves out. The earliest vitrified furnace lining with slag comes from a re-cut of an early ditch just south of Well 2 (G140), but not in sufficient concentrations to prove that iron working was taking place here at that time. More convincing evidence derives from a probably later sequence of surfaces, pits and the surviving bases of possible kilns or hearths inserted south of the same well in the line of the western droveway (G139: see section 3.2). The exact position of the iron working activity itself is only approximate, as the pit containing the furnace base was not itself burnt; the base could have been discarded from a nearby working area beyond the limit of excavation.

One pit here (G158) contained two big blocks of iron slag, others yielded vitrified furnace lining and at least three smithing hearth bottoms ranging in weight from

Fig 5.4 Distribution of residues from iron working, non-ferrous slags and jet offcuts from Iron Age contexts in the west of the site. Jet offcuts concentrate in boundary ditches in the east and the single copper-working residue in an early enclosed zone to the north of this, associated with Roundhouse 2. Other iron- and lead-working residues cluster in the west, in ditches south of Well 2. The possible silver-working residue lies in a subsidiary enclosure beside Roundhouse 3. *Drawing*: Helen Goodchild

303g to 2,008g. The latter comprise large plano-convex blocks of slag formed at the base of a smithing hearth, as components from the furnace, fuel and the iron objects combined in the heat. A single sample from these levels included pipe-like runs of slag, possibly an indicator of smelting. If so, areas of natural iron concretion or panning in the vicinity would have constituted a source of raw materials for such activity.

These elements are not well-dated, provably post-dating the palaeochannel that fell out of use before the start of the Iron Age (G135: see section 2.1), and pre-dating elements belonging to the end of that period. When set beside general hammerscale and slag evidence, however, they suggest that the intensive ironworking hereabouts dates to the final centuries of the Iron Age. Such activities happened either within the droveway leading up to Well 2 or in adjacent fields, with the residues of such work then discarded in the margins of this access route.

At a later point still, after the ditch bounding the droveway was re-cut, further metal-working pits and associated features (G158) were set into the top of this refurbished boundary. These final deposits include evidence from dribbles of vitrified furnace lining and two smithing hearth bottoms and run up to a date in the second century AD, if not just beyond. The implication is that artisan activity, alternating with boundary reinforcement and sometimes creeping into adjacent zones, ran seamlessly from the Iron Age into the Roman period. A concentration of iron slag and smithing hearth bottoms (G160) indicates another production area in a subsidiary enclosure c 40m east of Well 2 (see also section 2.3). This seems to be a late landholding development, suggesting that iron working was being increasingly controlled in the course of the Iron Age and beyond.

Finally, c 175m to the west of Well 2, in a trench extension with no intervening activity, lay a linear feature at least 8m long whose fill contained burnt cobbles and some probable hearth bottoms (G172). Although undated, it lay only 10m from a Roman cremation buried in an Ebor Ware jar of late first to early second century AD date (G171: see section 8.3). If the ditch is of a similar date, that would suggest that metal production may have taken place in this marginal area in the early Roman period.

Non-ferrous metal-working seems to be limited on the site, but four pieces of evidence are potentially important. An oval pit cut into the top of the surfaces generating intensive ironworking evidence of Late Iron Age date contained three large fragments of lead sheeting (G156). One had been folded and all seem to have been deliberately placed here, as only minor overlapping is evident (fig 5.5). This might suggest the recycling of lead

alongside the smithing, and perhaps smelting, of iron.

Also, a piece of lead casting waste came from material dumped above Well 2 late in its life (G170). This component, being derived from a context after a period of erosion and accumulation marking the demise of this waterhole in the Roman period, could have come from anywhere. Thus, its implications for lead manufacture in the immediate vicinity are unclear (see also section 8.3 for possible suspension gear and the nail group from this horizon, both possibly structured deposition).

More significant, spatially and chronologically, was what seems to be a rather roughly formed copper alloy ingot. This was derived from a context within the enclosure surrounding the large Roundhouse 1 (see section 6.2), the first enclosed space within the Heslington landscape and thus a zone with clearly controlled access. The material concerned was found immediately adjacent to the later, smaller building (Roundhouse 2), perhaps suggesting that such production occurred late in the occupation of this zone, after features had developed more intensively within it.

Finally, a collection of crucible fragments in a grey fabric, including one originally identified as a tuyère, came from within a small Late Iron Age enclosure, from the southern ditch beside the entrance into Roundhouse 3 (G153: see section 6.2). The fragments are too small to allow a thorough reconstruction, although one may be from the area of a lip and another part of a bowl-shaped vessel. Traces of vitrification confined to their inner surface indicate that heating was from above, paralleling Iron Age crucibles from Gussage All Saints and Glastonbury Lake Village.[7] Some had purplish deposits, perhaps hinting at a role in melting silver alloys.

If this identification is correct, production of this prestigious metal was confined within a roundhouse set

Fig 5.5 Lead sheeting deliberately placed in pit G156, perhaps suggesting the recycling of this material. © YAT

up in the corner of a sub-enclosure within a system of Late Iron Age landscape development – a closely controlled environment. This same zone, however, yielded evidence of vitrified furnace lining, together with similar material to the south east related to iron processing (G154). This would imply that this sector was not reserved exclusively for silver production.

Overall, evidence for lead, copper and proposed silver-working comes from more controlled landscape settings, the lead and silver elements being provably late in the sequence. This trend seems to match that seen with the smithing, and possible smelting, of iron. The latter is first evident in more accessible, open zones south of Well 2, and included some latitude in how residues were discarded. Later in the Iron Age, and arguably beyond, metal-working was taking place in more clearly defined, smaller spaces (see section 6.2 for further discussion in relation to structural development).

Jet is the final material type whose spatial distribution seems significant in prehistoric levels, clustering in two areas. The first lay 35m south of Well 2, in the western ditches of the droveway thought to run south from that water access point (G156 and G173). This included unworked jet blocks, perhaps made ready for shaping. A second zone comprised ditches on either side of the eastern droveway set up here in the Late Iron Age (G144, G147, G149, G151 and G167). The latter material ranged from individual items weighing only a few grammes to multiple offcuts: the fifteen items found in G151 weigh more than all of the others put together, for example (two jet fragments found in 'Roman' context G167 are assumed to have been re-deposited here when a drier was inserted into the line of an underlying droveway ditch: see section 4.2).

The differences in the numbers of jet fragments, the range of features into which they were deposited, and the fact that this material was discarded on both sides of the droveway imply that the working of jet was taking place in the area on a regular basis. This could have happened either in the immediate vicinity of the droveway or been generated by artisans working within the enclosed roundhouse to its north, their residues then regularly discarded into these ditches further south. The fact that shale offcuts, although less numerous, seem to match the distribution of their jet counterparts implies that both materials were worked contemporaneously, and perhaps by the same hands.

There can be little, doubt, therefore, that this site was concerned with specialist production in iron, precious metals and jet by the end of the Iron Age. Of these, iron production was clearly the most intensive and, whilst some of this can be understood in relation to the requirements of any farming, not all of it seems to fit those needs. This implication of specialisation is still more evident with the non-ferrous metal residues and jet offcuts. Two things are of note here. First, on spatial matters, the distribution of these residues is mostly in the west of the site, rather than in either Iron Age enclosure further east (although, see section 5.3). Further, in the latter area, its discard is clearly linked to the creation of boundaries on the site (see fig 5.4 and section 3.2), and may even have influenced the position and orientation of particular roundhouses and their associated, subsidiary enclosures (see section 6.2). Hence, one of the drivers behind the more complex field systems which eventually developed may have involved non-farming needs. Second, although dating can be hazy (see section 1.5), the origins of these more specialised manufacturing functions lie in the Iron Age, not with the coming of Rome (see wider discussion in section 9.2).

5.3 Early Roman production towards the east of the site

In the eastern part of the site, there is much less evidence for manufacturing activities in the Iron Age. This could be a function of levels of archaeological survival here. Yet, if pits and hearths like those seen in the west had been dug here, they would have survived later truncation, since shallowly founded circular buildings were excavated here (see section 6.2). Thus, the gap in human activity seems to be a real one.

The main exception to this picture concerns a shallow, sub-rectangular intrusion just north of Well 1 comprising a regular element in the north, perhaps wood-lined or even roofed, and a subsidiary channel along its southern edge (G76) (see fig 3.6). This was either a small, sunken-floored building or a covered working area: a concentration here of vitrified furnace lining, hammerscale (both flake and spheroidal) and lead spillage debris seems to relate to its functioning. Associated pottery includes some Flavian period samian ware from its lower levels, although material in its uppermost fill belongs to the fourth century AD. Either this feature was very long-lived, or some of its residues became mixed with later layers when an early Roman feature was backfilled to allow re-development (the latter is preferred in the light of activities above adjacent Well 1: see below). Seventeen fragments of disarticulated CBM were recovered from the general vicinity of this building, a surprisingly large number from an early context: either it came from the same late Roman tidying of the vicinity or this sunken structure had a tiled roof.

Fig 5.6 Early Roman timber features set into the top of Well 1, cut from the same oak tree felled between AD 53 and 89. © OSA

There is a hint of other changes nearby at this time. Thus, a pair of major timber uprights, set 2.5m apart, were inserted to the south-east above Well 1 (fig 5.6). They were cut from the same oak tree, felled between AD 53 and 89. In common with most of the timbers known from Roman York, these examples have stronger matches southward, rather than to the contemporaneous dendrochronological sequences from the higher ground to the north-west and west. The flat bases of these squared timbers show that they were not free-standing, suggesting the need for top plates to give them structural integrity (fig 5.7). Several roundwood timber branches and trunks of alder, yew and hazel were laid horizontally against the uprights. These exhibited few signs of working, apart from hewing of side branches. Whether they were part of the original structure or an alteration or repair is unclear. Either way, the primary timbers show that a major framework was inserted above this well at the start of the Roman period, either to allow a boggy zone to be crossed or to systematise water supply.

This development may be broadly contemporary with environmental changes within Well 1 itself. Here, a geoarchaeological horizon dated after 1981 ±28 BP/1957 ±25 BP (see section 2.3 and table 1.1, G199) suggests an increased waterflow at this time, alongside a significant

Fig 5.7 Flat base of one of the timbers seen in fig 5.6, showing that it was inserted as part of the frame, not driven into underlying strata. © OSA

increase in magnetic susceptibility readings (G199). This indication of a preponderance of heated materials and charcoal-rich sand suggests a nearby activity associated with burning, its residues flowing down into the springline. The next horizon, taking us into the second century AD, shows continued waterflow, but reduced burning. This implies that any adjacent production was a short-lived, and perhaps localised, event. Its timing, the second half of the first century AD, matches the point at which the oak framework was inserted above that Well 1, and when the sunken manufacturing area was created nearby (see section 6.2 for a possible relationship with Roundhouse 16).

In contrast, a second possibly enclosed area *c* 80m to the north-east suggests rather longer-lived production. First developed in the first or second century AD, it provides evidence for the insertion of a further series of less substantial, more sinuous features, also including pits or large postholes (G63). These new features were associated with signs of burning and so may represent some sort of artisanal production here. One associated piece of CBM comprises a *pedalis* in an unusual Roman fabric, R10. This appears to date to the third century AD or later, as do associated ceramics. An area of disturbance towards the southern end of these channels contained two large millstone grit blocks, one of which showed evidence for a socket for a vertical member (G64). The sheer size of these boulders, one being well over 2m across, suggests preparation for substantial structural development in the vicinity, although the exact position and nature of any such building was entirely unclear. Ceramics date an amorphous, stony spread just to the north-east of these stones to 360+ AD (also G64). This deposit also yielded an iron angle bracket thought to derive from building work. Although the exact implications of all this are uncertain, it seems clear that, at the very end of the Roman period or later, preparation for monumental construction was taking place here.

In sum, despite Roman conquest of the region having a mostly minimal impact on the Heslington landscape, there is evidence of the creation of a local, dedicated manufacturing zone beside Well 1 and further such activities to the north-east. The latter seems to have lasted throughout the Roman period, the former for a much more limited time span, perhaps only a few decades in duration.

5.4 Roman production in the centre of the site

At the centre of the site, a very different process of development was evident, not least because it was not preceded by any concerted Late Iron Age activity beyond the single enclosure with a roundhouse set along the springline (G205: see section 3.2). Any manufacturing emphasis here was very much concentrated in the Roman period, and perhaps beyond. In particular, north-west of the enclosure with associated crossroads (see section 3.3), the natural deposits of the hillside were differentially

truncated locally for the insertion of two interconnected hearths and associated postholes (G106). These, situated north of the end of Road 2 but pre-dating its insertion, were filled with profuse dumps of CBM fragments and concentrations of charcoal, the former sometimes associated with iron nails and, in one case, with three *in situ* flue tiles and an adjacent posthole. Another nearby cut seems to be associated with the use of these hearths, since it was also filled with substantial amounts of CBM, some of which appeared to rationalise into a distorted alignment of flue tiles. Their demise is marked by further substantial amounts of destruction debris.

These features are best interpreted as the remains of hearths, with a channel running between them, constituting either a single, large structure with various flues or two activity areas. This activity employed a particular form of box flue tiles not seen anywhere else on the site (and shorter than any recorded nationally[8]), being poorly made with uneven surfaces and no vents. This suggests a single batch made for a specific, specialist manufacture, here clearly associated with iron nails. Although the CBM represent a highly unusual group, their fabric matched that found in other, later examples, implying that the flues were not produced in a specialised factory.

Clearly, specialised artisanal production was being invested in here, yet its date is problematic. The finds from the features themselves belong to the first and second centuries AD and would thus represent the earliest Roman period activity in this part of the site. The directly overlying strata, however, comprise destruction debris seemingly associated with the demise of a masonry-founded building with probable timber superstructure, G106 (see section 6.4) just to the west dated to the third or fourth centuries AD. The most reasonable interpretation of this evidence is that specialist manufacture took place here at an early Roman date. If it did once spread further east, it was truncated by the insertion of the later building. The substantial depth of the surviving hearths makes their complete obliteration unlikely – this was an activity confined to a local area.

A second manufacturing area comprising layers of substantial cobbling set into scoops in the natural stratigraphy (G103) lay *c* 20m to the north-west of the zone described above. This created a roughly square platform at least *c* 10m across (its western limits are slightly uncertain) with an irregular surface. Clay post-pads and other postholes seem to be associated with this surface at certain points. Although they displayed no obvious spatial patterning, they suggest that it was surrounded by some sort of boundary fencing. A depression containing a profusion of charcoal in the surface of this cobbling near its north-east 'corner' might suggest a hearth position at this point.

Dating this second investment in manufacturing processes is problematic. Much of the material from its initial construction dates to the late second century AD. In the south, however, in one part of its use it does seem to underlie a ditch system (also G103) set up after the creation of Road 2 (see section 3.4) and backfilled in the late third century (it is clear from detailed evidence that this cobbled zone underwent phases of development). More generally, the cobbled area and this ditch seem to respect each other. The most convincing interpretation is that the cobbles were laid out at the end of the second century AD when the ditch to its south was first inserted, and that both continued in use through the third century.

Further east along Road 2, a series of stony deposits in shallow scoops, postholes and short slots lay on the northern flank of that thoroughfare (G216). Given the burning of the stones and the presence of charcoal in associated deposits, these features appear to be related to artisan production soon after the road was set out. Wood charcoal from their fills showed high proportions of oak, then a wide range of other trees; clearly, a number of environments was employed in collecting fuel for these activities, largely mature trees from hearth fills proper, but more immature woodland sources in associated pits, sometimes including dead or rotting wood. Another feature on this side, which cut a late road surface, contained substantial amounts of charcoal-capped fire-cracked cobbles discoloured by heat and representing another hearth (G124). Given these stratigraphic relationships, it suggests that manufacturing continued here up to the very end of the Roman period.

To the south of Road 2, there is very limited evidence for any corresponding activities, as perhaps befits a zone reserved for non-functional, prestigious purposes (see section 3.4). The one exception to this picture concerns an area due south of the hypocausted building (G1) (see section 8.5). Here patchy cobbled surfaces and hearths may have been set out in the vicinity of a possible contact spring, perhaps enclosed and entered from the north (G6 and G7: see fig 3.8). It is this area, as noted above (see section 5.1), that yielded direct evidence, uniquely on the site, of lead alloy repairs to Roman pottery. To the south lay a concentration of successive, shallow pits, together with a large irregular shallow cut and associated postholes, possibly a working hollow (G223). All cut into natural strata but contained material of third-century AD date and may be associated with a nearby scatter of late Roman pits (G222). Sometime in the fourth century AD this area was enclosed (G224), perhaps the point at which the possible spring to their north was also encircled. The

unusual character of this area seems, therefore, to have been retained through the fourth century AD.

To the east, just beyond the main boundary of the possible ritual zone but within the subsidiary ditch that flanked in on this side (see section 3.2), lay several scooped-out pits seemingly linked by a sinuous gully (G39). A concentration of metal-working residues here suggests artisan production. Stratigraphic evidence implies that this may have lasted over a period of time, perhaps starting in the early third century AD but continuing into the fourth. North-east of this lay a group of anomalous millstone grit fragments set in a slight scoop (G48). Their character seems to preclude a structural function, but might suggest processing of imported stone here in the late third century AD or beyond. The above evidence implies distributed foci of artisan activity, both on the northern edge of Road 2 and in the western and eastern zones to its south.

The sphere with the most concentrated evidence, however, lay 15m north of that road, a zone whose topographical organisation was fundamentally altered in the second half of the fourth century AD (see section 3.5). Perhaps uniquely at Heslington, this area constituted a designated artisanal zone. Activity started with the creation of a stone kiln structure up to 1.8m long, sunk 0.45m into the ground (G107) (fig 5.8). Some of its masonry was clearly re-used, notably a quern stone, but other stones included silicaceous sandstones and pink sandstone, both sourced from the Pennines and rare on the site, thus perhaps supplied for this particular structure. This good-quality kiln, with a stokehole to the east, is presumed to have had a domed roof at its western end. None of this survived, perhaps suggesting careful dismantling rather than simple collapse.

At some point, part of this feature had been repaired and perhaps extended, whether in one operation or successive periods of maintenance. This included modification of its stokehole, presumably an area of increased wear and tear. Black silt and charcoal within the body of the feature are a product of one of its early firings, not raked out afterwards, whilst similar, overlying material evidences its final use. This kiln obviously constitutes a major investment in this part of the site, modification suggesting a long life. Its position and stratigraphic relationships prove that it was created when this zone was terraced and topographically reorganised late in the fourth century AD (see section 3.5).

To the east of this kiln, several pits, ephemeral hearths and associated working area were set out on the opposite side of a boundary ditch (G108). One pit may have been dug for the mineral extraction (see section 2.2), thus implying that the drift geology here was sufficiently

Fig 5.8 Base of good-quality stone kiln, stokehole to east (right), employing both re-used masonry and rare stone from Pennine sources, perhaps indicating dedicated supply. The feature seems to have been carefully dismantled, rather than simply collapsing, at the end of its life. © DoA

visible at this time to be defined as a viable resource; the other features suggest a series of artisanal activities. CBM cross joins from different parts of the sequence of manufacturing suggest that these later actions may have disturbed their earlier counterparts.

The exact relationship, if any, between these activities and the use of the kiln to their west could not be securely determined. Yet, assemblages from both date to the closing decades of the fourth century AD and they are linked in their CBM profiles (albeit with the material in the kiln being re-used). Finally, they seem to have gone out of use at the same time, when covered by accumulations (G109). The creation of new terraces and ditch alignments in this zone, which happens immediately before the use of the kiln and quarrying/manufacturing commence, signals a much greater focus on artisan production here than hitherto.

Even after the extensive deposition of material sealed this zone, the emphasis on manufacturing continued. Small sections of cobbling appear across the area, suggesting the position of localised working areas and hearths (G110). Some of these seem to obey earlier, now-

backfilled boundary ditches, but others do not. Even after another general accumulation (G113) sealed these features, a final hearth and stokehole (G114 and G23) and associated cobbles (G25) were inserted before the whole zone was covered by post-Roman colluviation. This flourishing of production is most clearly demonstrated by the concentrations of spheroidal hammerscale in the vicinity (fig 5.9), evident in a range of pits and ditches here, but also spreading south in the uppermost fills of some of the larger landscape boundaries running south.

This late manufacturing episode concentrates mainly north of Road 2 and near Well 7, but is also apparent in ditches beside Road 2 and the eastern boundary of the late, 'monumentalised' enclosure between it and Road 1 (see section 8.5). A corresponding concentration occurs around Well 1 some distance to the east (see section 5.3, fig 5.9). Its northern and western limits are entirely unclear, but it is worth noting the recovery of three lead sheets from a late fourth-century AD ditch on the northern edge of Road 2 some 40m to the west of Well 7. Weighing 2.55kg in total, and thus representing a considerable resource in their own right, each was pierced

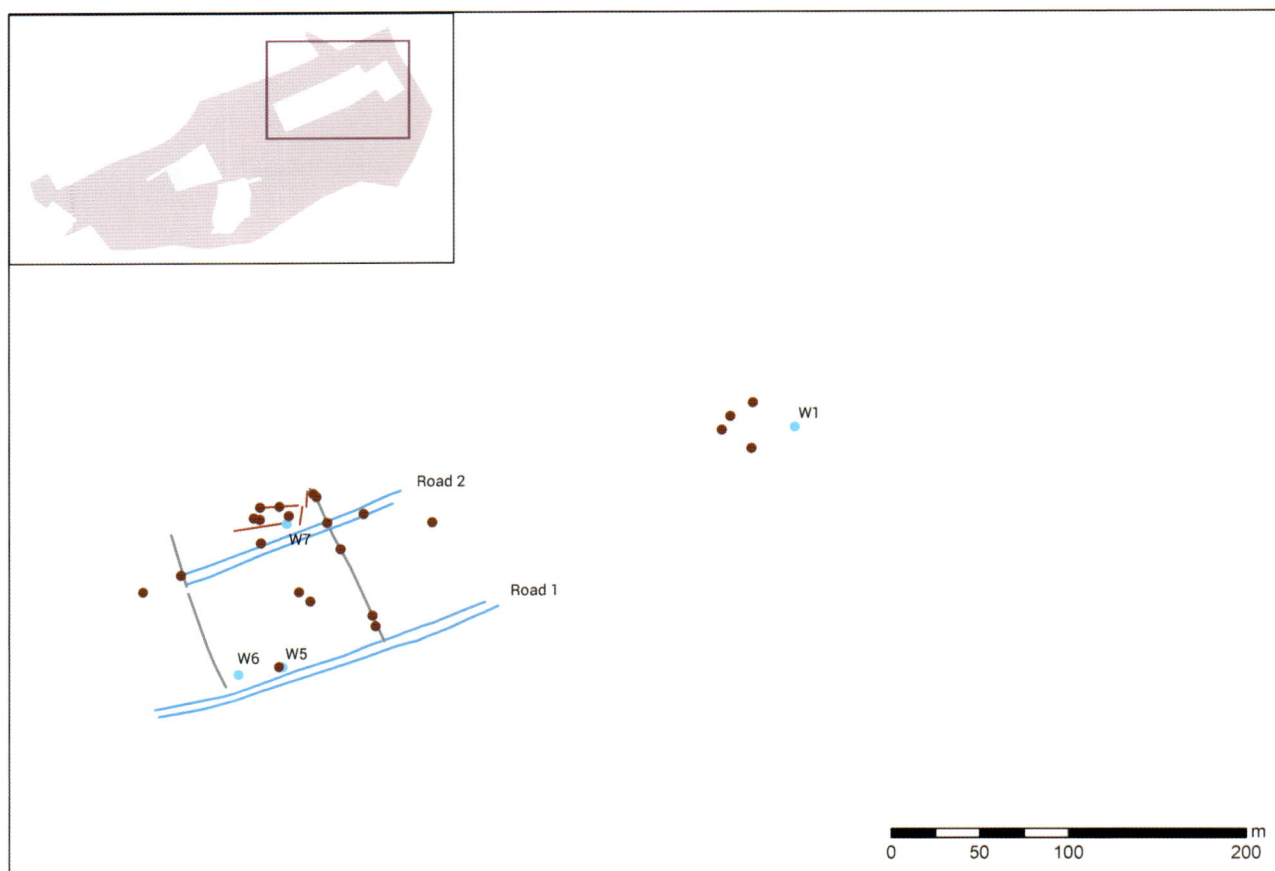

Fig 5.9 Manufacturing activity at the end of the Roman period, as evidenced by the distribution of spheroidal hammerscale in the latest levels in the cent-al part of the site (very late boundaries in red; see also fig 3.8). A second concentration of residues to the east may mark another such focus (see fig 3.6), although associated material here does not provably date so late in the fourth century AD. *Drawing*: Helen Goodchild

with a square nail hole, suggesting their original use as cladding before being cut or trimmed and, in one case, folded. This implies curation and preparation for recycling, whether for repair, plumbing or other architectural use. It is possible, then, that these 'industrial' processes were widespread, both spatially and in the range of metal-working functions performed. Such an artisanal focus fits circumstantial trends in widespread hammerscale recovered across some similarly late levels: this material, although mostly flakes, now included some spheroidal examples, arguably derived from objects being welded. Horizons dated to these decades also produced the greatest concentrations of hearth bottoms, non-diagnostic iron slag, slagged shale and vitrified hearth linings. This is also the time when lead alloy spillages identified in slag assemblages, when analysed by weight, were most evident. Finally, intensified manufacturing is hinted at in the general wood charcoal assemblage, which shows a growing emphasis on oak at the end of the Roman period, a trend perhaps linked to artisan production.

Both the direct and circumstantial evidence from the

tail-end of our sequences indicate three things. First, the focus on manufacturing in the late fourth century AD may be clear enough here but is not evident across the whole site in terms of both its character and intensity: the charred heather stems, sedge family rhizomes and, critically, culm bases present in a nearby ditch (G105) suggest that agricultural processes were still taking place nearby in this landscape at this time. Second, the use of these final features was interleaved with various extensive spreads. Sometimes these deposits obeyed pre-existing landscape divisions, yet, increasingly, such boundaries became less relevant in structuring operations. Indeed, the final hearth and associated cobbling (G113 and G114) seem to have been laid out on a fairly open hillside near Well 7, before post-Roman colluvial deposits began accumulating above them. Finally, concerning dating, the sequence of activity before accumulation G109 goes well into the fourth century AD, whilst overlying activities are securely dated to 370+ AD. Another set of accumulations and then the final hearths noted above in turn cut this horizon and must take us into the fifth century AD (see further discussion of dating in section 7.1). Thus, this site enters the post-Roman period with its agricultural base intact, but alongside an emphasis on manufacturing just north of Road 2, and perhaps at other nodes of production elsewhere. The latter activities, however, seem to occur in a landscape increasingly lacking clear boundaries. In sum, the demise of fourth-century monumental investment in the general area in the form

of a 'ritual' enclosure, entrance tower and hypocaust building (see section 8.5) led not to the end of human occupation but to a 'last hurrah' of metal-working. In the landscape beyond the specific zone, however, agricultural activities seem to have been prioritised once again. A more general context for these developments is presented in section 9.4.

Domestic landscapes – structures and household activities

6

This chapter considers domestic building development, especially changes in plan form and their social implications and associated activities (buildings thought to have non-domestic functions are considered in Chapter 8). It also discusses relationships with other themes such as landscape boundaries (see Chapter 3) and manufacturing processes (see Chapter 4). Description is divided between circumstantial evidence for prehistoric occupation on the site (section 6.1) followed by detailed discussion of roundhouses and related features set up here during the Iron Age (section 6.2). Circumstantial Roman evidence is then presented (section 6.3), followed by a description of two late Roman rectangular buildings and directly associated features (section 6.4).

6.1 Circumstantial prehistoric evidence

As noted previously, human activity at Heslington may have commenced in the Neolithic period, if not before, but became increasingly regular from the Late Bronze Age onwards and then moved definitively from mobile to sedentary forms of activity by the Late Iron Age. The focus of occupation seems to have shifted gradually from prehistoric nuclei nearer the western and eastern edges of the landscape to a much greater emphasis at its centre by the late Roman period. Its use in the medieval and modern periods, far more encompassing and consistent across its entirety, comprised exclusively non-domestic, mainly agricultural, activities. The early processes of changing human engagement with the landscape can be charted circumstantially by four forms of evidence: charcoal, flint, nails and worked wood stakes.

Using charcoal data to draw this picture in detail is challenging, partly due to the limited accuracy of dating (see section 1.5) and partly due to context. Thus, although occasional deposits are dominated by a high proportion of one taxon, perhaps indicating fuel selection, most charcoal assemblages represent the background noise of timber use on the site. Examples of more specialised contexts include the strong representation of ash in the fill of an Iron Age boundary ditch at the centre of the site (G205). This species produces good heat and can be burned as green wood without seasoning. Alder, a poor fuel wood until converted to charcoal, dominated in a broadly contemporary ditch elsewhere (G194). The latter's excellent preservation suggests carbonisation in an oxygen-reduced atmosphere and, given the low incidence of fungal hyphae, implies that good-quality timber was being converted into charcoal, rather than dead or rotting wood. During the Iron Age, then, sophisticated collection and processing of timber was possible and accompanied by specialised dumping of residues. Clearly, communities at this point were experienced in engaging with woodland environments and had the technology to match those abilities.

Flint offers a more specific route into early domestic activity, both via the specific functions of certain items such as saws and knives and via artefact condition, notably use ware, retouch and burning (the distribution of burnt flints is considered in the discussion of consumption practices: see section 7.3). The flint recovered from the site ran from the Mesolithic period (5 per cent) to the Neolithic (60 per cent, over half being Late) and Bronze Age (35 per cent, all thought to be of Early date). Based on its functional characteristics, activities such as hide scraping, typical of domestic sites, are well represented at Heslington, particularly from the Late Neolithic to Early Bronze Age, whilst other tools indicate a range of corresponding behaviours such as cutting and piercing. More specifically, two flint saws were recovered, one from topsoil and the second, more interestingly, from an Iron Age roundhouse (Roundhouse 1, see section 6.2). Examples of plano-convex flint knives, thought to be of Late Neolithic/Early Bronze Age date, come from a later ditch (G169) and from erosion or backfilling above the long-used Well 2 (an associated pit also yielded a much cruder knife: G158). The latter material is assumed to have been re-deposited from earlier occupation in the vicinity of these features (see section 9.1 on the increasingly focused character of activity with the move from mobility to sedentism in the course of the Neolithic and Bronze Age).

By the start of the Iron Age, nails and worked wood stakes had become much more common in all archaeological samples, perhaps implying the development of building on the site. Physical evidence of structural activity at this point remains elusive, however. One possible exception concerns an area south of Well 2. Here, consolidation of the ground included deposition of fire-cracked pebbles derived from Early Iron Age 'burnt mound' activity (see section 5.1). This dumping may have prepared this zone for the insertion of various pits and postholes (G138), including a variety of driven posts, one of oak 0.30m in diameter. Some postholes seem to form distinct alignments and to have been replaced on successive occasions. When combined, these features suggested to the excavators a rectilinear, post-built structure 2.5m long by 1.5m wide on a slightly different alignment from the dominant boundaries in the vicinity. If this is indeed a small structure, it would represent the earliest building on the site, created at the very start of the Iron Age on deliberately levelled ground – a significant investment. These features were, however, set directly above a large boundary ditch line running south from the well and could equally comprise a scatter of non-contemporary features amending or augmenting that alignment, rather than a separate structure laid out above

it. Such structural development remains unproven and is, we suggest, unlikely.

6.2 Iron Age roundhouses

By the Late Iron Age, there is more certain proof of structural development on the site, in the form of a number of roughly circular buildings – 'roundhouses'. Their levels of preservation varied hugely across the site, even to the extent of their actual number being uncertain: in what follows, sixteen have been identified and numbered as such (Roundhouse 1, etc, when first introduced, abbreviated to R1, etc, thereafter). This is a minimalist interpretation, given differential survival and limitations in the areas examined archaeologically (fig 6.1).

In no case did horizontal stratigraphy survive in association with these buildings, although the internal features such as hearths found within some and the existence of small stakeholes along certain boundaries imply that, in such places, later truncation may have been negligible. Unlike conditions in some adjacent waterholes (see sections 1.5, 2.1 and 2.3), organic survival in and around these buildings was minimal. Hence, this site does not add much to debates on building superstructures – for example, whether or not the non-domestic structures that can be recognised (see below) were roofed.[1] Equally, it has only a little more to say on their internal spatial organisation. The present account therefore concentrates on other aspects of the buildings: chronology, size, possible functions, and relationships with adjacent landscape spaces.

The majority of these buildings are in line with Iron Age equivalents in the region: surviving evidence suggested that their superstructure comprised the expected uprights placed in a circle supporting sloping rafters, with no central member.[2] Most structures were either kept clean during their lifetime or had evidence for internal occupation truncated by later activity. Thus, they are mainly dated from artefacts filling the ring ditches set out around them. Further, these finds only date final demise, and each roundhouse could have been kept clean for some decades, if not more, before filling up. Finally, some structures can be dated only by the fills of the enclosure ditches within which they seem to be placed. For all these reasons, therefore, there is insufficient chronological control to decide whether, over time, the roundhouses employed more regular timbers or developed more sophisticated entrance arrangements (as has been suggested elsewhere[3]).

Where their internal diameter could be measured or reasonably defined, it averaged c 5–6m, also in line with

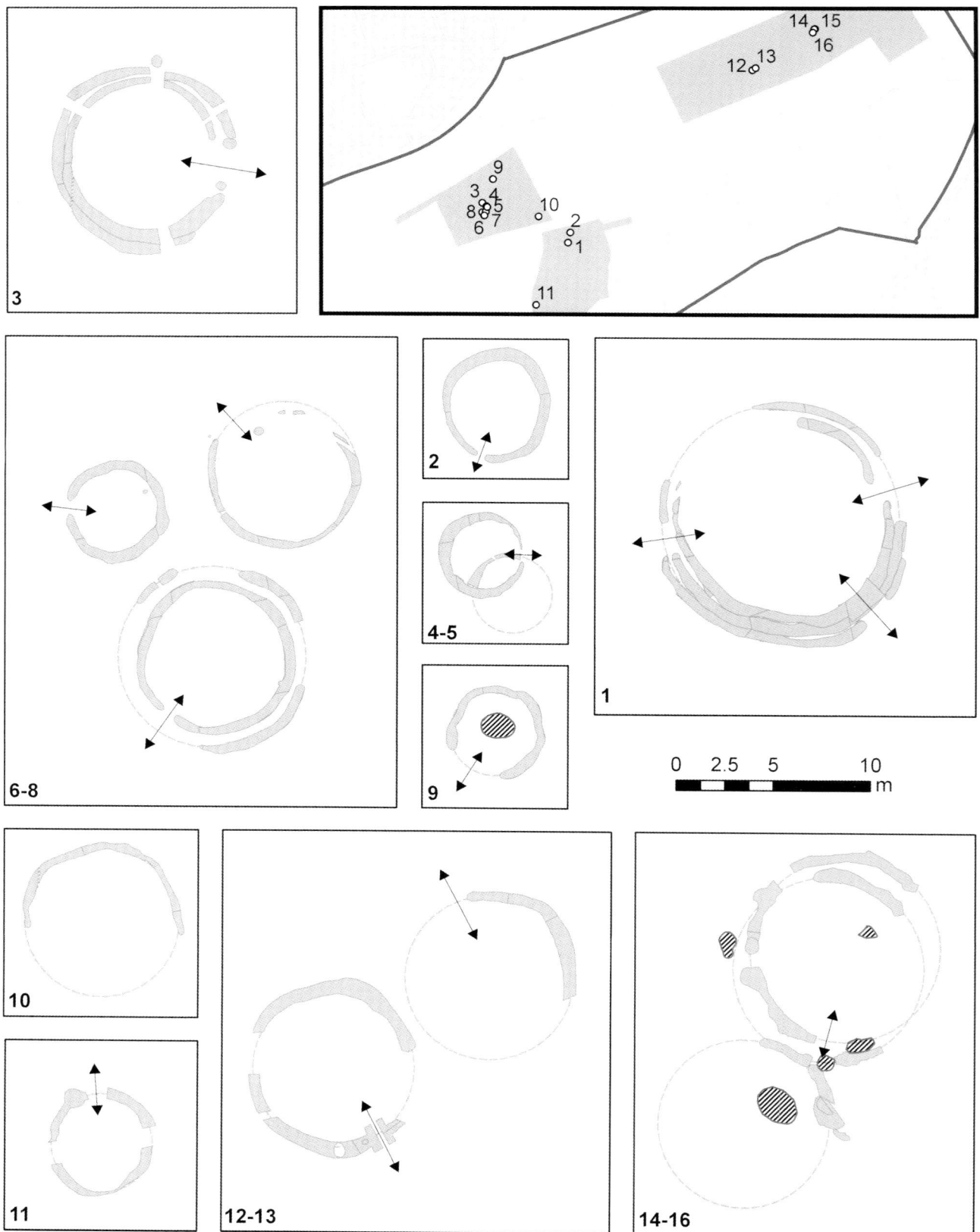

Fig 6.1 Roundhouse plan, form and distribution, drawn with common orientation and scale (north to top). *Drawing*: Helen Goodchild

other regional equivalents. When viewed in detail, however, the Heslington structures fell into three groups (table 6.1): those between 3.5m and 4.5m across (six),

between 6.7, and 7.7m (six) and between 9m and 10m (four). In what follows, these are termed small, medium and large roundhouses (although not all need to have

Table 6.1 Correlation of numbered roundhouses with size, diameter, orientation of entrance and date. Size categories (**L**arge, **M**edium, **S**mall) are as explained in the text. Date categories comprise Middle Iron Age (MIA), Late Iron Age (LIA) and early Roman (ER), or combinations of such.

Number	Size category	Diameter (m)	Entrance orientation	Approx. date of use	Comments
1	L	10	E, then E and W, then SE	MIA/LIA	Multiple phases, changes to entrance
2	S	4.5	SW	LIA/ER	Evidence for copper production alongside more general metal-working/heating
3	M	7.2	ESE	LIA/?ER	Controlled access to/inaccessible from south. Iron and ?silver processing. "Placed" vessel
4	S	3.5–4	unclear	LIA	Earlier version of R5, but evidence for heating activities in backfills
5	S	3.5	?E	LIA	Replacement of R4, but still with heating
6	M	7.2	SW	LIA	Some burnt material in inner and outer ditches, but discontinuous
7	M	?6.7	NW	LIA	Wide entrance—3.45m. less burnt material than R6
8	S	4.2	W	LIA	Narrow entrance, less burning evident than R6
9	S	4	SW	LIA	Central hearth, metal-working evidence
10	?M	?7.2	unclear, not N	unknown	Unenclosed, no Intensive burning
11	S	4.3	?N	unknown	Unenclosed, no Intensive burning, discarded jet fragment
12	M	7.7	SE	MIA/LIA	Replacement for R13 but changed entrance, set on central alignment of enclosure. In woodland setting
13	?	unknown	N	MIA/LIA	Replaced by R12, set on central alignment of enclosure. Also in woodland setting
14	L	?9	unclear	LIA/ER	Fragmentary survival, perhaps earliest of R14–16 group
15	L	9	E	LIA/ER	Hearth at rear, with further hearths just inside and outside doorway. Replaced by R16
16	L	?9	unclear, not E	?ER	Hearth at rear. Replaces R15

been 'houses', in the sense of purely domestic buildings – see further below).

Roundhouses 1 and 2 lay in the western part of the site, set up in a sub-enclosure measuring *c* 50m across within the earliest paddock here (see section 3.2). *Roundhouse 1* lay just inside and north-west of the gateway into this enclosed zone and was 10m in diameter internally, a discontinuous ring-ditch gully with a 1.1m-wide gap defined its primary entrance in the east (G146). This comprises the largest prehistoric structure uncovered on the site, the primary dwelling in this enclosure.

This building had a long history of development and use, perhaps reflecting the considerable investment that its originally large floor area implies. Thus, a second, slightly larger, version was constructed directly above the first, with its eastern entrance widened to 2.5m and a western counterpart, 1.6m wide, now added (G148). This

was, in turn, demolished and its replacement, of which only the southern half survived, set up with a 1.65m-wide entrance now placed on its south-east side: the fact that entrances were re-sited implies not just re-cutting of surrounding ditches but also wholesale recreation of the building's superstructure (G149). A flint saw was derived from the fill of the final drip gully of the latest roundhouse. Although this may be coincidental re-deposition, it is tempting to suggest that such an unusual item was employed when the latest building was in use, or even in the creation/modification of its timber superstructure.

The enclosure surrounding R1 also underwent various changes over time, including the re-cutting and modification of its surrounding ditches and, within that area, pit digging, the addition of curving ditches and other subsidiary divisions of space. Although the adjacent sequence of enclosure development could not be related stratigraphically to that of roundhouse 1, this long history fits with the extended life of that central building.

At some point in this process of later development, however, a small-sized *Roundhouse 2* was added 13.5m to the north of the main structure R1 (G148). This was 4.5m across internally, with an entrance to the south-west. A pit immediately adjacent to this building was backfilled with deposits containing frequent charcoal, fire-cracked pebbles and the previously mentioned copper alloy ingot (see section 5.2). Although the pit and house cannot be linked directly, both post-date a gully representing the initial use of this area. If the two were employed at the same time, both seem likely to be related to artisanal production, including copper manufacture (but not exclusively this – see discussion in section 5.2). This is backed up by the contents of other features in the vicinity whose fills included quantities of charcoal and burnt stones, one of which yielded an iron ring of indeterminate function (G146).

Perhaps the most convincing interpretation of this sequence is that a large, domestic structure, R1, was set up here initially: the primary feature in the first enclosed space on the site. Its subsequent modification, including altered entrance arrangements, is testimony to this continuing significance. These later developments included complex changes to the enclosed area, the most significant of which may have involved the development of specialist manufacturing, including not only pits and gullies, but a dedicated, roofed space in the much smaller

R2. As noted already (see section 5.2), jet offcuts were differentially discarded in the boundary ditches running south from this pivotal part of the landscape.

Finds from the earliest backfills within the enclosure around R1 date to the Iron Age. Finds from secondary features are not sufficiently diagnostic to say how much later in the Iron Age they were in use. It is noticeable, however, that material provably of Roman date is increasingly evident in these later phases. Unlike the occasional medieval or modern sherd also derived from these levels, which must be intrusive, it seems likely that some sequences of occupation ran into the first or second centuries AD. That said, there is no reason to suppose that the development of more specialist manufacturing development proposed above was imposed by external, Roman authority. Indeed, the tendency could easily have its origins in a period before the Roman conquest of this region in the late first century AD.

Roundhouses 3–5 were inserted in a subsidiary enclosure, 30m north–south by 25m east–west, itself in the south-west corner of a set of fields set out east of Well 2 (see section 3.2). Towards its south-east corner, this smaller compound had a narrow entrance (less than 2m wide) giving access to the unenclosed zone to its south. *Roundhouse 3* lay at the centre of this subsidiary enclosure and had a diameter of *c* 7.2m, thus medium-sized (G153). It went through several phases of development, its initial configuration incorporating a 2.8m-wide south-east entrance with a formal porch arrangement (fig 6.2). At

Fig 6.2 Roundhouse 3 in the course of excavation. © YAT

some point, the area north of this entrance was modified, possibly only a localised change. R3 then underwent still more substantial change, now being expanded to an internal diameter of *c* 8.5m and with a wider entrance, 6.1m across, still orientated to the south-east (G154).

The earliest fills of the ditches associated with this structure incorporated inclusions of fire-cracked cobbles and pebbles alongside charcoal flecks and fragments of burnt bone. Its later phases also yielded material displaying substantial signs of heating, but now including pieces of vitrified furnace lining and an ingot argued to be possible evidence for silver production (see section 5.2). The first modification of this roundhouse generated considerable numbers of pottery sherds, all of which dated to the Late Iron Age, together with a few sherds of Roman CBM from an upper fill, which could be post-abandonment in origin.

It seems that this medium-sized roundhouse, later expanded, was concerned with metal production, certainly iron and perhaps silver, from the start of its occupation. It was positioned in a small paddock, cordoned off within a larger field, one of three such evenly sized entities stretching to the east and created in a single act of development (see section 3.2). This arrangement included limited access to more open spaces to the south.

Roundhouse 4 (G154) survived only in a fragmentary form as the north-western part of a curving gully, indicating a building perhaps 3.5–4m in diameter, that is, in the small category (G154). Its silty, sandy backfill incorporated inclusions of fire-cracked stones, charcoal and burnt bone. Any entrance arrangements did not survive later truncation, partly due to modern ploughing and partly due to the insertion of its replacement, R5.

Roundhouse 5 was 3.5m across, thus also classified as small, with a possible entrance in the east, although this gap could be a function of later truncation (G154). It seems to act as a direct replacement for R4, although the two are not superimposed exactly so are considered here as two separate buildings. As with its predecessor, its backfill included frequent inclusions of fire-cracked stones, charcoal fragments and burnt bone, plus lumps of a reddish brown mineralised material not subjected to specialist analysis.

Successive structures R4 and R5 were inserted only 5m from the entrance into this subsidiary paddock, and thus would have mediated access to R3. Both are small in size and, the excavators suggest, may therefore have served as a hayrick or as housing for livestock, rather than human habitation. Given the characteristic burnt materials derived from the fills of both structures, and their resemblance to those of the medium-sized R3, they might, however, be better interpreted as part of the

artisanal activities taking place in a highly controlled, specialist zone. This sector was certainly in use in the Late Iron Age, with a hint, from a few fragments of CBM, that this may have continued into the Roman period.

Roundhouses 6, 7 and 8 (all G159) were set up in an apparently unenclosed area just south of the ditch bounding R3–5. *Roundhouse 6* was 7.2m in diameter, thus medium-sized, with a 0.65m-wide entrance to the south-west. An outer, discontinuous ditch in three segments may be a primary feature of the structure, as it respects the entrance. The fills of both inner and outer ditches contained burnt bone flecks, occasional pebbles and cobbles, in some zones showing burning and fire-cracking, but not in others. Stone inclusions were inconsistent, being concentrated in the inner south-east ditch. Considerable quantities of Iron Age pottery were evident in the outer ditch. It is evident, therefore, that this complex structure has a more variable history of backfilling, and perhaps use, than its counterpart to the north, R3: heating/burning is evident in both, but less consistently distributed in R6. On the other hand, much larger densities of pottery per soil volume were deposited in association with R6.

Roundhouse 7 lay just to the north-east of R6. Measuring 6.7m in diameter (the medium category), it included a 3.45m-wide entrance on its north-west side. Two postholes in this vicinity may relate to such access arrangements. Its ditch fills contained noticeably less burnt material than R6. *Roundhouse 8* lay just west of R7 and north-west of R6. Being 4.2m in diameter (and thus in the small category), it had a narrow, 0.70m-wide entrance in the west. The position of a single posthole symmetrically opposite this in the east may be coincidental. Its sandy ditch fills were generally devoid of heat-fractured materials.

Finds from all three buildings date to the Late Iron Age, and there can be no doubt that these were in use together as they are clustered in one small area with their entrances deliberately orientated to allow access from different directions – the parts where they back onto one another would have been too limited to allow doorways to be usefully situated on these sides. At the same time, there are clear differences between them. R6 and R7 are noticeably larger than R8, which may thus have had a subsidiary role. Furthermore, the doorway of R7 is much wider than the other two. Both variations hint at functional differences. In addition, some backfills of R6 contained burnt material, albeit discontinuously, thus resembling the domestic burnt elements seen with R3 in its earliest phase of activity, plus a lot more pottery. Both materials are less prominent in R7 and R8.

R6 could therefore be seen as a domestic structure, in

use at the same time as more specialist structures nearby that lack evidence for burnt material: R7 with its wider doorway and R8 with its small size. In this, they seem not only to have functioned differently from each other, but also from buildings just to their north, from which they were separated off: access to R3, involved with specialist metal-working, had its access 'protected' by R4 then R5.

Roundhouse 9 lay 50m north-east of R3 and comprised a feature 4m in diameter (thus, in the small category), with a doorway 2.6m wide on the south-west side (G160). The structure was set up in the south of a subsidiary enclosure, 20m wide and at least that in length. This had been inserted into the south-west corner of a field created as part of a series east of Well 2 in the Late Iron Age (see section 3.2). At the centre of the roundhouse, and orientated on its entrance, lay a scooped-out oval pit filled with significant amounts of fine pebbles and cobbles, some heat-fractured, and an associated smithing hearth bottom. The fills of surrounding ditches contained further burnt materials, whilst this general zone contained concentrations of slag. This evidence therefore suggests a single episode of activity, a Late Iron Age structure built in a closely controlled space specialising in metal working. In this it resonates with the use of R1, possibly there involving copper as well as iron production, and of R3, where an ingot (perhaps evidence of silver production) was discarded.

Roundhouses 10 and 11 were scattered more widely in this landscape. *Roundhouse 10* only survived as the northern part of a structure and was *c* 7.2m in diameter, (hence, medium-sized (G161)). Any entrance was not on its north side. Although it lay just west of a major north–south landscape division of known Iron Age date, it was not itself within an area bounded by surviving ditches. Its fills did not yield any concentration of burnt materials, but did contain a pottery sherd thought on site to be of Iron Age date.

Roundhouse 11 was 4.3m in diameter (thus small-sized) and also set in an apparently unenclosed area (G147). Its ditch almost petered out on the southern side, probably due to later truncation, but was elsewhere continuous except for provably later linear intrusions. Thus, its entrance is unclear, unless this relates to a 1m diameter, shallow 'posthole' on the northern ditch line. The fill of this feature lacked evidence for burnt material, but did yield Iron Age pottery and a jet fragment (see section 5.2 on jet production discarded in Late Iron Age ditch systems).

These two structures, apparently unenclosed, have no evidence for manufacturing processes, something which reinforces the notion that metal-working elsewhere only

took place in closely constrained spaces (spreads of burnt materials and dispersed pits containing such evidence elsewhere on the site may represent such activities but could not be linked stratigraphically or spatially to any structures, or indeed be dated by associated artefacts: G162 and G163). R10 and R11 may therefore be examples of circular structures related to agricultural practices. This is given slightly more credence by a curving feature 15m north-west of R11, a possible windbreak. It is paralleled by other features elsewhere in this western landscape (G161), whilst a Y-shaped configuration of ditches west of Well 2 could have a similar function, but is completely undated (G164).

In summary, this western part of the site sees a major, large roundhouse (R1) set up in its first enclosure towards the end of the Iron Age – a building that then retained its significance despite various changes: to its specific orientation, the original eastern access augmented with a doorway to the west, then altered entirely to create a south-east entrance; to the activities within its associated enclosure, which become increasingly involved with metal-working of various sorts and perhaps jet production, including the use of a new small structure R2; and to the landscape as a whole, when its immediate enclosure was retained but, beyond this, further, more focused fields were set out to the west and north, linking to the use of Wells 2 and 3 (see section 3.2).

This final change to a more enclosed landscape seems also to have signalled an increased division of functions, with high status and other metal-working evident in one medium-sized roundhouse, R3, and perhaps other activities involving burning in successive small structures, R4 and R5. R9 defines another zone where concerted metal production was concentrated. To the south of R3–5, in an unenclosed space, associated medium-sized roundhouses R6 and R7 and the smaller R8 lay in a cluster facing outwards, R6 perhaps used for domestic activity, R7 and R8 more specialised. Finally, in open areas beyond, R10 and R11 were also set up near boundaries, perhaps related more to agriculture than any domestic or manufacturing functions. Over time, therefore, what may have been a single household with an agricultural emphasis developed multiple functions, some of which included artisanal activities alongside still dominant farming practices (see further in section 9.2).

In the central part of the site, prehistoric development was far more limited, apart from the utilisation of contact springs (see sections 2.1 and 2.3). The one exception concerned the creation of a square compound on the springline, 35m across with an entrance to the east (see section 3.2, fig 3.5). This contained two roundhouses, 12 and 13 (both G205). *Roundhouse 12*, located towards its centre, had a diameter of 7.7m, thus was towards the top of the medium range in size. A 3.6m-wide entrance was present to the south-east, an associated posthole suggesting a more sophisticated doorway than in most roundhouses on the site (fig 6.3). *Roundhouse 13* to its east survived less well, but may have had a diameter of *c* 7m, placing it in the medium category. Its northern entrance was 1.25m across.

Given the position of the two structures and the alignment of the R12 entrance, they seem unlikely to have been in use together. R12 is well preserved across its whole width, so the limited survival of R13 in the west could have resulted from the construction of R12, rather than due to modern truncation. The fills of both features were generally devoid of finds, although a few sherds of Iron Age date were recovered from one associated gully. The character of both buildings and nature of deposition suggest a more conventional domestic and agricultural function for this zone compared the sector to its west containing R1–R11.

It is unclear whether the area surrounding R12 and R13 and their compound had been developed at this point. Possible tree-holes in the vicinity could have been dug then, as two of them contained material dating to the

same period as the compound itself (G209). The same may be true of a small number of intercutting features to the west and a nearby group of pits and short linear cuts (G214 and G219, respectively). Elsewhere, initial (undated) activity involved possible tree positions and two oval features produced by other natural processes (G118).

One of R12's gullies yielded charcoal that included oak, ash, beech, field maple, hazel, alder, wild/bird cherry, blackthorn, Pomoideae and poplar/willow. This shows a variety of environments being used for the collection of fuel, including open woodland, woodland clearings and margins, as well as scrub and areas of damp soils. It also encompassed a range of woodland stages: mature and immature trees, and dead or rotting timber. There is no certainty on how far occupants ranged to gather this material, but this breadth of wood types and species matches the evidence for nearby pit digging and tree-holes. Thus, this compound may have been set in a less intensively cultivated, more wooded environment, which lacked the major landscape divisions in what seems to have been a cleared landscape to the west.

Finally, concerning its date, it is unclear when in the Iron Age this compound and its roundhouses emerged. A re-cut of the enclosure ditch, therefore, already late in

Fig 6.3 Roundhouse 12 after excavation. Excavators are positioned around its periphery, with the surrounding enclosure delineated in yellow (see fig 3.5 for location in plan). © OSA

the sequence of activity, contained a small sherd of samian ware dating to the late second century AD. This could be intrusive, as there is clearly Roman activity in the vicinity, albeit mostly of a third-century AD or later date. Yet, early samian pottery is generally uncommon on the site, which might suggest that the associated boundary continued to be refurbished through the second century AD. If so, and even given the length of time suggested if R13 were replaced by R12, then the whole sequence of occupation here may date to the very start of the first millennium AD, thus rather later than the initial stages of development further west.

The only other sign of Iron Age activity occurred in the east of the site, on the springline just north of Well 1. This comprised the construction of Roundhouses 14–16, the least well-preserved examples recognised in the excavations and set up in a seemingly enclosed space just north-west of that contact spring (see section 3.2, fig 3.6). The earliest activity here involved the insertion of a curving ditch representing *Roundhouse 14*, of which only the north-east element survived extensive later truncation (G68). Based on the character of its replacement (R15), this may have formed a building of perhaps 9m diameter, thus in the large category. No dating evidence was retrieved from this structure.

Roundhouse 15 lay almost directly above R14 and was evidenced by a curving ditch of 9m diameter, the large category, which survived later truncation only as discontinuous elements (G69). Elements along its line included several postholes, two of which were placed at a definite break in the circuit and may indicate the position of a narrow, *c* 1.5m wide, entrance leading to the south-east. A pit containing fire-cracked stones was set just outside this putative access point. This may be a hearth but, if so, would have been situated dangerously close to the building's superstructure. It may have had a counterpart just inside the wall line to the north-east, where another feature showing signs of heating was recorded.

Material directly associated with R15 included a single Iron Age handmade sherd and a flint bladelet, the former perhaps dating the start of occupation here. Later fills and dumps above R15 yielded ceramics with a very wide date range, including three modern sherds (which must be intrusive) and material from the Roman period. The latter comprised imported, samian table wares and a concentration of Dressel 20 oil amphorae. The samian is securely dated to the first to early second centuries AD and, although the amphorae have a much wider chronological range, they are mainly concentrated in early Roman contexts. Although modern ploughing impacted severely on this area, it does not seem to be

disturbing a general spread of early Roman activity. In short, dumping of that date seems to have been confined to a zone directly above R15, suggesting that this roundhouse continued in use into the first century AD and perhaps later still. Its former site then saw the discard, and perhaps nearby use, of pottery vessels imported from outside Britain.

Several discrete episodes were evident within the area enclosed by R14 and R15, none of which could be directly related to the use of one building rather than the other (G70). These included a pit and cobbled surface and some postholes concentrated near the entrance of R15, perhaps situated to maximise daylight (although the entrance position of forerunner R14 is unknown). Other pits, post-pads and a probable hearth lay deeper within both structures and must belong to one or the other. Whatever their exact phase of use, they imply that the area inside R14 and R15 was much more intensively occupied than that which survived in the roundhouses R1–11 and R12/13 further west. The only piece of dating evidence from these internal features belonged to the Iron Age.

A set of features to the south-west, although much disturbed by later activity, suggests the position of a third roundhouse, *Roundhouse 16* (G72). This had a 9m projected diameter, in the large category, and no surviving entrance. It included clear evidence for a hearth near its north-east wall line, paralleling the feature seen inside R14/15. Pottery from the ring ditch of R16 included a handmade, presumably Iron Age, sherd but still more material dating to the first and second centuries AD. This included a rare South Gaulish samian ware vessel with a likely Flavian date. Material from R16's hearth dated exclusively to the late first to second centuries AD.

R15 and R16 cannot be related stratigraphically, yet are so close together that it is impossible to believe that they were occupied at the same time, especially given the doorway position of R15. However, the dating evidence in each, described in some detail above, provides one possible sequence of construction. Early Roman material is evident in the latest ditch fills of R15 and, although the R16 ring ditch contains one Iron Age sherd, most of its material is of that date too, and that in its hearth exclusively so. Thus, the most convincing explanation of this sequence is that R15 was constructed above the site of R14 during the Iron Age and in the early Roman period the former's site was sealed over with dumps of material, some of which percolated into its upper ditch fills, in order to prepare for the setting up of R16 to its south. Hence R16, containing a high proportion of this Roman material, suggests that it was built after the end of the Iron Age.

If this sequence is accepted – of R14 being replaced directly by R15 in the course of the Late Iron Age and the latter then dismantled to allow the construction of R16 immediately to its south early in the Roman period – then the similarities between all three buildings become yet more striking. Subject to the vagaries of differential survival, they are argued to have had similar diameters: all lie within the upper size range, and only the 'primary', and long-lived, R1 in the west of the site is of equivalent dimensions. Further, the hearths set inside each occupy very similar positions. The implications are important: roundhouses were being replaced here into the early Roman period, at a time when they were able to receive ceramic supplies from beyond Britain (see section 7.2). Yet, the type of houses being built then differed little from their forerunners, not only in size but even in their organisation of internal space.

As noted previously, this zone was modified when a sunken building associated with manufacturing processes was inserted nearby (G76: see section 5.3). This clearly took place before the third century AD and perhaps at the same time as an oak structure was added above Well 1 (G199). This was also the point at which the well itself saw a short burst of nearby activity involving an increased preponderance of heated materials and charcoal-rich sand. Three possible interpretations can be made: R16 was in use for a very short time, and the sunken structure, oak platform and heating activity all occurred together after that; the roundhouse, oak building and heated material all came from occupation in the late first century AD and were followed by the sunken building; or all four components were in use together.

The dating evidence is not good enough to distinguish with certainty between these scenarios, but the dates of associated assemblages do *seem* to militate against the first and second. Further, the sunken working area was set up beside the roundhouse, but did not intrude into it; so, spatially, the two could have been used together. This final scenario would have significant implications: a sunken manufacturing area dated to the first century AD and perhaps covered by a tile roof, would have been in use with a roundhouse whose spatial organisation was retained from its (clearly Iron Age) forerunners. Further such occupation was locked into early Roman ceramic circulation systems tied to continental sources: Iron Age/Roman transitions were clearly complex at this point.

Whatever the precise sequence of activity here, meaningful human occupation appears to have ceased in this vicinity by the end of the second century AD at the latest. However, statistical analysis of pottery groups implies a gap in deposition across the site in the Hadrianic to early Antonine periods. Thus, it is possible that this burst of production took place over a few decades, at most, at the end of the first century AD. This interpretation would fit with the fact that the enhanced magnetic susceptibility readings dated to the first century AD, above adjacent Well 1, a distinctive signature, were not evident in its second-century horizon. It would also fit the notion that Roman activity at the centre of the site only picked up properly in the last quarter of the second century AD at the earliest.

Further truncated features suggest other activities in the immediate vicinity of roundhouses R14–16 (G71, G73, G74 and perhaps G215, G217). Some seem to control movement into that area, yet others comprise pits, associated surfaces and a hearth. Unless these elements are an accident of survival, it could thus be argued that the areas outside these roundhouses were as busy as their interiors. These included one gully that yielded a CBM brick fragment with worn surface. This, if not intrusive, would imply a surprisingly early use of such building material in the vicinity. Another feature from this area, in the small gap between R15 and R16, yielded the earliest stratified nail on the site. Although nails will certainly have been used here before that time, it signals that they were becoming common enough to be either discarded or lost and not then reclaimed. More generally, twenty-four nails were recovered from early Roman deposits, 188 from their late Roman counterparts, in line with the volume of soil derived from each period. All activities in the vicinity of R14–R16, whether of Late Iron Age or early Roman date, seem to have been contained by the ditched enclosure with Well 1 at its south-east corner. Although the limits of extensive investigation across this zone should not be forgotten, there is no evidence for the surrounding landscape being divided into any sort of field system at this time.

In summary, there is a marked difference between the character of Iron Age occupation in the west of the site compared to its centre and east. In the former zone, a major roundhouse was set up in its first known enclosure, with this area later given over to metal-working and perhaps jet production. When more focused landscape divisions were inserted here late in the Iron Age, further metal-working was evident in often small roundhouses set up in the most controlled zones. Medium-sized houses lay in more open spaces beyond this, some probably domestic and others related to agricultural processes. Further east, in contrast, roundhouses with seemingly domestic functions on a more conventional Iron Age model were inserted in two enclosed spaces set up along the springline, one group 700m away and a second group 200m beyond that (excavation limitations mean, however, that intervening, un-investigated areas could also have been structurally developed at this point). The first, R12 and R13, seem to have been surrounded by woodland. The suite of taxa derived from gullies associated with the second, R14–16, or from nearby intrusions are typically weeds of cultivation or generally fertile disturbed ecotypes. This is a signature also seen in late Roman contexts, when we can be sure of adjacent agricultural activity. Thus, these easternmost roundhouses may have lacked evidence of landscape divisions outside their enclosure, but they were not set in a densely wooded environment.

6.3 Circumstantial Roman evidence

As argued above, the roundhouses in the west of the site seem to have fallen out of use at the start of the Roman period, whereas the central and eastern developments may have continued in use until at least the end of the first century AD and, in one case, perhaps were only built at that point. Some of the latter structures may even have been occupied for up to 100 years after that.

In contrast, structural development from the third century AD was confined entirely to the central part of the site. This tendency is very clear from the distribution of artefactual evidence, for example the common nail. As noted previously, nails and worked wood stakes were evident in Iron Age levels and, by the end of that period, had become common enough to be either discarded regularly on the site or lost and not reclaimed. This process continued into later centuries when, even taking into account the greater excavated soil volumes, nails become still more profuse. Most are 40–70mm long, and many seem likely to have been used in some form of structure. These are almost entirely absent from the western and eastern parts of the landscape.

Less common materials may also evidence this trend. Thus, finds of lead sheets, caulking and runoff, all of which could have been derived from building work, came from Roman contexts or had been re-deposited from such into later levels. It might be that some of the buildings involved were glazed, given the recovery of two window glass fragments: although one comes from a presumed residual context (G113), the other could relate to a nearby structure (G30); see further below on both. A triangular knife blade (G103) and carpenter's chisel or smith's punch (G224) might also indicate construction activity (or manufacture: see section 5.1). It is interesting that these last two items, although broken, had been discarded rather than their raw material being recycled to create

new tools. This suggests a new level of availability for iron.

Lighting is not strongly evidenced on the site, either in ceramics or metalwork. Pottery lamps are uncommon anyway in Britain, except in early military or urban sites, contexts that hardly match that of Heslington. Some rectangular-sectioned iron rings and a twisted rectangular strap from G88, if the two are associated, could represent a lamp hanger. Neither is complete, however, and they could equally be used to hang cauldrons or meat. They were not found in a proven structural context (but see further below on G30).

The position of other types of circumstantial evidence for building, notably stonework, is clearly much more significant. A partly intact, perhaps water-worn, millstone grit block was found in topsoil directly above the line of Road 2, near its eastern exposed limit. It employed features suggesting ambitious craftsmanship and might imply that a substantial piece of architecture, such as a water channel, once flanked that thoroughfare.

Three sets of stonework re-used in later wells have still greater significance. One group of three crudely worked voussoirs, of different sizes but with a consistent front– back dimension, were recycled in the lining of Well 5 (see fig 2.7). They were derived from an arch with a span of about 1.75m, forming a round-headed doorway such as might be found in an aisled barn or other agricultural building, or even making up the ribs or arches of a vault.

A second group from the same well are much more elaborate, comprising evidence for three dressed blocks originally from a structure using *opus quadratum* construction (fig 6.4), a technique in which rectangular stones were laid in horizontal courses without the use of mortar; here, they would have been bound together by iron clamps set in lead. Recurrent dimensions suggest that these stones came from a single structure. The technique is rare in British contexts, being confined to mainly to military bridges in the north, certain classical temples (for example, that of Sulis Minerva at Bath[4]) and mausolea (for example, at Shorden Brae at Corbridge[5]). As they had been re-used in a well lining, none need have been used originally on the Heslington site itself. It would not be difficult to transport them from the fortress or colonia at York, for example (but see further discussion in section 8.5).

Thirdly, a coarse-grained sandstone finial was incorporated into the structure of Well 7 (fig 6.5). At least 0.40m in height (it could have been topped originally by a ball or knob), its base included an elongated seating and off-centre hollow for placing on the roof line. In this, it resembles late Roman types in south-west Britain (none were known previously from the 'military' north[6]). Its re-

Fig 6.4 One of the stone blocks with features indicative of the *opus quadratum* construction technique. © OSA

use here has symbolic importance (see section 8.6) but, originally, it must have topped an important structure. There is no guarantee, however, that such an elaborate building occupied this piece of landscape, especially given the way in which it has been deliberately re-used.

Finally, information on structural development can be derived from studying the whole assemblage of Roman CBM from Heslington and its general distribution across the site. This includes not only examples of the usual *tegulae* and *imbrices* used for roofing, but also a possible chimney, bricks (*bessales* and *pedales*) and flues. Some were found *in situ*, and are discussed accordingly below, other were re-deposited in fills of cut features or dumped. Only one type, in Roman fabric R11, came from a securely stratified context. Hence, this was probably manufactured for a Heslington building, although certainly not as bespoke production: the fabric is known from elsewhere, notably in York itself.

CBM of all sorts concentrated almost entirely in the central part of the site. This emphasises how the western zone, which had experienced the most intensive prehistoric occupation, had now become marginal. The same low density is evident to the east, where the little material that was recovered mostly represents the 'background noise' of agricultural dispersal (see the above discussion of the sunken manufacturing building associated with R14–16 for a possible exception).

Within the central area, particular patterning is evident, perhaps with structural implications. Thus Type 7 flues, an early Roman form with combing in Roman fabrics R9 and R10, were derived from widely dispersed contexts (G35 and G123) and might imply the existence of good-quality buildings just outside excavated areas at

0.25m

Fig 6.5 Roof finial inserted asymmetrically into the lining of Well 7. © DoA

that early date. In contrast, the mainly single examples of generally later flue Types 4, 5/6, 7 and 8 that turn up elsewhere are more likely to be linked to nearby specialist production. Without more extensive fieldwork, it is difficult to know what to make of these tantalising glimpses.

Some CBM patterning is more coherent and may indicate, albeit still circumstantially, the position of buildings. Thus, the dumps sealing the line of a major late Roman boundary ditch (G30/G22) yielded an abraded fragment of a possible chimney (whether this was integral to a roof ridge line, free-standing, or even employed as a ventilator or lamp cover is uncertain). Corresponding contexts also contained worn floor tiles and stone roof tiles (G31 and G30), limestone debris and, as noted previously, a fragment of window glass and a possible lamp hanger (all from G30). As this large ditch was gradually being backfilled, it seems that some significant structures were being dismantled in its vicinity. As not all of these finds were derived from its latest fills, this process may have been an extended one.

Ditch G30 is significant, as it forms the eastern boundary of a specially 'reserved' area defined by a corresponding ditch and associated tower G91/96 in the west (see section 3.4). Both boundaries were backfilled with a range of atypical materials whilst Road 2, which formed the northern boundary of this zone, had its demise in the east marked by the dumping of further CBM (G125). The sheer volume of material discarded here might imply that the associated structures were nearby, as could sooted floor tiles from an adjacent large pit (G126). Of course, all of this material could have been deposited to simply discard building materials from redundant buildings. Yet, as this happens over time in boundary ditches that are also in receipt of other atypical assemblages, it could be seen as more than simply functional, for example, an act of structured deposition (see section 8.5).

Other building materials probably found their way onto the site having already been recycled several times. Thus, the late-flourishing manufacturing area north of Road 2 (see section 5.4) yielded a range of CBM. Some was re-used in a kiln (G107) and as hearth bases in an adjacent working area (G110), the rest being derived from an associated spread (G109). As well as the usual types, this assemblage included stone floor tiles (an uncommon find on the site, perhaps implying their use here only for thresholds), an extra-large (1.5 Roman feet) Lydion brick and two unusual flue tiles. Another Type 4 flue with rectangular vents was derived from a distant late Roman waterhole (Well 5, midway between Wells 4 and 6 and on the same springline: see section 2.3), showing that these recycling mechanisms extended across the site, and no doubt varied between zones.

The distribution of much more common roofing materials included *tegulae* and *imbrices*. A higher

proportion of the former would be expected on any site, yet they occurred in almost identical proportions at Heslington. Stone roof tiles were also prominent here, some re-used as packing in later structural features such as postholes, but most demonstrably in use with an excavated building (G106, discussed in detail below). If the latter's ridge line was capped with *imbrices*, this would explain the unusual ratio. A more likely reason, however, is that *imbrices* were being brought onto the site preferentially for re-use in other roles, such as water channels: *tegulae* are produced solely for roofing and only occasionally recycled (for example in burials).[7]

Although, generally, the weight of stone or *tegulae* was sufficient to ensure the structural integrity of the associated roof, nail holes were found on just six *tegulae*. Four had been inserted when the tile was wet, and so planned in the course of production, and two after firing, thus possibly as a later decision. This proportion matches the national average, as does the hole size, typically 7mm.[8] The nail holes in stone tiles ranged from 6–13mm in size, but were generally towards the lower end of that spectrum, thus similar to the *tegulae*. All but one of the latter holes seem to have been chipped out of the tiles, rather than drilled. Where this could be recorded, only five out of twenty-seven had centrally placed holes, the rest being decidedly off-centre (fig 6.6), a variation

Fig 6.6 Complete stone roof tile with nail placed off-centre, from the roofing of building G106. © DoA

presumably related to different ways of fixing them to the underlying roof timbers.

Overall, therefore, there is a considerable range of Roman building material from Heslington, some prestigious in character. Much, however, was being recycled here from elsewhere, whether to facilitate manufacturing processes, line wells or be re-deployed in other structural contexts. Some of this material is dumped in sufficient concentrations to imply the existence of prestigious structures just beyond the excavated areas, whilst in the case of building G106, discussed next, it derived from its collapsed stone-tiled roof.

6.4 Late/post-Roman structures

Various structures of late Roman date were investigated on the site (one perhaps being even a little later – see G112, below). Of these, a masonry tower to the west (G16 and G17) and a related building with hypocaust flooring (G1), although major constructions, are clearly monumental rather than domestic and are therefore

discussed under ideological landscapes in section 8.5. The remainder comprise three buildings, two of late Roman date and one at the transition into post-Roman centuries.

The first of these fell only partially within the site margins, so is least well understood. It comprised the south-west corner of a weakly bonded cobble foundation protruding from the eastern baulk of a central area trench (G47). At least 2m across, it lay at a different angle from the underlying Roman ditch (G46), implying a new phase of landscape development here in the third century AD or later. As noted previously (see section 6.3), concentrated dumping of building materials on site margins implies adjacent structural development, and this may be one such example just within the excavated zone. To the west, two further major rectangular structures were investigated, but here exposed *in extenso*. One lay on the line of, but pre-dated, Road 2 (G106) and the second (G112) lay to its north, set against that thoroughfare (fig 6.7).

Building G106 comprised, on its north side, a masonry feature made up of loose, clay-packed cobbles. Differences along this wall line suggest successive phases

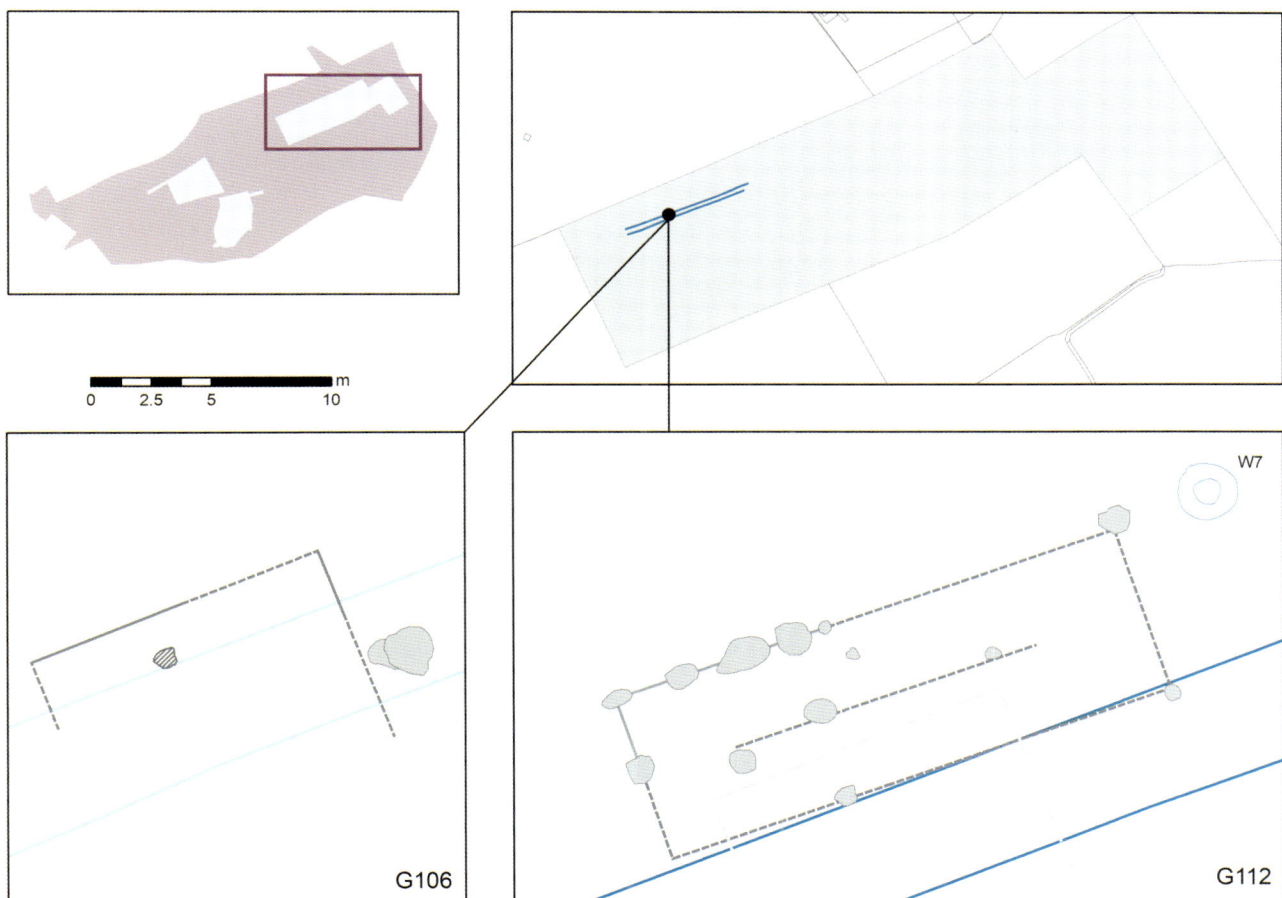

Fig 6.7 Plan of building G106 (left), its position later over-ridden by Road 2 (feint blue). Building G112 (right, with post positions delineated; see also fig 6.9) was set against Road 2 and perhaps linked to the use of Well 7 at its north-east corner. *Drawing*: Helen Goodchild

of development in this rough, insubstantial foundation. Its surviving surface level seems too consistent to be a simple product of later truncation, suggesting it represents a dwarf wall for a timber superstructure. The substantial post base found along its line gives further support for the notion of such a wooden framework. Further east, this northern boundary is defined by less substantial posts, perhaps implying a different form of superstructure here that terminated in the larger posthole defining its north-east corner.

The limits of this building on its other sides are less clear. Natural strata and earlier occupation layers seem to have been truncated to its west to allow for the building's insertion, but its southern limit is unknown, being cut away when hypocaust building G1 was terraced into the hillside (see section 8.5). What survives of G106 is sufficient to suggest a rectangular structure up to 13m long and at least 8m wide. Pebbly surfaces were laid around its eastern end and at its north-east corner, overlying the primary fills of a gully within the building and so seeming to be late additions. As both its extent and internal character are uncertain in the west, two interpretations of G106 can be offered: a building 9m long with a 4m 'lean-to' at its western end; or a 13m long structure with a major internal division at that intervening point: see further discussions of its roof, below (section 6.4).

Whatever its structural implications, the position of an internal division at this 4m point is important chronologically. Material derived from the construction phase of G106 yielded only ceramics belonging to the second half of the third century AD or earlier, yet this internal division co-aligns with the position of a ditch related to the fourth-century AD reorganisation of the hillside (G105: see section 3.5). So, the latter re-development respected a pre-existing building, and implying that this structure remained in use into the fourth century AD.

A hearth with a wattle and daub superstructure was in use with the adjacent gully where the latter changed from being regular and straight in the west to a meandering alignment. A fragment of an unusual glass flask dated to the second and third centuries AD was associated with the latest use of this channel, presumably curated for some centuries. Concerning the function of the structure, features on a quern stone fragment recovered from the building's west end were thought, when excavated, to imply its re-use as a potter's wheel. These are now better interpreted as related to feed-pipes facilitating the distribution of grain (see section 4.2). This suggests the structure's involvement with cereal processing (a co-joining, larger fragment of this same quern stone found in a later production area nearby (G110) implies that this building was encountered and disturbed or robbed subsequently).

At the west end of G106 lay a profusion of flat-lying stones and roofing stones capping its final occupation layers (fig 6.8). Stone tiles with a total weight of 112 kg were recovered, some partially articulated (90kg came

Fig 6.8 *In situ* roof collapse associated with building G106. © DoA

from a single horizon, representing 56 per cent of the total volume of roofing tiles from the site). These must represent roof collapse and, where surviving best, comprised elongated hexagonal tiles averaging 350mm long by 285mm wide and weighing *c* 3kg each (see fig 6.6). They were made of fine-grained, well-cemented, micaceous sandstone from a probable source in the Pennine Coal Measures Group to the west.[9] Seventy-four nail holes were recorded, so at least that number of tiles were present (only two had more than one nail hole). Their sheer weight suggests a substantial timber-framed superstructure above the masonry foundations to support the load. The third- or fourth-century AD date of this structure matches evidence from the core of York, where stone generally replaced tiled roofs from the middle of the second century AD[10] .

One stone tile from this collapse is notably different from the others, being both smaller and rectangular at the top, probably part of a hexagonal tile cut down to enable re-use following breakage. If this happened during manufacture, it would suggest that tiles were supplied roughly shaped, if fashioned at all, then finished on-site, a sensible strategy given the transport mechanisms and road surfaces at the time, which would have increased the chance of breaking completely finished items. Exceptionally, one pentagonal and one heptagonal stone tile, plus two fragments of Magnesian Limestone, were also recovered from this destruction horizon. Their implications are unclear, but, given the structure's long life, it would not be surprising for roof repairs to be needed over time, nor that these employed differently

shaped tiles and diverse geological sources.

It is difficult to determine how much of this building was roofed. A minimalist interpretation would be for a central part to be roofed along an east–west ridge line, with a lean-to to the west and an open-sided area to its east (for the latter to be open, but fenced off: some sort of distinction is implied by the different posthole types along its northern wall line). An alternative arrangement would see a north–south ridge line running the full width of the building spanning *c* 7.5m and an open area to its east. In the latter case, it is noticeable that the east–west channel within the building runs quite straight where it would then have been covered, but meanders/changes direction in what would have then become an external area.

An even greater weight of CBM (175kg) was recovered from the vicinity of this building, including examples of *bessales* and *pedales*. Many of these fragments were, however, recycled or comprised single examples such as flues. Some of the *imbrices* could have been used to cap the stone-tile roof (see section 6.3 on the high overall ratio of *imbrices* to *tegulae*), and other elements may have been used with the hearth and channel noted above. The remainder have no clear implications for the superstructure or functioning of the building. The wider interpretation of this building is set out below: see section 9.3.

The third structure, *Building G112*, was set up on top of the collapsed stone roof of building G106, but only after the latter's position had been sealed by a series of dumps and accumulations (G109), suggesting a

Fig 6.9 One of the post bases associated with building G112 in the course of excavation, showing cobblestone base and clay capping. © DoA

chronological gap between the two. The foundations of the new building comprised a series of intrusions up to 1.5m across packed with cobbles and clay (fig 6.9). Although wide, these cuts were only c 0.25m deep, thus constituting shallow scoops too insubstantial to have supported free-standing uprights. They must therefore represent large clay post-pads, the base for a rectangular, timber-framed building measuring perhaps 22m east–west by 7.5m north–south.

The character and position of these pads are highly consistent on the building's north and west sides but raise two issues elsewhere. The two pads that, on grounds of symmetry, should have lain towards its south-west corner were not identified in excavation, despite careful investigation. One would have been situated amongst the underlying manufacturing complex of hearths and channels (see section 5.4), and thus may not have been recognised for what it was. The other, which should have formed its south-west corner, lay in a zone of truncated natural strata. The later intrusive activity was thought to relate to the construction of earlier building G106, but parts of it might have happened later. That said, the pads may have been set in shallow scoops, but are quite distinctive and are thus unlikely to have been missed in excavation. If they are truly absent, this south-west corner could have been the position of a doorway allowing access into G112 from the immediately adjacent Road 2.

A second question concerns how much of G112 was roofed. The concentration of symmetrical post-pads towards its west end implies that this was a covered area, perhaps a 7.5m long east–west ridge supported by a line of central pads, hence with a span of 7.5m. For the eastern two-thirds, in contrast, there are hints of centrally placed pads but no consistent alignment, as would be needed if the same roofing arrangement was carried the full length. Either this part was either roofed in a different, less substantial, way or merely fenced off and uncovered. G112 follows the line of the natural hillside here and seems to have been built to respect the position of Well 7 to its north-east and set directly up against Road 2 to its south. G112 represents the final building development of this area, and indeed on the site as a whole.

The zone to the north of G112 saw the insertion of a possible cesspit (G12: this suggested function was not tested in later analysis) plus spreads of various materials and several oval-shaped scoops (G13). The latter intrusions might form the northern end of an ephemeral, rectangular building or, more likely, are just random features. Either way, they constitute the latest activity here and were perhaps in use when building G112 was occupied.

The suite of taxa that relate generally to this structure do not differ noticeably from the 'background noise' of the late Roman period, comprising weeds of cultivation and generally fertile, disturbed ecotypes. In contrast, however, artefactual and ecofactual assemblages directly linked to this building diverge markedly from the norm. Thus, relevant deposits lack any evidence for the utilisation of stone or CBM, except in packing or lining other features (a fragment of window glass from an overlying accumulation, G113, is assumed to be residual, its original context being entirely unclear). In addition, the ceramics associated with the building have unusually high proportions of beakers and dishes and low proportions of jars and bowls. To this can be added unusual Gauloise wine amphora sherds (also a fragment of Dressel 20 amphora, though this may be re-deposited), and the rare find of a ceramic tankard. Taken together, this could be seen as emphasising the discard of materials linked to feasting. By the same token, the proposed cess pit to its north yielded two important finds: a copper alloy spoon of fourth-century AD date (fig 7.1); and a fragment of a much earlier, unusual, glass jug perhaps only discarded here after lengthy circulation (see section 7.1). These artefacts reinforce the atypical nature of this this building.

A similar situation pertains to animal bone from here. The site's general faunal assemblage was highly fragmented, suggesting trampling and weathering. In contrast, material connected with building G112 was noticeably less eroded, maybe due to being covered soon after deposition, and less fragmented, perhaps because less disturbed (but it does come towards the top of the stratigraphic sequence, when such disturbance by human agents may have been minimal. In addition, these bones were more often butchered, implying different consumption practices, and less gnawed, suggesting different disposal practices. In various ways, therefore, this building marks itself out from other late Roman activities in this landscape. Understanding its date of construction and use is pivotal but complex, and is therefore considered in some detail below.

The building cut strata that date securely to the last quarter of the fourth century AD. A number of finds, seemingly of Anglo-Saxon date, were derived from this part of the site (their wider implications are discussed in sections 7.1 and 9.4). In particular, four items identified as pin beaters were recovered from hereabouts. Only one was complete, a cigar-shaped item used during weaving.[11] This is extremely rare within Romano-British contexts, but a regular find on early- to mid-Anglo-Saxon sites. A broken terminal in antler of what might be the same type of find was recovered from a lower fill of post pad 1113, one of the structural components of the G112 building.

Four explanations of this find are possible: as it only survives as a fragment, it may have been misidentified; the identification may be correct, but it could constitute one of the rare examples of this type of pin beater being used for weaving in the late Roman period; the find could be intrusive (but it was not in the uppermost fill of the feature concerned); or, it is correctly identified and dates to the early- to mid-Anglo-Saxon period. This last scenario would suggest that building G112 is of post-Roman date (and with it a later accumulation, G113, and overlying final hearth and stokehole, G114: see section 5.4). See further discussion of the end of the Roman sequence in section 7.1.

Whether this building was constructed and used at the end of the fourth century AD or some generations later, it shows a fundamental shift in the nature of activity at this time. The general character of the landscape here may not have changed, but only organic building materials were now being used. Further, feasting was being emphasised, and was still able to utilise long-distance imports from the Empire. Finally, faunal processing and discard practices had changed, and the only possible cesspit known from the site was now in use to its north. The wider implications of these trends for transitions between the Roman and post-Roman periods are taken up in section 9.4.

Consumption in the landscape – import, use and discard

7

This chapter draws in particular on evidence from site assemblages, mainly animal bones, ceramics and building materials but sometimes individual artefacts. The overall aim is to provide insights into how materials arrived in these landscapes, were then consumed, and finally discarded there. Their spatial and chronological patterning is first brought out at a general level (section 7.1), then details are discussed under a series of broad themes: exchange mechanisms at local, regional and long-distance scales of resolution, with implications for the shifting social status of the site (section 7.2); changing consumption patterns, notably in the course of the Roman period (section 7.3); and finally discard practices (section 7.4).

7.1 General patterns

The use of finds assemblages to characterise site activity is, of necessity, based on partial understandings due to a range of factors (see Chapter 1): horizontal stratigraphy rarely survived on the site, except where deposits were protected from later truncation by slumping into the top of large, gradually consolidating features such as wells or ditches (this is particularly important in any discussion of middens, whose position is largely a function of such fortuitous circumstances); certain materials, notably organics, did not survive in the ground; not all finds were gathered in excavation; and only some assemblages were subjected to detailed specialist analysis. It is therefore difficult to decide whether any spatial or chronological trends in this end-product are representative of what might have emerged if we could gather and analyse the full range of material culture for any one period. What we have seems unlikely to be representative of that whole, yet trends there are, and these are worth discussing in as much detail as the size and character of the different assemblages allow.

Information from well-dated finds has been incorporated into earlier discussions of site development, notably in Chapters 2 and 3, using information from flints and C14 dating for earlier periods, and ceramics and coins for the Iron Age and beyond. In summary, this suggests that, after some Mesolithic contact (5 per cent of flint tools), Heslington was visited regularly by humans from the Neolithic period onwards (58 per cent), with such visits becoming more focused on contact springs (see section 2.3) from the Bronze Age (38 per cent). Late in that period, contacts became more frequent and, in the course of the Iron Age, far more regulated (see section 3.2), culminating in sedentary occupation. The latter involved mostly agricultural production (see sections 4.1 and 4.2), but also more specialist manufacture (see section 5.2), alongside structural development (see section 6.2) from the end of the Iron Age. Occupation in the Roman period became still more intensive, before returning to agricultural activities in the medieval and modern eras. The recent building proposals that occasioned our own fieldwork will mean that extensive structural development will return to this landscape for the first time in 2,000 years (see section 9.5).

Much of this story can only be told in summary outline before the Iron Age, more substantial assemblages thereafter allowing a more detailed picture to be set out. Ceramics in particular show that there is a notable burst of activity at Heslington in the closing centuries of the first millennium BC, something continuing into the first century AD and considerably expanded thereafter. In contrast to the small numbers of Iron Age and Anglian ceramics from the site, Roman pottery allows us to chart this overall process with some statistical validity. Thus, just three per cent of secure groups of such ceramics date from the late first to early second centuries AD, here clearly overlapping with Late Iron Age handmade pottery. Nine per cent of this material dates to the late second to early third centuries and 23 per cent to the mid-third to early fourth centuries. It is the late fourth century, however, that generated the majority (60 per cent). If one considers the actual periods of time involved (the first three roughly seventy-five years each, the last perhaps only fifty years), these differences become still more striking, even accepting the different soil volumes involved.

Interestingly, finds of metal, shale, jet and bone do not correspond exactly with these trends. Whilst they do still demonstrate a similar paucity in the first and second centuries AD, followed by a third-century increase, finds of fourth-century date are less common than pottery profiles would lead one to expect. Objects of a later date are not absent, and some must date to the second half of the fourth century AD. The most obvious is a copper alloy spoon with traces of white coating that lacked the end of its handle and front of its bowl (discarded as no longer useful?), which may have been used by a left-handed person (fig 7.1). It is a type often found in late hoards such as Hoxne.[1] Some items may even date to beyond the fourth century: for example, a shale pendant and three iron penannular brooches (see further below). Yet, notable absences include personal ornaments such as copper alloy bracelets (only one late example was recovered, belonging to a tradition starting in the fourth century AD and continuing into the fifth) and small glass beads (of the seven beads recovered, the four from sieved samples all derive from early Roman contexts).

A similar lacuna is evident in the small group of datable vessel glass from the site (a surprisingly low number anyway, given the amount of excavation, and then rarely including diagnostic forms). The limited proportion of the bubbly light green glass typical of the fourth century AD contrasts with dominant blue/green vessels, indicating a focus in the first to third centuries AD. Importantly, three late vessels in colourless glass come from either an undated accumulation (G59, which also yielded a glass cup dating to the late third to early fourth century AD) or a provably late deposit (G113). One of the two glass vessels in a late context had been deliberately trimmed ('grozed'), implying recycling. In sum, the glass matches the stratigraphy but is simply being deposited in smaller numbers proportionately than the pottery, and is sometimes being recycled.

Metal-detected and unstratified material has a similar profile to the excavated material, containing little of exclusively fourth-century AD date. This implies that the contrast between pottery and the other finds is a real pattern, not an accident of recovery or deposit survival. At Heslington, finds made of glass, metal, shale, jet and bone seem to have been either supplied less regularly and/or curated for longer in the fourth century AD, implying a changed status for the site at this time. This could be because a large part of the excavated area was

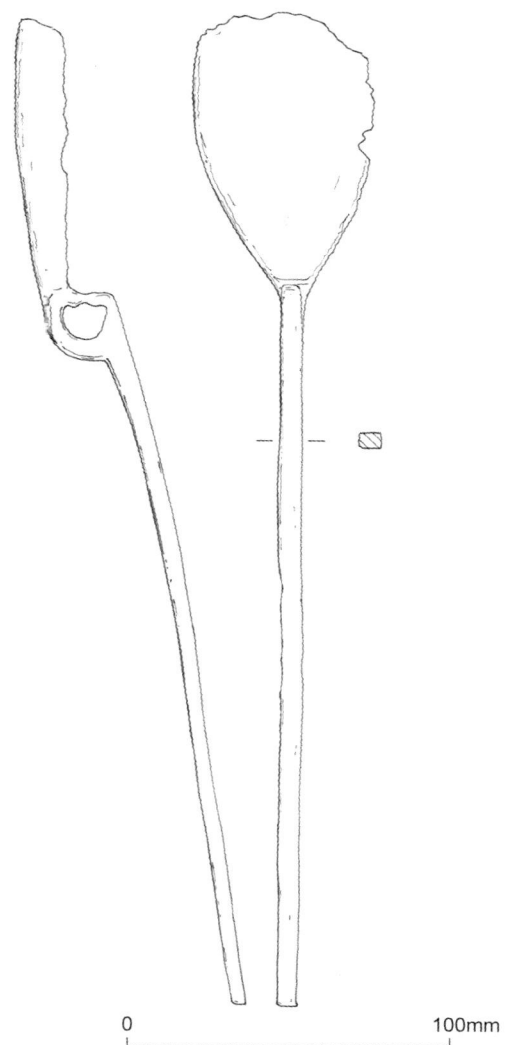

Fig 7.1 Copper alloy spoon of late Roman date among the copper alloy objects found. © DoA

now 'ritually enclosed' (see section 8.5) or because the most intensively occupied zone on its northern extremity was now increasingly given over to manufacturing processes (see section 5.4). Either factor could account for different depositional practices.

There is also a spatial dimension to these chronological changes. Thus, as noted previously, the earliest focused prehistoric activity at Heslington took place along the ridge of glacial moraine in the north of this landscape, then spread southwards to the springline over time. Next, the most intensive Iron Age development concentrated in the west of the site, with a smattering of occupation in the central and eastern areas adjacent to water sources. Iron Age and Roman finds assemblages, both 'small finds' and pottery, show how activity moved from this western focus to the central region (although not exclusively: a late Roman jet hair pin was derived from topsoil in this western zone). Again, ceramics are sufficiently abundant to allow meaningful quantification of this process: only 1 per cent came from the west, nearly all of Late Iron Age or early Roman date; 6 per cent from the east, with an early and mid-Roman emphasis; and the remainder from the central area, with a clear late Roman focus. The functional aspects of the ceramics mirror these trends, so it is date, rather than functional change, which underlies this spatial patterning.

A final issue to be tackled at this general level concerns whether activity continued into the post-Roman period. Here, the central area is of critical importance. Heslington differs from many sites in the Yorkshire region in that its ceramic supply seems to stop before the peak of calcite-gritted wares, thus implying a downturn in activity before the closing decades of the fourth century AD. This stands in contrast to Anglo-Saxon finds derived from the uppermost 'Roman' contexts on the northern margins of the site. Some of the latter could be funerary, suggesting a change of function here, but none *has* to be cemetery-related. Furthermore, others are more convincingly linked to domestic habitation. To reach meaningful conclusions, specific finds from around this transition have to be considered in detail.

Three plain penannular brooches with folded terminals, Fowler's Type D, derive from late site contexts and suggest a growing preference for iron over copper equivalents at this time, thus matching evidence from the latest, possibly post-Roman, levels at Wroxeter[2] and Lankhills cemetery at Winchester, dated to the late fourth or early fifth century AD.[3] Other finds from Heslington include a lead alloy dress pin of probable post-Roman date and a copper alloy wrist or sleeve clasp of the late fifth to seventh century AD (fig 7.2) – two other clasps of similar date were found from topsoil during metal detecting. Broadly contemporary bone finds include a pig's fibula pin, of a mid- to late-Anglo-Saxon form; pieces from two single-sided, composite combs (fig 7.3), which are most numerous in eighth to tenth century contexts;[4] a cigar-shaped pin beater (fig 7.4), most commonly found on early- to mid-Anglo-Saxon sites;[5]

Fig 7.2 Wrist clasp of Anglian date. © DoA

Fig 7.3 Single-sided comb of probable Anglian date. © DoA

and three broken pin beater terminals similar to this, two in antler and one in bone.

One of these items derives from the top of a late re-cut ditch just south of Road 2, and all others from either amorphous spreads or the uppermost fills of late Roman ditches in the central site near the northern limit of excavation (or, in one case, from a medieval furrow that disturbed such levels). None could be said to be well stratified (indeed, modern intrusive material was found in some of these contexts), but their distribution must be significant: they imply activity in this zone in the fifth to seventh centuries AD (and, with the bone pin and two single-sided combs, arguably beyond that: see also the

discussion in section 6.4 of the date of building G112, also situated here, for one of the broken antler pin beater terminals) (fig 7.5).

This spatial correlation becomes even clearer when the distribution of coins dating to the last quarter of the fourth century AD is compared to that of the above artefacts and of pottery thought to be of broadly 'Anglian' date.

There seems, then, to be a contradiction between the general Roman ceramic profile and possible post-Roman activity. The former pottery signature suggests a fall-off in activity before the very end of the fourth century AD, on the basis of the limited proportions of calcite-gritted wares in the overall assemblage. Yet, post-Roman finds in

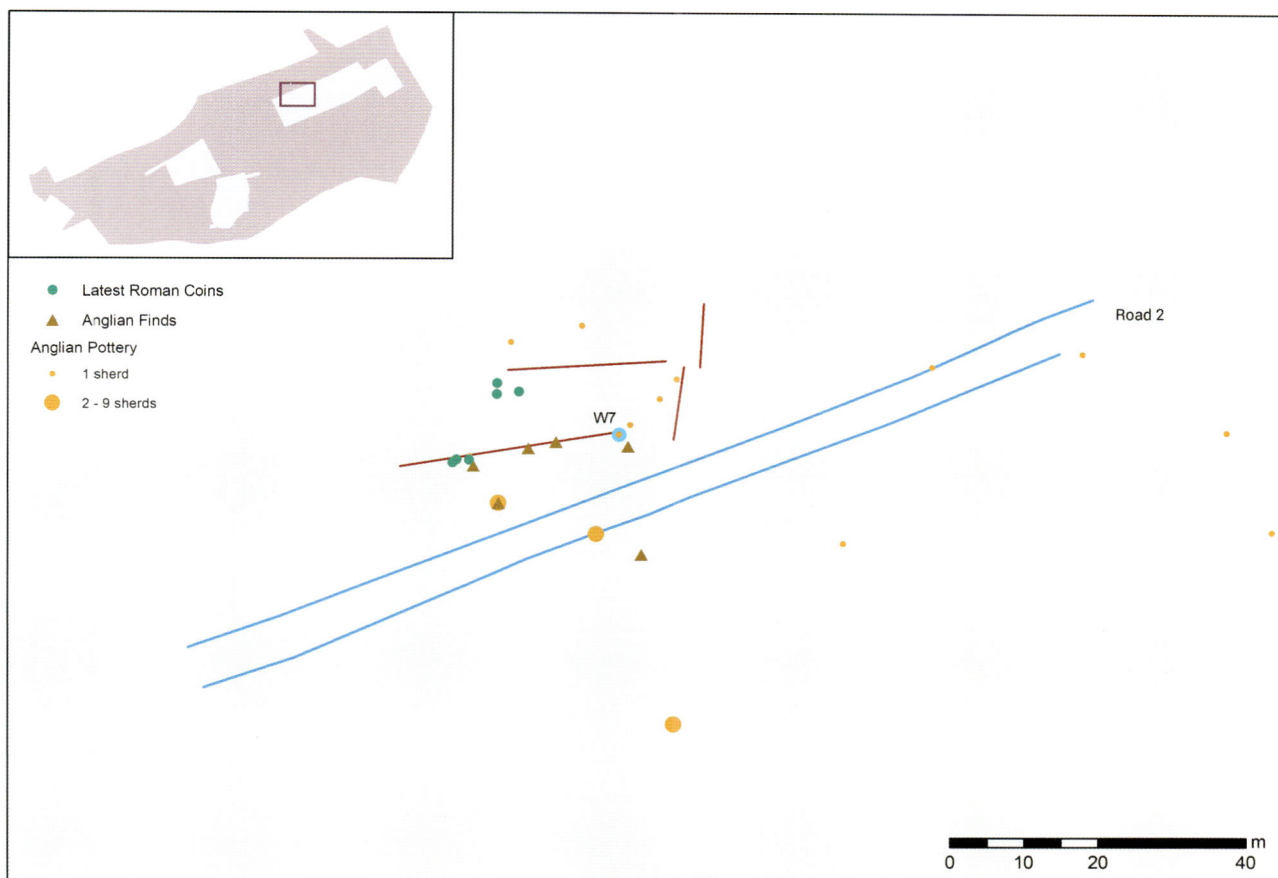

Fig 7.5 Distribution of features generating late fourth century coins, probable Anglian finds and proposed Anglian ceramics. *Drawing*: Helen Goodchild

one part of the site correlate with the distribution of the latest coins and with a sequence of late manufacturing activity (see section 5.4). This is also the area with evidence for late structural development in the form of building G112.

If one considers the proportion of calcite-gritted to Crambeck wares on a more focused, group-by-group basis, however, those in the particular zone noted above do actually conform to very late profiles. In particular, the reasonably sized ceramic assemblage from G113, the latest accumulation in this area, provides convincing evidence for activity here up to the very end of the fourth century AD. It is worth noting that this horizon was cut by features evidencing further manufacturing in the vicinity (see section 5.4), implying that this particular zone bridges the gap between 'Roman' and 'post-Roman' periods. The converse is also true: such transitional activity is not evident on any scale elsewhere on the site, where occupation seems to have fallen away some decades previously: continuity in one sector took place in an increasingly fragmented landscape setting (see further discussion in section 9.4).

7.2 Local, regional and long-distance exchange mechanisms

Beyond these broad trends, it is possible to consider the different ways in which specific types of material culture arrived at Heslington. Given the general lack of surviving organic materials on the site, this has to be discussed in terms of stone use (stone tools, querns and building stone) and ceramics (both building materials and, at greater length, pottery vessels).

As Chapter 2 makes clear, it is the local resources of this landscape, in particular water, that have had the most fundamental influence on human activity here in all periods up to the very recent. Nonetheless, from the Neolithic period onwards, its occupants enjoyed a range of wider contacts. In every case, it is easier to say what was brought into this landscape than what was leaving in return (and, in any case, there is no guarantee of a two-way flow – specific factors could have made the site a net exporter or importer in any particular sphere).

Stone tools demonstrate access to flint from coastal glacial tills to the east, whether arriving as raw material or as roughed-out/finished items (see section 5.1). A broken stone axe found on the site, dated to c 2000 BC, was made of dolerite from a dyke or a sill, most likely Whin Sill in the northern Pennines, some 150km to the north (see

section 8.1 and fig 8.1). At a subsequent stage, Late Iron Age roundhouses were engaged in the processing of iron, some of which could have been derived locally, and the manufacture of jet objects, seemingly over an extended period of time (see section 6.2) suggesting an ability to access these raw materials on a regular basis. Whilst exact sources for the Heslington material cannot be identified with certainty, the largest jet exposures in the region are found around Whitby on the North Yorkshire coast, c 80km north of the site.

Quern stones to facilitate grain processing arrive here from at least the Bronze Age (see section 4.2). All were found in re-used contexts, but most are so large that they are unlikely to have moved far: the prehistoric material, at least, was probably brought in to be used here. This collection is significant for the limited examples of beehive querns and high proportion of saddle querns, the size of the latter type being broadly consistent with those found in Neolithic contexts.[6] Unless recycling was taking place here over an extended period of time, however, most querns from Heslington are likely to be of later date: the earliest example identified from the site is a saddle quern from a probable Bronze Age context.

This early example is, unfortunately, from an unknown geological source, and just one prehistoric stone can be linked to a place of production, and then only tentatively. This poor-quality Iron Age quern, of the less-common beehive type, is thought to have come from the southern margins of the North Yorks Moors, 50km north of York, that is, considerably further away than the alternative millstone grit sources to the west. In the Roman period, disc hand querns were employed here for the first time. Some were manufactured from crinoid grit, from similar sources on the Moors to the earlier types noted above, and others from Pennine millstone, perhaps 25km to the west of York. About half of these disc querns, however, were made from Niedermendig lava. Presumably the latter material was imported via official channels, as such querns are found in various other state-related contexts, most obviously in London.[7]

The pre-Roman and early Roman quern assemblage at Heslington resembles that of civil sites elsewhere in the region, as does the change to the use of millstones in the late Roman period. The latter may signal a move from hand-milling at a household level to larger-scale processing at a central control point, thus implying that a vital point in crop processing was now being controlled by a higher authority (see section 9.3). If so, the geological sources used in this more controlled, supra-household, system are interesting. One of the large millstones is unambiguously of millstone grit, yet at least two others are derived from Jurassic exposures from the

North York Moors. As noted above, both of these regions were being exploited in previous centuries to supply pre-Roman saddle and beehive querns and early Roman disc querns. Even given the small number of examples, it seems clear that an investment in this new mechanical technology did not involve accessing new geological sources, or even a narrowing of that supply base: the site's quern trading links were still inclined northwards as much as westwards, as they had been for some centuries. Imperial authority may have developed more directly exploitative mechanisms to control milling, but it did not, or perhaps could not, control the sources of raw material needed to fashion the stones in the first place (see section 9.3).

Another item brought to the site during its later phases was building stone (see section 2.2). It is difficult to quantify the relative importance of local and more distant sources. This is in part because of the sampling strategies deployed in excavation and in part because of the diverse local drift geology of a region immediately in front of a glacial moraine which had made stone from distant geological sources accumulate briefly. Furthermore, the stone used directly in buildings was itself a very small proportion of the stone encountered in the work as a whole: for the former, see detailed discussion of Well 7 (section 2.3), kiln G107 (section 5.4), Building G106 (section 6.4) and tower G16/17 plus building G1 (both in section 8.5). At the latter, general level, limestone and sandstone from unknown sources predominate. Although a greater amount of such stone was re-used or re-deposited in late Roman features than in early equivalents, this is simply a product of the chronological focus of the site as a whole.

Alongside quarried stone, a few Roman structures incorporated purpose-built CBM into their fabric, although the vast majority of CBM recovered came from recycled contexts (see section 6.3). The general CBM fabric profile at Heslington matches that from York, probably because the main settlement either produced this material itself and/or articulated its supply, or was the place from which it was brought for re-use (although see below on signatures for a proviso to this statement). It is thus no surprise to see military influences in the stamped tile and tally mark evidence, although it seems unlikely that the army was concerned directly with supplying the site (see section 9.3 for military involvement more generally).

The evidence of CBM fabrics supports these general conclusions: those types not encountered at Heslington are anyway rare in the city, and the low levels of certain fabrics (R2, R3, R5, R9 and R10) and high proportions of others (R6 and R11) are, no doubt, a reflection of Heslington's late Roman chronological emphasis. Most of

the site's CBM assemblage, where real dimensions were measurable, is towards the smaller end of the size range, something also a product of its main period of occupation, the third and fourth centuries AD.

Also embedded in this material is evidence for its original manufacture. Seven fragments had signature marks, three of which add to Betts' typology.[8] Given that his research recognised forty-one marks in York, the proportion here of new (three) to known (four) types seems noteworthy. Either such signatures are very diverse and individual or, if different production centres used particular marks, some were involved with dedicated supply to rural sites such as Heslington and did arrive in York itself.

Knife trimming was evident on several tiles and smoothing lines parallel to the flange were present on one *tegula*. A second example had parallel lines on both edges, showing it was smoothed in two directions during manufacture. Single finger smoothing was most common, two fingers and the thumb being used only once each, implying considerable consistency in hand use. Twenty *tegulae* had lower cutaways of a type most commonly found in York and a single example had a thumb print on its surface. Upper cutaways were present on nineteen *tegulae*, in one case running the full thickness of the tile, possibly a manufacturing error. This does not seem to have stopped this item being used, or perhaps re-used, on the site.

Other fragments had batch marks (IX or XI depending on which way up it is meant to be read) and one a tally mark (XX). The latter is an unusual occurrence and perhaps associated with military production. Its site context did not mark itself out in any way, so it was probably recycled here for non-structural use. The assemblage also included fifteen examples of 'seconds'. Although it constitutes only a small proportion of the whole, less well-fired material was still being employed, despite most of the site's CBM being of a consistent standard. Flange profile and breadth did not correlate with fabric, implying random variation unrelated to any control of production

Finally, three bricks showed evidence for rain marks during manufacture, one for hail (fig 7.6). Others exhibited human or animal footprints (fig 7.7): one each of a sheep (or, less likely, a deer), a cat and a hobnail, and several of dogs (three) and chickens (two). These were caused by people or animals walking over the bricks whilst they were drying on the ground prior to firing and all are well attested in other assemblages.[9] Dogs could, of course, be guarding brick-making premises and cats kept to deal with vermin, whilst evidence for humans with hobnailed footwear (and finger prints) are unsurprising.

Fig 7.6 Tile with evidence for hailstones. © DoA

Fig 7.7 Tile with animal footprint. © DoA

The chicken and probable sheep remind us, however, that even such a specialist form of Roman manufacture was executed alongside the pastoral economy.

A second, much more substantial, type of ceramic evidence comprised various types of pottery vessel. These were introduced onto the site on a far more extensive basis than CBM, and for a considerable range of practices beyond structural development. They thus provide a much more detailed, and well-rounded, picture of changing trading relationships.

There was no proven Bronze Age or earlier pottery from the site, save that used in Bronze Age burials (see section 8.1) and just one sherd dated 900–600 BC from G138 (see section 3.1). None of the Iron Age material exhibited the angularity, decorative techniques or softer fabrics of pre-fourth century BC types. Hence, the vast majority of the site's prehistoric pottery arrived in the Late Iron Age, much seemingly on the cusp of the Iron Age and Romano-British periods (for the nature of this interface, see section 9.2). Within this assemblage, noteworthy are ten examples of small bead-rim and wedge-rim globular jars, conventionally dated to 100 BC–AD 100,[10] as are several jars with an S-bend profile, similar to examples found further east and conventionally dated there to the first century AD. Their implications for the social status of the site are unclear, although, as already noted (see section 6.2), the closing decades of the Iron Age saw the proliferating households in the west of the site develop from near complete dependence on the agricultural economy to some production of non-ferrous metals and jet (see section 5.2).

More striking is a remarkable group of highly burnished Late Iron Age vessels. These show considerable technical skills and appear to reflect improvements in kiln technology and potting techniques taking place in southern Britain at the end of the Iron Age. When found to the south within Yorkshire, they are assumed to be the result of cross-Humber contacts. The Heslington vessels are rather different in that their form may derive from local traditions but the skilful potting and burnishing techniques are foreign. It would seem that not just physical items but also ideas about ceramic production were crossing the Humber in the course of the first century AD, and that Heslington was a beneficiary of this interaction.

In the interface between Iron Age and Roman periods, some more prestigious items were also arriving on the site. These included two highly polished ornamental jet items, derived from the latest fills of a pit linked to metal-working in the vicinity of Well 2 (G158). These are probably earrings, an identification strengthened by their being found as a pair despite their slightly different cross-sections. A fragment of a shale earring was derived from another nearby pit of similar date (G158). Jet was used to make many other elements of female jewellery within Roman Britain and beyond (a distinctive medieval cross shows that jet was also available in later centuries: see further at the start of Chapter 8). Yet, shale and jet earrings are, surprisingly, absent from Roman period assemblages.[11] If this was a typically Iron Age jewellery item, its deposition in a context marking the transition between these periods could imply a symbolic act of closure, both of the two pits themselves and of general Iron Age activity in this zone (see section 8.3).

Two fragments of early Roman glass bangles were derived from the site. One, an unusual type, came from cleaning above a late Roman horizon at its centre and may have been retained in circulation as being interesting in its own right: only 10 per cent survived, and it had been made more striking visually by the addition of two deep blue trails covering the surface of its blue/green core. The second was found in the upper fills of a long-used Iron Age ditch in the west of the site (G166), that is, in a transitional context between Iron Age and the Roman Period. It was much more complete than the first, with about one-third of the circumference surviving. Although rare in terms of Heslington, this is a common Yorkshire type.[12] Hence, both jet earrings, archetypically Iron Age, and a glass bangle, archetypically early Roman, were being deposited at a point when activity was starting to decline in the west. Both may signal structured deposition, the one ending a tradition and the other ushering in its replacement.

Ceramics provide another way into exploring this Iron Age/Roman interface. In the first century AD most of Heslington's pottery took the form of handmade storage or cooking vessels in the local, pre-Roman traditions noted above. However, this element was soon overlain by a very different component. This comprised, in part, materials imported from beyond the province, such as samian tableware (at its highest supply point in these early levels), and Dressel 2–4 oil amphorae, both probably supplied via York. Yet, it also included other forms, such as 'military' rusticated Ebor Ware jars manufactured in York.

This profile, of local handmade vessels plus limited prestigious imports, might suggest that selected table wares were being used to tie the inhabitants of this landscape into a Roman power base: samian levels at Heslington are comparable to those of the fortress. The presence of particular rusticated Ebor Ware jars at Heslington is also noteworthy. Ebor wares in contemporary contexts in both fortress and early extra-mural settlement at York contain much higher proportions of oxidised wares. Thus, the Heslington material, none of which was scorched or sooted, appears to comprise a selected subset. Interestingly, the Hensall site,[13] although lacking samian imports, also received some rusticated Ebor Ware jars, again mostly reduced. This may be related to the Roman fort at Castleford, 20km to the west, acting as an intermediary. Two interpretations of this patterning can be suggested: either military establishments directly supplied specialised

foodstuffs in these vessels to adjacent communities shortly after conquest in an active promotion of nearby subsidiary settlement; or these particular jar types were the designated containers that authority used to articulate surplus extraction from those landscapes.

The evidence of ceramic lids may be significant here. These are common in Ebor Ware vessels in early second century AD levels, but disappear in the course of the next century. This trend is interesting for two reasons. First, the need for a lid itself signifies trade in foodstuffs, suggesting that, whichever way they flowed, food might have become less important over time. Second, lid concentration at Heslington is earlier than its third-century AD heyday in York. This pattern has been explained in York as the legionaries using casseroles on braziers in an 'African' cooking style.[14] The putative African vessels used to argue this case in York are, however, uncommon at Heslington. This may imply that the development has less to do with ethnic cooking practices among legionaries and more to do with mechanisms of food supply: perhaps it initially included York and adjacent landscapes, but later focused only on the fortress. Alternatively, the latter may have exploited only adjacent landscapes at first, but later derived influences from other places, too.

The Heslington landscape, bound to the York fortress initially in terms of ceramic vessels for serving food and latterly for its preparation, continued in similar vein thereafter. Thus, in the second century AD, the pre-Roman jar component still initially dominated, although these were gradually replaced by burnished equivalents from either York or, occasionally, Dorset. Other changes include lower proportions of samian, being replaced by Ebor tablewares, and the increased presence of amphorae, plus a wider range of prestigious tablewares either imported from Argonne and Cologne or from various parts of Britain. There is also evidence for the first mortaria which then continued to be supplied through to the end of the third century AD. In essence, gaps in the earlier supply system were now being plugged, intra-provincial sources filling the space between York-produced wares feeding in at the very local end of the spectrum and their continental counterparts.

Heslington may have been bound to York, but was still, it seems, a poor relation. A good illustration of this concerns thirty-four co-joining sherds from a pulley-mouthed, Ebor Ware flagon of late second/mid-third century AD date excavated from a considerably later context in Well 5. This vessel was reduced but had clear drip marks on the inside and traces of white slip on the outside, suggesting that the intention was for it to be fired in an oxidising atmosphere. Further, the rim was distorted and there were bubbles within the vessel walls. Sherds from another Ebor Ware vessel in this feature comprised a roughcast beaker that was rather reduced and overfired: clearly, Ebor Ware wasters were being supplied to the site. The profusion of sherds from a single flagon found in the same well suggests that this vessel was deposited there soon after breakage, but quite some time after original manufacture: this 'second' had remained in use for a considerable length of time.

In the third century AD, intra-provincial sources continued to expand, notably from suppliers in the Nene Valley and Mancetter-Hartshill. From within Yorkshire, calcite-gritted jars, developing out of local handmade traditions, became increasingly important at first, themselves later replaced by East Yorkshire grey wares from Norton and Holme-on-Spalding-Moor with a range of functions, a process seen on many other sites in the region at this time:[15] ceramics for cooking and storage were now mostly supplied from Yorkshire, but the site's tentacles could spread beyond this region to acquire particular table wares and food preparation vessels.

York's own networks were probably used to supply the more specialised vessels, as evidenced by the overall profile of material such as Nene Valley beakers, which reach a peak at the same time in York itself as in Heslington. At the latter, however, these vessel types often turn up in later levels than their date of manufacture would suggest. Given that site formation processes, especially disturbance and re-deposition, seem unlikely to vary between vessel types, this pattern suggests that these beakers were curated for longer here than their York counterparts: demand existed at both sites, but supply systems for non-Yorkshire products may have been more precarious on the immediate margins of York than in the centre of power itself, hence the need to use them for a longer period of time. A similar trend in continued circulation was evident with Gallic wine amphorae, but this seems more likely to relate to secondary uses of these large vessels – for example, by their being re-deployed as containers or in structural contexts such as packing postholes or lining gullies.

A series of five lead alloy fragments implying pottery repair were also excavated. One fragment is unstratified and the others are mixed by date and context. One is associated with the late Well 7, but the other three all derive from one zone, a cobbled working zone south of the prestigious building G1. Given the general paucity of finds from this area, their position seems to be significant and it appears that pottery was being repaired in the vicinity in the third or fourth centuries AD (see section 8.5).

At the same time, York's pivotal role in influencing

ceramic supply at Heslington seems to have been reducing over time. Not only do Ebor wares, samian and amphorae drop away and supplies from within Britain take their place in the course of the second century AD, but there is a much greater orientation on the increasingly powerful systems of East Yorkshire for supplying cooking and storage vessels in the third. In York at this time, Monaghan notes, on the basis of types of Ebor Ware, an emerging dichotomy between military ('African') groups at its core and civilian zones, implying tensions within that settlement.[16] Unsurprisingly, Heslington more clearly resembles the latter, suggesting that civilian areas are now more clearly linked to the nearby landscape than they are to the immediately adjacent fortress.

The fourth century AD is marked by the arrival of Crambeck wares, only to themselves decline as calcite-gritted wares increase towards AD 400. These in turn succumb, in the closing decades of that century, to handmade Huntcliff types and to vessels in fabric B18 (place of production currently unknown). The latter appear in small, handmade burnished jars and are distributed as far as Wattle Syke in West Yorkshire by the end of the century.[17] These are all common trends across the region, the general disappearance of beakers, flagons, serving bowls and dishes thus creating an assemblage close to the Late Iron Age profile seen at the end of prehistoric occupation. Heslington differs only in that Crambeck types continue to arrive here through most of the fourth century AD, but the site's general ceramic supply seems to stop before the peak of calcite-gritted wares (see section 7.1).

7.3 Consumption practices

In what follows, consumption is first discussed in relation to evidence for the distribution of burnt materials (flint for early periods, then pottery and bone for later ones). We then explore food production more directly, briefly through bones and, at considerably greater length, by means of ceramic and other artefactual evidence.

As noted previously (see section 6.1), flint shows that activities such as hide scraping and, to a lesser extent, cutting and piercing took place on the site during the Neolithic period and into the Bronze Age. Macro-wear is apparent on 26 per cent of the flint assemblage, notably scrapers, and micro-wear on 7 per cent, being especially heavy on knives and scrapers. None of this evidence, or that of flint with glossy surfaces or of heavily utilised retouched flints, has any diagnostic spatial distribution (a single retouched flake resembling a polished axe re-deposited in Well 2 relates to the earlier use of that waterhole: see section 2.3).

Almost 10 per cent of the flint was burnt, and it does seem to have some distinct patterning, with three types of concentration. First, such flints are strongly represented in and around Well 2 in the west (and in the ditches running south from this) and, further east, either near Wells 1 and 4 or, more likely, generally along the springline just east of latter (fig 7.8). This testifies to the long-term importance of water access discussed in section 2.3. Furthermore, given that the majority (60 per cent) is of Neolithic date, domestic consumption must have taken place here at that time, even though excavated features relate mainly to later periods (flints of proven Mesolithic date are too few to allow meaningful interpretation of their spatial patterning).

Second, there are further concentrations of flint in and around roundhouses R3–5 south of Well 2 and in their more dispersed counterparts R8–10, plus around R12–14 just north of Well 1. This could suggest that Iron Age domestic activity involved continuing flint use. It is much more likely, however, that this patterning is a result of the greater volume of soil excavated at these points and/or hearths used here in the Iron Age accidentally

scorching long-discarded artefacts (although R10 lacks clear evidence of a hearth, all other buildings generated evidence for concentrated burning, whilst the absence of burnt flints in other roundhouses seems to confirm their being less involved with heating functions: see section 6.2).

Finally, north of the springline at the centre of the site, only unburnt flints are evident across large areas exposed by excavation, most of which turn up in Roman ditches, presumably re-deposited there in the course of digging those boundaries. Yet, two burnt examples derive from the area to the west of this, their significance seemingly increased by a lack of unburnt examples in the vicinity. One is directly associated with an un-urned, Bronze Age cremation (see section 8.1), which could account for its being charred. The other one cannot, however, be explained in this way. Neither is provably of Bronze Age date and numbers are obviously small, yet there is a possibility that this is a sector in which consumption practices were concentrated in the Bronze Age, in and around the burials discovered there (see section 8.1).

Burning as an indicator of later consumption practices, in particular the preparation and cooking of food, can be derived from analysis of ceramic assemblages. It is only in Roman groups, however, that

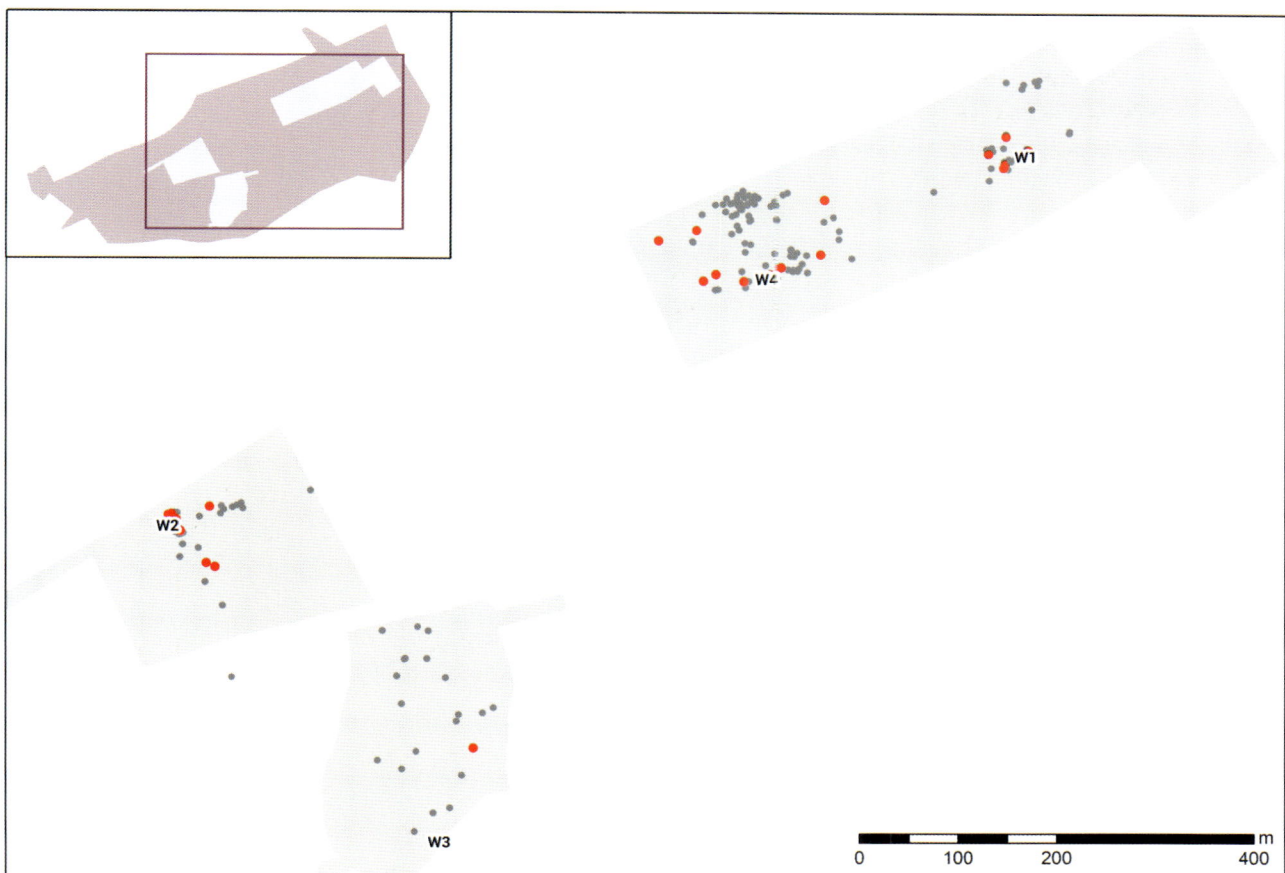

Fig 7.8 Distribution of flint artefacts across the whole site: burnt (red) and unburnt (grey). *Drawing*: Helen Goodchild

these occur in sufficient numbers to allow meaningful conclusions to be drawn. Scorching was most common on mortaria (perhaps surprisingly given their rarity and supply from often distant sources), then jars and finally bowls, these last two more so, as expected. Such burning was concentrated on body, rim, neck and flange. Two vessels had been exposed to so much heat that they had become distorted: they were clearly not wasters.

Burnt bone occurs at a very high level in prehistoric assemblages from the Bronze Age onwards, but especially in the latest Iron Age contexts, before declining. Although based on only a limited number of early samples, this suggests that food was cooked *in situ* up to the Roman period, then either prepared elsewhere or cooked in a way that did not generally char the animal bone concerned. Either of these trends would fit other evidence. The developed supply systems in Roman pottery noted above included, for example, possible provisions supplied in reduced, rusticated Ebor Ware jars. Equally, the proliferation of roundhouses within the Iron Age suggests domestic activity developed here with some intensity at that time (although the hearths in some buildings are probably linked to manufacturing processes, not food consumption: see section 6.4). There is no such clear evidence of domestic structures in the Roman period.

The changing proportions of animal species over time has been discussed in detail above (see section 4.1), showing sheep continuing their significance from prehistoric periods into early Roman horizons and giving way increasingly to cattle thereafter. It is argued that most of what was found at Heslington was consumed on-site, with no clear evidence for a market in meat at York affecting animal husbandry. Thus, there is no indication of beef or pork being made into joints for consumption elsewhere, although this might be hinted at in some sheep remains (or due to skin processing on-site). Finally, by the end of the Roman period, young animals were being consumed more regularly, which may indicate the circulation of more wealth and/or greater self-sufficiency.

Bones also show evidence for butchery, not just on the three expected main species, but also on horse, goat, goose and red deer, all of which were thus being dismembered for the removal of their meat. Most of the latter, however, came from the fills of Well 7 (which possible structured deposition may be atypical; see section 2.3). This includes the best evidence for horse butchery and the only evidence for skinning on cattle metacarpa. Cattle scapulae also from this feature show evidence for hanging to allow smoking (fig 7.9), although such a preservation method was also evident elsewhere, not only in another late Roman feature but also in an Iron Age context: the technique was employed over an

extended period of time. In contrast, a dump of bones that could have originated from the making of marrow or stock has no such specialised context and suggests that not only carcass reduction but also specialised processing took place somewhere on the site in the late Roman period (G31), evidence to be set at that time. The evidence can be set beside the previously mentioned indications of more 'industrial' activity at the very end of the Roman period.

Concerning artefactual evidence for consumption, the importance of accessing water at Heslington has been described in detail previously (see section 2.3), but the detailed mechanics of how it was obtained are generally lacking. One exception concerns the wooden bucket found in Well 7. Made with twelve staves of yew (*Taxus baccata* L.), set to create a tight fit and originally held in place by two iron hoops, it had a base of ash (*Fraxinus excelsior* L.). This timber had come from large trees (obtaining the ash is easily done, but finding yew trees of such a size may have been more problematic), then

Fig 7.9 Cattle scapula from Well 7, punctured to hang for smoking, with adjacent butchery marks. © DoA

carefully planed to make it watertight. The bucket's five-litre capacity makes it smaller than those from Dalton Parlours,[18] Skeldergate[19] and Rothwell Haigh,[20] and the use of yew is unusual.

The construction of this container suggests expert production with access to a specialised toolkit: a plane was used to smooth the stave edges; a small adze or round shave to prepare their inner faces; an axe to shape the outer stave faces, trim the base and hew the bevel around its edge; and, finally, a croze plane to cut the groove into the assembled staves to house that base. Although the Heslington bucket is largely intact, some pieces are absent (fig 7.10). The associated hoops survive only in fragmentary condition, but the handle is definitely missing. Given that the wear patterning evident on its staves is unlikely to be produced by an organic handle such as leather or rope, this was likely made of metal, and thus worth recycling. The mounts that fastened the handle to the bucket had not, however, been similarly re-used.

A virtually complete Huntcliff-type jar, a common type on the site, had been discarded with the bucket. This, uniquely among the ceramics, had external limescale, implying that such pottery vessels were also used to draw water (limescale was evident on the inside of twenty-nine vessels, mostly jars, suggesting that they were used to heat water). Interestingly, evidence for wear on jar bases is also mostly confined to this well feature. This suggests that, once filled, they were then used repeatedly in a particular way when holding that water.

Iron Age ceramic assemblages were dominated by jars, and this is also true of the Roman period overall (fig 7.11), where different jar types dwarfed tablewares (bowls predominated over other containers within the latter). Over time, however, this pattern varied considerably, with much greater diversity of vessel types in the first and second centuries AD, and a return to jar dominance by the fourth: a move between storage and consumption practices seen on many sites across the region. There are, however, many significant detailed changes within the overall trend. Thus, in the late first century AD, samian dishes and decorated bowls, with the occasional cup or beaker, were used to present and consume food, with handmade jars in pre-Roman traditions being employed to store or cook it (sooting is mostly evident on jars and confined to their upper parts: see above).

These imported table wares were augmented by amphorae during the second century, with Ebor Ware flagons and flasks then gradually replacing samian: Romanised dining now required the use of vessels made in York. Mortaria, arriving mainly from the second century AD onwards, suggest that new techniques of food preparation perhaps took a generation longer to change than how it was served (assuming, that is, that mortaria were indeed only used for grinding). Other approaches to Roman cooking are suggested by post-firing perforations evident on seven late vessels, which probably acted as colanders. Late, lid-seated Huntcliff-type jars also imply different food preparation or cooking.

Various forms of bowls and dishes for serving food continued to be prominent into later centuries, although always less important proportionately here than in York or other main towns. Most in the second century AD comprised Ebor Ware examples imitating samian forerunners, their place being taken in the next century by grey burnished ware flanged bowls, later enhanced in the fourth century AD by equivalents from Crambeck and the biconical bowls from East Yorkshire. The third-century AD examples derive inspiration, ultimately, from native traditions and their later biconical counterparts are not paralleled in York. If these vessels reflect a different way of eating, this might suggest that core 'Roman' practices increasingly incorporated local customs and, further, that this process was, in effect, bypassing York (see section 9.3 on changing town–hinterland relationships between York and Heslington). The wide-mouthed jars evident here in the third century AD have been claimed to suggest the serving of more liquid foods:[21] perhaps this was now being brought to the table as stews and soups from casseroles for collective dining, a fundamental shift away from arranging food on individualised flat vessels.

In contrast to bowls and dishes, specialist drinking vessels are generally rare in all periods. Deeper bowls, which become more common than flat dishes in the third century AD, could have been used for drinking, whilst lugged and narrow-mouthed jars, popular from that time, might also be interpreted as specialist liquid containers. The latter have no clear spatial link to wells, however, so do not seem to be connected directly to consuming water. Beakers and flagons reach a peak of 13 per cent of the assemblage by the early third century AD, in part due to the numbers of Nene Valley beakers now reaching the site (note possible curation: see section 7.2). It cannot be easily determined whether this implies a change in drinking habits, perhaps linked to the greater emphasis on Gallic wine amphorae at about this time, or simply a move from organic to ceramic containers.

Overall, therefore, we see a change from a ceramic emphasis on Late Iron Age jars to a diversity of Roman forms, but a return to jars by the end of the latter period. Yet, this overall Roman trend conceals a move from first-century AD types imported via York, to second-century

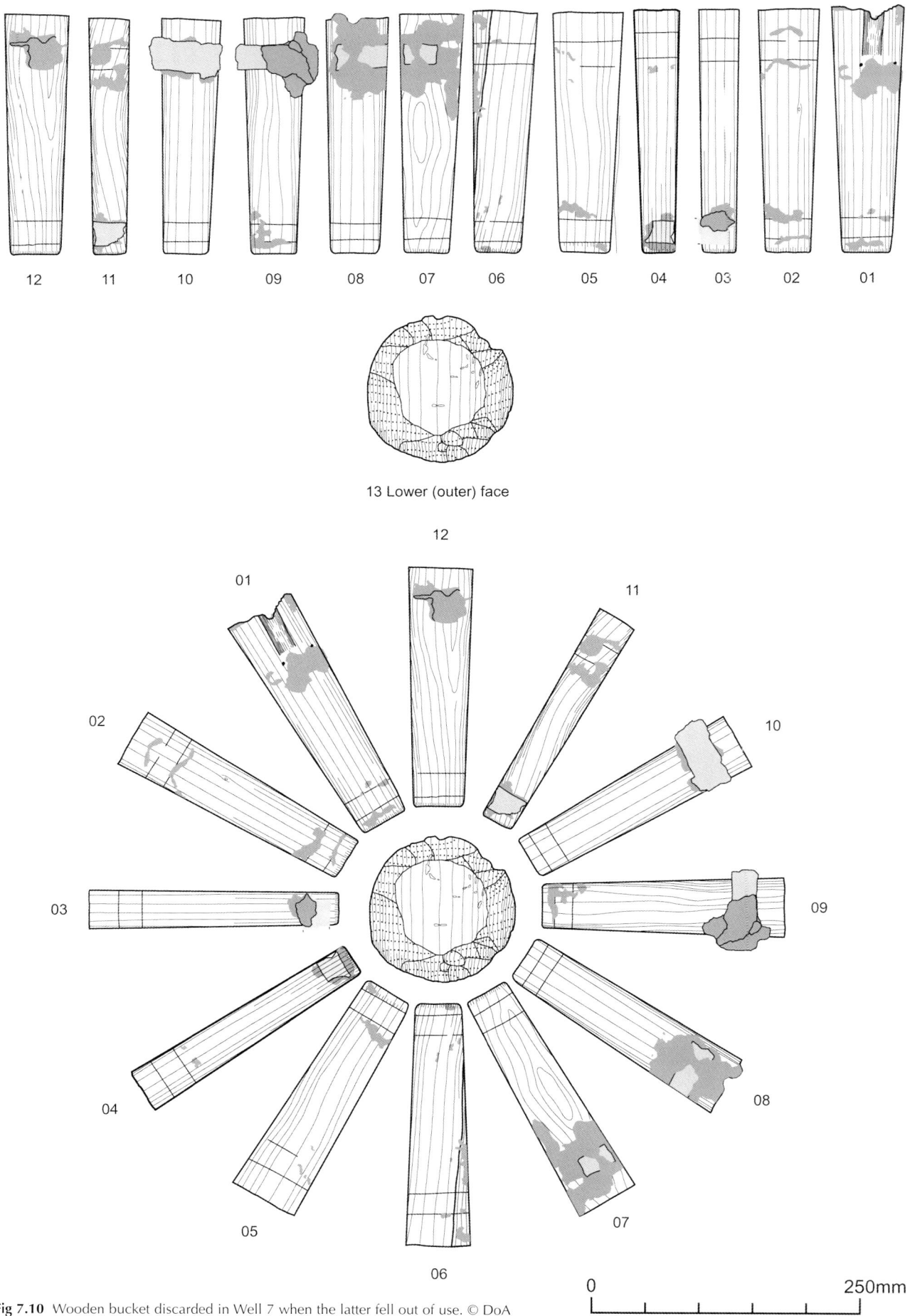

13 Lower (outer) face

Fig 7.10 Wooden bucket discarded in Well 7 when the latter fell out of use. © DoA

0   250mm

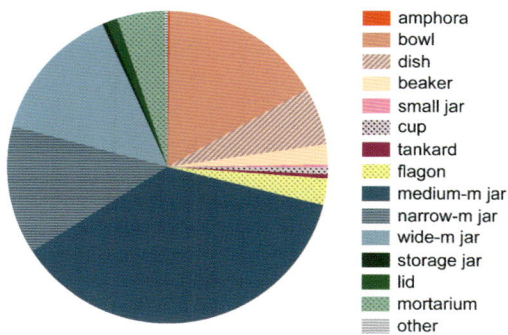

Fig 7.11 Overall quantification of Roman vessel types by EVES, showing high proportion of various jar types on the site compared to other storage vessels and table wares (wide-m jar = wide-mouthed jar; similarly, medium-m and narrow-m). *Drawing*: Neil Gevau

material produced in the city, to a regional orientation in the course of the third and fourth centuries. Thus, over time, the consumption practices of Heslington inhabitants drew inspiration increasingly from their locality, rather than from York itself (see section 9.3).

A rather different message on relationships with Roman authority derives from certain metal items from the site, notably brooches. These include three bow and two headstud brooches, all unlikely to be used much beyond the second century AD, and two bow brooches used during the later second into the third century (unlike early versions, seemingly worn by diverse sections of society, these were favoured by military communities after their civilian heyday). Finally, an uncommon enamelled plate brooch is of a type known mainly from military contexts in Britain and in its widespread continental distribution. In essence, therefore, these items suggest a distinct military emphasis.

To this can be added the evidence for two, perhaps adorned, baldric mounts. One, the possible edge of an openwork disc with internal scroll patterns, is similar to those used by soldiers in the late second and third centuries AD.[22] The second evidences a rivet type and decoration seen mostly in second-century AD military contexts. Equally, the copper alloy handle of an unstratified triangular-bladed iron razor, of third-century AD date, is most common in military contexts (although recent metal-detected finds might suggest a wider distribution and alter this pattern).

Despite weak stratigraphic contexts and sometimes imprecise dating, these finds suggest military influence on the site in the late second or third centuries. Such presence may, of course, be concerned with the process of landscape development, rather than military settlement *per se*. Allowing for a slightly longer-lived use of brooches by such personnel than their civilian counterparts, the

most obvious context would be the setting out of Road 1 and associated landscape divisions, something thought to have happened by c 250 AD (see section 3.3). Certainly, the next major change – the laying out of Road 2 and associated southern enclosure (see section 3.4), with its monumental western entrance and eastern gate (see section 8.5) – occurs c 300 AD, seemingly too late for the dating of some of these items.

In relation to other 'consumption' practices, a range of metal finds of third- and fourth-century AD date were distributed across this landscape, including various fasteners and fittings obtained from the disturbed tops of ditch fills. Hobnails are also most common in such levels (cf hobnails in one burial, see section 8.4, although the other examples probably constitute 'background noise' rather than disturbance of burials). Four late Roman finger rings, two silver and two copper, include one associated with an intaglio manufactured in the north and another could be an ornamental key-ring for locking a small box.

Finally, a jet hair pin with a diamond and triangle faceted cube head, a late Roman form, was obtained from modern topsoil in the west of the site, a zone generally lacking intensive occupation at this time. With the exception of this last item, any spatial or chronological patterning in these individual finds seems to reflect excavated soil volumes, and thus tells us only about the general status of the site, not specific activities or use within this. Having thus considered supply and consumption, we turn now to final discard.

7.4 Discard practices

The issue of extended circulation ('curation') has been raised above in relation to Nene Valley beakers and Gallic wine amphorae, the beakers related to problems with supply, the amphorae perhaps re-used in structural settings (see section 7.2). Curation may also explain the relative paucity of metal, shale, jet and bone artefacts of the fourth century AD, though supply problems seem more likely (see section 7.1).

For the purposes of post-excavation analysis, all features excavated at Heslington were allocated to one of several different types comprising 'open' and 'closed' cuts, deposits and 'structures' (see section1.5 for details). This system of classification allows, *inter alia*, for finds to be plotted against these (approximate) functional categories, whilst the site GIS allows spatial distributions to then be explored for functional and chronological patterning. The most significant results of such studies have been incorporated into earlier chapters where relevant, most clearly in understanding manufacturing processes (see Chapter 5).

Such classifications can also be used, however, to explore discard practices. In nearly all cases but the Roman period, patterning in the evidence simply reflects the period focus of different parts of the excavation and/or the volume of soil excavated (the occasional example in the Iron Age where discard seems significant has been mentioned previously – for example, the disposal of jet offcuts in droveway boundary ditches and the concentration of metal-working residues in certain roundhouses: see section 6.2). For the Roman period itself, bone and ceramic assemblages are large enough to have useful implications for rubbish disposal, and are thus considered next, briefly with respect to animal bones and in more detail with pottery.

An articulated animal burial was evident in a late Roman ditch flanking the north side of Road 1 (G218). It has a counterpart along this springline in a previously mentioned Late Bronze Age burial of two sheep/goat skulls and some feet bones deposited in a highly organic part of the springline between Wells 4 and 5 (G230). Whilst either burial might comprise structured deposition, the latter could equally represent primary processing or skinning waste, thus related to conventional animal husbandry. Concerning more general patterns, there is a hint of unusual animal bone disposal around late timber-framed structure G112, as noted previously (see section 6.4), and animal crania across the board are deposited more commonly in boundaries and trackway ditches than in other feature types. With these exceptions, bones were not discarded in any special way, most being highly fragmented and suggestive of trampling and weathering (perhaps after middening, as with the pottery described next).

Ceramics of Roman date are more informative, with about a third coming from boundary ditches, the rest being distributed between spreads, wells, pits and other ditches. Most patterning simply fits expected deposit volumes from the respective feature types. The exception is spreads that, at 25 per cent, show greater pottery densities than even the ditches, almost certainly a real pattern. It suggests that most pottery was discarded in rubbish dumps when it first fell out of use. No doubt, most of the accumulated material would later have been spread across the landscape during manuring, but the base of some middens seems to have been left in place (this chance survival reinforces just how unfortunate is the general lack of horizontal stratigraphy on the site: see section 1.2).

Within this broad pattern of ceramic discard, certain features mark themselves out still further and might imply a special form of discard. In one former Iron Age boundary ditch in the west, for example, fifty-seven sherds from a greyware flask suggest such deliberate deposition, in this case including the entire rim of the vessel (G153). In another, a later ditch in the northern central part of the site, a near-complete Knapton jar had been deposited (G103). Finally, much of a misfired or burnt pulley-mouthed flagon was recovered from a gully associated with Well 6 (although this could simply be linked to the use of that waterhole).

The density within unstratified groups lies between that of ditches and cobbled areas. The different volumes of modern topsoil surviving across the landscape and, especially, the variable collection practices between different parts of the project (see section 1.4) make such calculations difficult. Yet, this statistic seems to suggest that late ditch fills and surface deposits were mostly redeposited systematically into topsoil. This has the converse implication: that topsoil finds, especially from metal detecting, should be more representative of the upper fills of large ditches and of general middens than other feature types.

Moving beyond broad densities, large boundary ditches seem to favour the discard of particular items: more beakers, cups, flagons, dishes and specialist items such as Castor boxes, and fewer bowls and mortaria. Equally, flagons, cups and beakers were more often associated with pits than other feature types. This does not prove, however, that such features were purpose-built rubbish pits. Finally, structural features, a small category, are dominated by medium-mouthed jars, and walls by narrow-necked jars. This trend, although based on a limited sample, suggests that such liquid containers were being broken more often near to buildings.

Wells as a group are strongly associated with jars, notably narrow-necked jars used to carry liquids. However, this is entirely due to the large assemblage derived from Well 7. When these particular, and unique, assemblages are removed from such calculations, the material being discarded in other wells simply resembles the 'background noise' of ceramic discard on the site.

Overall, then, most finds were first discarded in middens, few of which then survived later truncation/redistribution into topsoil, and were then spread on fields. With the exception of particular finds intentionally placed in certain features, specialist vessels for serving liquids were more likely to be deposited in pits, and particular jars for holding liquids new to structures.

Ideological landscapes –
human burial, monumentality
and other specialised deposition

8

The following account discusses ideological aspects of human activity in the Heslington landscape, focusing in particular on evidence from the Bronze Age to Roman periods. Inevitably, evidence for human burial looms large (the end-date for burial evidence is dictated by the fact that the church controlled mortuary practices in the medieval period, here via St Paul's church from 1299, if not before). Discussion also includes evidence for monumental building and for types of structured deposition, notably in the placing of particular sets of finds in specific contexts to indicate complex social practices.[1] In what follows, it must be emphasised that discussion is mainly confined to clear ideological statements in the archaeological record: circumstantial evidence – for example, an unstratified copper alloy bell of Roman date, often linked to religious practices, or Roman vessel glass (G113), which is paralleled in burials around York – is mostly ignored, as is a distinctive medieval cross made of jet linked to Christianity. That said, the distinction between functional and ideological forces is by no means clear cut. To take recent exemplars, there are two listed buildings in the vicinity of the site. Heslington Hall, which housed the University of York in its early years, was clearly a statement of elite ideology when created as a manor house for Sir Thomas Eynns in 1568, and equally so when rebuilt to fulfil Victorian ideas in the mid-nineteenth century AD. Yet the nearby hospital, The Retreat, built in the eighteenth century AD for the 'moral treatment' of mental health, embodies in its architecture internal use of space and gardened landscapes not only a functional medical environment. It also expresses a set of Quaker ideas about psychological conditions and how to treat them: concrete functions and ideological imperatives are always intermixed in pre-modern periods as much as the recent past.

The account starts with a description of Bronze Age cremations (section 8.1), which are interpreted as signalling a change from markers influencing communities moving along the northern margins of the site to those beginning to settle more concertedly within it. A decapitation of Iron Age date (section 8.2) links to the point at which boundaries started to divide up this landscape, initially as a simple, single ditch aligned with a water source. An early Roman cremation and various forms of structured deposition above disused Iron Age features (section 8.3) mark the transition from the latter period whilst, in the Roman period proper, burials of neonates and adults (section 8.4) were inserted in relation to developments in contemporary agricultural practices. At the end of that period an entirely intrusive enclosure is created (section 8.5), with monumentalised entrance plus inhumations, a central prestigious building and associated burial, and the deposition of atypical assemblages into its eastern boundary ditch. Finally, masonry Well 7 (section 8.6) was inserted at a considerable distance from the springline on the site, symbolic elements being associated with both its construction and closure.

8.1 Bronze Age cremations and associated deposition

The drift geological development of the site has been described above in relation to a glacial moraine to its north, in which kettle holes developed *c* 11,000 BC (section 2.1). The first direct sign of human activity comprised an urned cremation inserted into or nearby this feature (unfortunately found off-site in 'watching brief' conditions: section 1.4). Recovered at a depth of 1.7m below the modern ground surface, only 20 per cent of the inverted urn survived later machining. This was sufficient, however, to show a ring-built vessel with random decoration, notable for its collar and over-hanging neck (possibly copied from basketry[2]). It was dated to *c* 2000 BC on typological grounds, which matches the C14 date of its associated context: 3554 ±20 BP (see table 1.1, G98), thus probably implying an overlap with Late Beaker usage.

This burial has parallels south of the Humber, plus some examples in Yorkshire (thirteen) and a few in Scotland (three).[3] The fact that it is one of the first from the Vale of York is almost certainly a function of site visibility there[4] compared, for example, to barrows on unencumbered landscapes of the Wolds to the south-east[5] and North York Moors to the north.[6] Examples in the latter landscapes are mostly found in association with round barrows, but any such feature would not have been recognised in the field here due to the circumstances in which the urn was encountered.

The bone fragments within this container were larger than those found in later Bronze Age or Roman cremations (81 per cent were above 10mm compared to *c* 30 per cent for other features) and most were identifiable (skull, rib, pelvis, tibia and humeri: 90 per cent vs 55 per cent for the Roman example), yet it was only 15 per cent complete. All of these factors are a probable result of the circumstances of its recovery, rather than a true reflection of past cremation practices. The age and sex of this individual are unclear, and no pathological examination was possible.

Only one item (fig 8.1) was found on the site itself that provably dated to the same period as this cremation, around the start of the second millennium BC. This comprised half of a butt-type battleaxe recovered from the upper fills of a sub-circular pit cut into the drift geology on the hillside just off the moraine towards the centre of the site (G98). This item, carefully polished and with a grooved shaft, was made of dolerite from a dyke or a sill, most likely the Whin Sill, a tabular layer of the igneous rock exposed near Hadrian's Wall, a considerable

distance north of York. The labour-intensive processes of grinding, perforating and then polishing involved with the production of this axe make it a prestigious object.

The Heslington pit is unlikely to have been dug specifically for disposal of the axe, as the find lay in an upper fill, positioned well below the top of the intrusion: it had not simply drifted into it at a much later date. Further such axes, when found elsewhere in the region, are mostly derived from burials. Some of the latter include rare bronze objects, a good example being a grave at Stanbury with a date range of 1960–1780 cal BC. A young male was buried here with a similar stone battleaxe (geological source unknown) plus a bone belt-hook and pin, a pair of copper alloy earrings and an accessory vessel.[7] Thus it is possible that a prestigious burial resembling that at Stanbury once existed at Heslington and was later disturbed, one of its grave goods then being placed in a nearby pit on the hillside.

The implication of the incomplete burial and the axe is that, around 1900 BC or a little later, several prestigious round barrows may have lain on the northern margins of the site (fig 8.2), at the southern edge of the glacial moraine that formed a routeway across the Vale of York at this time (an unpublished Bronze Age cremation from Lawrence Street in York, *c* 3km along the moraine to the west, although of later date (1380–1330 cal BC) may represent another such example, being situated in a prominent position on slightly higher ground at the edge of the moraine[8]). If interpreted correctly, such barrows would have formed prominent features in this landscape.

Some 35m to the south and west of this pit, thus further downslope from the moraine, lay two contiguous features (G98). One comprised a small circular cut containing an inverted, collared cremation urn. Just 0.2m to its north lay a second, sub-circular cut filled with

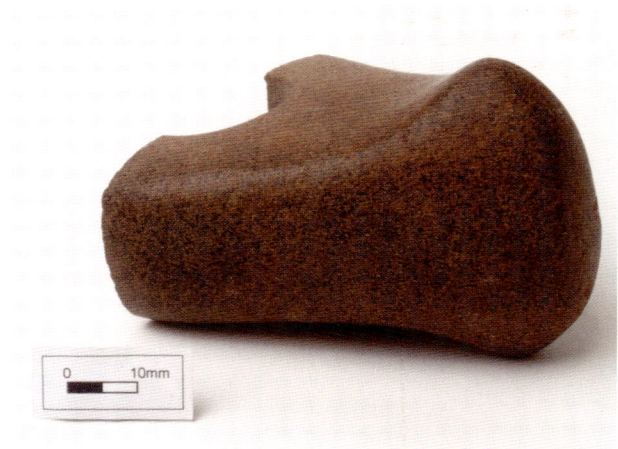

Fig 8.1 Bronze Age battleaxe made of dolerite, probably derived from Whin Sill, 150km north of York. © DoA

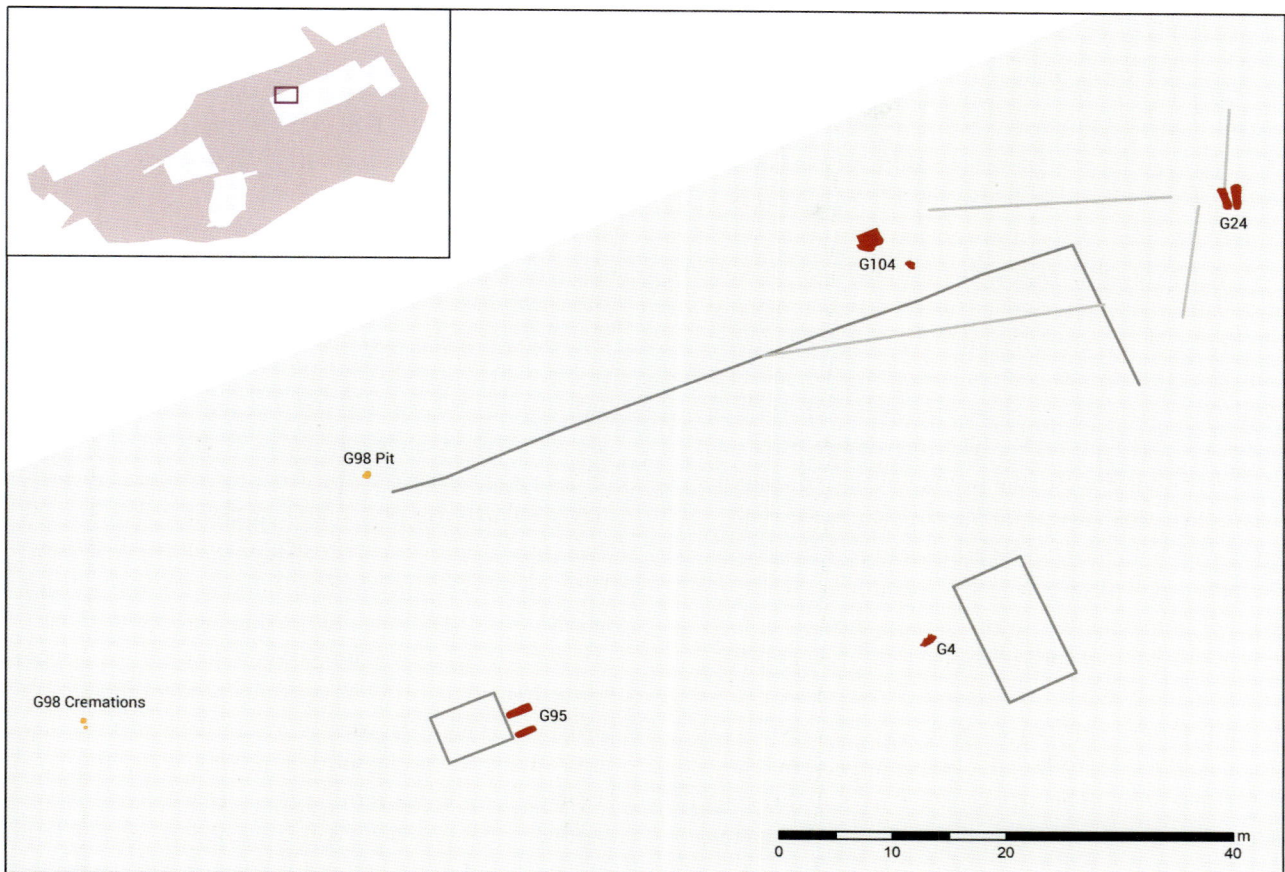

Fig 8.2 Location of burials in central northern area. Bronze Age activities included two cremations and a pit with axe (yellow: both G98). Roman burials included neonates G104 buried just north of the main site boundary at this point (dark grey); burials later inserted to their east (G24), which, in turn, seem to have influenced the setting out of a new, localised system of landholding to their west (light grey); and burials to their south set beside, respectively, tower G16/17 (G95) and prestigious building G1 (G4). *Drawing*: Helen Goodchild

charcoal-flecked silty sand including burnt human bone concentrated at its south-western edge: an un-urned burial. Although the two features could not be related stratigraphically, their proximity suggests that one was inserted when the position of the other was still known, thus implying that whichever comprised the primary burial was marked on the surface in some way. Investigation in the vicinity of the burials failed to locate any contemporary ditches within a 10m radius. This implies that neither burial lay beneath a barrow or, minimally, was not enclosed by a feature that involved digging very far into the contemporary ground surface. Thus, whatever marked the first burial (for example a post, as at Stanground, Peterborough[9]) was probably only visible locally, contrasting with the proposed notion of the earlier Bronze Age burials being prominent landscape features set along the moraine's southern margins.

The urned Bronze Age cremation of this pair was placed in a decorated vessel with a distinctive, 'slack' profile seen occasionally in local contexts and was dated by C14 to 3489 ±27 BP (1439, G98: see table 1.1). Its bone

content, weighing 438g, was excellently preserved and had been burnt to a high temperature (at least compared to the Roman cremation, G199, below). Just 27 per cent was identifiable, and pathology, sexing and metrics were not possible with the surviving remains. It did, however, clearly include two individuals, an infant 0–12 months and adolescent 14–16 years. It is not clear whether they had been intentionally mixed or become so when material was gathered up to be placed in the urn.

The cremation without an urn yielded a date of 3437 ±28 BP (1276, G98: see table 1.1), thus confirming the broad contemporaneity of the two, but without sufficient resolution to say with complete certainty which came first. It comprised the remains of an adolescent, 15–20 years at death, and was accompanied by a calcined flint knife, probably burnt in the cremation process rather than added as a post-pyre grave good. Meaningful information on sex, metrics and pathology could not be gathered. The bones in each burial were equally fragmented and, from their colouration, burnt at reasonably high temperature for an adequate length of time, allowing most of the bone to achieve full oxidation.[10]

Only 13 per cent of the non-urned assemblage was identifiable (vs 27 per cent) of the adjacent cremation and the level of bone preservation was less good ('moderate' vs 'excellent'). Further, this burial yielded 1,202g of human bone, substantially more than its urned counterpart (438g). As both features had been subject to the same amount of truncation, the latter difference must relate to their initial state. Hence, unless the bone within one was originally distributed in quite a different way from the other, the individuals concerned had not entered the ground in the same way. Such differences are probably due to it being easier to deposit a more complete bone assemblage into an open pit than to cremate two individuals, decant them into an urn, then invert and bury it. Yet care was still taken with both burials: the urned feature included, for example, small fingerbones. This might imply that the place of cremation was nearby for both burials.

The people with different ages in the urned burial – two individuals linked in the same bone container – contrast with its non-urned counterpart. It is interesting that only the latter contained a provable grave good signalling social differentiation: the flint knife, seemingly burnt during the cremation process. Hence, despite their proximity, these three people may have had different social relations with the community burying them. Whatever the exact situation, a simple equation of 'non-urned burial' with 'less important individual' is likely to be misleading.

It can be argued, therefore, that burial practice at Heslington from c 1900 BC shifted over a period of perhaps 400 years: from having an initial role in marking mobility in the landscape for people moving regularly along the raised moraine to its north, to allowing communities to make more local claims on the zone just down the hillside. Combining individuals of different ages in the later, urned burial implies a greater emphasis on intra-household relations at this time, which would also fit the notion of local cremation (due to the unfortunate recovery conditions of the earlier cremation to the north, we have no way of knowing whether it was cremated in the vicinity or at a distance). This pattern aligns with more general trends the second millennium BC, as individual mounds were increasingly replaced by group cemeteries.[11] In the case of Heslington, such a development would be linked to a shift from mobility to greater sedentism and the latter may have come with more complex social relations, plus distinctions within such (see section 9.1).

The above evidence shows that formal human cremation is evident in the Bronze Age over several centuries, yet not all disposal of human bodies took this form. Environmental evidence further south along the springline in the vicinity of Well 1 (see fig 2.2, section 2.3) shows that a palaeochannel set in a wooded landscape had been filling up over several centuries during the course of the Bronze Age. A fragment of adult skull was found in the fills of Well 1 here, in an Early Bronze Age context. This was extra-thick and had pitting along its sagittal suture, although the implications of these features are uncertain. Another skull fragment belonging to a juvenile or adolescent, with an occipital protuberance, was also found in the vicinity of Well 1, although could have been inserted after it demise. Taken together, these skull fragments imply that disposal of the Bronze Age dead in a damp, wooded environment well below the moraine took a different form from the (seemingly more formal) cremations, with or without urns, on the drier, overlooking hillside. Dating evidence is inexact for the lower skulls, but they are both probably of a general Bronze Age date. Attitudes towards the disposal of the human body in this period may have differed between the high, dry ground and its lower, damp counterpart (see section 9.1 on the wider context).

Elsewhere, a truncated organic deposit on the springline between Wells 4 and 5, dated 2733 ±30 BP (G230: table 1.1), and thus to the end of the Bronze Age, included two sheep/goat skulls and some feet bones (G230). If this is not simply discarded processing waste, this could comprise a structured deposit (but see further below). Equally, in the west of the landscape, a broken shovel was found within the Late Bronze Age lining of Well 2. Although only a rudimentary object, it would not have provided a very effective form of wattle lining for this feature and may have been linked to a red deer bone, interpreted by the excavators as having been caught in the weave of the well lining (see section 2.3). The palaeochannel south of Well 2, cut down in successive phases and filling up in the course of the Bronze Age (see section 2.1), contained the headless body of a red deer (*Cervus elaphus*). The channel may have been set in a wooded context, something disappearing in the general landscape. Deposition of a wild woodland resource may be linked to this process of change.

Although these possible examples of deliberate deposition in watery contexts in the Bronze Age are widespread, both spatially and chronologically, the deposition of human skull fragments is linked to the placement of unusual animal bones and atypical artefacts, in contrast to formal human burial beside the moraine. The human skull fragments in the south could be said to be integrated with animals from, and objects used in, the landscape: they are working with it, rather than intruding into it.

8.2 Iron Age decapitation and landscape division

Whilst water access had dictated human activity in this landscape from at least the Neolithic period into the Bronze Age (see section 2.3), it was still some centuries before any formal divisions were evident therein (see section 3.1). Ideological components related to these contexts are discussed next.

In the west of the site, the first tenuous evidence for controlling movement ran south of long-used Well 2. This took the form of paired pits in a possible alignment, dated to *c* 800 BC, their burnt pebble content representing possible production here (see section 5.2). More certain is the creation, some centuries later, of a boundary running for 25m south from the well: the first proper landscape division in the area (G138: see fig 3.1). This feature had a decapitated human skull inserted into its southern terminal dated to 2469 ±34 BP (G138: see table 1.1). The latter comprised a well-preserved cranium, mandible and the first two cervical vertebrae, totalling less than 25 per cent of an entire skeleton. It represented the head of a male, 26–45 years old (but more likely to fall into 26–35 year range), with an average skull shape but wide orbits and a long and narrow palate. This individual exhibited considerable evidence of dental calculus and mild gum recession, plus early osteoarthritis and may have suffered from anaemia or vitamin deficiency in life. The single adult phalanx found in the vicinity is not demonstrably associated with the decapitation. Hence, whilst there is clear evidence for some joint disease, it shows no signs of trauma, for example to imply amputation of a finger.

This man had been killed by long-drop hanging, which would have meant a quick death: the location of perimortem fractures to the axis vertebra represent a typical 'hangman's fracture'.[12] Hanging was followed immediately by careful, even surgical, decapitation using a thin-bladed knife inserted from the front of the throat and repeatedly pulled transversely across the neck. The head was then placed approximately face-down into what must have been a watery, anoxic environment. The speed of this whole process affected soft tissue decay, preventing the spread of endogenous bacteria via major blood vessels and the spinal cord and inhibiting autolysis. This unusual combination of circumstances has allowed the shrunken, but macroscopically recognisable, remains of the brain to survive in the absence of other soft tissues (fig 8.3).[13]

This evidence demonstrates that the insertion of the first clear boundary into this part of the site was commemorated in a highly significant way – the sacrifice, whether willingly or otherwise, of a human individual. There could be no clearer demonstration that the process by which this zone was to be developed to allow agricultural exploitation in increasingly complex ways (described previously: see section 3.2) was explicitly recognised at the outset as being of huge significance. It therefore required ideological investment (see section 9.1).

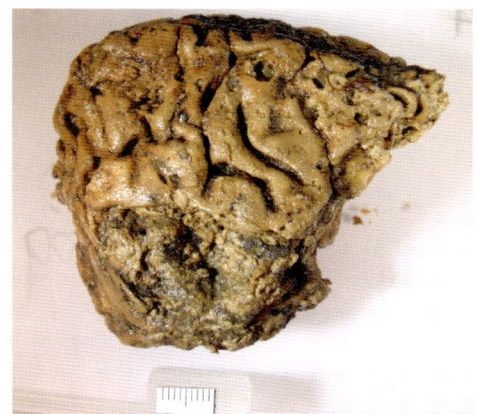

Fig 8.3 Decapitated skull in the course of excavation (left © YAT); and preserved brain tissue removed from the cavity during post-excavation analysis (right © S O'Connor)

8.3 Structured deposition at the Iron Age/Roman transition, including an early Roman cremation

Despite extensive exposure of later Iron Age field systems across this western zone, further pre-Roman burials are entirely lacking from the site, a common lacuna for this period:[14] either people were interred elsewhere, or funerary practices were in operation that left little archaeological trace (for example, exposure on platforms at the edge of settlements). Other forms of structured deposition may have still played a significant role here, however. Thus, the near-complete base of a ceramic vessel was deposited in the ditch terminal on the south side of the entrance into Roundhouse 3. In addition, diagnostic Iron Age jet earrings and a typically Roman glass bangle were deposited in watery places hereabouts (see section 7.2). There are even hints of similar activities near the eastern limits of the site, where the distal half of an adult/adolescent humerus was deposited in an early Roman ditch and an adult little finger in a large, broadly contemporary pit, both in the vicinity of Well 1. Due to the limited extent of exposure in this part of the site, however, each could equally have been disturbed from formal burial nearby.

Well 2, which was falling out of use at this point in the west of the site, evidenced a number of significant items in the natural formations accumulating above it (G170: see fig 3.4). These included a piece of lead casting waste, whose implications are unclear, and a piece of structural ironwork with two hooks, suggesting some form of substantial suspension gear. The latter may be related to the demise of the underlying well, whether as simple discard or as structured deposition (see also section 8.6). A copper alloy stud was also derived from this context (a second stud comes from a much later Roman ditch (G87) elsewhere).

At a much later date, in the fourth century AD, coins were deposited in the naturally formed horizon above the well, showing how long it took to accumulate and thus the now marginal status of this zone between the second and fourth centuries AD (G170). These coins formed two hoards dated to the mid-fourth century AD, thus broadly contemporary with three other hoards in the general vicinity.[15] Finally, two pieces of early Roman ard (see section 4.2 for agricultural implications) were found: one, in the west of the site (G167); and the second, much further east (G199). Both were broken in the same place, and may have been deliberately destroyed then

intentionally deposited. Clearly, therefore, the significance of both extremities of the site were now much reduced in terms of conventional settlement. Yet a range of meaningful material continued to be placed in the western, and perhaps even the eastern, zone.

The one example of a human burial belonging to this Late Iron Age/early Roman transitional period lay in the extreme west of the site (see fig 3.4). This comprised a deposit of charcoal and bone, mostly the former, filling a small, steep-sided pit inserted near a broadly contemporary hearth (G171: both features had been disturbed by a medieval furrow, so their relationship could not be ascertained). This fill yielded 426g of bone, of which half was identifiable as representing a human individual at least 18 years old. It was 25.6 per cent complete, but no sex or dental/skeletal pathology could be defined, in part due to post-depositional disturbance.

The pottery fragments found in this fill, comprising the base and lower body of a jar and sherds of a beaker, were discoloured and overfired respectively, probably due to their use during the cremation process either in the pyre or beside it.[16] The jar was an Ebor Ware type, dated to the late first to second century AD. The use of such a vessel links the burial to the fortress (see section 7.3 on Ebor Ware) and thus to Romanised practices. Given Roman law on human burial, this would suggest an absence of formal settlement nearby, something already implied by other evidence, although inserting this cremation need not preclude the continuing operation of the adjacent hearth. Given the incomplete nature of this cremation, comparisons with prehistoric counterparts elsewhere on the site are problematic. Yet, these bones are clearly less well burnt and more fragmented than the Bronze Age cremations described above (see section 9.3 on both this burial and the implications of the associated pottery vessel).

8.4 Burial of neonates and adults in relation to Roman landscape organisation

Another marginal zone that saw Roman period burials, but at a somewhat later date, lay near the centre of the site at its northern extremity (G104: see fig 8.2). Here evidence for the deposition of at least three perinates *in utero* were recovered. The best-preserved example was defined as an inhumation during the excavation and had 75 per cent preservation (described in fuller detail below). The second, its existence only established when human bone was recognised in post-excavation analysis, was derived from a feature seemingly first used as a hearth and had 15 per cent preservation (also detailed below). Finally, at least one other perinate is represented only as bones re-deposited when later deposits accumulated across this area (G108, G109). Even when all of the bones in the latter disarticulated assemblage are added together, they yield only a small percentage of the complete skeleton and all could belong to a single baby, a forty-weeks *in utero* perinate. It is clear, however, that this material did not derive from disturbance of the two better-preserved examples noted first – hence at least three perinatal individuals are represented here in total.

The first-mentioned articulated burial lay in an irregular, sub-rectangular grave up to 1.5m across but only 0.35m deep. The infant within had been laid out north–south in a foetal position, legs bent towards the chest and arms bent away from it, with head to north and facing east. Dated to 1730 ±25 BP (G104, 757: see table 1.1), it represented a forty-weeks perinate with ten tooth positions, including five tooth buds. Several nearby flat-laid stones may have once capped the grave, whilst two iron nails and what was identified later as an iron angle bracket came from its fills. The latter metalwork may represent coffin furniture, although the items were not clearly *in situ* when excavated (such an interpretation would make sense only if other nails and brackets had been lost to later disturbance: a likely event, as discussed further below).

Four metres to the west of this grave lay an east–west oval scoop *c* 2.2m long and just 0.22m deep. When first discovered in excavation, its reddened base and the charcoal content of its fills suggested the remains of an ephemeral hearth, and this may still be true, in part. Later analysis, however, also showed that its upper fills yielded the remains of a second infant skeleton, either disturbed after burial or inserted in a non-articulated state. The bones had not been burnt, so may have been placed in a disused fireplace for convenience (but perhaps still carefully positioned – see below). Dated to 1736 ±25 BP (G104, 2139: see table 1.1), so within the same date range as the first burial, it evidenced a perinate, 38–40 weeks, with no tooth positions. A lead sheet, rolled into a cylinder, was associated with this burial and seems likely to be deliberately included, perhaps a protective amulet. A fragment of blue/green vessel glass also from the grave could be similarly interpreted, although could equally be a chance inclusion in the fill or a product of later disturbance.

Although the second burial seems to have re-used a former hearth, the first cut into the natural drift geology

of the hillside in a zone largely unused up to that point. As both were inserted in only shallow scoops, each was easily disturbed by later activities (the process that seemingly generated the third, mixed assemblage of further perinatal bones). Yet, some care had clearly gone into placing both babies on the hillside: the first burial generated hints of a stone capping and of coffin furniture, whilst the second included possible amuletic grave goods. Given the evidence for three burials, and that two of them, at least, were carried out carefully and with due reverence, this suggests something more than opportunistic selection of a vacant zone to discard new-born babies: here, we are clearly far from the notion of casual infanticide.[17]

The fact that two of the three were subsequently disturbed, however, might lead one to question whether this constituted a formally defined, long-term burial ground. Broadly contemporary ditch systems to the south initially stopped just short of the burial positions (G101: see section 3.3), so the zone chosen for these inhumations may have been immediately outside this bounded zone, reflecting the connection between neonatal infants and the living community in general, and perhaps the mother in particular (something perhaps inherited from pre-Roman contexts[18]). Later in the third century AD, agricultural needs meant that farming activity now needed to expand northwards (G108: see section 3.3), and the former burial area was not of sufficient significance to prevent this from happening. One result was that at least one of the individuals interred there became jumbled with those later activities.

At a later date still, two inhumations were inserted towards the east of this central zone (figs 8.2 and 8.4), comprising two sub-rectangular features set above a co-aligned boundary ditch (G24). One intrusion was 2.5m long and up to 1.4m wide, with eight rounded stones, possible packing, evident towards its sides. This contained the badly-preserved remains of a slightly flexed and supine man, with both arms and legs extended and head to the north. He was aged at least forty-six years and was dated by C14 to 1707 ±30 BP (G24: see table 1.1). This man's eleven surviving teeth showed calculus on three and caries on one.

Abutting this burial to the west lay a second sub-rectangular cut 2m in length and up to 0.85m in width. It contained the better-preserved remains of an extended and supine woman, with head to north, arms crossed and legs parallel. Some hobnails recovered from around her feet imply that she was buried in shoes (cf section 7.1 on general hobnail distribution). She was aged at least forty-six years, her teeth showing evidence of calculus

Fig 8.4 Acjacent extended inhumations G24 of third-century AD date, showing local differential survival. Their insertion into the landscape affected the alignment of later field boundaries in the vicinity (see fig 8.2). © DoA

on just one (males tend to have a greater proportion of dental calculus, as is the case here) but with caries on eight and abscesses on two, plus dental enamel hypoplasia due to stress in childhood. Possible brucellosis is indicated by lesions on both hips, perhaps a result of consuming unprocessed dairy products, whilst the degenerative joint disease evident on her right foot and first cervical vertebra may indicate habitual squatting.

Although the two graves converged to be almost touching at their southern limits, not enough evidence survived to allow a stratigraphic relationship to be established securely between the two. They have different arm positions and the woman was buried with shoes and perhaps surrounded by a rudimentary stone cist, whilst the man was seemingly unadorned. Such diversity is, however, common with contemporary burials and so

does not greatly distinguish the two, especially when one considers the male's limited state of preservation. Both date to the mid-third century AD and one was set up to respect the other. Overall, they have more in common than they have differences.

Their position, exactly above and co-aligning with a ditch that marks the first time that such boundaries were extended into this area, suggests that both were inserted to reinforce the validity of this newly defined claim on the landscape. The demonstrably hard life of at least the woman – dietary stress in childhood, possible consumption later of unprocessed dairy products, degenerative joint disease due to habitual squatting – implies someone who was *of* the landscape and who was then buried *in* that landscape as part of a process of expanding into pastures new. It could be thus be seen an example of how the impact on the body of a 'taskscape' in life was then carried through into death.[19] Finally, when this zone was being re-organised in the fourth century AD, these burials still influenced the new system of landholding, which was confined to the area to their west (see section 3.4).

Not all treatment of human bones was of the formalised nature noted above. The finding of an adult left radius in a late Roman feature near Well 5, for example, may be the result of simple disturbance and random deposition, rather than anything ritualised yet it was inserted alongside an unusual Ebor Ware flagon, deposited long after its date of manufacture, and a tile in an atypical fabric (see section 2.3). The mundane, nonetheless important, burials described above contrast with evidence for prestigious Roman burial in the vicinity, thus probably telling us how often Roman burials have been missed due to a lack of formal monitoring of ground disturbance in past decades (see section 1.2).

8.5 A late Roman enclosure with monumental features and structured deposition

Something altogether more monumental is evident on the site in the form of a rectangular unmortared cobble foundation measuring 7m north–south by c 5m east–west (G16). Its thick walls suggest that this was designed for a substantial superstructure, whether masonry or timber (fig 8.5). The monument was subsequently reconstructed, involving a complete rebuilding of its western side, extending it by c 3m in that direction (G17). The magnitude of these changes suggests that any roofing must have been dismantled to allow for the re-modelling. The level to which the foundations survived and the lack of disturbed stonework in immediately adjacent areas suggest that its superstructure was systematically removed at the end of the structure's life. Similarly, the absence of

Fig 8.5 Cobble foundations of tower G16 and G17, in the course of excavation. © DoA

105

diagnostic CBM signatures in the fills of adjacent cut features suggest either that its roof was also methodically removed or that it employed different building materials.

A little distance north of this foundation lay a scooped-out pit containing two point-dressed masonry pieces made of millstone grit (G94). One was partially worked, with a hollow in its worked surface, perhaps the site of a 0.30m diameter column, whilst the other's surface included a 50mm deep depression. Both might have been employed in the superstructure of the cobble foundation. Sixty-five metres to the south-east of this tower, Well 5 used recycled stones in its lining (see fig 2.7). These comprised three crudely worked millstone grit voussoirs, probably from a simple arch with a span of *c* 1.75m, unsurprising in an agricultural context.

However, a second, more elaborate, group evidenced the use of *opus quadratum* on the site. As noted previously (see section 6.3), this masonry resembles that used in the tower-tomb mausoleum at Shorden Brae,[20] albeit at a smaller scale. Thus, the Heslington structure could be the source of these recycled materials and have had a similar mortuary function.

Two east–west rectilinear features (fig 8.6). were cut into the area immediately to the east of the tower and must be linked to its use (G95). That to the north was 2.40m long and 0.80m wide, with a maximum depth of 0.55m. It contained skeletal remains comprising a single fragment of left femur and, at its west end, a poorly preserved skull facing south. This was a possible male, 26–35 in age, with calculus on four of his sixteen

Fig 8.6 Graves G95 set in front of tower G16/17. © OSA

Fig 8.7 Detail of skull in a G95 grave with iron nails 'pinning' it to the ground. © OSA

surviving teeth. Three large nails were found driven into the earth immediately adjacent to the skull, with eight others elsewhere, some re-used (fig 8.7). This grave is noticeably bigger than strictly necessary for the skeleton, which might suggest that it was once laid on a wider wooden platform to be displayed.

To the south of this grave, at 1.2m, lay a second intrusion 1.90m long, 0.65m wide and 0.87m deep. Its burial comprised skull fragments and a possible clavicle towards the west, but otherwise little evidence for any other post-cranial material. The deceased was aged at least twenty-six years and may have been a male. Calculus was evident on sixteen of his nineteen teeth and *ante-mortem* tooth loss in one. The burial contained twenty-three nails, again concentrated around the cranium. The fills at the eastern end of both burials were cut by a shallow, irregular north–south feature 4.30m long, 0.63m wide and up to 0.15m deep. Voids and angular stones in its fill suggest that the feature was open and subject to weathering for some time after its creation. A nearby oval intrusion seems to be linked to this slot and both are best interpreted as marking the graves

It is not clear whether the two bodies there were interred at the same time, but they clearly adopted very similar burial rites (skull position, use of nails adjacent to head) and were commemorated together on the surface

(the proposed grave marker was inserted after both cuts had been backfilled). Their exact relationship with the adjacent tower is also uncertain, but the burials and monument are clearly linked, reinforcing the notion of a prestigious mausoleum being set up here (fig 8.8). Accelerator mass spectrometry (AMS) dating of the burials was unsuccessful due to the poor bone collagen preservation, but the tower seems to have been built in the late third century AD or afterwards and was certainly modified late in that century or into the fourth.

This investment in a mortuary monument took place in a significant landscape setting. It flanked the south side of recently defined Road 2, where it entered a newly defined enclosure set up north of earlier Road 1 (see fig 3.8). As argued previously (see section 3.4), the ditches flanking the enclosure to the east included a post-built gateway. This controlled movement from the east, just as the proposed mausoleum mediated access in the west. Atypical inhumations that were marked on the surface, and one possibly displayed initially, were used to further reinforce its architectural authority.

Within the area defined by this enclosure, activity was also qualitatively different from what was evident elsewhere. In particular, a terraced area measuring at least 15m across east–west (southern limits unclear) was inserted just south of Road 2, the material cut away in the

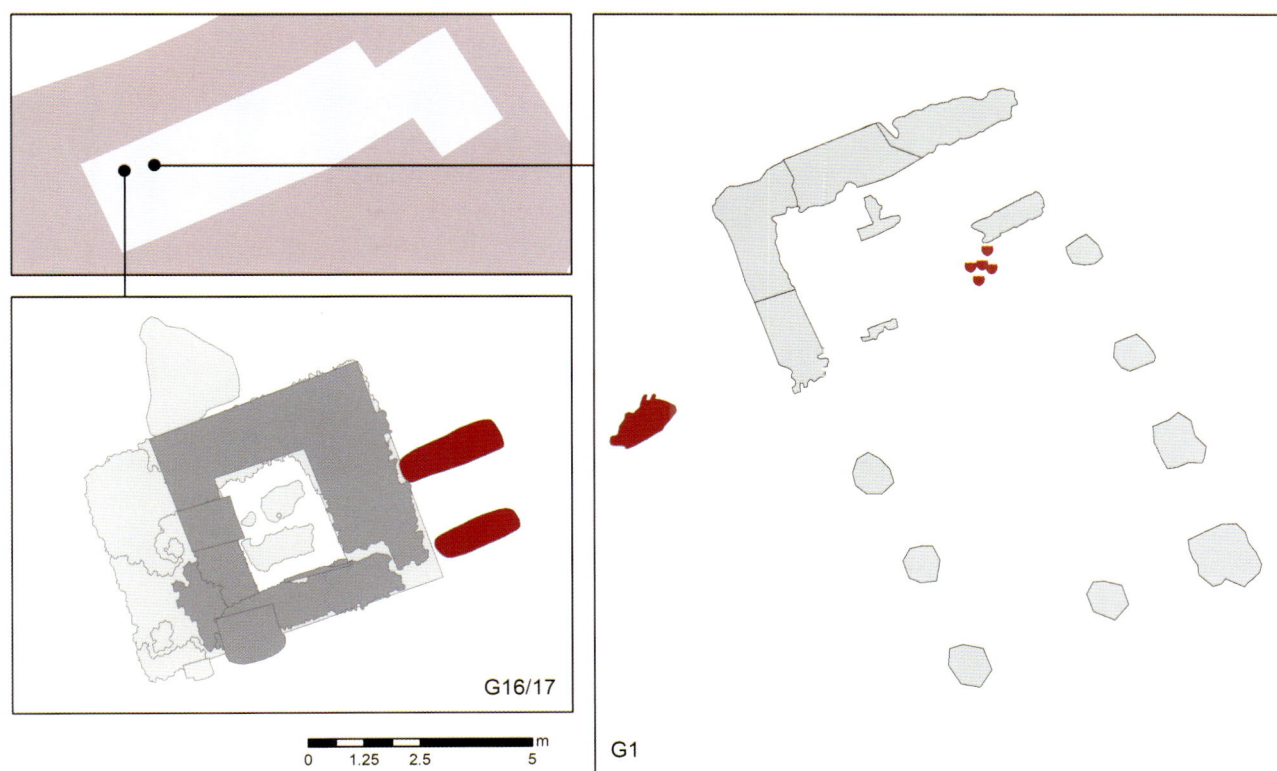

Fig 8.8 Position of tower G16/17 (left: original extent, darker; rebuilt, lighter) with adjacent burials G95 (purple). Building G1 (right) was linked with the insertion of 'ritual' ceramics (purple) (see also fig 8.10) and an adjacent burial G4 (purple) (see also fig 8.11). *Drawing*: Helen Goodchild

Fig 8.9 Building G1 in the course of excavation, with hypocaust tiles and masonry dwarf walls. © YAT

north being used to raise the ground to its south and thus form a levelled area for future building. A good-quality, rectangular structure then set up here (fig 8.9) measuring, externally, 12.5m north–south by 7.25m east–west (G1: see fig 8.8). Given that building G106 to the north (see section 6.4) was dismantled when it was set up, a construction date in the last quarter of the 3rd century AD or later seems likely. The pottery associated with this structure was dated to the third to fourth centuries in general, mostly derived from the earth-moving to prepare for its construction. Yet accumulations in its immediate vicinity, which generated sizeable ceramic assemblages, lacked any elements that must date to the fourth century AD. Thus, notwithstanding the investment involved, either the building was not in use for long or, more likely, diagnostically contemporary pottery was rarely deposited near it.

The building's structural components in the north comprised a cobble masonry foundation set in firm brown clay, with a secondary addition/repair of angular limestone towards its north-east corner. This created a single room, floored with *opus signinum* and heated by a furnace inserted at its north-east corner, with stokehole to

the east (exposure to heat here may explain limestone repairs to this zone). To the south, its walls took the form of substantial paired clay and cobble post-pads, with a 1.5m-wide entrance point in the west where the masonry foundation stopped and post pad construction started.

Five sets of *pilae* bonded with a good-quality pinkish cream mortar were placed symmetrically across the northern room to create a hypocaust system. Each base was constructed in a similar fashion: a larger tile measuring 320mm by 280mm at the base, then up to three smaller square tiles 200mm across set on this (sizes conform to Romano-British averages). Most of the *pilae* were left *in situ*, but all tiles that could be sampled were made from the same R6 fabric, including a single, extra-large 'Lydion' brick forming part of the access arrangement (a single factory would be expected to produce tiles with different functions). However, a ceramic pipe of unknown purpose incorporated into one its walls came from a different source. If flue tiles played a part in the heating arrangements, none survived the building's demise.

The best surviving *pilae* column had a surface 0.18m above the *opus signinum* floor, below the level of the adjacent walls. It is unclear whether this hypocaust was a primary feature of the room or an addition, although the *opus signinum* flooring was continuous beneath the base of each set of *pilae*. The nature of any flooring set above the *pilae* is also unclear. If this comprised a mosaic pavement or a second concrete floor, this had been systematically removed, with no keying being evident on the surrounding walls. Perhaps this suggests the use of a tiled or wooden floor, which would be capable of systematic removal and re-use without leaving any traces.

Five jars in Black Burnished Ware Fabric 1 were inserted within the building (fig 8.10). These are uncommon on the site, especially compared to broadly contemporary York groups, and their positioning here implies some sort of ritual purposes beside the hypocausted room at this time. A very large (110mm long) bolt from its vicinity also suggests an atypical attitude to security, or perhaps relates to the building's prestigious nature.

Just to the west of this structure, an anomalous human burial was placed in a shallow, ill-defined scoop, some possibly associated stones implying a lining or covering (G4). This comprised a skeleton lying north-west–south-east in a flexed position on its right, with the right arm extended above the rest of the skeleton (fig 8.11). It generated a C14 date of 1648 ±39 BP (G4: see table 1.1), but was buried with a spindle whorl made from a sherd of white Ebor Ware, a pottery type long out of circulation before the end of the third century AD. The remains, 85 per cent complete (the most of any skeleton from the site, despite being just below modern

ploughsoil), were of a 1.63m-tall male, 26–35, whose dental evidence showed small wisdom teeth, considerable calculus (26/31) and moderate periodontitis. Analysis of long bones suggested B12 deficiency and muscle injury on both fibulae. In particular, lesions affected the lumbar vertebrae, the sacrum and, especially, the left iliosacral joint. In addition, abscesses were identified in the lumbar vertebrae. Some of these changes were degenerative and their distribution and location are likely to be due to gastrointestinal tuberculosis.

In sum, this individual had clearly been cared for in his community for enough time to allow evidence for tuberculosis to be apparent on his bones. He had then been buried in a seemingly privileged position, next to a high-status building (the structure had hypocaust heating) with ritual airs (the Black Burnished Ware 1 jars) and with unusual forms of pottery deposition nearby. It thus seems possible that this whole compound, access to which was mediated by a gateway in the east and proposed mausoleum in the west, may have had a dedicated ritualistic function.

Within this enclosure, but due south of the above building, lay a series of patchy cobbled surfaces, possible hearth and probable boundaries (G6 and G7). They formed a funnel either side of a possibly water-worn channel in which sands and gravels later accumulated (G8). These features are unremarkable in themselves and their function is difficult to interpret, yet this zone also marked itself out in artefactual terms. It was a place where the repair of pottery with lead alloy was concentrated (see section 5.4) and from which two linked

Fig 8.10 Ceramic jars inserted within hypocausted Building G1, evidencing its link with 'ritual' activities. © YAT

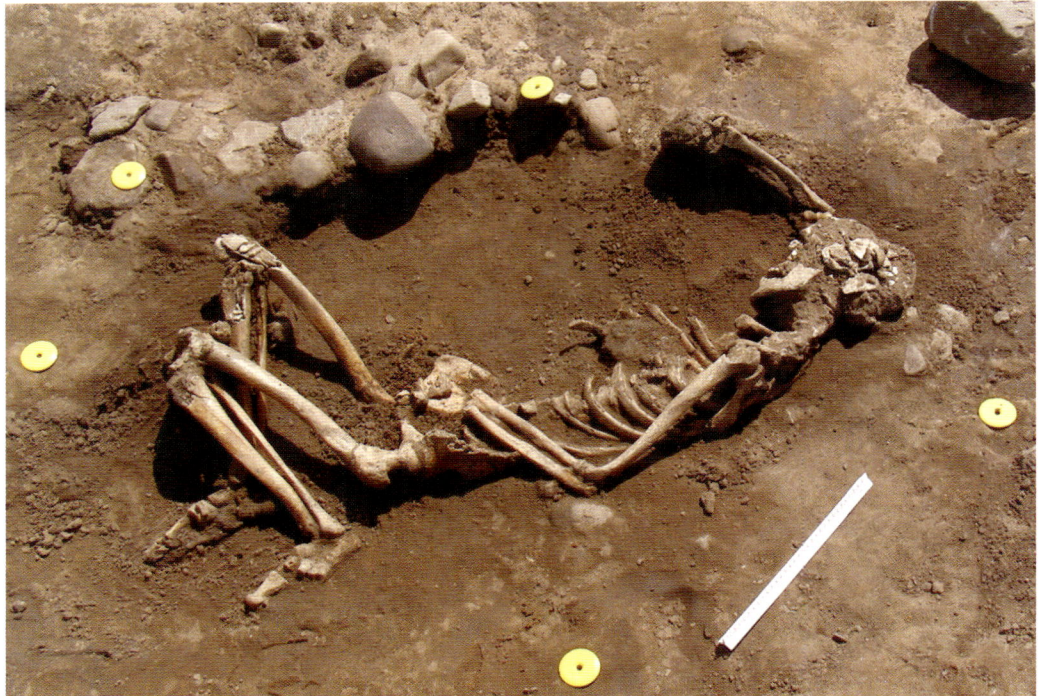

Fig 8.11 Crouched burial G4, with possible gastrointestinal tuberculosis. © DoA

iron objects for hanging something were recovered. The latter may be for a cauldron or for flesh but, given the small size of the rings, are most likely related to a lamp. It is also in this area that a concentrated deposit of carbonised field maple was dumped in a small pit, the likely product of a fire using such fuel (G6: see section 4.2). On a variety of grounds, therefore, this zone might be interpreted as being reserved for special activities.

Assemblage evidence also marks out the enclosure's eastern boundary (G30, G31 and G38: it is unclear whether the western boundary was also favoured in this way, as too little of its fill was examined to provide meaningful comparisons). As discussed previously (see section 7.4), large boundary features on the site generally favour certain types of ceramic find: extra beakers, cups, flagons, dishes and specialist items such as Castor boxes, yet fewer bowls and mortaria contained one of only two fragments of head pot from the site (fig. 8.12). The other example, from a ditch to the north (G12) included only part of the incised bosses forming the hair, so may be less significant. It also yielded *tazze* and abnormally high proportions of samian ware, plus a *tegula* with a sixth legion stamp and some other CBM, and items connected with transport. High proportions of 'Anglian' ceramics, including two joining sherds, sealed the northern terminal of this eastern boundary, perhaps suggesting a focus for post-Roman activity here.

Some of these characteristics could simply be due to the feature being adjacent to particular types of domestic activity, but not all of these activities can be explained

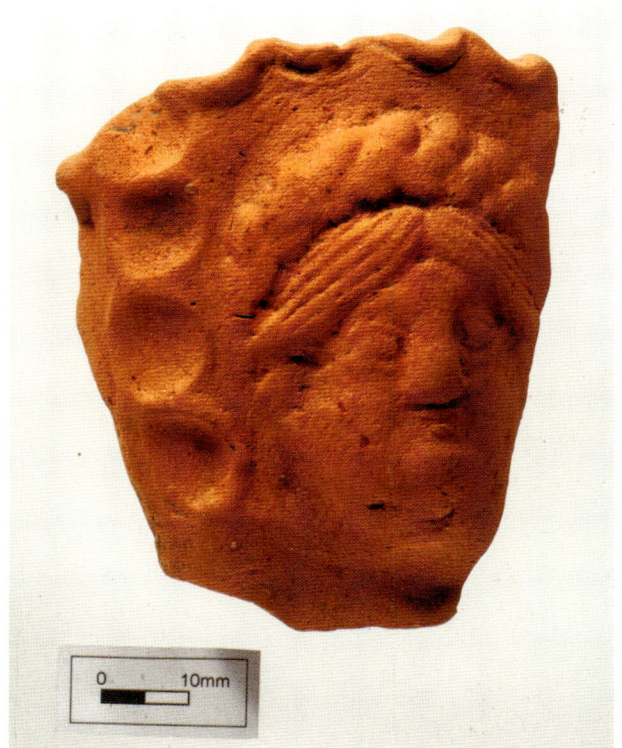

Fig 8.12 Head pot fragment from ditch G12. © DoA

simply as 'functional' discard. The CBM, for example, was found a long way from any known structures. Equally, the samian sherds, which must have been long outmoded when deposited, were concentrated in the ditch terminals either side of the gated access point. Finally, co-joining sherds from a dish were found in both this ditch and in a spread within earlier building G106 to its west (see section 6.4). We know that the latter structure was disturbed in later activity (for example, when part of an associated quern stone in its immediate vicinity was re-used as a base for manufacturing processes). Here, however, part of a simple dish originally related to the occupation of the building had been recovered from it and then found its way into a later boundary 40m away. All of these items, therefore, could constitute the structured deposition of carefully selected materials along this boundary and, with the samian, had been placed at the gateway, a critical transition point in the landscape.

Something similar may be evident with faunal assemblages from this ditch. As noted previously (see section 7.4), animal crania were generally more common in boundary and trackway ditches, something perhaps linked to a concern with stock control. Yet this eastern boundary also saw the deposition of a pig comprising the head of an old animal and body of much younger one (fig 8.13), inserted towards its southern limit where it approached the springline (G38). This activity differs markedly from a broadly contemporary animal burial in a late Roman ditch flanking the north side of Road 1 (G218) and, for that matter, from the burial of the articulated bones from two young sheep/goats and feet bones from the same animals in the Late Bronze Age (G230; whilst this faunal group could comprise structured deposition, it could equally represent primary processing waste, with the dressed carcass deposited

elsewhere, or skinning waste). The deliberate mixing of animal ages above the enclosure ditch might suggest a concern with issues of fertility at this time, in contrast to the more conventional discard of animal bone seen elsewhere on the site.

In sum, therefore, the period around 300 AD saw the creation of an entirely new element in the Heslington landscape. Up to that point, human burial could be linked to parochial needs, whether Bronze Age cremations signalling the change from communities passing by the site to those engaging with it on a more local scale; an Iron Age decapitation marking the creation of the first major boundary here; an early Roman cremation being situated in relation to marginal production processes; later Roman neonates being laid out just beyond the formally bounded zone; or, at a slightly later date still, adults being used to reinforce landscape divisions.

After that point, however, an enclosure was created with monumental activity at its entrance points, reinforced by abnormal human burials inserted beside a masonry tower in the west and by structured deposition along its eastern boundary ditch, especially at its gateway. A prestigious building with hypocaust was constructed at its centre, again accompanied by a unique inhumation. The general presence of a lamp, *tazzes*, Castor boxes, face-neck flagons, a possible unguent pot and fragments of head pot seem to reflect a focus on ideological dynamics within this area, in contrast to more obviously agricultural practices beyond. Up until this point, most of the developments seen on the site in prehistory and at the

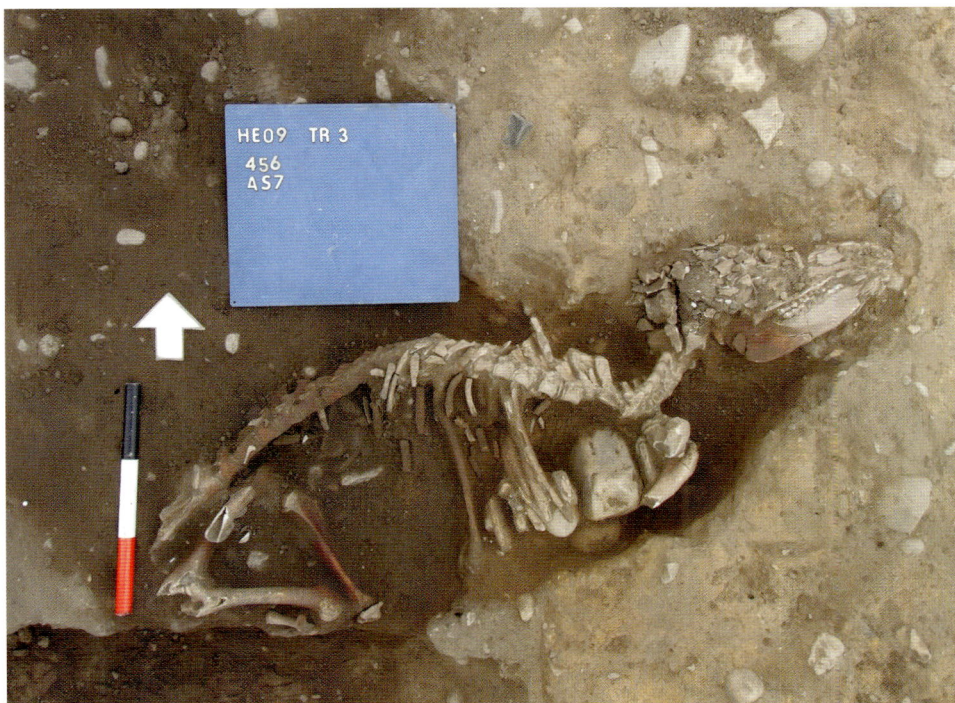

Fig 8.13 Burial, comprising the head of an old pig and body of a younger one, inserted into the southern end of a major boundary ditch G38. This deliberate mixing of ages might suggest a concern with fertility and pastoral reproduction processes. © DoA

start of the Roman period can be understood in terms of the changing demands of the pastoral and agricultural economy that operated here (see sections 4.1 and 4.2; although note the hints at specialist manufacture at certain points and periods in this landscape: see chapter 5). It is difficult to avoid the conclusion that these monumental developments, in contrast, were generated by something other than internal needs. Whether they were welcomed by, or imposed on, the inhabitants of the landscape is discussed more fully below (see section 9.3).

8.6 Late Roman masonry Well 7 and associated symbolism

A final act clearly related to ideological needs in this landscape relates to the construction of the masonry-lined Well 7. As noted previously, accessing water has had a fundamental influence on human activity at Heslington and was concentrated in those areas with easiest access – either along a springline at a height of *c* 22m OD in the centre of the site or in a palaeochannel further west. This mostly took the form of either unlined pits or timber-lined features, although at least one Roman well (Well 5) employed re-used stone for its lining (see section 2.3).

Well 7 marks itself out from the above trends in terms of its stone-built character and its position, situated at a height of 26.5m OD, *c* 75m upslope from the springline (see fig 2.2). It thus represents a major monumentalisation of this part of the hillside. Set in a circular cut 3.2m across and 4.35m deep, thus allowing a well with an internal diameter of 1m to be built, it was lined with newly quarried facing stones of squared-off, roughly hewn, oolitic limestone blocks (fig 2.9). These stones, curved on their outer surface, were set in carefully defined, regular courses, not formally bonded but packed with silty clay. The base of the well was composed of triangular limestone slabs set directly on natural clay at the springline, such engineering suggesting an intimate understanding of the subsoil (fig 8.14). Stratigraphically, the well must have been dug in the second half of the fourth century AD and associated ceramic assemblages imply its demise by the end of that century.

The construction of this feature seems to have employed the use of several nails that were much longer than any evident elsewhere on the site, perhaps related to the workings of its well head. It was also anomalous in its re-use of a high-quality roof finial in its lining (see section 6.3 for details and fig 6.5). This clearly interrupted the symmetry of the well and was meant to be seen to be doing so: something originally meant to be viewed atop a major building was now cast into the depths, a fall from grace that would have been deliberately displayed to those using the well.

The lowest fills of the well suggest that it was kept fairly clean initially, the amphorae in these levels, larger than elsewhere, and associated bones suggesting low-level, unintentional discard. This was followed by an episode marking the well's demise: two adult female pig skulls, which must have fouled the water source, were deposited at a time when scrub and heathland were evident in the vicinity and insects and frogs/toads were falling into the well. A wooden bucket and virtually complete jar, best interpreted as the discard of water-raising equipment, also came from this horizon.

The next fills, forming at a time when there was wasteland vegetation in the general vicinity and including further pitfall insects and frogs/toads, seem to have been deposited in a single action. This included a very large cobblestone, which clearly precluded any water access, and the bones of butchered cattle and horse, immature deer, dog and calf, plus the sacrifice of a large antler, valuable raw material. These deposits yielded far less pottery than underlying strata, but did include an unusual long-necked beaker and a complete grey ware jar, perhaps already rather old when deposited. In combination, such items suggest the deliberate closure of the well. Post-closure deposits formed in stagnant or slow-moving water, interleaved with the gradual collapse of part of the well's stone lining, before the latter's complete demise. Layers of a much later date then accumulated above the site of the former well, one generating a pot with an unusual roundel decoration. They relate to the very different forms of activity taking place here in the post-Roman period (see section 6.4, Building G112, and section 7.1 for discussion of post-Roman trajectories).

It is striking that, whilst the well represents a monumental intrusion into this area of landscape, all of the material found in its fills, whether use, demise or closure, would have been familiar to those inhabiting this landscape. Thus, these ceramics circulated here widely and, whilst some jars found in its fills may have been connected directly to water usage, most were not. Equally, the sheep, cattle and horses are found in other contexts on the site, albeit in different forms and proportions. The particular faunal material related to the well's closure, although it involved an interesting combination of young and old animals (the cow and calf bones related to farming, the sub-adult red deer and large antler to hunting), could have come from, respectively, within and near this landscape: they attest locally derived, well-understood, 'mundane' elements.

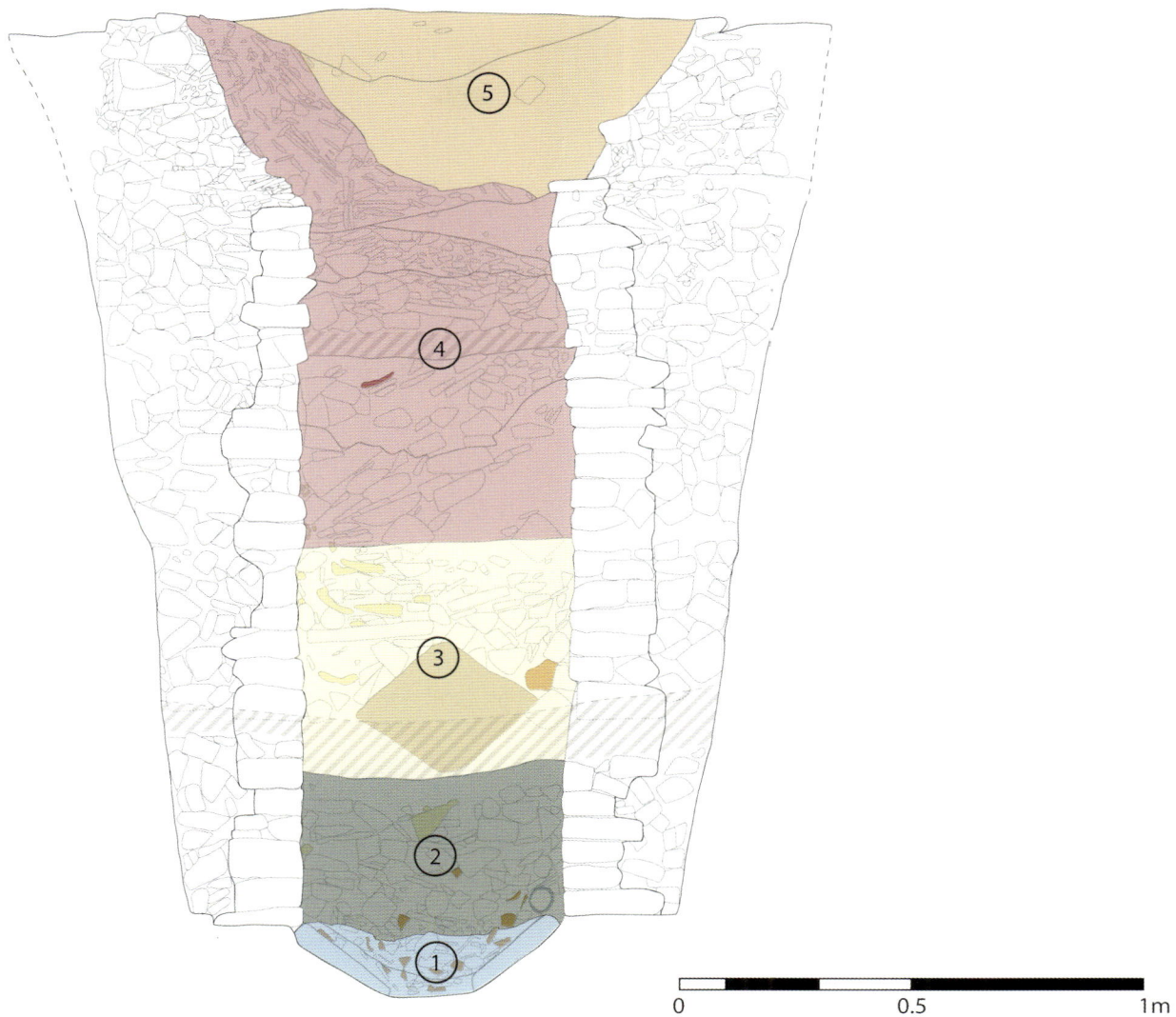

Fig 8.14 Profile of Well 7, G111, indicating stages of filling: primary usage (light blue), demise (green), closure (yellow), gradual collapse of lining (purple), and post-Roman accumulations (orange). *Drawing*: Helen Goodchild

Thus, although some of both the ceramics and animal bones were deliberately placed in the well as symbolic performance, it is a performance related to local agricultural cycles and fertility practices, not to 'external' needs. The closure of this monumental investment – a feature lined with newly quarried stone and positioned 75m north of a springline that had been employed to obtain water here for centuries – could be interpreted, therefore, as the inhabitants of this landscape reasserting the primacy of agricultural practice.

In sum, therefore, the site experienced a series of ritualistic acts from the Bronze Age onwards, initially in the form of cremations interpreted as making claims on this landscape by mobile communities moving along the northern margins of the site. Later Bronze Age cremations suggest that people were then either starting to settle more concertedly within this landscape or at least visiting it with greater regularity. The first formal boundaries here, of Iron Age date, were marked by the insertion of a decapitated skull, whilst an early Roman cremation and various forms of structured deposition signal transition into the Roman period. Later in the latter era, neonatal and then adult burials were inserted in connection with landholding. If all acts thus far can be viewed as intimately connected to landscape needs, then the last century of Roman rule proved an exception: a ritual enclosure with monumentalised entrance and a central prestigious building, each with associated inhumations, was then set out, with evidence for 'structured deposition' along its eastern boundary. A masonry well inserted high on the hillside at the end of the Roman period incorporated symbolic elements in its construction and seems similarly out of harmony with rural needs. Ceramic and bone deposition marking its closure, however, suggests a return to the influence of agricultural exploitation.

9

Transitions in the landscape – change within and between conventional periods

As explained at the outset of this publication, we have chosen to discuss the detailed evidence from this site under a series of themes concerning landscape engagement (chapters 2–8), their order being based on the principle that archaeologists need to understand the material context of using resources, creating boundaries and producing food and artefacts (chapters 2–5), before considering structures, consumption and ideological facets (chapters 6–8). At the same time, we acknowledged that the processes of development embedded in the very core of the excavated stratigraphic sequences should still be explored. Yet we noted that pivotal step changes in forms of landscape engagement at Heslington do not fit easily into the period-based divisions conventionally used to describe various prehistoric periods or Roman, medieval and modern developments (fig 9.1). We now confront the latter dilemma directly, by concluding with a discussion of suggested key points of transition in landscape activity here: from mobility and sedentism (section 9.1); between the Iron Age and Roman periods (section 9.2: in our case, a 'non-transition'); within the Roman period (section 9.3); between the late Roman and the sub-Roman/Anglian periods (section 9.4); and between the medieval and modern periods (section 9.5). Our hope is that our newly emerging evidence, by implicitly questioning current chronological frameworks, might facilitate the emergence of more convincing alternatives.

9.1 Transitioning from mobility to sedentism

To contextualise the above transition at Heslington, it is necessary to consider regional trends. Prehistoric archaeology in Yorkshire has been investigated over a long period of time, extending from barrow diggers and finds collectors in the nineteenth century, with a particular focus on Neolithic and Bronze Age periods, to multi-period landscape research in the twentieth century and more recent rescue work, for example the current project. The most recent synthesis of conventional wisdom on Yorkshire's prehistory starts with cave sites possibly occupied in the Late Upper Palaeolithic,[1] then early Mesolithic activity at Star Carr[2] and in a wider range of settings thereafter.[3] For present purposes, however, it is the later sequences that are most relevant. Manby, King and Vyner[4] propose that long barrows are evident in better-preserved landscapes from *c* 3500 BC (if not a few centuries earlier[5]), accompanied by more widespread contemporary flint assemblages in other areas. They also suggest an increased emphasis on the construction of henges from *c* 3000 BC, some accompanied by Grooved Ware assemblages. After *c* 2500 BC, circular barrows and prestigious metalwork are said to arrive, increasingly replaced by cemeteries of collared-urned cremations in the course of the Bronze Age. By the end of the latter period, the first hilltop enclosures appear, for example at Paddock Hill.[6]

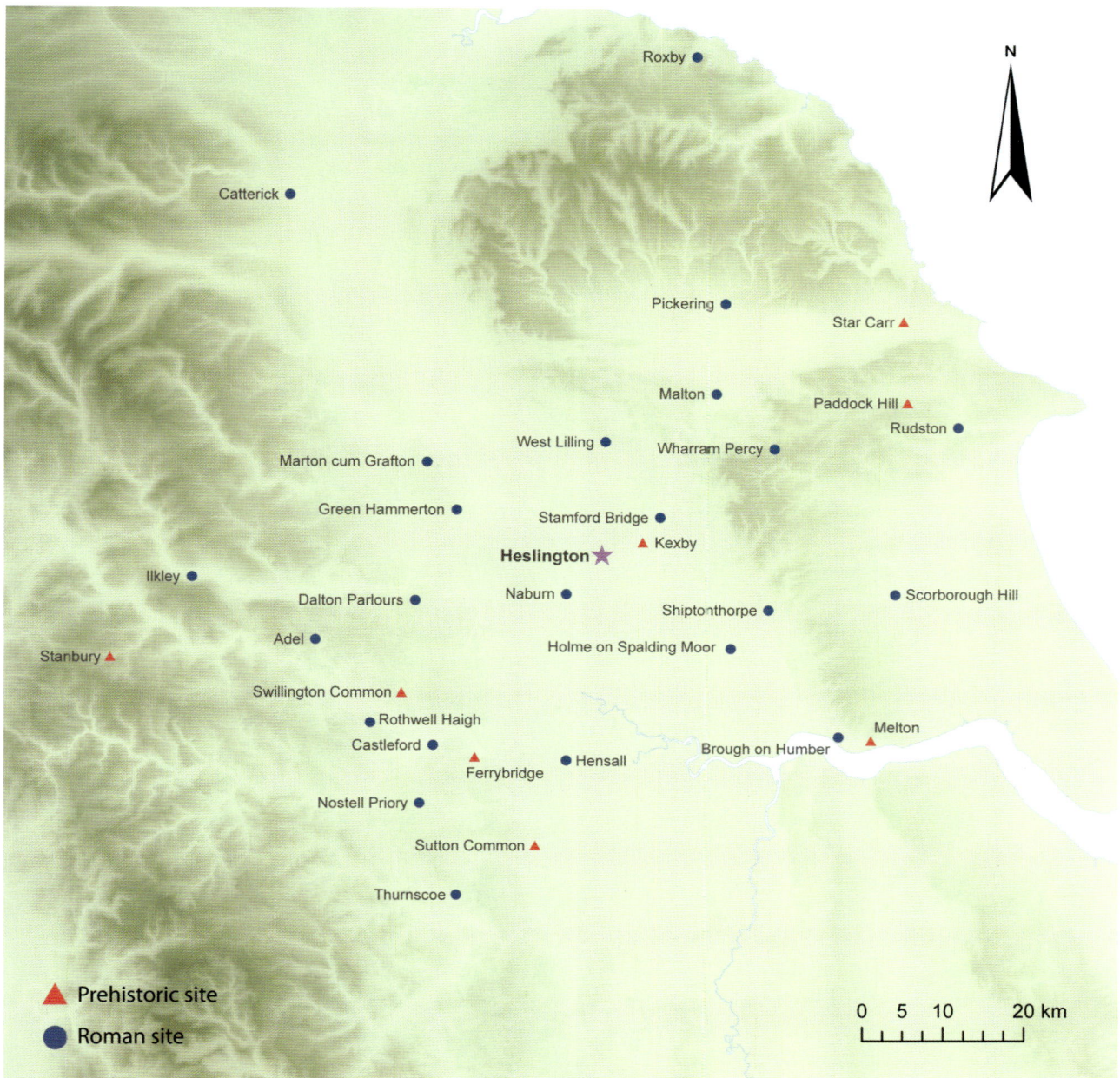

Fig 9.1 Map of main prehistoric and Roman sites mentioned in the text. *Drawing*: Neil Gevaux

Naturally, as with any such sketch, there are issues of gross over-simplification, and reality was certainly more complex in terms of chronology and ecological impact, let alone the question of what such trends might mean for overall social development. For a start, these northern sequences would, no doubt, be tightened further if the monuments concerned were to be subjected to the sort of Bayesian analysis of C14 dates carried out for the Neolithic period in general[7] or for early enclosures in southern Britain within this.[8] Equally, the transition from 'Mesolithic mobility' to 'Neolithic sedentism' was once thought to represent a straightforward change from hunting groups to settled communities, with the latter

perhaps involving immigrant peoples and having significant impact on wooded landscapes. Yet recent work demonstrates an overlap of some centuries between the two periods and suggests possible disarticulation, even conflict, between the communities involved.[9] In addition, even if the questionable notion of a Neolithic 'package' of animal domestication and agricultural development is accepted, the consumption of wild plants and hunted animals remained common until well into the Bronze Age.[10]

Further, whatever the timings, the process of development was not a story of inexorable change. Stevens and Fuller,[11] for example, have put forward a stop/start interpretation of Neolithic farming, with the 'real' revolution in Britain deferred until the Bronze Age. Not only this hypothesis, but its relationship, if any, with climate events is still contested,[12] as is the link between a Mesolithic/Neolithic transition and 'elm decline' in the region.[13] More recent commentators, for example, have stressed the complex relationship between human activity and woodland change[14] and noted that the timing of woodland clearance may vary hugely, even along the length of a single valley.[15] Similar reservations are likely to arise concerning Berg's suggestion of a link between a 'lime decline' and the impact of climate change at the end of the Bronze Age.[16]

It is important that chronological details are refined and ecological relationships understood, yet, for present purposes, a much more relevant barrier is that current syntheses have been constructed on the basis of archaeological findings from the best-preserved parts of the region's landscapes, notably the central Pennines, Yorkshire Wolds and North York Moors, rather than the Vale itself. Narratives derived from these adjacent areas have had a profound effect on the interpretation of evidence from the less accessible zone between them. This influence is at its clearest in terms of proposed east–west trade networks. The well-known Thornborough henges may have been gathering points for communities exchanging greenstone axes from Langdale, in Cumbria, to the west for flint from the east (and, no doubt, swapping ideas and having other forms of social interaction in the process). It is clear that East Yorkshire both exported raw material to Cumbria and received more such axes than anywhere else.[17] Yorkshire also evidences the greatest concentration of Grooved Ware pottery outside Wessex and Orkney. The mechanics of how flint, axes and pottery were moved across the landscape are disputed, however. Whereas most commentators favour routes across the Vale using glacial moraines,[18] Vyner's critique of this position maintains that such monuments are rather part of a long-lived 'Great North Route' running up its western flank in which traffic, if anything, avoided crossing the difficult conditions of that lower ground.[19] If the role of the Vale in Neolithic and Bronze Ages is contested, so must be that of the moraines.

Ian Roberts and colleagues have begun to test and enhance conventional models by deploying intensive aerial photographic evidence augmented by geophysical survey, fieldwalking and excavation on the Magnesian Limestone.[20] This exposure, a zone threatened by modern farming and quarrying, lies at the foot of the Pennines on the western edge of the Vale. Their research suggests that Neolithic henges were placed at points

where the Aire, Wharfe and Nidd rivers flowed into the Vale, thus laying foundations for development into the Bronze Age. The Ferrybridge 'ritual landscape', for example, started *c* 3,000 BC with a possible long barrow followed by timber circles, then saw round barrows constructed from *c* 2000 BC before pit alignments and associated field systems emerged by the end of the Iron Age. Breaks in monumental activity within general processes of landscape evolution should not be forgotten however, for example here the gap from within the Bronze Age until towards the end of the Iron Age.[21]

In moving from the Vale as a whole towards the specific Heslington evidence, it is useful to consider prehistoric material recovered in and around York. Despite the surrounding area being rich in prehistoric crop-marks,[22] only a limited amount of evidence from the city was available for discussion by Radley,[23] most of it generated during nineteenth-century railway construction work there. He noted a hoard of Neolithic flint axes and blades from Holgate on the edge of the city, alongside individual axes and flint implements from the vicinity plus several 'Beaker' period pottery sherds and proposed Iron Age burials. This material, together with a pre-Roman cist burial beneath Clifford's Tower in central York, has been used to suggest a general Neolithic presence under the historic town, with Bronze Age occupation on dry ridges overlooking its rivers, and perhaps a small Iron Age agricultural settlement beneath the nineteenth-century railway. The overall distribution of these activities suggested to Radley the significance of the moraine and the rivers throughout prehistory. Developer-funded fieldwork since Radley's synthesis has augmented this picture, showing a concentration of prehistoric lithics at the Ouse/Foss confluence.[24] Larger archaeological exposures across the city continue to generate Neolithic and Bronze Age artefacts from time to time. The latter include an assemblage of arrowheads, scrapers and part of a polished stone axe from Hungate,[25] and Mesolithic to early Bronze Age flint tools near the River Ouse at Blue Bridge Lane.[26] Undated features have also been revealed at the base of Roman horizons and may be of pre-Roman date, for example a linear feature in Little Stonegate, and ditches and stakeholes at the St Leonard's Hospital site.[27]

On the Heslington side of York, evaluation work ahead of a community archaeology project at Kexby,[28] *c* 6 km to the east of the site, revealed evidence for a 43m diameter henge. Its inner ditch with eastern entrance and outer ditch with possibly opposed entrances to north-east and south-west resemble the hilltop enclosure at Paddock Hill (above), whilst its final ditch fills are of Iron Age date (a second nearby ring ditch, 30m in diameter, could be a

Bronze barrow and is discussed further below). Just 1.5km to the west of Heslington lay 'Siward's Howe',[29] once interpreted as a Neolithic long barrow.[30] It is, however, better viewed as a post-medieval windmill mound.[31] More promising is a double bank and ditch earthwork at Green Dykes Lane west of the howe, suggested to be an Iron Age cross-ridge dyke controlling movement along the moraine.[32] Dating is unclear, but its long-term significance (which, of course, may not mean antiquity) is suggested by the fact that it was first mentioned in fourteenth-century accounts of the city's ridden boundaries and later formed the border between the townships of Heslington St Lawrence and Gate Fulford (although nineteenth-century disputes between the two parishes suggest the boundary had been levelled by then). Limited excavations across the line of the dyke ditches reached 1.2m, but were unbottomed when still generating post-medieval pottery, whilst possible primary bank collapse here contained a probable Neolithic flint flake. This find, plus the sheer scale of the feature implied by finding post-medieval pottery at a considerable depth, might suggest a major prehistoric landscape division. Certainly Ramm saw the dyke as being Iron Age in date and related to a hypothetical contemporary settlement south-west of the Ouse, beneath modern York.[33]

Considered in the round, therefore, the distribution of prehistoric artefacts from beneath York tells us more about the vagaries of recovery, often in less than ideal conditions, than about meaningful patterns of past activity. In the vicinity of the Heslington site, the henge at Kexby was recorded only in initial evaluation work, in the event an opportunity not then taken up. Hence the Green Dykes boundary is the best candidate for a prehistoric feature near Heslington, implying the importance of controlling movement along the moraine (notwithstanding the question of whether such east–west traffic was of secondary importance to a main north–south route to the west: see above).

This same moraine, it has been argued (see sections 2.1 and 8.1), was fundamental to understanding early mobility at the Heslington site, forming a solid route along its northern boundary. This ridge was punctured by kettle holes at several points locally, with palaeochannels running down from it in the west and an east–west line of contact springs originally set in woodland some 100m down slope to its south (see fig 2.2). When human presence was first registered on the site, a wetland environment existed in the south and east, contrasting with more open grassland elsewhere (see section 2.1).

The clearest evidence for that early human activity comprises flint artefacts showing burning, use ware and retouch. Such items mostly came only from the fills of later ditches and long-used wells, but were almost certainly disturbed from nearby (see section 7.1). They suggest human visitors in the Mesolithic period, then more regular presence from the Neolithic onwards. Later Neolithic flints, recognised on the basis of their cores being consistent with Grooved Ware associations,[34] indicate concerted activity here up to 500 years before any actual features are apparent. This early date is backed up by evidence for knapping, the form of which suggests a pre-Bronze Age date. Activities such as hide scraping are well represented in these flints, plus cutting and piercing, perhaps meat preparation or skin/fur processing: all could thus be linked to hunting. Apparent concentrations of this early burnt flint are, however, simply a product of excavated soil volumes, degree of disturbance by later features or charring from Iron Age hearths. Equally, no spatial patterning is evident on the macro-wear seen on scrapers and micro-wear on these and knives. Finally, flints with glossy surfaces or heavily retouched are equally widespread. Thus, no specific foci can be recognised in such early activities (see section 5.1).

These Neolithic visitors enjoyed a wide range of contacts, their tools demonstrating access to flint sources from coastal glacial tills to the east, whether arriving as raw material or as roughed-out/finished items. Retouching and knapping are evident, sometimes using an anvil but mostly hammering. Only a small proportion comes from primary core reduction, however, suggesting a supply of fist-sized, roughed-out nodules with most cores then worked to exhaustion. This, together with evidence of core rejuvenation flakes, might imply pressure on such external sources of supply. In all of these facets, our evidence fits the regional trends summarised above: evidence, from c 4000 BC, for the construction of earthworks and funerary monuments, cereal cultivation, pastoralism and woodland management.[35] Yet few domestic structures are known from the region in this early period, and habitation appears to be limited, dispersed and episodic, presumably because of the continuing mobility of the communities concerned. This situation probably continued well into the Bronze Age.

At the same time, among this background noise of flint use, there are hints at more concerted Neolithic activity at Heslington (see section 5.1). In the east of the site, near Well 1, one of two scoops filled with burnt cobbles yielded a burnt fragment of a possible leaf-shaped arrowhead, suggesting a hearth of early Neolithic date. At the western edge of the site, due east of Well 2, lay two features devoid of finds, an absence that, in itself, may be indicative of an early date (fig 9.2). To the south of this well lay several more pits whose undated fills contained haematite, perhaps linking them to Late Neolithic sites

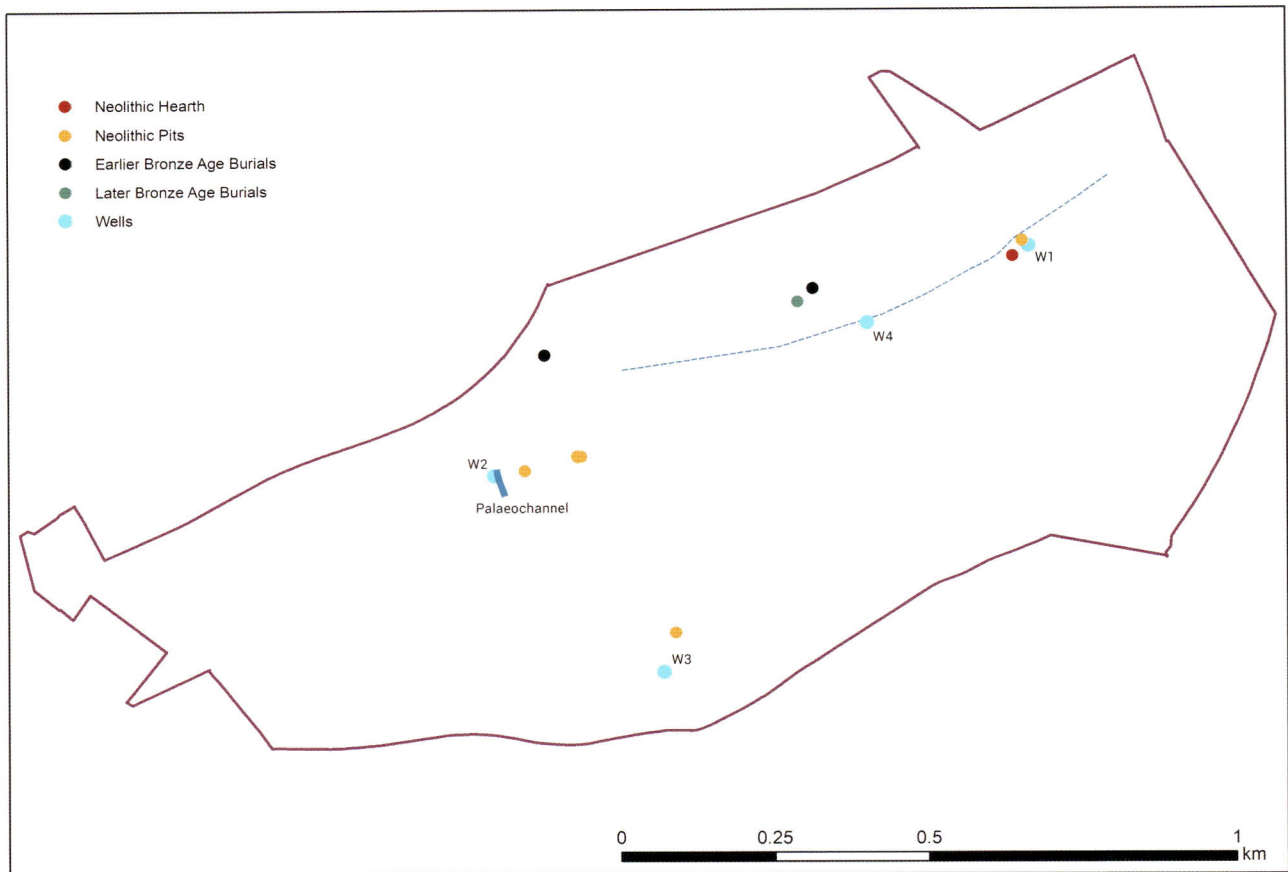

Fig 9.2 Summary of main pre-Iron Age features on the site, showing possible Neolithic pits and a hearth, plus Bronze Age burials, related to wells that seem to have been in use during these periods. *Drawing*: Helen Goodchild

with such pottery (see section 5.2).[36] The most convincing early feature, however, lay north-east of Well 3. It comprised an isolated, circular pit containing a broken stone axe (see fig 5.2) and a jet offcut. Clearly of Neolithic date, the pit represents a type commonly, if not regularly, found across the region and studied recently by Carver.[37] Despite the lack of concerted Neolithic settlement in Yorkshire noted above, pits containing broken pottery, flint debitage, and plant and animal remains are widespread here, interpreted variously as being related to quarrying, grain storage or rubbish disposal. Such pits concentrate in places favourable to settlement and favoured by monuments, in contrast to the much more widespread surface finds.[38] Most contained a single fill with high concentrations of flint debitage and fragmented pottery, sometimes mixed with other materials. They suggest rubbish disposal during occupation or the cleaning up after such. Either way, detailed engagement with the landscape is implied, perhaps marking it for future return: abandoned need not mean forgotten, as Pollard's discussion of Neolithic place-making makes clear.[39]

The Heslington pit, involving the disposal of just an

unused, perhaps prestigious, broken axe and a jet offcut, fits into that minority of Carver's types that were relatively empty, some of which contained complete items (others included human bone and food or drink offerings in their contents, perhaps related to funeral practices[40]). If all deposition in Neolithic pits can be interpreted as moving 'beyond the mundane',[41] the Heslington feature, with its single prestigious axe and jet offcut, must be doubly so. It implies, minimally, that people were starting to mark visits to 'their' landscape, and perhaps leaving it in such a way as to prepare for re-visits.[42] In short, in the course of the Neolithic period, the site was becoming involved with the creation of 'ancestral geographies'.[43]

This process of engagement took a step forward during the Bronze Age. Activity at first still appears to focus on accessing water, rather than settling formally. In this, the Heslington evidence matches that elsewhere in the Vale of York, where direct evidence for Bronze Age settlement is vanishingly rare (Swillington Common, 35km south-west of York, is a notable exception[44]). In contrast to such habitation, hoards of bronze metalwork are well attested in the York area,[45] mostly with a Late Bronze Age emphasis.[46] To this picture can be added the large number of stone axe-hammers from the Vale, conventionally allocated to the early part of the Bronze Age and interpreted as indicating woodland clearance.[47] If correctly dated and interpreted by Radley, they might suggest the opening up of landscapes (if these items are seen as being only symbolic of clearance, they would still suggest an ideological concern with tree-removal). It is even possible that the cutting back of woodland was a prerequisite for the wider circulation of metal.

In the specific Heslington landscape, one of the moraine's kettle holes had been filling up during the Bronze Age, to be replaced by a palaeochannel (see fig 2.3), perhaps in a wooded landscape (see section 8.1). These features were augmented by evidence for accessing water sources further downslope (see section 2.3). One, the long-lived Well 1 in the east, was clearly used early in the Bronze Age (and evidenced Neolithic activity nearby) and the other, the more centrally placed Well 4, was definitely in use in the Middle Bronze Age (and may have been originally of Neolithic date: see section 2.2). In sum, settlement may have been lacking here, but water was being retrieved with increasing regularity.

Apart from collecting water, the Bronze Age also saw the first formal burials appearing on the site. Interpreting mortuary practices at this date is fraught with problems. Late Bronze Age burial rites are much less visible in the archaeological record than earlier ones, complicating chronological interpretations.[48] Such gaps could be explained by denied funerals, inaccessible corpses or dead bodies displayed above ground.[49] A greater interpretative challenge concerns the once-common assumption that the Bronze Age saw the development of an 'ideology of the individual' in burial practice, as opposed to an emphasis on interpersonal connections in the Neolithic. Brück argues, in contrast, that grave goods do not simply flag individual ownership but also represent mechanisms for linking the dead and the living.[50] This applies equally whether such items were produced for mortuary display, concealed to control or obscure, or symbolically destroyed. Further, whilst burial is no simple mirror of social relations and expresses an emotional encounter, it takes place in a powerful arena through which status, power and inequality in the living can be structured.[51]

Alongside social attributes, such arenas had physical properties, a landscape setting that shaped, and was shaped by, the people who dwelt there. Such a link is implied by the use of material from diverse sources in barrow-making to create different connections to place,[52] something critical in any move towards settling in the landscape.[53] The impact of mortuary monuments on a landscape was immediate with the act of interment, but could also be long term, as seen at the Melton site,

situated on the south edge of the Yorkshire Wolds.[54] Here a Bronze Age round barrow was constructed and seemingly kept free of deep vegetation afterwards, before having cremations of c tenth-century BC date cut into it. Some centuries later, the barrow influenced the setting out of a large, triple-ditched linear boundary to its east that formed a major landscape, perhaps even territorial, division here between the Wolds and the Humber estuary. Finally, it affected Iron Age burial practice, notably the positioning of a square-ditched barrow inhumation and four-posters, perhaps places for excarnation. It may even have influenced the positioning of some Anglo-Saxon inhumations in its vicinity many centuries after this.

Bronze Age burials from the Heslington site (see section 8.1) also had implications for activity in the wider landscape. Two prestigious round barrows seem to have appeared on its northern margins c 2000 BC or a little later, inserted just on the edge of the glacial moraine running across the Vale. One, an urned burial of this date unfortunately recovered in watching brief conditions, provides direct evidence of mortuary practices. The second is suggested on the basis of a broken, dolerite axe dated to c 2000 BC (see fig 8.1) placed in a pit. The axe resonates with a better-preserved, Early Bronze Age burial from Stanbury, West Yorkshire,[55] suggesting reburial after disturbance of the original cremation.

This Heslington evidence can also be set beside that of another, slightly later, Bronze Age urned burial on the edge of the moraine 3km to the west,[56] plus two collared urn fragments from Poppleton, on the western edge of York,[57] which occupy a similar, morainal position. Finally, 7km to the east of Heslington, the 30m diameter ring ditch at Kexby noted previously,[58] although on the large side, could be another such barrow. Taken together, these imply a series of burials set up on the raised ground of the moraine. There is little doubt that this glacial feature facilitated movement in both Mesolithic and Neolithic periods, latterly, as claimed above, in the creation of ancestral geographies. From soon after 2000 BC, however, people appear to have been moving along this route with a regularity that allowed, or perhaps necessitated, its being marked with mortuary monuments. The use of the cremation rite would mean that the bodily remains of the deceased could be transported over long distances, to be inserted in landscape settings distant from that of their life, or their place of death.[59]

By c 1500 BC, more localised claims are apparent within the Heslington landscape (see section 8.1). Two contiguous burials were inserted near, but just off, the moraine, seemingly after cremation had taken place nearby. One, an urned burial, contained people of different ages and the second, non-urned, example included a burnt flint knife as a presumed grave good: the two burials were spatially linked but socially differentiated. It seems that they were not then covered by a large mound, as was surmised for their predecessors discussed above. Yet, they appear to have been marked on the surface in some way, thus remaining visible from a local position after interment (unless whatever feature marked their position was of considerable height, they are unlikely to have been visible to people moving along the high ground of the moraine to their north). The differentiation between the two burials, yet mixing of ages in one of them, is clearly significant. The former aspect suggests some complexity within the community making mortuary decisions at that time. The latter recalls, for example, the site at Stanground, Peterborough, where twelve double burials were identified, each containing the remains of at least one child, usually alongside one adult or an adolescent/adult.[60] Generally, non-adults are less likely to be buried alone than adults of either sex.[61] Such intentional mingling of age sets could be interpreted as emphasising intra-household relations over the commemoration of an adult 'head of household'.

The period from *c* 1500 BC has been portrayed generally by Bradley as evidencing movement into marginal areas, often initially on a seasonal basis.[62] This was a time at which burials were increasingly set up close to settlements and sometimes in cemeteries; barrows became smaller and metalwork was more rarely interred with the dead. Evidence from Heslington has some resonances with these trends, here related to an increasing focus on immediate locality as part of a shift towards greater sedentism. These burials, as argued above, suggest a greater emphasis on household relations and mixing of age sets, plus the incorporation of social diversity within such emerging communities. Such interpretations would suggest an integral relationship between burial practice and general landscape development, arguably the point at which people stopped just moving along the moraine and started to occupy adjacent areas immediately downslope more concertedly.

Equally, there appear to be spatial limits on this process. Roughly 65m to the south of these formal burials, for example, a fragment of adult human skull was deposited in an early Bronze Age context in Well 1, with another piece of skull in a later fill (see section 8.1). The deposition of human bones in watery places aligns with the placing of unusual animal bones and artefacts in such contexts. Thus, it might be suggested that burials in the north were diagnostically human and meant to be seen as such, whereas, downslope, attitudes differed to the disposal of the human body and to the relation between human and other animals: ideological boundaries seem to

have existed down the hillside, before any evidence for physical ones. Bronze Age investment in waterholes has been associated elsewhere with the creation of field systems, sometimes alongside acts of special deposition (for example, at Burghfield in Berkshire[63]). The above interpretations of changed burial practice around 1500 BC have been suggested, admittedly on purely circumstantial grounds, to signal the point in time something more permanent might be expected. No fields, or even boundaries, of Bronze Age date were evident within excavated areas at Heslington, so our understanding of human/landscape interaction at this pivotal point remains partial: a major lacuna. Yet, part of a red deer was incorporated into the lining of Well 2 and a beheaded animal of the same species was placed in the palaeochannel to its south in what may have been one of the few remaining wooded zones in this landscape. This might imply that the significance of this opening up of the landscape was recognised at the time, and was being acknowledged.

Towards the start of the Iron Age a fence line was set out in the west of the site, running south from Well 2; the first proven linear boundary on the site (see section 3.1). This was later reinforced and extended south by a ditch and a metalled routeway laid out alongside it. This extension of territorial control was marked by the deposition of the decapitated skull of an adult male at its southern terminal (see section 8.2). Then the area west of the well was being divided up at this time, a development recognised as being of profound significance, requiring what can only be interpreted as a human sacrifice, willing or otherwise: a man was killed quickly in a long-drop hanging, then beheaded, with the head placed immediately in the ground.

The start of this process, dated by a small amount of pottery to *c* 900–600 BC and by C14 to 2730 ±60 BP (G138: see table 1.1), signals a definitive change in landscape engagement: from visits, however regular, to concerted occupation. Access to water was now being controlled more fully, the alder cylinders from near Well 2 (see fig 5.3) implying that this fundamental resource was being channelled elsewhere and/or stored in some way (see section 5.2). Finally, broadly contemporary pits containing heat-shattered pebbles might be interpreted as truncated versions of 'burnt mounds', whether derived from saunas or cooking activity.[64] Better-preserved examples elsewhere (such as in the Dales)[65] are generally believed to be of Bronze Age date, thus somewhat earlier than the Heslington features. There is, of course, no reason why an eminently sensible mechanism for heating water/making steam should not have been used over an extended period of time. The wooden channels and burnt pebbles imply that water, although accessed in the Neolithic period and increasingly so in its Bronze Age counterpart, was now being used in new ways.

The creation of physical boundaries can be linked to indications of more general changes in the landscape. By the start of the Iron Age, livestock clearly played a significant role at Heslington. Foul water/dung assemblages from the base of Well 4 imply watering of animals, whilst coleopteran remains linked to dung and decay, derived from pits near these contact springs, suggest that grazed ground then existed in their vicinity into subsequent centuries (see section 4.1). The ditch with decapitation noted above (the latter element dated to 2469 ±34 BP; G138: see table 1.1) seems likely to relate to the control of livestock accessing that water source. Hence, although no enclosures were evident at this time, this implies the need to separate animals, and perhaps the emergence of distinct herds. A saddle quern (an unusual type in a period when beehive querns predominate[66]) was derived from an Early Iron Age context in Well 4 (see section 4.2). Hulled barley but limited wild plants and weeds dominate this early cropping regime. The beetle remains noted above also indicate fertilised ground near wells, and thus that crops were being used in conjunction with animals: a mixed farming regime operated here from the start, surely the norm in the region.

As noted above, this change in focus involved intervening in the landscape on an increasing scale, by inserting fences and digging ditches. A hint at the increasing importance of being able to intrude into the ground is provided by the broken shovel re-used in the side of Well 2, found alongside a red deer bone (see section 2.3). The shovel would not have provided a very effective form of lining and the single deer bone seems unlikely to represent an animal simply caught in the well. Both may therefore have been deliberately deposited, the one signifying a new investment in taming nature, the other representing a continuing link to the wild. The well itself is, of course, another example of a community attempting to tame a 'wild' contact spring.

In Britain as a whole, the end of bronze production has been seen as creating a crisis and ushering in a new age from c 800 BC.[67] This is thought to have involved a greater emphasis on food production and on enclosed settlements, with large-scale open landscapes linked to mixed farming superseding coaxial fields, and later hillforts suggesting a new scale of surplus storage. Whatever the effect of an end to the circulation of prestigious metal work elsewhere, and whether it impacted on all levels of society or just a restricted elite, no such crisis can be recognised at Heslington. In its

place we see evolving levels of engagement with the landscape. Furthermore, the timing of changes within this sequence of development does not map onto conventional divisions of prehistory in any meaningful way. Rather they fall at points more in line with the spirit of Bradley's general synthesis noted above: mobility along the moraine over millennia, becoming more regular by c 2000 BC; an indication, from the evidence of burials and water supply, of more local engagement off that moraine by 1500 BC (with or without any field systems: see above); followed by the first proven attempts to divide up the landscape from c 900 BC, and the more concerted insertion of ditch lines from perhaps 500 BC. This final change became increasingly intensive in the course of the Iron Age, a process described next.

9.2 Transitioning between late prehistory and the Roman period

The preceding section described the move from mobility to sedentism at Heslington, involving increasingly focused engagement with that landscape, perhaps from the Mesolithic period into the Bronze Age, deploying a combination of practical and ideological mechanisms to make such claims. The mixed farming regime that emerged from this process culminated in setting out fences and then ditches from about the start of the Iron Age, the first tentative step towards diving up this landscape. How these foundations were built upon in later centuries is discussed here (fig 9.3).

Initial organisation in the west of the site took the form of an open funnel-like ditch arrangement, later replaced by an enclosure to its west (see fig 3.1, section 3.1). Both sets of boundaries were created in order to facilitate controlled access to Well 3 to their south-west and seem likely to be related to the movement of stock. Also at some point towards the end of the Iron Age, the long-lived Well 2 to their north-west was enclosed and a stone well head, tank and steps added to its facilities, together with surfaces in its vicinity: water access here was being further regularised. These last changes were quickly followed by the creation of a system of large paddocks to the east of the well. The latter scheme included the first true enclosure, its ditches creating a c 45m square feature with an entrance to its south (see figs 3.2 and 3.3). This contained the first roundhouse (see further below).

Development still later in the Iron Age involved a system of even smaller fields, one set running due east

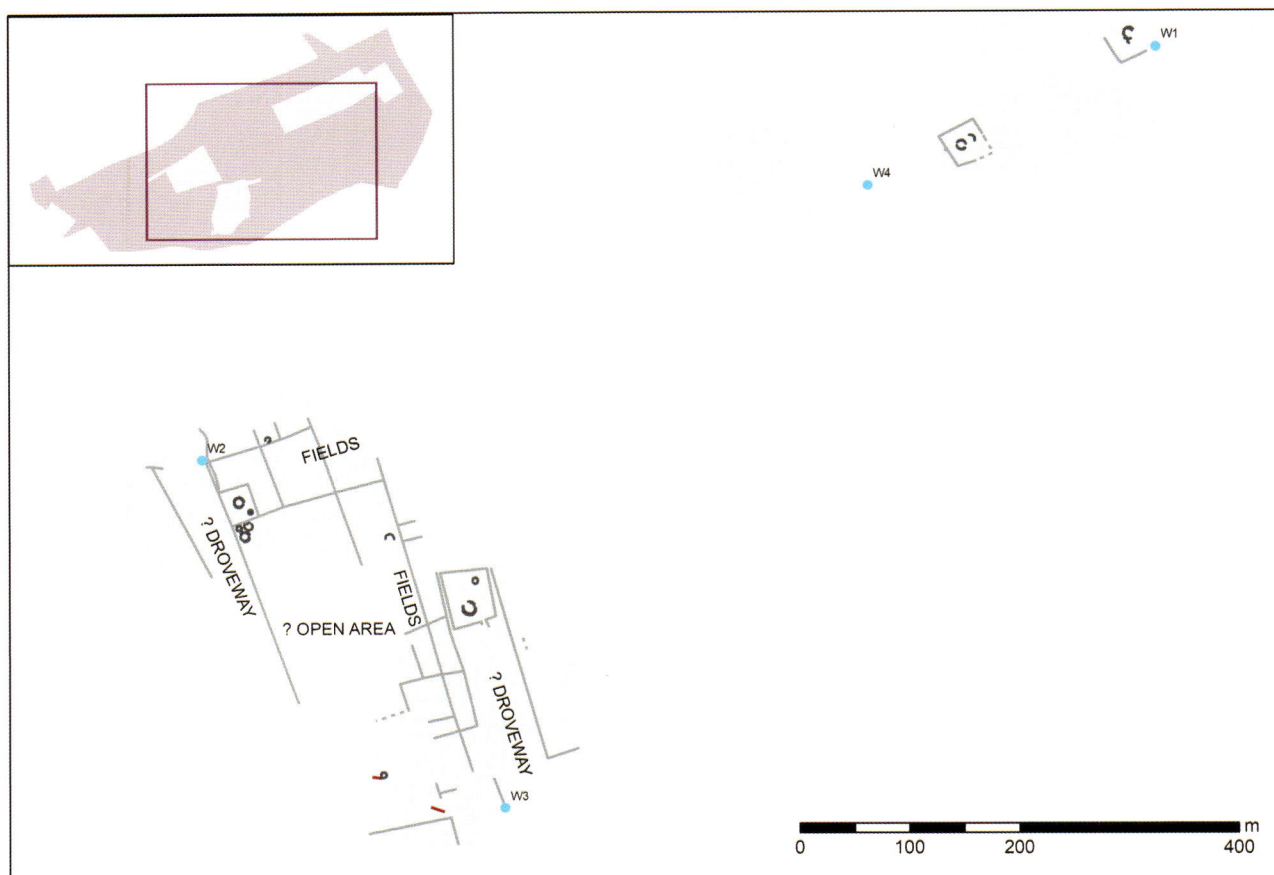

Fig 9.3 Summary of processes of transition between the end of the Iron Age (grey) and early Roman (red) periods. *Drawing*: Helen Goodchild

from Well 2 and a second at its eastern limit running down towards Well 3 to the south. As a result of these changes, two probable droveways were created. That in the west led up to Well 2 and that further east ran north from Well 3 up to the primary enclosure. A possible open area may have existed between the field systems and the western droveway. Activities here included the construction of a range of roundhouse buildings, both within sub-divided fields and immediately beyond them. Activities in the retained enclosure at the north end of the eastern droveway became more diverse and involved further construction, some of which seems to have been related to the production of metal and jet items (see further below).

The case has been made above for a mixed, and inter-dependent, farming regime existing here from at least the Bronze Age, and this continued into later centuries. Concerning crops, hulled barley still predominated, but six-row barley and spelt wheat and emmer wheat also started to appear. This profile parallels evidence from the nearby sites at Sutton Common,[68] Swillington Common South[69] and Manor Farm.[70] Further afield within Iron Age Yorkshire, hulled barley is still the most frequently recovered crop, with spelt wheat introduced at the beginning of the Iron Age and more common in the south of the region, and emmer wheat in the north (spelt is associated with a less intensive agricultural regime of manuring and hoeing than its emmer counterpart[71]). In Britain as a whole, the gradual adoption of a range of crops in the course of the first millennium BC has been related to agricultural expansion onto heavier soils.[72] The diversity of landscapes where the trend is evident, Heslington included, might rather suggest that wider social forces, not just simple soil type, played a role in this process.

Although ploughing must have been occurring in this landscape for many centuries (see section 4.2), the finding of parts of two ards in subsequent early Roman contexts, perhaps ritually broken, provides explicit evidence for tilling the soil at this time. Equally, contemporary charcoal samples show increasingly sophisticated timber collection and processing mechanisms, alongside specialised dumping of burnt residues (see section 6.3): communities were becoming yet more experienced in engaging with woodland environments from the first centuries BC into the first centuries AD, and had the technology to match. On the pastoral side (see section 4.1), increased stock control is seen in the course of the Iron Age with the move from funnels to paddocks, then to smaller fields set out with respect to droveways; all are articulated in relation to the continuing need to access water. Finally, dung beetles attest to the increasing concentrations of stock in this landscape. Animals may have been more numerous and moved about/contained in more regulated ways, yet overall spatial organisation at this time does not suggest that large numbers were being moved off-site on a regular basis.

The Late Iron Age is also the point when the first proven structures appear on the site. This is evidenced circumstantially by the increasing numbers of nails and worked stakes in samples from the start of that period (see section 6.1) and by the flint saws found here, one directly associated with such a structure. It is directly attested by clusters of roundhouses within and beyond the enclosures mentioned above (sixteen in all, R1–R16: see section 6.2). Where definable, the superstructure of most buildings employed a circle of upright posts supporting sloping rafters and no central post, in line with regional equivalents.[73] Limited levels of survival mean that little else can be added to this picture, for example on whether more regular timbers or sophisticated entrances developed over time, as has been suggested elsewhere.[74] The sizes of these houses, by diameter, fell into three groups: 3.5–4.5m (six), 6.7–7.7m (six) and 9–10m (four).

R1, the earliest and one of the largest structures, was positioned to control access into the first proper enclosure on the site (see above). It was long-lived, its superstructure being replaced and doorway re-orientated on successive occasions. The surrounding enclosure was itself also modified, with its boundaries re-cut, and pits and curving ditches dug inside. Part of these changes involved the construction of the smaller, 4.5m-diameter building, R2, to its north. The latter was associated with a copper alloy ingot, whilst jet offcuts were discarded in the droveway running south from the compound containing both R1 and R2: what seems to have started as a domestic structure in a dedicated enclosure thus became linked with prestigious artisan activities later in its life, R2 perhaps housing such a specialist function (see section 5.2).

To the north-west, variously sized roundhouses R3–5 were set up within the later system of smaller fields noted above, positioned in a cordoned-off zone with limited access to open areas to the south. This group was associated with a profusion of burnt material, initially charcoal and bone, and latterly with vitrified furnace lining and a possible silver ingot. The distribution of these residues suggests that initial domestic activity,

perhaps focused on R3, was replaced by iron manufacturing and perhaps prestigious metal working in R4 and R5. Access to this artisanal sector seems to have been increasingly restricted over time, as would befit those working with silver. Finally, 50m north-east of these, R9 was inserted in its own small enclosure, also generating evidence for the working of iron, and perhaps copper, in association with its dominant central hearth: another closely controlled production zone.

This picture of intensified metal production is supported by the concentrations of hammerscale and slags in broadly contemporary samples from around Well 2, augmented by vitrified furnace lining and iron slag blocks here, some concentrated in pits. This implies that smithing hearths may have intensively occupied the margins of the proposed droveway leading south from that well. One of these samples yielded slags with pipe-like runs, which might imply smelting of iron, presumably drawing on the natural iron pan known from the vicinity. Finally, an oval pit from this area contained lead sheeting, thus hinting at the working of this material. In the unenclosed zone just to the south of R3–5, in contrast, R6–8 implied diverse, mostly domestic, functions, whilst R10 and R11, incorporated into open spaces well beyond this, were probably linked to agricultural functions and may not even be proper houses; these incomplete ring ditches could have been used as windbreaks, for example.

Overall, therefore, domestic and agricultural functions dominated this western landscape and were chronologically primary in the first enclosed area, yet the latter zone was then a focus for the production of copper objects and the manufacture or repair of jet items. A second enclosed zone to the north-west, near long-used Well 2, involved the working of iron and perhaps silver, with the open area to its west evidencing smithing on an intensive scale, and perhaps even iron production. Finally, an enclosed outpost to the north-east was concerned with further iron and copper working. The latter two sectors seem to have been planned for artisanal use from the outset. The earliest levels containing these residues are securely dated to the Iron Age, but the latest horizons include material of the first and second centuries AD, and thus are, formally at least, of 'Roman' date.

Iron smithing might be expected in any agricultural settlement at this time, but hints of iron smelting and the working of copper and silver are much less common. The way in which the latter, more specialist processes are positioned – set in distinct enclosures with surveillance of access arrangements – matches with the notion of high-status production: if the movement of prestigious items between people was to play a critical role in reinforcing social relations, as befits a prestige goods economy, then the artisans making them would have to work in carefully defined circumstances. Such activities are paralleled elsewhere in the region in the Iron Age. Copper working is recorded in a single roundhouse at Ferrybridge to the west of the Vale[75] and iron at Roxby on the northern edge of the North York Moors.[76] Smithing and smelting was evident in a roundhouse with a central furnace (although the paucity of associated slags here might imply that such production was limited or quickly failed).

Jet is a rare and precious substance, warm to the touch and perhaps valued for its electrostatic properties (thus seen as magical?). Its production at Heslington, then, is worthy of wider consideration. Jet has been found in various prehistoric contexts in Britain, starting with elliptical beads from early in the fourth millennium BC.[77] Almost from the outset, both Whitby jet and, as imitation, cannel coal was used for making 'jet-like' items. By the Bronze Age, it is thought that a range of jewellery was being created in Whitby by skilled specialists using flint saws to cut raw material, then perforating and polishing artefacts to allow the finished items a wide distribution.[78] The Heslington evidence suggests that equivalent production flourished into the first millennium BC.

This proposition is backed up by finds from another roundhouse at the Roxby site noted above, a building yielding evidence for the working of jet and glass – whether repairing old items or creating new ones.[79] The economy at Roxby was based on mixed farming, and the roundhouses involved in manufacturing were in use from the Late Iron Age into the Roman period, two characteristics paralleled at Heslington. Yet Roxby lies within a few kilometres of coastal jet sources at Whitby, whereas our site is some 80km distant. At Heslington, unworked jet blocks ready for shaping, a valuable resource, had been discarded in the earliest, jet-bearing stratigraphic levels south of Well 2 (see fig 5.4). The later ditches flanking the eastern droveway, in contrast, generated only smaller offcut fragments. Systematic, long-lived jet manufacture would have required organised supplies and, it seems, by the end of the Iron Age, raw material was being used up completely: either there was more pressure on supply systems by that later point in time, or artisans were now working with greater expertise and creating fewer wasteful by-products.

In essence, then, this western area seems to have developed from an enclosed roundhouse, likely a single household, focused initially on agricultural practices. Clearly, sufficient surplus was produced here even at this formative stage to allow that small community to engage with wider exchange systems, as evidenced by the ceramics it received. As further households became evident in this zone during the Iron Age, surrounding landscapes became increasingly enclosed, including the creation of probable droveways and larger numbers of smaller fields. This more complex rural economy involved multiple households. Most were still reliant on agricultural processes, but a few dedicated at least part of their time in contributing to the production of items made of not just iron, as would be expected in such a rural setting, but also of more precious metals and of jet.

In contrast to this combination of agricultural and specialist functions in the west, the Iron Age enclosure 700m further east seems more typically domestic (see section 3.3). Straddling the springline here, it contained successive roundhouses R12 and 13 and generated a few non-descript Iron Age pottery sherds but no metallic residues (see section 6.2). There are hints that this enclosure occupied a more wooded landscape than the western zone, to judge by the range of timber species it could use for fuel and the naturally-formed gullies evident in its vicinity, which would not have survived in heavily-ploughed landscape. Its latest levels contained early Roman imported pottery, attesting to its continued occupation into that period.

Two hundred metres east of this, just north of Well 1, lay another group of large roundhouses R14–16, each with at least one central hearth (see section 6.2). The first two structures were of Late Iron Age date, but the last, although modelled quite exactly on the form and spatial organisation of the others, seems to have been built in the early Roman period. Its use relates to that of an adjacent sunken, perhaps tile-roofed, building whose content of vitrified furnace lining, hammerscale and lead spillage debris implies a concerted role in manufacture (see section 5.3). An oak framework was laid out above nearby Well 1 at this time (see figs 5.6 and 5.7), that waterhole then becoming filled with charcoal-enriched sands. This newly developed production zone was surrounded by a fertile, disturbed ecotype, so contrasting with the woodland context surrounding the roundhouse enclosure to its west. The ditches laid out around these buildings contained material of Roman date, although it is unclear whether these boundaries were created then or simply falling into decay at that point.

Overall, the Late Iron Age landscape at Heslington comprised ditches defining increasingly focused field systems and compounds containing roundhouses, all tied to the mixed farming economy that had been developing here in previous centuries. In one sphere in the west, however, there was clearly an investment in the controlled production of both iron and more prestigious metalwork, plus jet items. This development, starting towards the end of that period, then continued into the first century AD and beyond (the only hint at later modification comprising two small sections of obliquely-running ditch of early Roman date just west of Well 3; see section 3.2, fig 3.4). A second enclosure with roundhouses to the east was also converted into a manufacturing zone, thus impacting on adjacent landscapes. In this case, however, the manufacturing focus commenced only at the end of the first century AD.

This picture of continuity into the opening century of the Roman period is also true of water supply, a fundamental aspect of landscape engagement here from much earlier centuries (see section .2.3). Thus Well 1 in the east, in use from at least the start of the Bronze Age, was last employed in the early Roman period. In the west, Well 2 had been employed throughout the Iron Age but only perhaps a century or so into the Roman period. The disuse of this major water source, fundamental to how the Iron Age landscape had been organised here, is particularly interesting. Its demise was seemingly marked by the deposition of Iron Age jet earrings and Roman glass bangles above its latest silting (see section 8.3). Both artefact types circulated widely in their own periods, but are unknown in the other. Although these items were not deposited in exactly the same place, they could be interpreted as an act of closure that symbolically acknowledges the transition between Iron Age and Roman eras. Structured deposition above the site of this former well then continued into later centuries, including the discard of lead casting waste, structural ironwork, copper alloy studs, a wooden ard and fourth-century AD coin hoards.

The surrounding landscape was also used for a further symbolic action: the insertion of a single cremation in the early Roman period (see section 8.3). Cremation procedures may have taken place in the immediate vicinity, as its container was scorched in the process (cf Brougham[80]). The vessel concerned was an Ebor Ware jar, a type conventionally linked to the fortress (see discussion below). Thus, the burial deploys explicitly Romanised practices and 'military' material culture, yet this cremation zone was not otherwise marked in any special way, at least any that survived. This suggests that what mattered under Rome were pre-cremation rituals, rather than the actual acts of burning and burial, in contrast with Bronze Age cremations (see section 9.1). Such differences in attitude may be reflected in the actual 'standard' of the firing process: the Roman cremation is burnt much less consistently and at a lower temperature than its Bronze Age counterparts.

The Iron Age/Roman interface has been looked at spatially and structurally above, but can also be explored using assemblages, notably ceramics (see section 7.1). The earliest sizeable pottery groups include types also found in transitional prehistoric/Roman horizons in East Yorkshire, for example at Scorborough Hill.[81] Highly burnished vessels from these levels show that jars in local traditions were produced using improved potting skills and kiln technology known to the south of the Humber River at this time: ideas, as well as pots, were moving across that estuary at this formative stage. These elements were, however, soon mixed with imports from outside Britain, notably samian dishes and bowls. For some decades, it seems, vessels for serving food sat alongside local jars for storing and cooking it. The initial use of samian vessels at Heslington reached levels comparable to those of the York fortress itself, attesting how much the site was bound into centrally-organised distribution systems at this stage.

By the start of the second century AD, however, rusticated Ebor Ware jars became increasingly common at Heslington. This pottery type was locally produced, either manufactured beside the fortress, where wasters have been found,[82] or a little further out, at Lawrence Street or at Appletree farm, both on the edge of York. Such wares could have been produced at more than one place, of course, but this last site has the most convincing evidence, with kilns, wasters and clay extraction pits dating to the first half of the second century AD.[83] Ebor Ware vessels are conventionally interpreted as food containers fulfilling 'military' needs. Interestingly, however, the Heslington jars differ somewhat from their counterparts in York. More of them had lids, few were scorched or sooted, and oxidised fabric types were under-represented: such vessels must have been differentially selected for discard.

Two explanations of such patterning might be suggested: either foodstuffs were being supplied here in an attempt to promote a subsidiary settlement, presumably under the direction of York as the central authority, or particular types of Ebor Ware jar (lidded and non-oxidised) were recognised by that administration as being the designated containers for taking foodstuffs from Heslington households. If Rome did remove food from the Heslington landscape in this way, the overall continuity in its organisation implies that such surplus was being extracted only after local communities had decided on the mechanics of its production, not following any shift in the fundamentals of landholding. Deciding which of these explanations appeals might depend, in part, on one's attitudes towards imperial authority: the evidence, as it stands, allows for both possibilities.

These inhabitants were securely tied into archetypical 'Roman' exchange systems at this formative period. In this, Heslington resembles contemporary sites such as at Scorborough Hill,[84] 50km to the east: the latter's ceramics, although rooted in pre-Roman dynamics, now incorporated a 'prestige overlay' in the form of imports from across The Humber. In contrast, the sites at Hensall,[85] 30km away from York, and Lingcroft Farm, Naburn,[86] just 5km south of Heslington, continued to receive 'native' jars but lacked any such imports: clearly, central authority could have an impact on lower order settlements, yet it did so selectively and not on the basis of simple geographical distances from, or ease of communication with, that core.

In the course of the second century AD, the pre-Roman ceramic component was gradually replaced by burnished jars, and the imported samian table wares gave way to their locally-produced, Ebor Ware equivalents. It is only now that the first mortaria became evident. This implies that some food *serving* was modified almost immediately with the arrival of the army, including the use of tableware imported from outside the province, yet new ways of food *preparation* took another generation or two to become embedded. Charred bone (see section 7.3) provides another insight into cooking practices. Such material is increasingly evident from Bronze Age into Iron Age levels, as domestic activity developed and households proliferated over time (see section 9.1), yet is virtually absent from Roman horizons (and, even where it is found, it may have been re-deposited from earlier contexts). Either meat was now being cooked elsewhere and brought to site, or it was prepared in new ways or its bone residues were being disposed of differently. There is not sufficient chronological resolution in the faunal assemblages to decide whether this change matched that seen in serving and in cooking, as implied by ceramics. It is, however, a development belonging to the first or second centuries AD.

Heslington's ceramic signature at this point suggests that it retained a higher status than nearby Lingcroft Farm[87] and Kexby,[88] plus settlements even further away such as at Armthorpe near Doncaster.[89] In addition, its traded finewares, albeit present in only small quantities, serve to make a contrast with settlements such as Marton site 26 and Stockton-on-the-Forest.[90] At the same time, Heslington has some regional comparators: it resonates with an unpublished assemblage from a Fulford site only 4km to the west,[91] and the breadth of its ceramic range resembles that of sites such as Green Hammerton[92] and West Lilling.[93] The latter three sites are interesting in that the first lies directly on the road from the York fortress, the second has been claimed to be a villa, and the third incorporates kilns for pottery production: they already mark themselves out from the rural norm in terms other than their ceramic signatures. One reason why Heslington might find itself in a group with a somewhat elevated, early Roman status concerns its character when imperial authority first encountered this Iron Age landscape. The single roundhouses in separate enclosures distributed along its springline may have been common in the region (although precious few have been excavated, presumably due to restricted site visibility in the Vale: see section 1.2). In the west, however, a proliferation of roundhouses were set among complex field systems and, although inhabitants as a whole must have remained reliant on farming, some households here were concerned with not just iron production for agricultural needs, but also the working of precious metals and jet.

That said, although Heslington may have marked itself out ceramically at first, its signature began to diverge from that of the fortress in the course of the second century AD: it may have been privileged somewhat initially, for whatever reason, but was still a poor relation. This is graphically illustrated by the finding of a 'second' of an Ebor Ware flagon, and of an overfired Ebor Ware beaker. These inferior items not only arrived at the site, but the latter seems to have been circulating there for some time before being discarded. The Iron Age/Roman interface at Heslington, therefore, suggests a clear contrast between landscape organisation and ceramic circulation. Agriculture, plus an element of manufacture, suggest continuity into the first and second centuries AD, whereas Roman pottery types not only augmented pre-Roman material culture but, in some spheres, later replaced it. Further, in doing so, they signalled not only changing relationships with long-distance and local exchange networks, but also significant developments between York and this part of its hinterland.

Unsurprisingly, the nature of this transition has been of considerable interest across the Yorkshire region[94] and well beyond. Previously, it has mostly been portrayed as an abrupt change, in part due to a concentration of fieldwork on military features such as roads, forts and signal stations.[95] This conventional picture has often been underpinned by the notion of a 'pro-Roman' Parisi tribe in the east contrasting with more rebellious Brigantes to the west,[96] with forts at York, Malton, Brough, Hayton and Stamford Bridge being needed to control relationships between the two.[97] In deploying such evidence, sharp distinctions between native and Roman become inevitable – a self-fulfilling prophecy, rather than the testing of competing models.

More recent rescue archaeology ahead of modern development has fed a wider range of sites into the equation, and added new types of evidence, notably from the analysis of environmental data. Sometimes these later investigations have supported the notion of a marked change after conquest. Thus, a synthesis of results from the previously-mentioned investigation of the Magnesian Limestone belt west of the Vale describes the development of mixed farming from the Neolithic period, culminating in field systems set in cleared woodland plus a hint at greater specialisation late in prehistory.[98] This scheme was clearly disrupted by the insertion of roads and forts after the Roman conquest, for example with the fort at Newton Kyme set up to oversee a crossing point of the Wharfe, and similarly with Castleford, Ilkley and Adel too. The different nature of crop processing evident near forts and *vici* suggests that the impact of central authority sometimes went beyond settlement development to encompass some control of landscape production.[99]

Yet there seem to be limits on such intervention. Beyond new road systems, landscape organisation west of the Vale shows little evidence of change and, where such exists, it is in zones of only marginal interest to Iron Age communities.[100] A similar picture has been suggested to the east. The road and associated enclosures at Shiptonthorpe, for example, have been interpreted as representing a 'narrow corridor of opportunity' rather than an attempt to dominate whole swathes of landscape beyond these thoroughfares.[101] For the most part, pre-Roman continuities held sway or, if attempts were made to impose changes, they failed.

The corresponding picture on sites closer to Heslington also favours continuity across the Iron Age/Roman interface. Thus, the aforementioned site at Lingcroft Farm, Naburn, only 5km to its south-west, saw Iron Age settlement develop within rectilinear enclosures in the form of large roundhouses with a central hearth, and smaller ancillary buildings.[102] These households received a greater range of material culture, including Roman pottery types, in the course of the second century AD. Yet landscape divisions were not altered in this process, and one roundhouse was even built at that late date (cf the discussion of Heslington Roundhouses 14–16; see section 6.2). The apparent lack of droveways at Naburn might indicate a more arable economy here than at Heslington, but in all other respects the landscape sequences run along parallel lines. There are also hints at Naburn of settlement consolidation, and perhaps depopulation, towards the end of the second century AD, something also seen in the western landscape at Heslington. Just to the east of Heslington, the previously-mentioned site at Kexby, with a long history of prehistoric development, saw re-cutting of boundaries within both Late Iron Age and early Roman periods and perhaps the use of a granary structure and two possible bread ovens. Whilst activity continued into the third century AD, it

employed very different, posthole buildings.[103]

Investigations at a landscape level, as at Naburn and Roxby, are rare (and even these are partial: the one not formally published, the other comprising only initial reconnaissance in a project that did not come to fruition). Further afield in the Vale it is difficult to find large amounts of evidence due to limited site visibility. The landscapes of the Yorkshire Wolds, *c* 35km north-east of York, suffer from neither problem. They have been subjected to extensive survey, their chalk outcrops being very accessible to aerial photography,[104] to geophysical prospection and to detailed investigation in both the Iron Age[105] and later[106] periods. For present purposes, work at Wharram Percy[107] in the north of these landscapes and at Melton[108] just off the Wolds in the south, near the Humber Estuary, are the most relevant.

Fenton-Thomas describes how prehistoric trackways, often articulated in relation to pre-existing Bronze Age barrows (cf previous discussion in section 9.1), first dictated long-distance movement across the Wolds.[109] In the course of the Iron Age, this landscape became increasingly arable and, from the fourth century BC, square-ditched barrows were used to make claims on the landscape, especially in contexts close to water, trackways and boundaries. Some of these claims took the form of 'cart burials' and are assumed to evidence the emergence of a social elite.[110] By the end of the Iron Age, these tracks had developed into droveways, with contiguous sets of enclosures set out beside the routes ('ladder settlements').

Work at Wharram Percy shows that these ladder settlements were retained in use well into the Roman period.[111] The settlement may have received increasing amounts of Roman ceramics from early in the second century AD, but faunal assemblages show that it remained an economy based mostly on sheep for wool and milk, plus cattle for milk and traction. Meat from these animals, alongside that from pigs, was generated only after each beast had played another role in the agricultural economy. The third century AD, in contrast, saw the demise of the ladder settlements at Wharram Percy, replaced by larger, discrete enclosures. This constituted the most fundamental shift in landscape organisation to have occurred here since the development of the prehistoric trackways mentioned above. One of these new enclosures was the site for a higher status structure building with tiled roof and mosaic pavement (a 'villa'), set up in a position to oversee the new system of landholding. Despite a continuing emphasis on sheep over other animals, the third century was also the point at which prime beef production and specialised culling of sheep became visible, together with specialised disposal of faunal remains. It could be argued, therefore, that the period around 200 AD was a watershed, the point in time at which an external authority such as the Roman state had sufficient control over this landscape to define new production processes and re-direct any surplus. The converse is also true: before that point, it had been unable to impose its authority on these producers.

A similar picture can be suggested for Melton, situated just off the south end of the Wolds.[112] Here, as noted previously (see section 9.1), a round barrow dictated the positioning of a major, triple-ditched linear feature forming a territorial boundary running from the Wolds down to the Humber estuary. This boundary influenced landscape development over successive centuries, notably with the insertion of an 11m-wide trackway running to its east and facilitating movement along the base of the Wolds scarp. The enclosures that had developed beside this track by the end of the Iron Age formed a classic ladder settlement as seen on higher ground to their north-west, here with roundhouses developing within such compounds. This organisation of the landscape continued, with only minor changes, into the early Roman period.

It is assumed that this Iron Age floruit on the Wolds was, at least in part, a product of 'industrial level' development of iron production in Foulness Valley, which utilised the advantages of local bog ore, timber from managed woodland and creeks for water transport systems.[113] It might be expected that such control of iron would create wealth and social differentiation, but elites are not obvious in the settlement record. If they existed but were dispersed across this landscape, this might explain the focus on elite transport seen in the cart burials noted above. Yet, the timing of this Wolds-based intensification of Iron Age production, in the closing centuries of that period, matches a similar process at Heslington, far from Foulness sites. This suggests that, whatever the cause, it involved something deeper than just the availability of particular local resources. The forces involved were powerful enough, both on the Wolds and in the Vale, to ensure fundamental continuity of landholding into the Roman period, even if 'Romanised' ceramics circulated extensively and increasingly on these sites over time.

The tenacity of Iron Age landscape organisation in the face of Roman conquest of the region should not surprise us. Giles describes the way in which the fenced enclosures of the Wolds ladder settlements defined relationships between neighbouring households.[114] Equally, Atha and Roskams discuss how Iron Age rhythms of routine, for example in inter-household collective ditch digging alongside major trackway boundaries and intra-household renewal of individual enclosures,[115] would

have created long-standing 'taskscapes'[116] among these Wolds communities. Thus, defining and maintaining these systems would have been bound into the social fabric of those who farmed the landscape. Remaking that fabric would have been resisted on various levels: whatever the tablewares used and the artefacts worn, these underlying forces took many decades to undermine and replace. In the case of both the Wolds and the Heslington site, it was not until at least the end of the second century AD that such shift occurred (see section 9.3).

9.3 Transitioning within the Roman period

In the course of the Roman period, the focus of activity shifted significantly across the Heslington site, from a general emphasis on prehistoric and early Roman activity in the west, plus specific foci further east (see sections 3.3 and 9.2), to a concentration in the central area from the third century AD onwards. This is most graphically illustrated by the distribution of the total ceramic assemblage: only 1 per cent came from the west, nearly all of Late Iron Age or early Roman date; 6 per cent from the east, with an early Roman and mid Roman emphasis; and the remainder from the central zone, with a clear late Roman focus (see section 7.3). Chronological assemblages of securely grouped Roman ceramics back these trends, with 3 per cent dating from the late first to early second centuries AD (overlapping with handmade pottery of Iron Age date), 9 per cent to the late second to early third centuries, 23 per cent to the mid-third to early fourth centuries, and 60 per cent to the late fourth century. These proportions are striking, even when adjusted for excavated soil volumes, and match the chronological profile of non-ceramic finds (except in the fourth century, which may relate to trajectories of development in its closing decades: see section 9.4).

Within these broad-brush trends, ceramics show important patterning by sources (see section 7.2). Initially, Roman-period pottery supplies embodied a combination of local and imported wares, with little in between. From the second century AD, however, these gaps were plugged by intra-provincial wares, notably bowls and dishes from regional production centres such as Nene Valley and Mancetter-Hartshill, presumably traded via York. Disposal practices were patterned (see section 7.4), with flagons, cups and beakers differentially common in pits, drinking vessels discarded near buildings (perhaps linked to Gallic amphorae, although numbers concerned are small) and Nene Valley cups in particular curated and more likely to be discarded in boundary features; in sum, the ceramic types produced elsewhere in Britain, used for eating and, particularly, drinking, were gradually becoming more prominent and once on-site were used and then dumped in specific types of place. In this intra-provincial reorientation, the site matches an emerging dichotomy between soldier and civilian in York,[117] the Heslington profile matching that of the non-military areas. Thus, rather than cultural differences between 'African' legionaries and local civilians as once suggested,[118] the York trend seems likely to be a product of wider socio-economic forces.

During the third century AD, the mediating role of York seems to reduce. Thus, bowls inspired by native traditions, and later biconical vessels, become more common here than in either *colonia* or fortress. Wide-mouthed jars, thought to imply collective dining on stews rather than individualised eating, suggest that not just economic connections but eating practices were at stake, with local customs bypassing the urban core. Products from within Yorkshire, notably calcite-gritted jars then grey wares from Norton and Holme-on-Spalding-Moor[119] (ceramics for cooking and storage), continued this trend for urban/rural separation.

The fourth century AD was marked by the arrival of Crambeck wares, then calcite-gritted and fabric B18 jars. Both trends are common across the region, but the appearance of the latter jars, increasing at the expense of dishes and bowls elements, were slightly delayed at Heslington beyond the norm. Lid-seated Huntcliff-type jars might again imply changed food preparation or cooking strategies; types also rare in the fortress. One might expect greater social integration between soldier and civilian at this time, for example between genders with legalised marriage, something suggested on archaeological grounds by the finding of baby burials and women's jewellery within the fortress.[120] The implication of the Heslington evidence seems to be, instead, that food preparation there maintained these Roman/native distinctions.

In continuing to acquire small quantities of a broad range of traded fine wares throughout these late centuries, Heslington contrasts with lower status settlements such as Marton site 26 and Stockton-on-the-Forest.[121] At the same time, it resembles sites at Green Hammerton and West Lilling.[122] The former is claimed to be a villa and the latter definitely included pottery kilns. Hence, both have an enhanced status that they share with Heslington, sufficient to distinguish all three from the lowest-order sites. Yet, their fine ware profile is still insufficient to align with that of York and proven villas: Heslington seems, for the most part, to occupy an

intermediate position at this point, even if the jar to bowl/dish profile in the early fourth century AD lifts it, temporarily, to a position closer to urban and military centres and villas (fig 9.4).

Ceramic signatures may show complex changes in the relationship between the site and its environs, but general discard practices suggest overall continuity (see section 7.4). Thus, animal bones of Roman date, especially crania, were more commonly discarded in boundaries and trackway ditches than in other feature types, but all were highly fragmented, suggesting trampling and weathering after middening (except around building G112: see section 9.4). Discard of Roman ceramics also favoured boundary ditches, alongside spreads, again probably related to discard in a midden before disposal in manuring

Coinage appears to be part of the same background noise of deposition as the bone and pottery assemblages, with the understandable exception of coins deposited as hoards. Two hoards of fourth-century AD date were inserted into silting above the now disused Well 2 in the west of the site (see section 2.3). These were of a similar date to that recovered just below Heslington Hill when the university was first developed and to two others found nearby in the nineteenth century.[123] The circumstances of the latter's recovery, unfortunately, precludes any understanding of their context of deposition, in particular whether they too were placed in watery locations. What is clear is that a feature used throughout the Iron Age into the early Roman period, which had been pivotal not just for supplying water but also in organising field systems here, retained a significance long after it had ceased to operate as a water source (see section 8.3). This parallels the fourth-century AD waterhole at Shiptonthorpe, initially used to water stock following the placement of a shoe as a possible foundation deposit. After it silted up, articulated animal bones were laid out above this feature, perhaps placed ritually on a gravel platform.[124]

Beyond general assemblages, landscape organisation in the opening century of Roman rule, as already noted (see section 9.2), changed little. Before the start of the third century AD, however, there were very significant changes. The formerly vibrant Iron Age and early Roman zones in the west and the broadly contemporary enclosures along the 22m OD springline all fell out of use and the main focus of activity moved to the centre of the site – a major settlement shift. An east–west, ditched thoroughfare at least 115m long, Road 1, was laid out in the late-second or third centuries AD along that springline (see section 3.3). This routeway not only formalised movement along the hillside but, for the first time, served

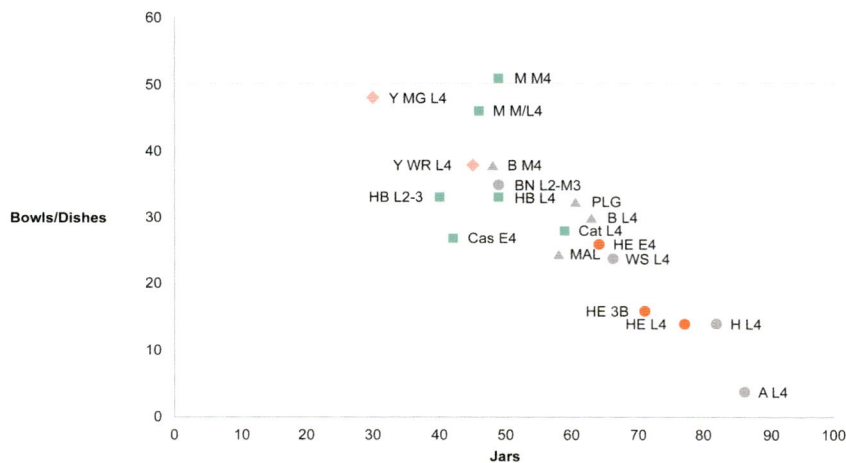

Fig 9.4 Relative proportions of bowls/dishes to jars at Heslington East (HE (red circles) in the mid-3rd century AD (3B), early 4th (E4) and late 4th (L4) centuries compared to a range of other site types (their dates abbreviated similarly). The latter comprise Marton (MAL: Leary unpublished d); Micklegate, York (Y MG: Monaghan 1997); Wellington Row, York (Y WR: Monaghan 1997); Healam Bridge (HB (L2-3): Leary unpublished e); Beadlam (B: Evans 1993); Castleford (Cas: Evans 1993); Catterick (Cat: Bell and Evans 2002); Malton (M: Evans 1993); Heslerton (H: Evans 1993); Healam Bridge (HB (L4): Evans 1993); Bank Newton (BN: Leary 2011); Green Hammerton (PLG: Leary unpublished d); Aberford (A: Leary unpublished f); Wattle Syke (WS: Leary 2013). Blue squares = urban and military sites; orange diamonds = York; grey triangles = villa/probable villa sites; grey circles = rural sites. *Drawing*: Neil Gevaux/Ruth Leary

to lead traffic off the site at either end, rather than simply navigate within it. Thus, it represents a new level of engagement with adjacent areas. At the same time, water sources underwent significant alteration (see section 2.3). The demise of Well 2 in the west has been noted above, taking place alongside that of Well 3 to its south. Along the springline itself, long-used Well 1 in the east, first used in the Bronze Age, if not before, and again in the Late Iron Age and early Roman period, now fell out of use, to be replaced by Wells 5 and 6 further west. The latter, in particular, seems to have influenced the laying out of a major enclosure (see section 3.4) to the north of Road 1 (fig 9.5).

Such investment in systematic movement might be expected to match other Roman roads in the vicinity of Heslington. Unfortunately, not all Roman thoroughfares said to exist on this side of York are founded on solid evidence. One account, for example, argues that a major route once ran south-east from the fortress towards the 'small town' of Throlam, near Holme-on-Spalding-Moor.[125] This idea is based solely on a straight parish boundary thought to be a long-lived landscape feature, yet no such road was evident in excavations beside York[126] and its very existence must now be doubted.[127] More convincing was a metalling of uncertain alignment, perhaps a minor Roman road, revealed at Belle Vue Street to the west of Heslington, which may have formed a route along the moraine here.[128] Even if such a routeway did exist, however, this was no guarantee of successful roadside development. In 2008, a sizeable area was exposed between the Heslington site and the possible

road at Belle Vue Street. Despite being on elevated, well-drained ground, and apparently near a spring in the environs of Heslington church, this archaeological work revealed no evidence of occupation, Roman or otherwise.[129]

The main impact of Heslington's Road 1 occurred in its immediate environs. Here, by *c* 250 AD, it formed the southern limit of a large enclosure (see section 3.3). Subsidiary north–south ditches within this enclosure defined a track channelling movement down the hillside to the road, whilst east–west elements created a crossroads with this channel, perhaps using natural cobbles here to aid mobility. Macrofossils suggest damp ground and grasslands in the vicinity of these subsidiary ditches, perhaps derived from grassy field margins or plants collected from grassland or meadows as hay for fodder. This, alongside the general configurations, suggest that the new enclosure and its internal divisions were designed to control the movement of stock. Other discrete enclosures to west and east of the crossroads may also be related to pastoral needs.

There are additional signs that other activities in this central zone were becoming more organised at this time. Thus, early in the third century AD, three badly-preserved perinatal burials were inserted into natural geology on the northern margins of the site beyond the enclosed zone (see section 8.4). The best-preserved inhumation, lying in a foetal position, contained nails and a possible coffin fitting. The second, nearby, yielded a rolled lead sheet and a fragment of glass. The third example was too disturbed by later activity for anything

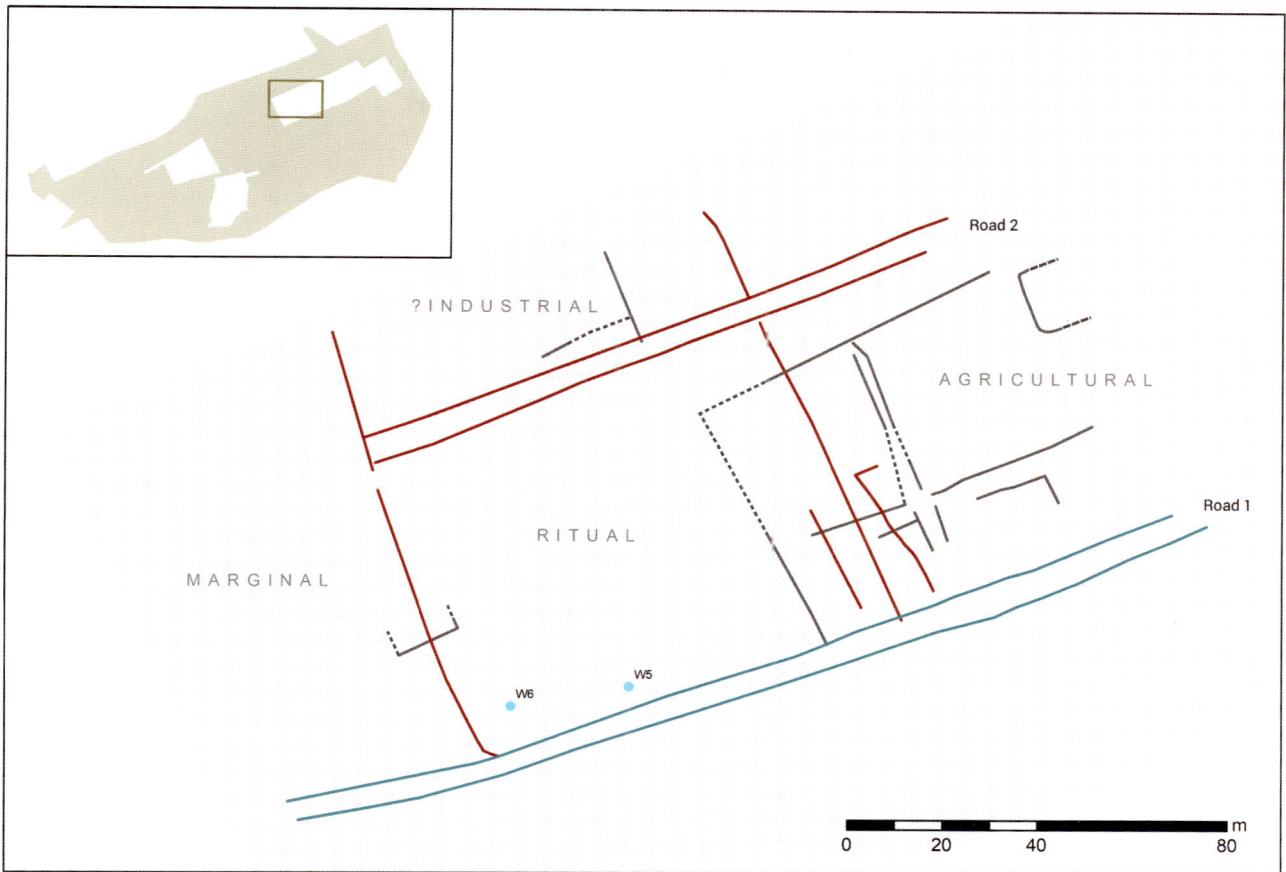

Fig 9.5 Summary of main transitions within the Roman period, in which a main enclosure with central crossroads (grey) north of Road 1 (blue) was partially replaced by a larger 'ritual' enclosure in the west, with Road 2 added to its north (all in red). *Drawing*: Helen Goodchild

other than the recognition of human bone, post-excavation.

Grave goods for young people are less standardised than for adults,[130] and Cool has argued that the very young may have needed increased protection in death.[131] The choice of lead here could thus be deliberate.[132] Lead 'scrolls' are known as grave goods elsewhere,[133] one certainly being a lead curse tablet.[134] The Heslington cylinder, although not a tablet, could have been strung as an amulet. Even the iron nails in the first burial could have amuletic significance.[135] Extra nails are often found in cremation burials where functional explanations are lacking.[136]

Thus, rather than a product of casual infanticide, as has been suggested in other cases,[137] these new-born babies had been buried with care. Their positioning, just beyond the activities of the living community, suggests a deliberate choice to maintain links to that community, presumably first and foremost with, and thus via, the mother.[138] At the upper echelons of Roman society, funerary monuments convey information on individual lives, expressing affiliations and gendered behaviour, especially in frontier regions.[139] The driving force at

Heslington, in contrast, seems to be the need to signify the 'failure' of a small section of rural society to reproduce itself, and the grief, individual and collective, which would have resulted.

The zone in which the perinates were buried was disturbed when human activity extended into this area, suggesting that, whilst burial of the new-borns was carried out respectfully, other material needs remained paramount in the longer term. Even at this later stage, however, human burial was an integral part of landscape claims. Two co-aligned inhumations were inserted here later in the third century AD (see section 8.4, fig 8.4), their position then influencing boundary development into much later decades. One, a man aged at least forty-six years, was badly preserved but had teeth showing signs of calculus and caries. The other, a woman with a similar age range, was better preserved. She wore shoes in death and her teeth showed not only signs of calculus and caries, but of hypoplasia, suggesting nutritional stress in childhood. She also exhibited evidence for brucellosis, perhaps through the consumption of unprocessed dairy products, and of degenerative joints, maybe related to habitual squatting. Clearly, these individuals had led hard lives, presumably a result of working the land in the immediate locality: the (sometimes romantic) notion that communally-performed 'taskscapes'[140] generated social cohesion within and between household units (see above and section 8.4) should not blind us to the rigours of the work involved.

A final issue concerns the driver behind the need to set out a road and new landscape divisions across this part of the site. Several 'military' finds seem to be related to the initial development of the northern hillside, and some others to its reorganisation late in the fourth century AD (see section 9.4). More generally, brooch types and baldric mounts from elsewhere on the site, plus the profile of samian ware imports, suggest army connections here in the late second or third centuries AD, roughly when the above changes took place. Beyond these artefactual hints, however, the features concerned seem very much a product of local, agricultural and pastoral needs. Historically, commentators on Roman Britain have emphasised the pivotal role of the army in promoting 'Romanisation'.[141] What the Heslington evidence suggests is that, in so far as the Roman state and its armed personnel played a role in this landscape, it was in deploying surveying expertise, rather than in directing landscape exploitation. Although lacking any long-term military connections, the laying out of Road 1 at Heslington represented a qualitative change in that it was accompanied by a system of enclosures involving the movement of animals off-site. This contrasts with simply controlling their access to water within the landscape, as seen in landscape configurations from prehistory up to the third century AD.

This Heslington evidence provides an interesting comparison with that at Shiptonthorpe, where a Roman road was laid out by the mid-second century AD, after tree clearances but in an already-developed Iron Age landscape. Military finds may have derived from soldiers using the road, but the thoroughfare itself seems to have been maintained locally.[142] Clearly, Roman roads can be symbolic of centralised power and present an opportunity for further development: a source for information, cultural interaction or new forms of consumption. Yet, a road may have only 'novelty' value, with adjacent activities remaining embedded in pre-Roman social relations.[143] More generally, a combination of pre-existing trajectories and the need for new communications networks seem to have driven development at Heslington, rather than purely military factors.

Faunal data (see sections 4.1 and 7.3) clearly has a role to play in the wider exploration of this landscape in the late Roman period. Apart from the main domesticates, goat, goose and red deer were all being dismembered for meat removal at that time. Red deer antler was used here in various periods, the absence of roe deer after the Iron Age perhaps suggesting forest clearance and/or over-hunting by that point (see section 2.2). Generally, neither these animals nor fish were of great significance in the Roman period (the absence of such fauna in sieved samples of this date implies that such scarcity is not a simple product of recovery methods). Unfortunately, pre-Roman faunal samples are too few to allow meaningful conclusions concerning the use of 'wild' resources beforehand, so it is difficult to decide whether or not their general avoidance in the Roman period represents a change of attitude.

Alongside Road 1 and its associated enclosure, greater investment in animal control at this time is suggested by evidence for penning elbow in goats, backed up by finds of bridle bits and an ox goad (as ever with artefactual evidence, we are dealing with small numbers of objects, but the fact that they are found at all, presumably after being discarded rather than recycled, might imply more widespread usage). Equally, specialised carcass reduction, whether for marrow or stock, alongside the large-scale dumping of bones, shows that processing of animals was also changing at this time (the skinning seen on one cow and several horse bones was derived, however, from 'specialised' deposition in Well 7, and may thus be atypical: see section 8.6). The wide distribution of several ceramic cheese presses, mostly of late Roman date, implies that the processing of milk products was also taking place here. That said, not all animal processing involved innovative practices: evidence for smoking of cattle scapulae (see fig 7.9) comes from both pre-Roman and Roman contexts.

Within the main domesticates using this landscape, pigs were killed at the optimal point for meat consumption, as would be expected. Other than swine, the Roman period is often portrayed as marking an end to an Iron Age emphasis on sheep over cattle.[144] This trend is indeed evident at Heslington (see table 4.1), but based on only small assemblages for the pre-Roman and early Roman periods. More significant, then, might be the point, based on an end to the transmission of congenital problems, when cattle reproduction here moved from a small, 'founder population' to a much greater level of interbreeding, thus adopting the kinds of strategies seen in medieval and modern cattle populations. This change, implying an opening up of herd management and perhaps signalling the arrival of a market in beef, only occurred in the late Roman period. Whether such diversification involved the import of new breeding stock into Britain, as has been claimed for one part of south-east Britain,[145] is unclear. What is certain, however, is that this change was happening at about the time that Road 1 and its associated enclosure were set out.

Presumably, part of any such market would have been orientated on the nearby inhabitants of York. It is striking, therefore, that faunal assemblages from both fortress and *colonia* show little evidence for being supplied with selected joints of meat.[146] The scale of beef production at Heslington may have increased and diversified from the third century AD, with that proportion now consumed elsewhere facilitated by the laying out of Road 1. Yet, York could not dictate culling patterns in its immediate hinterland:[147] if this constituted a dedicated beef market, its reach remained limited.[148] The profile of sheep at this time suggests a breeding population at Heslington, the absence of lambs matching their presence at York. Yet, even this profile may not prove that 'market demand' *per se* from York was dictating sheep culling patterns at Heslington. It is equally possible that the latter's inability to over-winter large flocks of new-born animals required the slaughter of a significant proportion of the new arrivals and that York was an obvious source of willing consumers.

Finally, there is no evidence for an increase in animal height in these centuries, as might be expected with innovative breeding programmes. Animals may have been produced and moved in new ways, and perhaps their carcasses processed (see section 4.1) and discarded (see section 7.4) differently, but change did not extend to developing the productive base of the pastoral economy or to dis-embedding the fundamentals of stock management. Overall, the pre-existing drive to use animals for manure production and traction, then cull superfluous beasts as necessary, remained paramount throughout the Roman period.

As noted above, cropping regimes were an integral part of animal husbandry strategies at Heslington (see section 4.2) and can therefore be considered in relation to the above trends. This evidence, unlike its faunal counterpart, has sufficient data sets from prehistoric horizons to distinguish meaningful patterning, as has been described previously (see section 9.2). In summary, it showed that hulled barley, and some spelt and emmer wheat, were cultivated in the Iron Age contexts at Heslington, a profile paralleled by contemporary sites in the region.

The Roman period here is distinguished by an increased emphasis on spelt wheat and the presence of 'bread wheat', thus matching evidence from other sites transitioning into the Roman period, such as Dalton Parlours[149] and Dragonby.[150] The presence of large quantities of 'bread wheat' at Roman period sites is, however, unusual. The rich assemblages at Heslington are probably the result of parching accidents in crop dryers, and thus are unlikely to be representative of the agricultural economy as a whole. Yet, this assemblage does demonstrate that 'bread wheat' was an important crop here during the later Roman period, not simply a contaminant of other crops, and may suggest innovation[151] and a higher status than other contemporary sites in the region.[152]

'Bread wheat' produces higher yields and is winter hardy, yet more vulnerable to pests and disease and requires a greater degree of soil fertility than other wheats.[153] It is not a Roman introduction, being present in small amounts on Iron Age sites,[154] but hulled barley and spelt wheat always dominate such earlier contexts.[155] Beyond the specifics of the crop record, taxa associated with fertile disturbed ecotypes were evident in late Roman levels in the vicinity of damp springs and ditches, perhaps attesting the increasingly fertile conditions that 'bread wheat' cultivation would require. Finally, such a change might be hinted at in the finding of a rake, originally with wooden beam and stepped prongs.[156] This must have been a common tool in such a landscape in all periods, but our one example derives from a late Roman context. If not simple happenstance (see argument above on bridle bits and a goad with respect to pastoral production), it could suggest an intensified cropping regime.

Certain physical features at Heslington can be directly related to crop processing, most obviously two late Roman crop driers, one square and the other T-shaped (see section 4.2). Such features, widespread in the south of Britain,[157] are also evident across the north, for example at Wharram Percy,[158] Nostell Priory,[159] Thurnscoe[160] and Catterick.[161] Where datable, these northern examples belong to the third or fourth centuries AD, thus being consistent with late intensification of processing. The greater incidence of stinking chamomile at Heslington, a plant of heavy clay and clay loam soils, may also be related to agricultural expansion in the later Roman period. Its increasing occurrence in archaeobotanical assemblages of Roman and later date in England has been linked to the introduction of plough technology that would have enabled more efficient cultivation of heavier clay soils.[162]

Such a change is also suggested by the wood that fuelled these driers. Those at Heslington used oak, a long-burning species producing good heat, which must have been supplied on a regularised basis in order to make the investment in a drier worthwhile (the Nostell Priory feature used hazel, also an excellent fuel for such contexts[163]). Some support for such a role for oak is provided by evidence from the Shiptonthorpe site; here, the most common timber species is blackthorn, thought to come from trimming underwood/hedges rather than from woodland management, yet oak, the second most popular timber source, was derived from coppicing on a short, 3–5-year cycle.[164] Such systematic supply on a short cycle implies that this species might have had as important a role here as at Heslington. There are, therefore, several grounds to suggest the intensification of rural production from the third century AD: 'bread wheat' becoming more significant; the arrival of more fertile ecotypes; greater investment in crop drying; and perhaps regularisation of timber supply.

A similar case can be made for milling (see section 4.2). The various types of hand-mill seen here in pre-Roman and early-Roman assemblages resemble those from civil sites in East Yorkshire, in particular Newbridge Quarry near Pickering.[165] From the third century AD, however, these were increasingly replaced by large millstones, perhaps driven by mechanical power. This would have allowed larger quantities of grain to be processed in less time,[166] and could be viewed simply as a move towards greater efficiency. Yet, the change from hand-milling, presumably at a household level, to larger-scale processing, with millstones set up at central points, was also an opportunity to gain more control of crop processing, The Shiptonthorpe roadside settlement may be another example of such a mechanism being in operation. The sheer volume of Roman querns found there suggested to the excavators that, by the end of the Roman period, flour was being exported from the site, perhaps accompanied by the removal of surplus sheep.[167] They also proposed that other activities, such as small-scale smithing and meat processing, plus evidence for writing and the circulation of coins, indicate that this landscape was now incorporated into regional taxation systems.

Interestingly, at York, large millstones are rare in both the *colonia* and, especially, the fortress, suggesting that both soldiers and civilians there received rural outputs as flour or bread, not as grain. Importantly, the granary known from Coney Street, just outside the fortress, fell out of use before the end of the third century AD,[168] at about the time that millstones were first evident at Heslington. Perhaps the risk-buffering mechanism of a granary, needed at the start of the Roman period, was no longer required once processing could be controlled at arm's length, reflected in the move from hand to mechanical milling. This would give the state a clear role in agricultural practice, facilitating the extraction of surplus from the landscape in the process. If this claim, admittedly based on a series of tentative lines of argument, is accepted, then much more than inserting

new ditches was at stake at Heslington: landscape reorganisation was part of a battle over who managed and controlled cropping regimes, and agricultural practices more generally.

Such a perspective puts into context the general tenacity of pre-Roman landholding systems noted previously (see section 9.2). Change not only threatened inherited social relations within and between households, but also the control of rural surplus on which those social structures depended. This pattern in cropping practices parallels evidence for the similar intensification in broadly contemporary faunal profiles and for the first indications of roadways being set out to allow movement of people, stock and, no doubt, other products such as wheat off the site. Thus, a package of changes were involved. Two things should be noted about this process, however. Firstly, the attempt to impose external authority on the landscape, if correctly interpreted, is only evident after the fortress at York had been in place for at least a century. If doing so was part of an imperial hinterland policy, it was long deferred, for whatever reasons. Secondly, it was only partially successful: cropping regimes may have been re-orientated and communication infrastructure developed, but, in meat production at least, there is no evidence for improving animal sizes and most beasts were still dispatched here only after a long life in the rural economy.

Thus far, the main emphasis here has been on changes in Heslington's rural economy and their relationship with central authority beyond the site. At around the start of the fourth century AD, however, a new enclosure was created here (see section 3.4) and, as will be argued below, this was very much a non-agricultural imposition on the landscape. By the start of the fourth century AD, an east–west cobbled routeway with flanking ditches, Road 2, had been set out along the hillside 70m north of Road 1, with a 90m-wide enclosure created between these two thoroughfares. A large millstone grit block, suggesting ambitious craftsmanship, lay beside the road (see section 6.3) and, although not found *in situ*, might have once formed an associated water channel. The limits of this enclosed zone were defined to east and west by substantial ditches, with subsidiary features on both sides. Entrance into this new compound in the east was controlled via a 2.5m-wide, eastern timber gateway, whilst that in the west was mediated by a masonry tower and associated inhumations in marked graves, their skulls seemingly nailed into place (see figs 8.5–8.7). More broadly, access to water in this newly cordoned-off zone was retained by incorporating Well 6 at its south-west corner, yet the crossroads for stock movement to its east, argued above to be a pivotal element in the third-century landscape, was now superseded entirely.

The tower only survived as a cobbled foundations (see fig 8.5), but stonework later used to line a well elsewhere on the site included material re-used from a single structure employing *opus quadratum* construction (see fig 2.7). This is a rare technique in Britain, confined mostly to military bridges on Hadrian's Wall,[169] classical temples, such as Bath,[170] and mausolea, for example that at Shorden Brae, Corbridge.[171] Thus, it may be that this tower was also a mausoleum (the fact that its superstructure was then recycled within the fourth century would imply that the original building was in use for decades, not centuries). Such a mortuary monument would parallel other evidence for prestigious Roman burials from the vicinity, for example the female sealed with gypsum placed in a stone coffin recorded east of St Paul's church in Heslington, one of several 'Interesting Remains in Heslington Field' noted by Wellbeloved following disturbance by gravel quarrying in 1831.[172] The coffin was presented to the Yorkshire Philosophical Society, whilst a second coffin was then used as a planter outside Heslington Hall. Given these imperfect recovery conditions, any less monumental burials here would have been missed (an isolated, unaccompanied inhumation south-west of Siward's How (YAT site 1980.1029) is an example of what would be recorded today). Hence it is unclear whether the stone coffin was part of a cemetery or the isolated burial of a prestigious woman.

Within the new enclosure on the Heslington site, the zone just south of Road 2 was terraced for the construction of a masonry-founded building with hypocaust (see fig 8.9), its timber colonnade to the south overlooking the lower slopes of the enclosure and beyond (see section 8.5). The lines of complete pots (see fig 8.10) inserted immediately south-east of this structure imply ritual offerings here, whilst an associated burial just to its west (see fig 8.11) was of a male with a grave good of a spindle whorl made from a curated Ebor Ware vessel. He was a frail individual whose medical condition included degenerative changes suggesting tuberculosis: this is someone who enjoyed 'care in the community' for long enough to allow a disabling disease to become apparent on his bones. The fact of having to be cared for might explain the choice of a spindle whorl, a grave good conventionally linked to a 'female' pursuit. We might wonder whether this was someone who, of necessity, found himself mostly in the company of care-giving women, a context which thus came to define his gender in death. And was such care even repaid, in part, by his involvement with textile production? Being catered for by the rest of society when partly disabled need not mean being unproductive.

Hence on a variety of grounds, notably atypical burials, monumental and prestigious construction, this development marks itself out from all previous activities on the site. Further, it incorporates features lacking any obvious, material links to the productive exploitation of the landscape and moves away from critical features of the rural economy, as shown by the demise of the crossroads for stock movement (above). This enclosed zone is also different in its associated discard practices. General disposal on the site, as noted previously (see section 7.4), mostly comprised middening of artefacts and animal bones, then spreading them further through manuring. To the south of the hypocaust building described above, beside a possible springhead, lay an area that generated evidence for using lead alloy to repair pottery. This probably represents specialist activity rather than an act of structured deposition. More interestingly, the filling of the eastern boundary ditch of the new enclosure included the mixed burial of a pig with an old head and a younger body (see section 8.5, fig 8.13). Other animal burials of both Roman and earlier date are known along the springline, for example the deposition of sheep/goat skulls and feet bones in the Bronze Age. Yet, although these interments may still comprise deliberate ritual acts, they can be understood in terms of the dynamics of conventional animal husbandry. The mixing of ages, in contrast, suggests a particular concern with animals reaching maturity, and thus with fertility (mingling young and old is one thing, the finding of a sheep body and calf head at Tiel-Passewaaijse, Holland,[173] takes matters a stage further; it could imply a questioning of animal classification itself, perhaps re-evaluating the relationship between nature and culture).

Concerning Roman approaches to animal fertility in general, it has already been noted that production of the main domesticates was being intensified and reorganised in the Heslington landscape, but that this did not extend to programmes to breed larger animals. Here it is interesting to note that, on the basis of metrical data, the Roman period evidences the emergence of two distinct dog sizes.[174] This development, interpreted as indicating a distinction between hunting and lap dogs, would thus imply the rearing of pets. If correct, it shows that Rome, on occasion, had the ability to create dedicated breeding programmes. Yet this intellectual energy went into creating what were, essentially, statements of prestige, but not into improving the animals that supplied manure, traction and meat in the landscape. This would constitute an important statement about priorities under Rome, and the limitations on its ability, or inclination, to intervene in the fundamentals of pastoral production.

Unusual deposition in this eastern boundary is also

evident in other assemblages. As noted above, large boundary features favour certain types of ceramic find. Yet, within such general trends, this ditch yielded *tazze* and abnormally high proportions of samian ware, plus items connected with transport (see section 8.5). Some of this material could simply be due to the character of adjacent activities, but the samian sherds, long outmoded when deposited, were concentrated in the ditch terminals either side of the gated access, a critical point of transition. The same ditch contained one of only two fragments of head pot from the site (see fig 8.12), here comprising much of its face (the other example, from a ditch to the north, included only part of the incised bosses forming the hair in such a vessel, so may be less significant). This choice of facial feature is paralleled at Piercebridge, where sherds of a head pot with lip, eye and nose features were thought to form a 'ritual' deposit in a ditch.[175] This vessel type, first evidenced in burial contexts in the Rhineland, derives more often in Britain from domestic ritual contexts and has been interpreted as linked to military influence, a 'Germanic' link perhaps retained into later centuries.[176] Whatever its origins, the fabric of later Yorkshire products suggests local sources, and perhaps an equally local protective deity,[177] rather than a product of African military identities (see above on such military identities in general).[178] Hence this fourth-century enclosure marks itself out not only in the buildings and associated burials involved in its construction, but also in its use for pottery repair and in the distinctive ceramic materials deposited into its eastern boundary ditch, especially near its associated gateway.

In contrast to the above, the zones beyond this new enclosure generated no such evidence for dispersed ritual activity. To the north of Road 2, dumps of building materials included three *in situ* flue tiles implying an early specialised production area with, to its north-east, fenced-off cobbled platforms with hearths of much later date (see section 5.4). Further east, similar features suggest artisan activity stretching along both sides of the road, some of these activities perhaps predating that thoroughfare but others demonstrably not. In the second half of the fourth century AD or later, a still more concentrated production zone operated here, starting with the construction of a badly-preserved rectangular, timber-framed building with a stone tile roof, G106 (see section 6.4). The gully and hearth(s) inside it suggest an industrial or agricultural function, the building resembling, in scale and character, a broadly contemporary aisled structure at Shiptonthorpe. The better preservation of the latter demonstrated structured use of internal space (a cleaned zone near the road, and less clean part elsewhere), plus infant and animal burials

associated with boundaries.[179] It is unclear whether the Heslington building embodied dualities such as living/dead, male/female and civil/private. The proposed manufacturing function of this zone is supported by the general distribution of artisanal residues, for example the lead sheets, caulking and associated runoff coming from this zone, plus a knife blade and a carpenter's chisel or smith's punch (see section 6.3). The latter two items imply that iron was now common enough not to require recycling, something reinforced by the discard of iron nails and wooden stakes in much greater numbers than hitherto in these late levels.

The zone to the west of the new enclosure remained marginal, a place where trees grew and sinuous gullies formed. On its opposite side, in contrast, farming activity may have continued unabated, with some other evidence here appearing to attest the continuing prosperity and productive capacity of this part of the site. Thus, a range of CMB were derived from this eastern zone, including roofing tiles, part of a possible chimney and worn floor tiles. The fabrics of these items generally match the profile seen in York at this time. That said, the number of new signature marks found on Heslington roof tiles and not previously recorded in York might suggest dedicated supply, rather than simply feeding off urban mechanisms. So, rather than recycled from York to be used as hearth bases or channel lining in manufacturing at Heslington, these items may have been used in prestigious construction somewhere nearby in the fourth century.

Such indications of prestigious habitation cannot solve an underlying lacuna for the site. The evidence described above has been used to argue that, when the focus of activity shifted here in the third and fourth centuries AD, roads were set out, the production of crops and animals intensified and a vibrant industry occupied the zone north of Road 2: people were working here. What is not at all clear is where these people lived. The simple explanations are either that such habitation left no traces in the excavated sectors or, more likely, that they lay beyond those areas. Arguments have already been rehearsed on why the changes seen in the late Roman period would not have been simply accepted by producers, but struggled over. As Roman power was, it seems, finally successful, it is possible that producers were then removed from this landscape and lived elsewhere. If so, this would not fit easily alongside the positioning of human burials inserted into this landscape. Both neonates interred at the start of the third century and adults some decades later resonate with landscape organisation at those times. Equally, reverence afforded to the former and the hard life indicated by the latter suggest they were part of that local community. If they were dispossessed of landscape control and lived elsewhere, why would they be returned to that landscape in death?

Whatever the details of habitation, it is clear that, although little altered here at the start of 'the Roman period', from *c* 200 AD, a series of step changes occurred at Heslington. These included alterations to ceramic supplies and the regionalisation of associated exchange systems and a shift in settlement focus to the centre of the site, using boundaries to define new landholding, sometimes integrated with burial practices. The new boundaries facilitated intensification of stock control and the moving of surplus off-site, alongside a greater emphasis on cattle (but not stock improvement). Similar intensification is evident in 'bread wheat' production, the latter perhaps related to the introduction of mechanical mills, arguably as a mechanism for the state to intervene in the landscape and draw it fully into taxation systems. Early in the fourth century AD, a ritual enclosure with monumentalised entrance arrangements and 'Romanised' central building, both associated with atypical burials, was imposed in this area, the first feature not directly related to agricultural processes in this landscape. Beyond this, however, stock was still managed and crops processed. The surplus thus generated was sufficient to tie Heslington into local, regional and even some intra-provincial pottery exchange systems, with a hint that its ceramic profile in the early fourth century AD (see fig 9.3) aligned more with signatures seen at villas, towns and military centres than mundane rural settlements. Although the latter prominence may not have lasted through that century, Heslington remained a vibrant economic entity for most of that period.

The notion of a second/third century AD watershed, as suggested for Heslington, is by no means uncommon in the Yorkshire region. Halkon notes, for example, that economic development is most evident in Roman East Yorkshire from that time,[180] the point at which long-lived 'ladder settlements' on the Wolds were finally replaced by new systems of landholding,[181] and perhaps in landscapes beyond this.[182] Equally, Ottaway's recent description of Roman Yorkshire as a whole,[183] if read in a certain way,[184] presents a lot of corresponding evidence for the timing of such a change. It can also be argued that this period marked a fundamental shift in the character of town–hinterland relationships generally within the region.[185]

Such pervasive change suggests that much more than local dynamics are at play here: it could be argued that the third century AD is the time when imperial power first managed to impose its authority on pre-existing Yorkshire society. Even within this model, however, there seem to be limits to such imposition in terms of Heslington's pastoral economy, for example the absence of full blown market in

meat and lack of evidence for stock improvement. Also, as the ceramic evidence shows, change was a two-way process, with intra-provincial, then regional, dynamics quickly overtaking a simple core–periphery set of relationships between Heslington and York.

The fact that a fundamental shift at this date is rarely acknowledged in general commentaries must owe a lot to the impact of chronological classifications based on the very notion of a 'Roman period' in Britain. The concept of an era designated as 'Late Antiquity' is much more common in continental scholarship than here. Such a category may have been constructed in relation to political imperatives concerning a 'United Europe',[186] but does resonate with patterning in archaeological evidence from Yorkshire. In any case, AD 200 is the date which Esmonde-Cleary has chosen to start his recent account of the Roman West,[187] something that would accord closely with the Heslington sequence. His choice of end date, AD 500, is something to be explored, implicitly, in the next section.

9.4 Transitioning between the late Roman and the sub-Roman/Anglian periods

The above discussion described processes of site development at Heslington from a sea-change at the start of the third century AD, when settlement shifted to the centre of the site and landscape exploitation increased, into the fourth century AD, at the start of which a monumentalised ritual enclosure was set out over part of this zone. This sequence of development naturally raises the question of whether or not such trajectories continued into the fifth century and beyond, a time usually seen as a turning point in social and economic relations in northern Britain.

Given the complexities of dating in these critical decades – C14 dates have too much latitude to chart developments with the necessary accuracy; material culture such as pottery is unchanging or terminally residual; new coin types are no longer circulating in the region, or even arriving in the province – one way to explore such trajectories is to consider general assemblage profiles, most obviously in ceramics. Ceramic supply at Heslington towards the end of the fourth century shows a much greater emphasis on jar types, a common regional signature which thus created an assemblage close to the high proportions of jars seen in Late Iron Age horizons some centuries earlier. At Heslington, however, supply of such jars seems to have stopped before a clear peak of those made in calcite-gritted fabrics, the type of profile that would be expected for any settlement running into the fifth century (see section 7.1). On the other hand, although they are proportionately under-represented, the site did receive *some* very late fourth-century types, notably handmade jars of Huntcliff type and in fabric B18. Also, occupation could simply have continued here using older types of containers due, for whatever reason, to a relative lack of access to enough of this material. The finding of a curated flagon in the latest levels of Well 6 may be an example of this pressure on supply.

Interestingly, the overall profile of non-ceramic finds from the site, which had matched that of the pottery throughout most of the Roman period, began to diverge from it in the course of the fourth century AD. This is evident in the relative paucity of personal ornaments such as copper alloy bracelets, small glass beads and datable vessel glass (and even the late glass vessels that can be identified at Heslington are sometimes trimmed, suggesting that they may have been brought onto the site for recycling, rather than domestic use: see section 7.1). This relative lack of provably fourth-century small finds is equally true of unstratified material recovered by metal detecting in topsoil, suggesting a real pattern rather than material in uppermost horizons being lost to medieval/modern plough disturbance. Of course, such trend need not suggest a reduced population – personal ornaments might simply be better curated – but it at least implies a change of site status, cultural preferences or depositional practices at this time.

Another indicator of change in these closing decades, which might also be interpreted as stress on supply mechanisms, here of food, derives from faunal evidence (see section 4.1). Red deer, whose antlers had been used in various earlier periods as a source of raw material for artefact production, were first used as food only in the very latest Roman levels (though the sample is biased by the bones deposited in Well 7: see section 8.6 and below). The previously-noted move from an emphasis on sheep to cattle, underway from the start of the Roman period (see table 4.1), but perhaps especially from the third century AD (see section 9.3), also reached its conclusion at this point. The profile at Heslington now resembled the high proportion of cattle seen on central sites in both fortress and *colonia* in York.[188] Although very old animals still comprised 30 per cent of the cattle total, it seems possible that prime beef stock was now being exported from the site.

Among other domesticates, sub-adult sheep were also in evidence, patterning in their culling perhaps implying smaller breeding flocks, with meat now being valued over secondary wool or milk. Pigs, despite being bred only for

meat, show an increased proportion of sub-adults at this late date. Even if simply due to random survival or particular discard practices, this perplexing pattern implies an uneconomic production process (admittedly something easily corrected in pigs, which can be quickly bred back to former levels). It does make an interesting comparison with the parts of two old sows thrown into Well 7 (see section 8.6), which suggests that a concern with maintaining pork production remained important to farming strategy in this landscape. Further afield, the 'small pig horizon' under York Minster, perhaps evidence for feasting there into the sub-Roman period,[189] implies unsustainable consumption practices: urban hinterland strategies may have been under pressure. Finally, evidence for horses, although based on a limited data set, was lower in the Roman period than in prehistoric horizons levels (see table 4.1), yet a large shale pendant from a very late Roman level, perhaps used to decorate a horse harness (see section 4.1), implies that these animals may have had some considerable status at this late stage.

The above trends from the closing decades of the fourth century AD and beyond indicate a pottery supply increasingly focusing on storage jars and diverging from non-ceramic finds profiles. Pressure at this time on the exploitation of pigs and red deer for food, just as cattle, and perhaps sheep, show signs of developing a market in meat, suggest fundamental tensions in process of landscape exploitation. It is possible that, as certain food sources were being supplied to customers off-site, local inhabitants had to move towards alternative sources, and did so in ways that were not sustainable in the long term. At the same time, the general physical, stratigraphic and spatial character of the site does not seem to change: most areas continued to function broadly along the lines established at the start of the third century AD.

One zone north of Road 2 provides an exception to this picture of continuity, however (fig 9.6). At a late stage it was terraced and new boundaries were set out at an oblique angle to both the hillside and the earlier landscape divisions (see section 3.5). This innovation in landholding seemed to obey both earlier inhumations to the east (see section 8.4) and the position of pre-existing, stone-roofed building G106 to the south (see section 6.4). Hence, it seems likely to comprise only a local modification of the wider landscape. Within it lay a stone-founded kiln (see fig 5.8: repaired and so probably long-lived), a clay extraction pit and a range of more ephemeral hearths, all indicating artisanal production. At certain stages, these features became sealed by more general soil accumulations, only for these deposits, in turn, to have further manufacturing features inserted into them (see section 5.4).

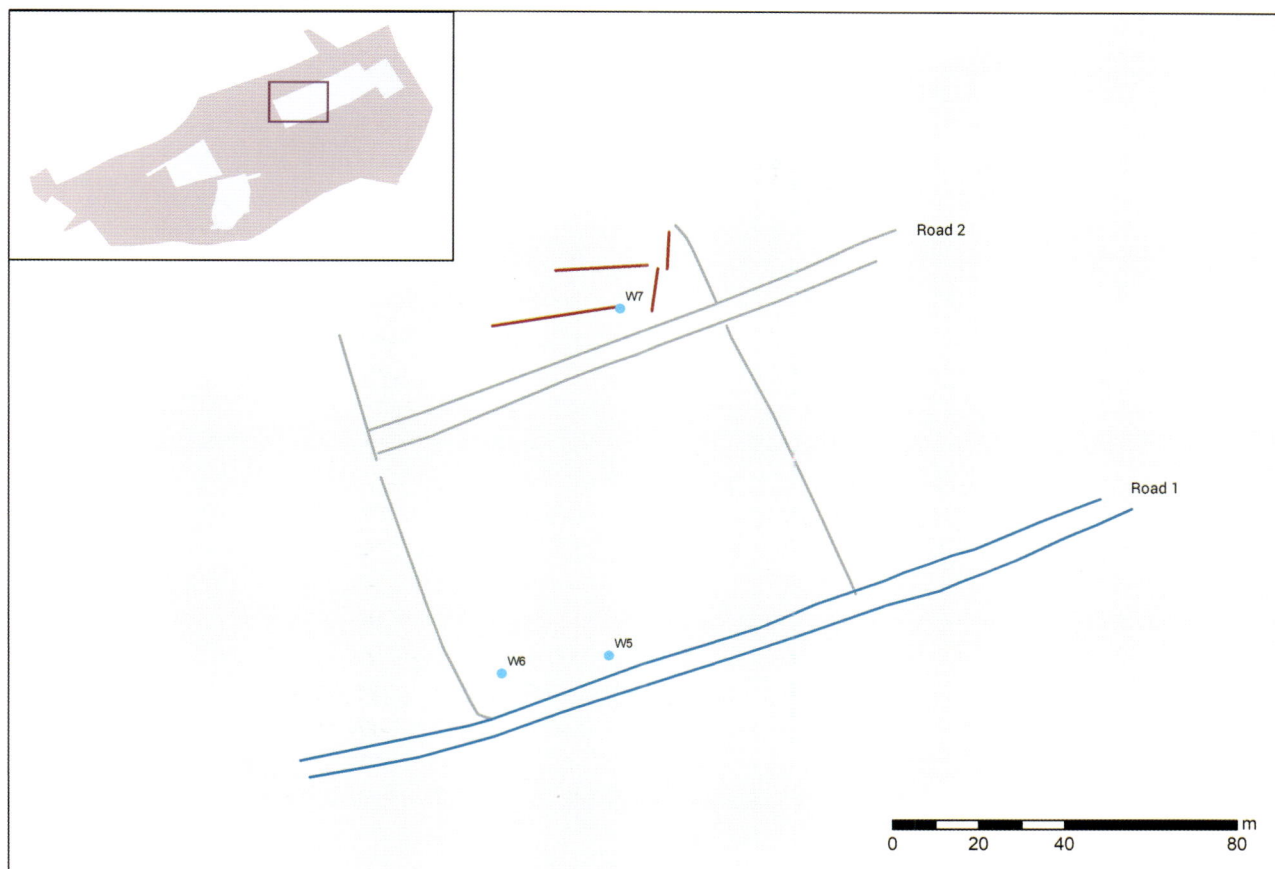

Fig 9.6 Summary of main transitions at the end of the Roman period, in which Road 1 (blue), and Road 2 plus 'ritual' enclosure (grey) were retained, but a differently-aligned system of terraced landholding (red) defined a new organisation of a localised zone at the northern edge of the site. *Drawing*: Helen Goodchild

The uppermost elements in this sequence had ceramic profiles of very late fourth-century types and, given that the start of manufacturing here dates to the second half of the fourth century AD, such activity probably extended to the end of that century if not beyond. The initial developments here were clearly set up in relation to existing boundary ditches in the vicinity but, over time, these limits were increasingly ignored and the final features seem to have been used in what was, essentially, an open area. There is much less residuality in assemblages from these very latest deposits than in those below, suggesting that, once formed, they underwent little further disturbance, presumably due to protection by the colluvium of medieval date that formed above them across the hillside (see section 2.1).

Finds from these horizons attest the significance of production processes here (see section 5.4). These include a bone rough-out, increased amounts of hammerscale (mostly flake, but some spheroidal, the latter perhaps suggesting welding), vitrified hearth linings and bottoms, and concentrations of iron slag, slagged shale and lead alloy spillages. Given the profusion of successive features

and concentrations of residues, it is surprising that the proportion and frequency of oak in these late levels reduces; one might expect it to be employed in such heating processes. It may be that manufacturing at this intensive level could not be sustained by local woodland. Charred plant macrofossils suggest the possible use of turves as fuel for the first time at this late stage, perhaps a strategy to get around this problem (although turves are hardly the ideal way to create high temperatures for metal working). Although this newly defined sector as a whole concentrated on manufacture, the fills of a nearby late ditch yielded evidence for charred heather, sedge and, critically, culm bases (see section 5.5), suggesting that agricultural production continued in the immediate vicinity. The manufacturing focus, even if limited in extent, could explain the reduced emphasis on personal ornaments in late assemblages noted above; artisans may have had different tastes and needs from the general population (although their ceramic preferences do not appear to have changed: see above).

Stone-lined Well 7 (see section 2.3) was inserted into this reconfigured, industrial zone. It was opened and closed with 'ritual', structured deposition: respectively, a re-used finial incorporated into its stone lining, and the placing of a combination of young and old animals linked to both farming and wild resources above its primary silting (see section 8.6). The positioning of this feature, some 65m up from the much more accessible water sources of the springline used from the Bronze Age onwards, required this well to be dug to a depth of over 4m to reach the water table. This level of investment suggests that it was positioned here to meet manufacturing needs, not vice versa.

Rectangular building G112 was set out to the west of Well 7 and, seemingly, linked to its usage (see section 6.4). It was constructed above the stone-roofed structure G106, itself of fourth-century date, but only after a gap during which soil had time to accumulate. G112 comprised clay and cobble post-pads as the base for a timber-framed superstructure, perhaps only roofed at its western end. Associated ceramics suggest a link to feasting and its associated animal bone assemblage was less eroded and fragmented than the average, and more often butchered and gnawed. The fills of a possible cesspit to its north, the only example of such a feature known on the site, yielded a copper alloy spoon (see fig 7.1) and sherds of an unusual, curated glass jug. Thus, although the general environment around this building had not changed, human consumption and discard practices in its immediate vicinity, perhaps including the disposal of human waste, had altered.

It is likely that building G112 and Well 7 fell out of use together. Artefacts from the latter's demise were different from the rest of the site in size and condition, whilst faunal material was also unusual.[190] This assemblage thus constitutes something other than standard domestic rubbish, characteristics paralleled in distinctive material from wells at Dalton Parlours[191] and Rudston.[192] On the other hand, its ceramics contrast with the tablewares and food preparation vessels from wells at Rothwell Haigh[193] and Shiptonthorpe.[194] Perhaps most striking is the familiarity of most of the material used to backfill Well 7: its jars circulated widely in this landscape, whilst the cattle and horse found there also occur in other contexts on the site. Even the young dog and deer could have come from, respectively, within and fairly near the site. They therefore attest locally-derived, well-understood, 'mundane' elements, yet they were now being deposited in symbolic performance related to agricultural cycles and fertility practices, whether at annual, generational or longer-term points of transition. If Well 7 and Building G112 fell out of use at the same time as the industrial zone beside them ceased, this act of closure might imply that, after an 'industrial' interlude,

there was a perceived need to return to an agricultural economy.

The restricted zone described above, with its focus on manufacture, distinctive water supply and structural development, may have continued in use into the post-Roman period, given the extended sequences and approximate ceramic dating. This suggestion is reinforced by the corresponding distribution of 'Anglian' ceramics with a domestic signature (see fig 7.5). Particular finds from this manufacturing zone include an intaglio, perhaps indicating some 'official' connections, and a key for a box, maybe signifying a focus of security. Beyond these specifics, iron penannular brooches are favoured in these final deposits over their copper equivalents, something seen in late levels at both Wroxeter[195] and the Lankhills cemetery, Winchester.[196] This sector thus marks itself out from most of the rest of the site. Some of the items found here, notably brooches, wrist clasps and incised ceramic vessels, are common on cemetery sites, but none need to be exclusively confined to such contexts and could simply relate to domestic habitation.

In trying to understand the changes here at the local landscape level, it is virtually impossible to decide which side of 400 AD the main developments might lie and by how much. The issue here is not so much whether we might be able to develop more accurate mechanisms to make an informed decision on such dating in the future, rather that the distinction between the very late Roman and sub/post-Roman period(s) may not be entirely relevant. What is certain is that, in the course of the last decades of the fourth century AD, at least one part of the Heslington landscape began to show signs of tensions in its artefact supply systems, both ceramic and non-ceramic, and inconsistencies in its production and/or export of meat. It also developed a much greater focus on manufacturing processes alongside a burst of structural development and insertion of a new type of well. The later elements of these production processes seems to have increasingly ignored ditched boundaries, before returning to an agricultural focus within an open landscape later covered by hill wash of medieval date.

This turn to localised manufacture at Heslington occurred following the demise of an early fourth-century enclosure involving a masonry tower and hypocaust building, each associated with unusual burials. Such a reversal of monumentalisation recalls what must be broadly contemporary events seen at the core of Roman power in the region, the *principia* at the centre of the York fortress. Here, as the architectural unity of that building fragmented and it took on 'ritual airs',[197] metal-working activity appeared in ancillary rooms beside what remained of the (?still columnated) hall,[198] perhaps at the same time as the aforementioned 'small pig horizon' accumulated nearby. The seeds of decay in both cases are planted within the second half of the fourth century AD, with metal-working and atypical, unsustainable consumption practices involved in the process of fragmentation.

Beyond this specific manufacturing zone, a high proportion of 'Anglian' ceramics were derived from a midden accumulating above the eastern exit of the ritual enclosure c 30m to its south-east (see section 8.5). This concentration of finds, if not just a chance survival of horizontal strata, might suggest another focus of post-Roman activity. Equally, the area around Well 1, a considerable distance further to the south and east, could have been brought back into use at this time, given the date of several linear and curvilinear features near this water source. Such evidence does not suggest once widespread occupation in the post-Roman period, rather a few, localised *foci* in an otherwise deserted landscape. In this, our Heslington site may have come to resemble what has been claimed for Anglian development at Heslington Hill, less than a kilometre to the west.[199] These authors have sought to decouple their assemblage profile from the type of funerary contexts seen on cemeteries such as at Heworth and The Mount on the periphery of York.[200] If their arguments are accepted, sites such as this, and our own, can henceforth be more readily recognised for what they were: rural populations practising a largely subsistence economy, set out piecemeal in separate nodes along this part of the moraine. Some were set up in pristine landscapes, as at Heslington Hill, others like our own developed above places that evidenced occupation in preceding centuries, aspects of which may have remained visible at this time, if only as hollows in the ground. Superposition, however, does not imply any form of continuity, and these small homesteads were themselves later deserted as activity moved downslope into the adjacent Vale in the course of the medieval period proper. In Heslington's case, this took the form of hill wash (see section 2.1), followed by ploughing of medieval and modern date (see section 3.6).

9.5 Transitioning between the medieval and modern periods

The final transition at Heslington is best explained by comparing the medieval period, when surplus was extracted from direct producers as rent or labour service under feudal relations,[201] to capitalist systems, where wage labour forms the fundamental mechanism for exploiting producers. The latter system embodies commodity production in all economic spheres including, critically for present purposes, agricultural landscapes. In replacing artisan production with new forms of industrialised manufacture, it has alienated labour in various ways: from the land, from nature and from the self. Finally, within this overall trend, capitalism has gone through several significant changes over time. Those most relevant to this discussion are, first, the middle of the twentieth century, when nation states took on a new role in facilitating the running society (in Western Europe: in education, housing and health provision after World War II) and, second, the 1980s onwards, when, in attempting to increase the rate of exploitation after world-wide crises, states were forced to adopt neoliberal economic agendas in a (currently failing) attempt to rescue that system from further catastrophe. It is argued below that these alienating forces in general, and state intervention followed by neoliberalism in particular, can be recognised both in the recent developments seen on the Heslington site and in how the site was investigated archaeologically. Such influences also explain how the new university development there has been conceived and resourced, and how it will be carried through.

Within the Heslington landscape, the colluvium that accumulated above the latest Roman and Anglian stratigraphic horizon on the site (see section 2.1) was cut by furrows of broadly medieval date, evidenced in excavation, geophysical survey, aerial photography and the 1857 Enclosure Map (see section 4.2). Most furrows ran north–south, down the hillside, but a later east–west group was evident on flatter ground in the west of the site. The straight-sided form of this ploughing suggested to Perring a fairly late, perhaps sixteenth-century, date following medieval 'strip farming' (fig 9.7).[202]

Beyond this evidence for ploughing, it is necessary to deploy documentary sources to summarise the development of the Heslington parish during such time. What follows draws heavily, if selectively, on the Victoria County History account of that parish.[203] Although not directly seen in the excavated areas, it is clear that open fields in the vicinity of the site were increasingly impacted by the creation of 'closes' from the seventeenth century. Still more focused spatial divisions were evident by the late eighteenth century, before the advent of extensive and concerted enclosure in 1857, employing the 1836 Act. By the latter point, however, there had already been some divergence from customary cropping regimes here, with turnips, potatoes, mustard, flax and chicory all being produced in the vicinity before 1800. To some extent,

Fig 9.6 Summary of main transitions at the end of the Roman period, in which Road 1 (blue), and Road 2 plus 'ritual' enclosure (grey) were retained, but a differently-aligned system of terraced landholding (red) defined a new organisation of a localised zone at the northern edge of the site. *Drawing*: Helen Goodchild (contains OS MasterMap® Topography Layer [FileGeoDatabase geospatial data], Scale 1:1250, Tiles: GB, Updated: 1 November 2017, Ordnance Survey (GB), Using: EDINA Digimap Ordnance Survey Service, <http://digimap.edina.ac.uk>, Downloaded: 2018-05-29 11:49:34.438)

therefore, improvement, or at least increased diversity of planting regimes, preceded full landscape reorganisation.

A 7m-wide track with side ditches laid out in a low-lying, eastern part of the site (see section 3.6) is one of the few medieval features here beyond the aforementioned furrows. This suggests an investment in moving animals off-site in the medieval period, perhaps part of the far-flung network of droveways known to have existed in the region at that time, a product of the need to supply burgeoning medieval towns with food. The degree to which Heslington was tied into these extensive systems is, however, unclear: stock could have been mainly moving from here directly into York, or destined for a more local settlement, most obviously Heslington village (see below). It is thought that nearby medieval landscapes included a combination of arable land, meadow and common pasture, the lower parts of which flooded. This may have required designated droveways to ensure that stock crossed such boggy ground safely. Our excavated section of track could be one such example.

Turning to the development of medieval settlement in the vicinity of the site, the most relevant places comprise,

just to the west, Heslington village, with its church, agricultural facilities and, latterly, school, and the immediately adjacent Heslington Hall. The village is a classic, planned settlement of 'two-row' medieval properties flanking a broad, central 'street-green': Main Street.[204] Domesday records landholdings here of the Archbishop of York, Count Alan of Brittany and Hugh, son of Baldric. By 1148, some land had been given to St Peter's (later St Leonard's) hospital in York, hence splitting the then village between two parishes either side of Main Street (recombined in 1869). The position of any manor house is unknown, whilst the name itself, Eslington in Domesday, suggests a possible Anglian origin: 'farmstead near the hazel trees' or 'settlement of the people of the water hall'.[205] This has led to the bold claim that Heslington is indeed an Anglian settlement.[206] The status and size of Heslington at Domesday are unclear, but assarting of land is evident in its vicinity in the late twelfth century AD, alongside the supply of labour service and goods in kind, thus reflecting the dynamics of feudal socio-economic relations.

The church at Heslington, dedicated to St Paul, is first

documented in 1299 (rebuilt in 1858 and further restored in 1973), whilst a tithe barn, undated but thought to be situated nearby, attests the role of religious authority in legitimating large-scale grain storage, alongside taking a proportion of that surplus. A windmill is mentioned in this area in 1530, and two windmills are indeed shown on the moraine north-east of Heslington village in a 1787 image, one atop Siward's How. Such structures suggest increasing control of grain processing after agricultural improvement. An ice-house situated on a farm north of Heslington Road at this time implies an investment in storing meat over winter, perhaps another indicator of greater landscape productivity in the vicinity, whilst the nearby bleach works, 'lately built' in 1804, similarly implies flax retting on a new scale, in this case for use by linen cloth makers in York. Finally, a gravel-dealer was operating in Heslington by 1840, using pits dug into the moraine (in the process, disturbing Roman burials: see above). All of these developments imply that new scales of agricultural activity were emerging under capitalist relations.

The most prominent structural development later in these centuries, however, was Heslington Hall, an elite residence built in 1565–8 for Sir Thomas Eynns, a prominent member of the Council of the North and one of Henry VIII's commissioners. Although this development does not seem to have impacted on landholding in its immediate vicinity, it did lead to the setting up of Village Farm. The house itself was then bought by Sir Thomas Hesketh of Lancashire, another member of the Council of the North, who established alms houses to the west of the village and further buildings along Main Street. When the hall passed to Ann Yarburgh in 1708, its formal gardens were redesigned, including planting the yew trees that occupy the present site. Major Henry Yarburgh, who succeeded in 1789, dismantled the dilapidated alms houses and rebuilt them as Hesketh Cottages using capital from the sale of Castle Mills in York to the Foss Navigation Company: profits derived from urban industry were now facilitating rural change, and enhancing local aristocratic charitable reputation into the bargain.

A school, now called Lord Deramore's, was constructed north of the village in 1795. A gift to help educate the populace, it taught increasing numbers of both girls and boys in the course of the nineteenth century. School playing fields were set out nearby above medieval ploughing to show that both body and mind were to be catered for. The school was further expanded in both 1957 and 1965, its pupils now separated more formally by age, an expression of state involvement in education in the second half of the twentieth century.

Finally, in 2017, the school was subject to a near total rebuilding, a product of its conversion to an academy under the auspices of the South York Multi-Academy Trust.[207] This new institutional position not only formalises its role as a feeder for a designated secondary school nearby, but distances it from Local Authority control (a process of privatisation and new build that has its equivalent in higher education: see further below).

The trends in centralised agriculture processing and storage in the eighteenth and nineteenth centuries noted above in relation to windmills and the ice-house, plus industrialisation implied by the flax bleach works and large-scale extraction of gravel, were reflected in the excavations by the replacement of the occasional late medieval stone land drain by modern ceramic equivalents (see section 4.2). These recent drainage schemes were conceived on a larger scale than hitherto and employed more consistent materials, both elements being a product of the mechanisation of farming post-World War II. In its latest incarnation, drainage on the site has seen plastic pipes replace their ceramic counterparts, demonstrating how the by-products of the oil industry now inculcate themselves into farming, as in so much economic activity.

The mechanised ploughing that went alongside the above developments was a major factor in the destruction of archaeological remains in this landscape, and in many other parts of the British countryside. As noted previously (see section 1.1), this was one of the several threats that comprised a driving force behind the 'Rescue' movement in British archaeology in the long economic boom after World War II. Countering such destruction led, in turn, to the creation of a government-funded fieldwork profession and a planning process involving the use of 'the expert' to make decisions about future development. Such procedures, which increasingly removed decision-making from the local community, are evident across Europe (cf section 1.1 and the notion of 'qualified practitioners' embedded in the Valletta Convention[208]).

In the 1990s, this UK fieldwork profession underwent fundamental changes. Work once undertaken by centrally-resourced organisations with regional responsibilities became the province of 'roving' commercialised units whose businesses thus ebbed and flowed with the vagaries of the wider economy (a relationship at its most traumatic, perhaps, in Ireland after the 2008 recession[209]). It has also generated attempts to re-establish links between fieldwork practitioners and local communities, and thus decentre the expert.[210] These latest trends provide the context within which the competing commercial organisations YAT and OSA operate on this project, but also led to our attempts at community engagement at Heslington (see section 1.4).

Alongside mechanised ploughing, the area under investigation also expressed other recent changes to agricultural practices. Thus, of late, different zones in the development area have been used: as a semi-formal rubbish tip, an expression of the inability of the modern world to keep up with the discard of the waste materials which it generates; for a Park-and-Ride scheme, a rear-guard action to promote public transport over the private car and thus stop atmospheric degradation and building decay in the historic core of York; as a place for local residents to walk their dogs on a regular basis, particularly people from the adjacent housing estate of Badger Hill; and as somewhere to plant maize annually in different formations to create a 'maize maze' recreational route, allowing paying customers to engage with crop growth in an entertaining way.[211] This last use of the landscape was not only a market opportunity for a modern farmer trying to overcome the vagaries of increasingly specialised world food markets by diversifying agricultural practices, it was also, together with dog walking, an informal opportunity for local people to attempt to close a 'metabolic rift' opened up between the natural and cultural worlds under modern capitalism.[212]

This rift is reflected in a current lack of cognitive ownership of the Heslington landscape by those communities who live and work nearby. The government advocacy of a 'localism agenda'[213] has made only limited inroads into ameliorating these fundamental tensions, not least because that policy was partly driven by neoliberal forces seeking to withdraw the state from systems of social support.[214] Our own community programme (see section 1.1) was successful in many ways, but left untouched other anxieties (for example, the objections of the Parish Council to a road being driven close to their church as part of the overall university development, or those dog walkers who used wire cutters to break through fences around the development zone in order to have continued access to the landscape that they had been using for decades before the re-development was planned). Recently, Smith has been a powerful advocate of heritage managers needing to challenge the Authorised Heritage Discourse set up by state authorities to pass down 'the heritage' to the public.[215] She argues that this approach needs to be replaced with an alternative that facilitates community engagement, in which local people can decide what is significant about 'their past'. In attempting to help implement such practices at Heslington, our experience shows just how difficult it is to avoid tokenism in confronting authorised discourse directly, rather than seeking to subvert it piecemeal.[216]

The most obvious interaction between this general landscape and the modern world, however, concerns the university itself. The establishment of academic institutions always occurs in the context of wider social forces, whether centres of learning in the medieval period or organisations developed later in relation to state formation and the economic needs of industrial capitalism, especially in nineteenth-century Europe.[217] In the case of York University, that context comprised state intervention in society in general, and in education in particular, after World War II (cf Lord Deramore's primary school noted above). This is most clearly expressed in the Robbins Report,[218] which proposed setting up a number of new Higher Education institutions and put forward the idea of universities needing to not only foster the creation of technical skills but also produce cultivated people, and balance research with teaching and promote a notion of common citizenship.

Before World War II, Heslington village was, in essence, a quiet rural retreat with its local aristocracy and about twelve working farms. Piped water and gas had arrived in the interwar years, whilst the outbreak of World War II saw the Deramore family evacuated and the Royal Air Force take over Heslington Hall as the headquarters of No. 4 Group Bomber Command. This was the context on which the university imposed itself in the 1960s. Other developments in the vicinity included building council houses within Heslington village and larger estates at Newlands Park to the north and Badger Hill to the east, all a product of trends in housing provision in post-war decades. Yet, in the long term, it was the university that ushered in the most fundamental shift in the character of the area. Funded by central government and based initially at Heslington Hall, it soon expanded by draining large areas of the surrounding landscape to erect buildings for teaching and student accommodation. Speedy structural development was thought essential, leading to the use of a then-innovative construction technique, the 'CLASP' method.[219]

Church Green, which occupies the zone between Heslington Hall and St Paul's church, had been variously divided up in the nineteenth century, in part to take account of the sensibilities of those living in the Hall by enhancing their privacy. Before the development of the university, J B Morrell had bought up the Hall and associated land to fulfil a long-cherished ambition to create a folk park, including village green with maypole, gypsy camp and water mill.[220] This plan was overtaken when the university acquired this land in 1964 and used it for recreation such as an annual firework display: a proposed invention of bucolic tradition involving a village community gathering round a representation of springtime agricultural significance (the maypole) was replaced by a real community of students coming together in autumn to commemorate a distant political event using pyrotechnics of increasing, and latterly electronic, sophistication. Such displays were later curtailed by a combination of financial and health and safety considerations, equally common aspects of current social change.

The impact of the university is clear in population figures. At the end of the nineteenth century, Heslington parish included c 500 people and this stood at c 880 by 1951. A few years after the university had been founded, it had risen to 2,000,[221] and to 4,000 by the end of the twentieth century. The decision to double the size of the campus by developing Heslington, the proposal that occasioned our own archaeological work there (see section 1.1), will boost these figures still further. In the process, the landscape known at the start of our investigations, dedicated to agricultural production with added elements of recreation, rubbish dumping and a transport node, will be turned into a zone occupied by a proliferation of substantial monuments, the first time this has happened here since the late Roman period (see section 8.5).

This new development, although portrayed as being founded on Robbins' educational principles developed in the early 1960s, derives its detailed form from the very different circumstances experienced by higher education establishments fifty years on: a type of 'knowledge factory'. At the time Robbins was writing, 10 per cent of the British population went to university; today, there has been a threefold increase,[222] explanation enough perhaps for why more space might be needed by York University. Unprecedented student numbers are now coupled, however, with greater government regulation and compliance requirements, and the need to demonstrate societal and, especially, economic impact: in essence, then, higher education is increasingly shaped by the needs of big business with neoliberal agendas.[223] Driven by the requirement to promote a 'knowledge economy' that turns new ideas into commercial goods and services, universities have moved from places of scholarship to centres of profit that compete for student 'customers'. The latter now pay for their degrees via individualised loans, rather than the government grants of the 1960s, and are taught in the context of higher staff/student ratios than in other developed economies.[224] Teaching 'excellence' will soon be assessed by using two measures: student satisfaction surveys filled in soon after teaching has been delivered (ie without proper opportunity for a considered assessment) and graduate income levels. Further, greater numbers of non-academic managers now oversee the

work of lecturing staff, and many of these university teachers are employed on increasingly precarious contracts.

From its inception, alongside educational facilities, the new campus design incorporated private franchises, for example to supply fast food conveniently to students. In addition, a 'Sports Village' now occupies the east of the site. Costing £9 million (£5 million from university loans, £3 million from York City Council and the remainder from sports organisations[225]), it contains 'state of the art' facilities open to both staff/students and members of the public. The intention is that, despite its peripheral position, it will become a sporting hub for the whole of York. Indeed, that very position makes it accessible from the adjacent ring road, a typical example of how edge-of-town facilities function in many cities today.

Finally, the sizeable zone now available between that Sports Village in the east and more conventional educational facilities in the west seems destined to be used, at least in part, to accommodate future 'spin off' companies related to the university (see fig 9.7). Over 120 such companies in the science and technology sectors, from 'start-ups' to international corporations, already occupy the existing York Science Park. This crowded space to the north of the original campus is run by an arm's-length company, York Science Park Limited.[226] The centre of the newly-created zone at Heslington, now cleared of its archaeological 'problem', will allow further, light-industrial expansion. A good example already located there is the York Robotics Laboratory. Established in 2012 as a joint venture between the Department of Computer Science and Department of Electronics, it is dedicated, in part, to conventional academic research and teaching, yet is also 'keen to work with a wide variety of sectors from business'.[227]

Hence, the impactful architecture of the Heslington development, which has received several awards,[228] together with its integral commercial outlets and 'state of the art' accommodation and sports facilities, should not be understood simply as a vanity project for university leaders. Rather, it is part of the way in which this institution will compete for future student customers. Alongside the European monies, it has been funded by a combination of bank loans, which will need to be repaid, and commercial enterprises, which will make their profits from the development in the fullness of time. And the use of space which eventually emerges there will be as much concerned with outputs spinning off into the wider economy as it is with purely educational goals: the neo-liberalised 'university-scape' of the 2000s at Heslington East will be a very different place from that which developed to its west in the 1960s.

Notes

Chapter 1

1   Rahtz 1974.
2   Roskams 2001.
3   https://www.coe.int/en/web/conventions/full-list/-/conventions/treaty/143 (accessed 25 September 2019).
4   http://webarchive.nationalarchives.gov.uk/+/http://www.communities.gov.uk/publications/planningandbuilding/ppg16 (accessed 25 September 2020).
5   Carver 2003, 61.
6   For example, on prehistoric sites see Cooper 2012.
7   Perring 1999.
8   Webley et al 2012.
9   Demoule 2002.
10 Schlanger and Aitchison 2010.
11 See Ronayne 2008 for an Irish example; trajectories in countries such as Romania and Poland, where EU infrastructure schemes have softened the blow, show how effects might be ameliorated.
12 English Heritage 2000.
13 Ministry of Housing, Communities and Local Government 2019.
14 Faro Convention 2005.
15 Neal and Roskams 2013.
16 Ibid.
17 Perring 1999.
18 Fell 2006.
19 Reeves undated.
20 RCHM(E) 1962 (called Road 2).
21 Ibid (called Road 1).
22 FAS 2003.
23 Thurnam 1849.
24 Ramm 1966a.
25 Perring 1999.
26 Evans 2002; Mason and McComish 2003.
27 Mason and McComish 2003, 8.
28 Challis et al 2009.
29 Kendal 2003; Mason and McComish 2003.
30 Bartlett 2003; Bartlett and Noel 2003, 2004a and 2004b.
31 MacNab 2004.
32 Ottaway 2011b.
33 Historic England 2006.
34 https://www.york.ac.uk/archaeology/research/current-projects/interarchive/ (accessed 25 September 2019).
35 Bayliss 2015.
36 O'Connor and Evans 2005.
37 Gwilt 2006.
38 Carver 2003.
39 https://doi.org/10.5284/1019860 (accessed 25 September 2019).
40 http://www.iadb.co.uk/iadb2017/iadb2017.php.
41 Roskams 2020.
42 Whittle 1988, 38.
43 See Roskams 2019 for references and critique.

Chapter 2

1   Jarvis et al 1984.
2   Natural England 2012.
3   Bateman et al 2001, 14.
4   Fenton-Thomas 2005, 48
5   Perring 1999.
6   Innes and Blackford 2003.
7   Benn and Evans 1998, 244.
8   Simon Price pers comm.
9   Rackham 1990, 76.
10 Edgeworth 2011. See also Franconi 2017 for Roman fluvial landscapes in general.
11 See Roskams 2019 for a wider discussion of Roman approaches to the control of water and its implications for culture/nature relationships and, beyond this, for the limitations of postmodern frameworks of social interpretation in archaeology.
12 Roskams et al 2013.
13 Roskams (2019) discusses water use in this wetland landscape, and its wider implications for theorising the relationship between natural and cultural processes.

Chapter 4

1   Perring 1999.
2   Oswald et al undated.
3   O'Connor 1988
4   O'Connor 1988.
5   Huntley 2002, 88.
6   van der Veen 1992, 74.
7   Jones 1981, 106.
8   Manning 1985, 59.
9   Perring 1999.
10 Scott 1951, 198; Fenton 1978, 377.
11 Hillman 1982, 138; Monk 1987, 135.
12 Jones 1981, 108.
13 Hillman 1981, 153–4.
14 Monk 1987, 223.
15 van der Veen 1989.
16 Rahtz and Watts 2004, 85ff
17 Simmons 2013, 65.

18 Gwilt 2006.

19 Buckley 2001, fig 62.

20 Brun and Boréani 1998, figs 25 and 28.

21 Perring 1999.

22 Short 1994.

Chapter 5

1 Hamilton and Whittle 1999.

2 Lawton 1993; Monaghan 1997, 869.

3 Barton and Bergman 1992, fig 4.23.

4 Isbister 2000.

5 Cunnington 1923.

6 Barfield and Hodder 1987.

7 Spratling 1979; Mortimer and Starley 1995.

8 Brodribb 1987, 74.

Chapter 6

1 Romankiewicz 2018.

2 Harding 2009.

3 Cunliffe 2004, 269.

4 Cunliffe and Davenport 1985.

5 Gillam and Daniels 1961.

6 Lowther 1976; Blagg 1977.

7 Philpott 1991.

8 Brodribb 1987, 11.

9 English Heritage 2012.

10 Carver et al 1978, 41.

11 Walton Rogers 2007, 33.

Chapter 7

1 Bland and Johns 1993.

2 Corbishley et al 1997, 211.

3 Booth et al 2010, 193.

4 MacGregor et al 1999.

5 Walton Rogers 2007, 33.

6 Cruse 2013.

7 Morris 2010, 106ff.

8 Betts 1985.

9 McWhirr 1979; Betts 1985; Brodribb 1987.

10 Rigby and Ambers 2004, fig 7.

11 Allason-Jones 1989, 29.

12 Price 1988, 351.

13 Leary 2009.

14 Monaghan 1997, 872ff; Swan 1992.

15 Evans 1985.

16 Monaghan 1997, 869ff.

17 Leary 2013a, 136.

18 Wrathmell and Nicholson 1990, 206.

19 Hall et al 1980.

20 Allen 2011.

21 Cool 2006, 155.

22 Bishop and Coulston 1993, fig 91.

Chapter 8

1 See Garrow 2012 for a discussion of the development of this concept.

2 Hurcombe 2008.

3 Manby et al 2003.

4 Vyner 2018.

5 Fenton-Thomas 2005.

6 Spratt 1993, 92–120.

7 Richardson and Vyner 2011: clearly it is the grave goods, rather than any urn, that makes this burial prestigious.

8 Reeves undated.

9 Ellison 1980.

10 McKinley 2004.

11 Bradley 2007, 185.

12 James and Nasmyth-Jones 1992.

13 O'Connor et al 2011.

14 Cunliffe, 2004, 543.

15 Carson and Kent 1971.

16 Evans 2004.

17 Mays 2000.

18 Millett and Gowland 2015.

19 Cf Ingold (1993) on the concept of taskscapes and Roskams (2019) for the limitations of this notion.

20 Gillam and Daniels 1961.

Chapter 9

1 Manby 2003.

2 Milner et al 2018.

3 Manby 2003.

4 Manby et al 2003, table 3.

5 Roberts et al 2010.

6 Manby et al 2003, 65.

7 Bayliss et al 2007.

8 Whittle et al 2011.

9 Griffiths 2014a, 2014b.

10 Manby et al 2003, 105.

11 Stevens and Fuller 2012.

12 Bishop 2015; Stevens and Fuller 2015.

13 Smith 1981; Berg 2001, 7. See Parker et al 2002 for the wider context.

14 Bishop et al 2018.

15 Fyfe et al 2003.

16 Berg 2001, 8.

17 Edmonds 1995, 52–3.

18 For example, Radley 1974, 10.

19 Vyner 2007.

20 Roberts et al 2010.

21 Roberts 2005.

22 Addyman 1984, 10–11.

23 Radley 1974.
24 Fell 2006.
25 Vyner 2018.
26 Spall and Toop 2005.
27 Vyner 2018.
28 Stirk 2006.
29 Ramm 1966a.
30 Short 1994, 19.
31 Oswald *et al* 2016.
32 Ramm 1966b.
33 Ibid, 590.
34 Hamilton and Whittle 1999.
35 Manby *et al* 2003.
36 Isbister 2000.
37 Carver 2011.
38 Ibid, 115.
39 Pollard 1999.
40 Carver 2011, 130.
41 Anderson-Whymark and Thomas 2012.
42 See Garrow *et al* (2005) for another example of repeated and persistent activity not equating with continuous occupation.
43 Edmonds 1999.
44 Howell 2001.
45 Whyman and Howard 2005, 21.
46 Manby *et al* 2003, 94–6. The under-representation of previous centuries reinforces the significance of an early bronze spearhead found in Heslington Field in 1889: Elgee and Elgee 1933, 240.
47 Radley 1974, 21.
48 Brück 1995.
49 Weiss-Krejci 2013.
50 Brück 2004.
51 Stutz and Tarlow 2013.
52 Brück 2004.
53 Cooper 2016.
54 Fenton-Thomas 2011.
55 Richardson and Vyner 2011.
56 Reeves undated.
57 Vyner 2013.
58 Stirk 2006.
59 Oestigaard 2013.
60 Caffell and Holst 2012.
61 McKinley 1997, 142.
62 Bradley 2007: the 'Late Bronze Age' category listed in his table 4.1.
63 Brossler *et al* 2013.
64 Barfield and Hodder 1987.
65 Laurie 2003.
66 Cruse 2013.
67 Bradley 2007, 226.
68 Boardman and Charles 1997.
69 Howell 2001.
70 Holden and Hastie 2001.
71 van der Veen 1992, 145–53.
72 Jones 1981.

73 Harding 2009.
74 Cunliffe 2004, 269.
75 Roberts 2005.
76 Inman *et al* 1985.
77 Smith 1974.
78 Sheridan and Davis 2002.
79 Inman *et al* 1985.
80 Evans 2004.
81 Leary 2016.
82 RCHM(E) 1962.
83 Lawton 1993.
84 Leary 2016.
85 Leary 2009.
86 Jones *et al* undated.
87 Ibid.
88 Stirk 2006.
89 Leary 2008.
90 Respectively, Leary unpublished a and unpublished c.
91 MAP 1996.
92 Leary unpublished b.
93 Precious and Vince 1999.
94 Ottaway 2013.
95 See the critique in Roberts *et al* 2010.
96 Ramm 1978.
97 Halkon 2013.
98 Roberts *et al* 2010.
99 Richardson 2001; cf above on the absence of such indicators of fundamental change at Heslington.
100 Roberts *et al* 2010.
101 Millett 2006, 321.
102 Jones *et al* undated.
103 Stirk 2006.
104 Stoertz 1997.
105 Giles 2007.
106 Fenton-Thomas 2005.
107 Atha and Roskams 2012.
108 Fenton-Thomas 2011.
109 Fenton-Thomas 2005.
110 Dent 1983; Stead 1991 – although also see Giles 2012.
111 Atha and Roskams 2012, 7.
112 Fenton-Thomas 2011.
113 Halkon 2013.
114 Giles 2007.
115 Atha and Roskams 2012, 77.
116 Ingold 1993.
117 Monaghan 1997.
118 Swan 1992.
119 Evans 1985.
120 MacGregor 1976; Ottaway 1993.
121 Leary unpublished a and unpublished c.
122 Leary unpublished b; Precious and Vince 1999.
123 Carson and Kent 1971.
124 Millett 2006, 314.
125 RCHME 1962, 1 and fig 2, named 'Road 1' in the latter.
126 Ottaway 2011a, 261.
127 Oswald *et al* undated.

128 Ottaway 2011a, 258–9.
129 Oswald and Pollington 2012, fig 7.
130 Philpott 1991, 100.
131 Cool 2011, 310–1.
132 Tomlin 1988, 81.
133 Philpott 1991, 164.
134 Westell 1931, 290 no. 5789.
135 Dungworth 1998.
136 Black 1986, 223; Cool 2004, 452.
137 Mays 2000.
138 Millett and Gowland 2015.
139 Carroll 2013.
140 Ingold 1993.
141 See Mattingly 2007 for a recent critique.
142 Millett 2006, 305.
143 Ibid, 325.
144 Albarella 2007.
145 Albarella et al 2008.
146 O'Connor 1988.
147 Perring and Whyman 2002.
148 Cf Parkins (1997) on the nature of town–hinterland relationships and Whittaker (1995) on particular models.
149 Murray 1990, 190.
150 van der Veen 1996, 197.
151 van der veen and O'Connor 1998, 130.
152 van der Veen 2016.
153 Jones 1981, 106.
154 van der Veen 1992, 74; Huntley 1995, 41, and 2002, 85.
155 Huntley 2002, 88.
156 Manning 1985, 59.
157 van der Veen 1989.
158 Rahtz and Watts 2004.
159 Simmons 2013, 63.
160 Giorgi 2004, 65–6.
161 Huntley 1996, 295.
162 Jones 1981.
163 Simmons 2013, 65.
164 Millett 2006, 304.
165 Heslop and Cruse 2012.
166 Monk 1987, 217.
167 Millett 2006, 307.
168 Kenward and Williams 1979, 48.
169 Breeze 2006.
170 Cunliffe and Davenport 1985.
171 Gillam and Daniels 1961.
172 Wellbeloved 1842.
173 Groot 2008.
174 Grant 1989, 145; Brück 2003.
175 Cool and Mason 2008, 310.
176 Braithwaite 1984.
177 Halkon 1992.
178 Swan and Monaghan 1993.
179 Millett 2006, 309.
180 Halkon 2013.
181 Atha and Roskams 2012.
182 Chadwick 2007.
183 Ottaway 2013.
184 Roskams 2015.
185 Roskams 1999.
186 James 2008; Wood 2008.
187 Esmonde-Cleary 2013.
188 O'Connor 1988.
189 Roskams 1996; Gerrard 2007.
190 See Roskams et al (2013) for details.
191 Wrathmell and Nicholson 1990.
192 Stead 1980.
193 Leary 2013a.
194 Millett 2006.
195 Corbishley et al 1997.
196 Clarke 1979.
197 Phillips and Heywood 1995
198 Roskams 1996
199 Spall and Toop, 2008.
200 Ibid, 13.
201 Hilton 1990.
202 Perring 1999.
203 Baggs et al 1976, who provide detailed references to the primary literature being used.
204 Colley 1992.
205 Ibid, 3.
206 Baggs et al 1976.
207 https://southyorkmat.co.uk/ (accessed 25 September 2019).
208 Ibid.
209 Ronayne 2008.
210 Schofield 2013.
211 http://www.yorkmaze.com/ (accessed 25 September 2019).
212 Empson 2013.
213 Jackson et al 2014.
214 Neal and Roskams 2013.
215 Smith 2006.
216 Neal and Roskams 2013.
217 Callinicos 2010.
218 Robbins 1963.
219 https://www.york.ac.uk/about/history/1960s/ (accessed 25 September 2019).
220 https://www.york.ac.uk/about/history/foundations/ (accessed 25 September 2019).
221 Baggs et al 1976.
222 https://www.ons.gov.uk (accessed 25 September 2019).
223 Collini 2017
224 https://www.ucu.org.uk/article/4624/Studentteacher-ratios-in-higher-and-further-education (accessed 25 September 2019).
225 https://www.york.ac.uk/about/history/2000s/ (accessed September 2019).
226 https://www.york.ac.uk/business/partnerships/science-park/ (accessed September 2019).
227 https://www.york.ac.uk/robot-lab/
228 https://www.york.ac.uk/about/history/2000s/ (accessed 25 September 2019).

Abbreviations and bibliography

Abbreviations

ABG	associated bone group	Heslington	Heslington East site
ArcGIS	architecture geographic information system	MoRPHE	Management of Research Projects in the Historic Environment
Architect Archaeol Soc Durham Northumb	Architectural and Archaeological Society of Durham and Northumberland	NAA	Northern Archaeological Associates
		OD	ordnance datum
BAR Brit Ser	British Archaeological Reports British Series	OSA	On-Site Archaeology Ltd
		OSL	optically stimulated luminescence
CBA Res Rep	Council for British Archaeology Research Report	PPG	planning policy guidance
		Proc Prehist Soc	*Proceedings of the Prehistoric Society*
CBM	ceramic building material	VCH	Victoria County History
DoA	Department of Archaeology, University of York	WYAS	West Yorkshire Archaeological Service
EVES	estimated vessel equivalents	YAS	Yorkshire Archaeological Society
GIS	geographic information system	YAT	York Archaeological Trust

Bibliography

Addyman, P 1984. 'York in its archaeological setting', in P Addyman and V Black (eds), *Archaeological Papers from York Presented to M W Barley*, 7–21, York Archaeological Trust, York

Albarella, U 2007. 'The end of the Sheep Age: people and animals in the Late Iron Age', in C Haselgrove and T Moore (eds), *The Late Iron Age in Britain and Beyond*, 393–406, Oxbow Books, Oxford

Albarella, U, Johnstone, C and Vickers, K 2008. 'The development of animal husbandry from the Late Iron Age to the end of the Roman period: a case study from South-East Britain', *J Archaeol Sci*, 35, 1,828–48

Allason-Jones, L 1989. *Ear-rings in Roman Britain*, BAR Brit Ser 201, BAR Publishing, Oxford

Allen, S 2011. 'The wooden artefacts', in Richardson 2011, 25–47

Anderson-Whymark, H and Thomas, J 2012. *Regional Perspectives on Neolithic Pit Deposition: beyond the mundane*, Oxbow Books, Oxford

Atha, M and Roskams, S 2012. 'Prehistoric and Roman transitions at Wharram Percy', in S Wrathmell (ed), *A History of Wharram Percy and Its Neighbours*, 63–82, University of York, York

Baggs, A, Kent, G and Purdy, J 1976. 'Heslington', in K Allison (ed), *A History of the County of York East Riding: Vol 3, Ouse and Derwent Wapentake, and part of Harthill Wapentake*, 66–74, VCH, London, online <http://www.british-history.ac.uk/vch/yorks/east/vol3/pp66-74> (accessed 20 December 2019)

Barfield, L and Hodder, M 1987. 'Burnt mounds as saunas, and the prehistory of bathing', *Antiquity* 61 (233), 370–9, online <https://dx.doi.org/10.1017/S0003598X00072926>

Bartlett, A 2003. 'University of York Heslington East development archaeological geophysical survey phase 1', unpublished report, GeoQuest Associates

Bartlett, A and Noel, M 2003. 'University of York Heslington East development archaeological geophysical survey phases 1 and 2', unpublished report, GeoQuest Associates

Bartlett, A and Noel, M 2004a. 'University of York Heslington East development archaeological geophysical survey phases 1, 2 and 3', unpublished report, GeoQuest Associates

Bartlett, A and Noel, M 2004b. 'University of York Heslington East development archaeological resistivity survey in field 9', unpublished report, GeoQuest Associates

Barton, R and Bergman, C 1992. 'The Late Upper Palaeolithic site', in B Cunliffe and R Barton (eds), *Hengistbury Head, Dorset: Vol 2, the late upper Palaeolithic and early Mesolithic sites*, 78–95, Oxford University Press, Oxford

Bateman, M, Buckland, P, Frederick, C and Whitehouse, N (eds) 2001. *The Quaternary of East Yorkshire and North Lincolnshire Field Guide*, Quaternary Research Association, London

Bayliss, A 2015. 'Quality in Bayesian chronological models in archaeology', *World Archaeol*, **47** (4), 677–700, online <https://www.tandfonline.com/doi/full/10.1080/00438243.2015.1067640> (accessed 7 January 2020)

Bayliss A, Bronk Ramsay, C, van der Plicht, J and Whittle, A 2007. 'Bradshaw and Bayes: towards a timetable for the Neolithic', *Cambridge Archaeol J*, **17** (S1), 1–28, online <https://dx.doi.org/10.1017/S0959774307000145> (accessed 11 December 2019)

Bell, A and Evans, J 2002. 'Pottery from the CfA excavations', in P Wilson (ed), Cataractonium. *Roman Catterick and its hinterland: excavations and research, 1958–1997 (Part 2)*, 352–416, CBA Res Rep 128, Council for British Archaeology, York

Benn, D and Evans, D 1998. *Glaciers and Glaciation*, Edward Arnold Publishers, London

Berg, D 2001. 'The physical environment', in Roberts *et al* 2001, 3–9

Betts, I 1985. 'A scientific investigation of the brick and tile industry of York to the mid eighteenth century', unpublished PhD thesis, University of Bradford

Bishop, M and Coulston, J 1993. *Roman Military Equipment from the Punic Wars to the Fall of Rome*, Batsford, London

Bishop, R 2015. 'Did Late Neolithic farming fail or flourish? A Scottish perspective on the evidence for Late Neolithic arable cultivation in the British Isles', *World Archaeol*, **47** (5), 1–22, online <https://dx.doi.org/10.1080/00438243.2015.1072477> (accessed 11 December 2019)

Bishop, R, Church, M, Lawson, I and Roucoux, K 2018. 'Deforestation and human agency in the North Atlantic region: archaeological and palaeoenvironmental evidence from the Western Isles of Scotland', *Proc Prehist Soc*, **84**, 145–84, online <https://dx.doi.org/10.1017/ppr.2018.8> (accessed 11 December 2019)

Black, E 1986. 'Romano-British burial customs and religious beliefs in south-east England', *Archaeol J*, **143** (1), 201–39, online <https://dx.doi.org/10.1080/00665983.1986.11021133> (accessed 11 December 2019)

Blagg, T 1977. 'Schools of stonemasons in Britain', in J Munby and M Henig (eds), *Roman Life and Art in Britain*, 51–74, BAR Brit Ser 41.1, BAR Publishing, Oxford

Bland, R and Johns, C 1993. *The Hoxne Treasure: an illustrated introduction*, British Museum Press, London

Boardman, S and Charles, M 1997. 'Charred plant remains', in M Parker-Pearson and R Sydes (eds), 'The Iron Age enclosures and prehistoric landscape of Sutton Common, South Yorkshire', *Proc Prehist Soc*, **63**, 221–59

Booth, P, Simmonds, A, Boyle, A, Clough, S, Cool, H and Poore, D 2010. *The Late Roman Cemetery at Lankhills, Winchester: excavations 2000–2005*, Oxford Archaeol Monogr 10, Oxford Archaeology Ltd, Oxford, online <https://library.thehumanjourney.net/607/1/WINCM_AY21.pdfA.pdf> (accessed 11 December 2019)

Bradley, R 2007. *The Prehistory of Britain and Ireland*, Cambridge University Press, Cambridge

Braithwaite, G 1984. 'Romano-British face pots and head pots', *Britannia* **15**, 99–131

Breeze, D 2006. *Hadrian's Wall*, English Heritage, London

Brodribb, G 1987. *Roman Brick and Tile*, Sutton, Gloucester

Brossler, A, Brown, F, Guttmann, E, Morris, E and Webley L 2013. *Prehistoric Settlement of the Lower Kennet Valley: excavations at Green Park phase 3 and Moores Farm, Burghfield, Berkshire*, Thames Valley Landscape Monogr 37, Oxford Archaeology Ltd, Oxford

Brück, J 1995. 'A place for the dead: the role of human remains in Late Bronze Age Britain', *Proc Prehist Soc*, **61**, 245–77

Brück, J 2003. 'Different types of dog at Roman Godmanchester', *Archaeol Rev from Cambridge*, **16** (1/2), 75–92

Brück, J 2004. 'Material metaphors: the relational construction of identity in Early Bronze Age burials in Ireland and Britain', *J Social Archaeol*, **4** (3), 307–33, online <https://dx.doi.org/10.1177/1469605304046417> (accessed 11 December 2019)

Brun, J-O and Boréani, M 1998. 'Deux moulins hydrauliques du Haut-Empire romain en Narbonnaise: Villae des Mesclans à la Crau et de Sainte Pierre/ Les Laurons au Ares (Var), Gallia', *Archaeologie de la France antique*, **55**, 279–326

Buckley, D 2001. 'Querns and millstones', in A Anderson, J Wacher and A Fitzpatrick (eds), *The Romano-British 'Small Town' at Wanborough, Wiltshire: excavations 1966–76*, 156–50, Britannia Monogr Ser 19, Society for the Promotion of Roman Studies, London

Caffell, A and Holst, M 2012. *Osteological Analysis, Stanground South, Peterborough, Cambridgeshire*, unpublished Osteoarchaeology Report 1,212, York Osteoarchaeology, York

Callinicos, A 2010. *Universities in a Neo-Liberal World*, Bookmarks, London

Carroll, M 2013. 'Ethnicity and gender in Roman funerary commemoration', in Stutz and Tarlow 2013, online <https://www.oxfordhandbooks.com/view/10.1093/oxfordhb/9780199569069.001.0001/oxfordhb-9780199569069-e-31> (accessed 11 December 2019)

Carson, R and Kent, J 1971. 'A hoard of Roman 4th century bronze coins from Heslington, Yorks', *Numismatic Chron*, **11**, 207–25

Carver, G 2011. 'Pits and place-making: Neolithic habitation and deposition practices in East Yorkshire *c* 4000–2500 BC', *Proc Prehist Soc*, **78**, 111–34

Carver, M 2003. *Archaeological Value and Evaluation*, Societa Archeologica Padana, Mantova

Carver, M, Donaghey, S and Sumpter, A 1978. *Riverside Structures and a Well in Skeldergate and Buildings in Bishophill*, Archaeology of York 4, CBA, London

Chadwick, A 2007. 'Trackways, hooves and memory-days: human and animal memories and movements around Iron Age and Romano-British rural landscapes', in V Cummings and R Johnston (eds), *Prehistoric Journeys*, 131–52, Oxbow Books, Oxford

Challis, K, Kincey, M and Howard, A 2009. 'Airborne remote sensing of valley floor geoarchaeology using Daedalus ATM and CASI', *Archaeol Prospect*, **16** (1), 17–33, online <https://dx.doi.org/10.1002/arp.340> (accessed 11 December 2019)

Clark, C, Evans, D, Khatwa, A, Bradwell, T, Jordan, C, Marsh, S, Mitchell, W and Bateman, M 2004. 'Map and GIS database of glacial landforms and features related to the last British Ice Sheet', *Boreas* **33** (4), 359–75, online<https://doi.org/10.1111/j.1502-3885.2004.tb01246.x> (accessed 7 January 2020)

Clarke, G 1979. *Pre-Roman and Roman Winchester. Part II: the Roman cemetery at Lankhills*, Winchester Studies 3, Oxford University Press, Oxford

Colley, A 1992. *Heslington: a portrait of a village*, Neville Publishing, York

Collini, S 2017. *Speaking of Universities*, Verso, London

Cool, H 2004. *The Roman Cemetery at Brougham, Cumbria: excavations 1966–1967*, Britannia Monogr 21, Society for the Promotion of Roman Studies, London

Cool, H 2006. *Eating and Drinking in Roman Britain*, Cambridge University Press, Cambridge

Cool, H 2011. 'Funerary contexts', in L Allason-Jones (ed), *Artefacts in Roman Britain: their purpose and use*, 293–312, Cambridge University Press, Cambridge

Cool, H and Mason, D 2008. *Roman Piercebridge: excavations by D W Harding and Peter Scott 1969–1981*, Architectural and Archaeological Society of Durham and Northumberland, Durham

Cooper, A 2012. 'Pursuing "the pressure of the past"': British prehistoric research, 1980–2010', *Proc Prehist Soc*, **78**, 315–39, online <http://dx.doi.org/10.1017/S0079497X00027183> (accessed 13 December 2019)

Cooper, A 2016. '"Held in place": round barrows in the Later Bronze Age of lowland Britain', *Proc Prehist Soc*, **82**, 291–322, online <http://dx.doi.org/10.1017/ppr.2016.9> (accessed 13 December 2019)

Corbishley, M, Bird, H, Barker, P, White, R and Pretty, K 1997. *The Baths Basilica Wroxeter Excavations: 1966–90*, English Heritage, London

Cruse, R 2013. 'Easington 1996–8 ERAS excavations', unpublished Yorkshire Quern Survey Assessment, East Riding Archaeological Society, Hull

Cruse, R and Heslop, D 2013. 'Querns, millstones and other artefacts', in L Martin, J Richardson and I Roberts (eds), *Iron Age and Roman Settlements at Wattle Syke: archaeological investigations during the A1 Bramham to Wetherby upgrading scheme*, 165–83, Yorkshire Archaeol 11, WYAS, Leeds

Cunliffe, B 2004. Iron Age Communities in Britain: an account of England, Scotland and Wales from the seventh century BC until the Roman conquest, Routledge, London

Cunliffe, B and Davenport, P 1985. *The Temple of Sulis Minerva at Bath*, Oxford University Committee for Archaeology Monogr 7, Oxford

Cunnington, M 1923. The Early Iron Age inhabited site at All Cannings Cross Farm, Wiltshire, George Simpson & Co, Devizes

Demoule, J-P 2002. 'Rescue archaeology: the French way', *Public Archaeol*, **2** (3), 170–7, online <https://doi.org/10.1179/pua.2002.2.3.170> (accessed 7 January 2020)

Dent, J 1983. 'The impact of Roman rule on native society in the territory of the Parisi', *Britannia*, **14**, 35–44, online <http://dx.doi.org/10.2307/526339> (accessed 13 December 2019)

Dungworth, D 1998. 'Mystifying Roman nails: *clavus annalis, defixiones* and m*inkisi*', in C Forcey, J Hawthorne and R Witcher (eds), *TRAC 97: proceedings of the seventh annual theoretical Roman archaeology*, 148–59, Oxbow Books, Oxford

Edgeworth, M 2011. *The Archaeology of Flow*, Bloomsbury Academic, Bristol

Edmonds, M 1995. *Stone Tools and Society*, Batsford, London

Edmonds, M 1999. Ancestral Geographies of the Neolithic: landscapes, monuments and memory, Routledge, London/New York

Elgee, F and Elgee, H 1933. *The Archaeology of Yorkshire*, Methuen, London

Ellison, A 1980. 'Deverel-Rimbury urn cemeteries: the evidence for social organisation', in J Barrett and R Bradley (eds), *Settlement and Society in the British Later Bronze Age: part 1*, 115–26, BAR Brit Ser 83, BAR Publishing, Oxford

Empson, M 2013. Land and Labour: Marxism, ecology and human history, Bookmarks, London

English Heritage 2000. *Power of Place: the future of the historic environment*, English Heritage, London

English Heritage 2012. Strategic Stone Study Database, online <http://www.bgs.ac.uk/mineralsUK/buildingStones/StrategicStoneStudy/EH_project.html> (accessed 13 December 2019)

Esmonde-Cleary, A 2013. *The Roman West, AD 200–500: an archaeological study*, Cambridge University Press, Cambridge

Evans, D 2002. 'Campus 3 development, University of York, York: report on an archaeological desk top study', unpublished YAT report 2002/58, YAT, York

Evans, J 1985. 'Aspects of later Roman pottery assemblages in northern England', unpublished PhD thesis, University of Bradford

Evans, J 1993. 'Pottery function and finewares in the Roman north', *J Roman Pottery Stud*, **6**, 95–119

Evans, J 2004. 'The pottery vessels', in H Cool, J Bond and L Allason-Jones (eds), *The Roman Cemetery at Brougham, Cumbria: excavations 1966–67*, 333–64, Society for the Promotion of Roman Studies, London

Faro Convention 2005. *Council of Europe Framework Convention on the Value of Cultural Heritage for Society*, online <https://www.coe.int/en/web/conventions/full-list/-/conventions/treaty/199> (accessed 13 December 2019)

FAS 2003. 'Heslington Hill, Heslington: a post-excavation report', unpublished Field Archaeology Specialists report

Fell, D 2006. 'A window on the prehistory of Yorkshire: a study in the application of geographical information systems for mapping prehistoric artefact distributions within their natural and archaeological environments', unpublished Masters dissertation, University of York

Fenton, A 1978. *The Northern Isles: Orkney and Shetland*, John Donald Publishers, Edinburgh

Fenton-Thomas, C 2005. *The Forgotten Landscapes of the Yorkshire Wolds*, Tempus Publishing, Stroud

Fenton-Thomas, C 2011. Where Sky and Yorkshire and Water Meet: the story of the Melton landscape from prehistory to the present, On-Site Archaeology, York

Franconi, T (ed) 2017. Fluvial Landscapes of the Roman World, *Journal of Roman Archaeology* Supp Ser 104, JRA, Oxford

Fyfe, R, Brown, A and Coles, B 2003. 'Mesolithic to Bronze Age vegetation change and human activity in the Exe Valley, Devon, UK', *Proc Prehist Soc*, **69**, 161–81, online <http://dx.doi.org/10.1017/S0079497X00001298> (accessed 13 December 2019)

Garrow, D 2012. 'Odd deposits and average practice: a critical history of the concept of structured deposition', *Archaeol Dialogues* **19** (2), 85–115, online <http://dx.doi.org/10.1017/S1380203812000141> (accessed 13 December 2019)

Garrow, D, Beadsmoore, E and Knight, M 2005. 'Pit clusters and the temporality of occupation: an earlier Neolithic site at Kilverstone, Thetford, Norfolk', *Proc Prehist Soc*, **71**, 139–57, online <http://dx.doi.org/10.1017/ S0079497X00000980> (accessed 13 December 2019)

Gerrard, J 2007. 'Rethinking the small pig horizon at York Minster', *Oxford J Archaeol*, **26** (3), 303–7

Giles, M 2007. 'Good fences make good neighbours? Exploring the ladder enclosures of late Iron Age East Yorkshire', in C Haselgrove and T Moore (eds), *The Later Iron Age in Britain and Beyond*, 235–49, Oxbow Books, Oxford

Giles, M 2012. A Forged Glamour: landscape, identity and material culture in the Iron Age, Windgather, Oxford

Gillam, J and Daniels, C 1961. 'The Roman mausoleum on Shorden Brae, Beaufront, Corbridge, Northumberland', *Archaeol Aeliana*, **4** (39), 37–62

Giorgi, J 2004. 'The charred plant remains', in P Neal and R Fraser, 'A Romano-British enclosed farmstead at Billingley Drive, Thurnscoe, South Yorkshire', *Yorkshire Archaeol J*, **76**, 6–92

Grant, A 1989. 'Animals in Roman Britain', in M Todd (ed), *Research on Roman Britain 1960–89*, 135–46, Britannia Monogr 11, Society for the Promotion of Roman Studies, London

Griffiths, S 2014a. 'A Bayesian radiocarbon chronology of the Early Neolithic of Yorkshire and Humberside', *Archaeol J*, **171** (1), 2–29, online <https://www.tandfonline.com/doi/pdf/10.1080/00665983.2014.11078260> (accessed 7 January 2020)

Griffiths, S 2014b. 'Points in time', *Oxford J Archaeol*, **33**, 221–43, online <http://dx.doi.org/doi:10.1111/ojoa.12035> (accessed 13 December 2019)

Groot, M 2008. 'Surplus production of animal products for the Roman army in a rural settlement in the Dutch

River Area', in S Stallibrass and R Thomas (eds), *Feeding the Roman Army: the archaeology of production and supply in NW Europe*, 83–98, Oxbow Books, Oxford

Gwilt, A 2006. 'The querns', in M Millett (ed), *Shiptonthorpe, East Yorkshire: archaeological studies of a Romano-British roadside settlement*, 206–20, YAS Roman Antiq Sect, East Riding Archaeological Society, Leeds

Halkon, P 1992. 'Romano-British face pots from Holme-on-Spalding Moor and Shiptonthorpe, East Yorkshire', *Britannia* **23**, 222–8, online <http://dx.doi.org/10.2307/526112> (accessed 13 December 2019)

Halkon, P 2013. *The Parisi: Britons and Romans in eastern Yorkshire*, The History Press, Stroud

Hall, A, Kenward, H and Williams, D 1980. *Environmental Evidence from Roman Deposits in Skeldergate*, Archaeology of York 14, CBA, London

Hamilton, M and Whittle, A 1999. 'Grooved ware of the Avebury area: styles, contexts, meanings', in R Cleal and A MacSween (eds), *Grooved Ware in Britain and Ireland*, 36–47, Oxbow Books, Oxford

Harding, D 2009. The Iron Age Round-house: later prehistoric building in Britain and Ireland, Oxford University Press, Oxford

Heslop, D and Cruse, J 2012. 'Querns', in J Richardson (ed), *Iron Age and Roman Settlement Activity at Newbridge Quarry, Pickering, N Yorks*, 54–6, WYAS Publ 12, WYAS, Leeds

Hillman, G 1981. 'Reconstructing crop husbandry practices from charred remains of crops', in R Mercer (ed), *Farming Practice in British Prehistory*, 123–62 , Edinburgh University Press, Edinburgh

Hillman, G 1982. 'Evidence for spelting malt', in R Leech (ed), *Excavations at Catsgore 1970–1973: a Romano-British village*, 137–40, Western Archaeol Trust Excav Monogr 2, Western Archaeological Trust, Bristol

Hilton, R 1990. *Class Conflict and the Crisis of Feudalism: essays in medieval social history*, Verso, London

Historic England 2006. *Management of Research Projects in the Historic Environment: the MoRPHE project managers' guide*, Historic England, London

Holden, T and Hastie, M 2001. 'Manor Farm: the charred plant remains', in Roberts *et al* 2001, 221–2

Howell, K 2001. 'Swillington Common', in Roberts *et al* 2001, 47–68

Huntley, J 1995. Plant and Vertebrate Remains from Archaeological Sites in Northern England: data reviews and future directions, Architect Archaeol Soc Durham and Northumb, Durham

Huntley, J 1996. 'The biological material', in P Busby, P Evans, J Huntley and P Wilson, 'A pottery kiln at Catterick', *Britannia* **27**, 293–7

Huntley, J 2002. 'Environmental archaeology: Mesolithic to Roman period', in C Brooks, A Harding and R Daniels (eds), *Past, Present and Future: the archaeology of Northern England*, 79–96, Architect Archaeol Soc Durham and Northumb Res Rep 5, Durham

Hurcombe, L 2008. 'Organics from inorganics: using experimental archaeology as a research tool for studying perishable material culture', *World Archaeol* **40** (1), 83–115

Ingold, T 1993. 'The temporality of the landscape', *World Archaeol* **25** (2), 152–74

Inman, R, Brown, D, Goddard, R and Spratt, D 1985. 'Roxby Iron Age settlement and the Iron Age in north-east Yorkshire', *Proc Prehist Soc*, **51**, 181–213

Innes, J and Blackford, J 2003. 'Yorkshire's palaeoenvironmental resource', in T Manby, S Moorhouse and P Ottaway (eds), *The Archaeology of Yorkshire: an assessment at the beginning of the 21st century*, 25–30, YAS Occas Paper 3, YAS, Leeds

Isbister, A 2000. 'Burnished haematite and pigment production', in A Ritchie (ed), *Neolithic Orkney in its European context*, 191–5, Orkney Heritage Society Cambridge, McDonald Institute for Archaeology, Cambridge

Jackson, S, Lennox, R, Neal, C, Roskams, S, Hearle, J and Brown, J 2014. 'Engaging communities in the 'Big Society': what impact is the localism agenda having on community archaeology?' *Historic Environment: Policy & Practice*, **5** (1), 74–88 online <http://dx.doi.org/10.1179/1756750513Z.00000000043> (accessed 13 December 2019)

James, E 2008. 'The rise and function of the concept "Late Antiquity"', *J Late Antiquity*, **1** (1), 20–30

James, R and Nasmyth-Jones, R 1992. 'The occurrence of cervical fractures in victims of judicial hanging', *Forensic Sci Int*, **54** (1), 81–91, online <https://doi.org/10.1016/0379-0738(92)90083-9> (accessed 13 December 2019)

Jarvis, R, Bendelow, V, Bradley, R, Carroll, D, Furness, R, Kilgour, I and King, S 1984. *Soils and Their Use in Northern England*, Bull 10, Soil Survey of England and Wales, Harpenden

Jones, M 1981. 'The development of crop husbandry', in M Jones and G Dimbleby (eds), *The Environment of Man: the Iron Age to the Anglo-Saxon period*, 95–127, BAR Brit Ser 87, BAR Publishing, Oxford

Jones, R, Clarke, S and Rush, P undated. 'Lingcroft Farm: material change and social continuity: The Iron Age and Romano-British community at Lingcroft, Naburn, Near York', unpublished typescript, Department of Archaeological Sciences, University of Bradford

Kendal, T 2003. 'Campus 3 development, University of York, York: report on archaeological fieldwalking', unpublished YAT report 2003/22

Kenward, H and Williams, D 1979. *Biological Evidence from the Roman Warehouses in Coney Street*, Archaeology of York 14 (The past environment of York), CBA, London

Laurie, T 2003. 'Researching the prehistory of Wensleydale, Swaledale and Teesdale', in T Manby, S Moorhouse and P Ottaway (eds), *The Archaeology of Yorkshire: an assessment at the beginning of the 21st century*, 223–53, YAS Occas Paper 3, YAS, Leeds

Lawton, I 1993. *Appletree Farm, 1987–1992: an Ebor Ware kiln site*, YAS Bull 10, YAS, Leeds

Leary, R with Evans, J, Hartley, K and Ward, M 2008. 'The Iron Age and Romano-British pottery', in J Richardson (ed), *The Late Iron Age and Romano-British Rural Landscape of Gunhills, Armthorpe, South Yorkshire*, 25–45, WYAS Publ 10, WYAS, Leeds

Leary, R 2009. 'The Romano-British pottery', in M Rose and J Richardson (eds), 'Hensall Quarry, Hensall, North Yorkshire', 12–26, unpublished report

Leary, R 2011. 'Romano-British pottery', in Richardson 2011, 4–14

Leary, R 2013a. 'The Romano-British pottery', in L Martin, J Richardson and I Roberts (eds), Iron Age and Roman Settlements at Wattle Syke: archaeological investigations during the A1 Bramham to Wetherby upgrading scheme, 120–54, Yorkshire Archaeol 11, WYAS, Leeds

Leary, R 2013b. 'The Romano-British pottery', in R Gregory, P Daniel, F Brown, H Anderson-Whymark and A Staewardson (eds), *Early Landscapes of West and North Yorkshire: archaeological investigation along the Asselby to Pannal natural gas pipeline 2007–8*, 176–90, Oxford Archaeology North, Lancaster

Leary, R 2016. 'Romano-British pottery', in G Glover, P Flintoft and R Moore (eds), *'A mersshy contree called Holdernesse': excavations on the route of a national grid pipeline in Holderness, East Yorkshire*, 174–200, Archaeopress, Oxford

Leary, R 2017. 'Romano-British pottery', in C Ambrey, D Fell, R Fraser, S Ross, G Speed and P Wood (eds), *A Roman Roadside Settlement at Healam Bridge: the Iron Age to early medieval evidence: Vol 2, artefacts*, NAA Monogr 3, NAA, Barnard Castle

Leary, R unpublished a. 'Roman Pottery from Marton, Site 26'

Leary, R unpublished b. 'Roman Pottery from Green Hammerton'

Leary, R unpublished c. 'Roman Pottery from Stockton-on-the-Forest'

Leary, R unpublished d. 'Report on the Romano-British pottery from excavations at Marton to Acomb Landing', unpublished report for NAA

Lowther, A 1976. 'Romano-British chimney-pots and finials', *Antiq J*, **56**, 35–48 online <https://doi.org/10.1017/S0003581500019612> (accessed 13 December 2019)

MacGregor, A 1976. *Finds from a Roman Sewer System and an Adjacent Building in Church Street*, YAT fascicule 17/1 , CBA, York

MacGregor, A, Mainman, A and Rogers, N 1999. Craft, Industry and Everyday Life: bone, antler, ivory and horn from Anglo-Scandinavian and medieval York, Archaeol York ser 17 (2), CBA, York

McKinley, J 1997. 'Bronze Age 'barrows' and funerary rites and rituals of cremation', *Proc Prehist Soc*, **63**, 129–45, online <https://doi.org/10.1017/S0079497X00002401> (accessed 13 December 2019)

McKinley, J 2004. 'Compiling a skeletal inventory: cremated human bone', in M Brickley and J McKinley (eds), *Guidelines to the Standards for Recording Human Remains*, 9–13, IFA Paper 7, Institute of Field Archaeologists, Southampton and Reading

MacNab, N 2004. 'Heslington East, Heslington, York: a report on an archaeological evaluation', unpublished YAT report 2004/23

McWhirr, A 1979. *Roman Brick and Tile: studies in manufacture, distribution, and use in the Western Empire*, BAR Int Ser 68, BAR Publishing, Oxford

Manby, T 2003. 'The Upper Palaeolithic and Mesolithic periods in Yorkshire', in Manby *et al* 2003, 31–3

Manby, T, Moorhouse, S and Ottaway, P (eds) 2003. *The Archaeology of Yorkshire: an assessment at the beginning of the 21st century*, YAS Occas Paper 3, YAS, Leeds

Manby, T, King, A and Vyner, B 2003. 'The Neolithic and Bronze Ages: a time of early agriculture', in Manby *et al* 2003, 35–116

Manning, W 1985. Catalogue of the Romano-British Iron Tools, Fittings and Weapons in the British Museum, British Museum, London

MAP 1996. 'Germany Beck, Fulford: archaeological sample excavations, interim report', YORM1996.352, MAP Archaeological Consultancy

Mason, I and McComish, J 2003. 'Campus 3 development, University of York, Zone E: report on an archaeological desk-top study', unpublished YAT report 2003/29

Mattingly, D 2007. An Imperial Possession: Britain in the Roman Empire, 54 BC–AD 409, Penguin Books, London

Mays, S 2000. 'The archaeology and history of infanticide, and its occurrence in earlier British populations', in J Sofaer Derevensk (ed), *Children and Material Culture*,

180–90, Routledge, London

Millett, M (ed) 2006. *Shiptonthorpe, East Yorkshire: archaeological studies of a Romano-British roadside settlement*, YAS Roman Antiq Sect, East Riding Archaeological Society, Leeds

Millett, M and Gowland, R 2015. 'Infant and child burials rites in Roman Britain: a study from East Yorkshire', *Britannia* **46**, 171–89, online <https://doi.org/10.1017/S0068113X15000100> (accessed 13 December 2019)

Milner, N, Taylor, B, Conneller, C and Schadla-Hall, T (eds) 2018. *Star Carr: a persistent place in a changing world*, White Rose University Press, York

Ministry of Housing, Communities and Local Government 2019. *National Planning Policy Framework*, online <https://assets.publishing.service.gov.uk/government/uploads/system/uploads/attachment_data/file/6077/2116950.pdf> (accessed 17 December 2019)

Monaghan, J 1997. *Roman Pottery from York*, Archaeology of York 16/8, CBA, York

Monk 1987. 'Archaeobotanical studies at Poundbury', in S Davies and A Ellison (eds), *Excavations at Poundbury, Dorchester, Dorset 1966–1982. Vol 1: the settlements*, Dorset County Museum, Dorchester

Morris, F 2010. 'North Sea and Channel connectivity during the Late Iron Age and Roman period (175/150 BC–AD 409)', unpublished PhD thesis, Oxford University

Mortimer, C and Starley, D 1995. 'Ferrous and non-ferrous metalworking', in J Coles and S Minnitt (eds), *Industrious and Fairly Civilized: the Glastonbury lake village*, 138–43, University of Exeter Press, Exeter

Murray, J 1990. 'The carbonised plant remains from selected deposits', in S Wrathmell and A Nicholson (eds), *Dalton Parlours: Iron Age settlement and Roman villa*, 18–94, WYAS, Leeds

Natural England 2012. *NCA Profile: Vale of York*, online <https://doi.org/http://publications.naturalengland.org.uk/publication/3488888> (accessed 17 December 2019)

Neal, C and Roskams, S 2013. 'Authority and community: reflections on archaeological practice at Heslington East, York', *Historic Environment: Policy & Practice* **4** (2), 139–55

O'Connor, S, Esam, A, Al-Sabah, S, Anwar, D, *et al* 2011. 'Exceptional preservation of a prehistoric human brain from Heslington, Yorkshire, UK', *J Archaeol Sci* **38** (7), 1,641–54, online <https://doi.org/10.1016/j.jas.2011.02.030> (accessed 17 December 2019)

O'Connor, T 1988. *Bones from the General Accident Site, Tanner Row*, Archaeology of York 15 fascicule 2 , CBA, London

O'Connor, T and Evans, J 2005. *Environmental Archaeology: principles and methods*, Sutton, Stroud

Oestigaard, T 2013. 'Cremations in culture and cosmology', in Stutz and Tarlow 2013, online <https://www.oxfordhandbooks.com/view/10.1093/oxfordhb/9780199569069.001.0001/oxfordhb-9780199569069-e-27> (accessed 17 December 2019)

Oswald, A and Pollington, M 2012. 'Commonplace activities: Walmgate Stray, an urban common in York', *Landscapes* **13** (2), 45–74

Oswald, A, Goodchild, H and Fitton, T 2016. 'Earthwork and geophysical surveys of Siward's How and its environs, Heslington, in 2015–16', unpublished archive report, Department of Archaeology at University of York, York

Oswald, A, Goodchild H and Roberts, D undated. '*Veni, non vidi, sed vici*? A positive outcome from a sceptical re-assessment of York's "Roman Road 1"', unpublished report, University of York

Ottaway, P 1993. *Roman York*, English Heritage and Batsford, London

Ottaway, P 2011a. 'Belle Vue Street', in P Ottaway, *Archaeology in the Environs of Roman York: excavations 1976–2005*, 258–69, YAT fascicule 6/2, CBA, York

Ottaway, P 2011b. 'Heslington East research objectives', unpublished, Heslington archive

Ottaway, P 2013. *Roman Yorkshire: people, culture and landscape*, Blackthorn Press, Pickering

Parker, A, Goudie, A, Anderson, D and Mark R 2002. 'A review of the mid-Holocene elm decline in the British Isles', *Prog Phys Geog*, **26** (1), 1–45, online <https://doi.org/10.1191/0309133302pp323ra> (accessed 17 December 2019)

Parkins, H 1997. *Roman Urbanism: beyond the consumer city*, Routledge, London

Perring, D 1999. 'Heslington campus, City of York', unpublished report, University of York

Perring, D and Whyman, M 2002. *Town and Country in England: frameworks for archaeological research*, English Heritage Res Rep 134, CBA, York

Phillips, D and Heywood, B 1995. *Excavations at York Minster: Vol 1*, RCHME, London

Philpott, R 1991. *Burial Practices in Roman Britain*, BAR Brit Ser 219, BAR Publishing, Oxford

Pollard, J 1999. '"These places have their moments": thoughts on settlement practices in the British Neolithic', in J Brück and M Goodman (eds), *Making Places in the Prehistoric World: themes in settlement archaeology*, 76–93, UCL Press, London

Precious, B and Vince, A 1999. 'Pottery from West Lilling (Site BPTSEP 169): assessment report', AVAC Rep

1999/019, Alan Vince Archaeological Consultancy, York

Price, J 1988. 'Romano-British glass bangles from East Yorkshire', in J Price and P Wilson (eds), *Recent Research in Roman Yorkshire*, 339–66, BAR Brit Ser 193, BAR Publishing, Oxford

Rackham, O 1990. *Trees and Woodland in the British Landscape*, Dent, London

Radley, G 1974. 'The prehistory of the Vale of York', *Yorkshire Archaeol J*, **46**, 10–22

Rahtz, P 1974. *Rescue Archaeology*, Penguin, Harmondsworth

Rahtz, P and Watts, L 2004. *Wharram: a study of settlement on the Yorkshire Wolds*, University of York, York

Ramm, H 1966a. 'The site of Siward's How, York', *Yorkshire Archaeol J*, **41**, 584–7

Ramm, H 1966b. 'The Green Dykes: a forgotten York earthwork', *Yorkshire Archaeol J*, **41**, 587–90

Ramm, H 1978. *The Parisi*, Duckworth, London

RCHM(E) 1962. *An Inventory of the Historical Monuments in the City of York. Vol 1: Eburacum, Roman York*, HMSO, London

Reeves, B undated. *27 Lawrence Street*, publication currently embargoed: apply to YAT for permissions

Richardson, J 2001. 'Conclusions', in Roberts *et al* 2001, 246–8

Richardson, J (ed) 2011. *Rothwell Haigh, Rothwell, Leeds: excavation report*, WYAS, Leeds, online <http://archae-ologydataservice.ac.uk/archiveDS/archiveDownload?t=arch-941-1/dissemination/pdf/archaeol11-92831_1.pdf>

Richardson, J and Vyner, B 2011. 'An exotic Early Bronze Age funerary assemblage from Stanbury, West Yorkshire', *Proc Prehist Soc*, **77**, 49–63, online <https://doi.org/10.1017/S0079497X00000621> (accessed 17 December 2019)

Rigby, V and Ambers, J 2004. *Pots in Pits: the British Museum East Yorkshire Settlements Project 1988–1992*, East Riding Archaeologist 11, East Riding Archaeology Society, Hull

Roberts, I 2005. *Ferrybridge Henge: the ritual landscape*, Yorkshire Archaeol 10, WYAS, Leeds

Roberts, I, Burgess, A and Berg D (eds) 2001. *A New Link to the Past: the archaeological landscape of the M1-A1 link road*, WYAS, Leeds

Roberts, I, Deegan, A and Berg, D 2010. *Understanding the Cropmark Landscapes of the Magnesian Limestone: the archaeology of the magnesian limestone and its margins in South and West Yorkshire and parts of North Yorkshire and north Nottinghamshire*, WYAS, Leeds

Robbins, L 1963. *Higher Education: report of the committee appointed by the Prime Minister under the chairmanship of Lord Robbins, 1961–63*, HMSO, London

Romankiewicz, T 2018. 'Room for ideas: tracing non-domestic roundhouses', *Antiq J*, **98**, 17–42, online <https://doi.org/10.1017/S0003581518000148> (accessed 13 December 2019)

Ronayne, M 2008. 'The state we're in on the eve of world archaeological congress (WAC) 6: archaeology in Ireland vs corporate takeover and a reply from University College Dublin', *Public Archaeol*, **7** (2), 114–31, online <https://doi.org/10.1179/175355308X330016> (accessed 17 December 2019)

Roskams, S 1996. 'Urban transition in early medieval Britain: the case of York', in N Christie and S Loseby (eds), *Towns in Transition: urban evolution in Late Antiquity and the early middle ages*, 159–83, Scholar, Aldershot

Roskams, S 1999. 'The hinterlands of Roman York: present patterns and future strategies', in H Hurst (ed), *The Coloniae of Roman Britain: new studies and a review*, 45–72, Journal of Roman Archaeology Supp Ser 36, JRA, Oxford

Roskams, S 2001. *Excavation*, Cambridge University Press, Cambridge

Roskams, S 2015. 'Book review: *The Parisi: Britons and Romans in eastern Yorkshire* by P Halkon, History Press, Stroud, 2013; *Roman Yorkshire: people, culture and landscape* by P Ottaway, Blackthorn Press, Pickering, 2013', *Britannia*, **46**, 433–5, online <https://doi.org/10.1017/S0068113X15000288> (accessed 17 December 2019)

Roskams, S 2020. 'The post-excavation analysis and archiving of outputs from complex multi-period landscape investigations: the example of Heslington East, York', *Internet Archaeology*

Roskams, S 2019. 'The limitation of water flow and the limitations of postmodernism', *Theoretical Roman Archaeology Journal*, **2**(1), 6, online https://traj.openlibhums.org/articles/10.16995/traj.371/ (accessed 8 April 2020)

Roskams, S, Neal, C, Richardson, J and Leary R 2013. 'A late Roman well at Heslington East, York: ritual or routine practices?', *Internet Archaeol*, **34**, online <https://doi.org/10.11141/ia.34.5> (accessed 17 December 2019)

Schlanger, N and Aitchison, K (eds) 2010. *Archaeology and the Global Economic Crisis: multiple impacts, possible solutions*, Culture Lab Editions, Tervuren, Belgium

Scott, L 1951. 'Corn-drying kilns', *Antiquity*, **25**, 196–208

Schofield, J 2013. *Who needs experts? Counter-mapping*

cultural heritage, Ashgate, Farnham

Sheridan, A and Davis, M 2002. 'Investigating jet and jet-like artefacts from prehistoric Scotland: the National Museums of Scotland project', *Antiquity*, **76** (293), 812–25

Short, R 1994. 'The survey of Siward's How, York', unpublished undergraduate dissertation, University of York, held in York HER

Simmons, E 2013. 'Charred plant remains and charred wood remains', in D Pinnock (ed), *The Romans at Nostell Priory: excavations at the new visitor car park in 2009*, 62–6, On-Site Archaeology Ltd, York

Smith, A 1981. 'The Neolithic', in I Simmons and M Tooley (eds), *The Environment in Prehistory*, 125–209, Duckworth, London

Smith, I 1974. 'The jet bead from Fengate, 1972', in F Pryor (ed), *Excavation of Fengate, Peterborough, England: the first report*, 40–2, Royal Ontario Museum, Toronto, Canada

Smith, L 2006. *The Uses of Heritage*, Routledge, London

Spall, C and Toop N 2005. *Blue Bridge Lane and Fishergate House, York: report on excavations July 2000–July 2002*, APC Monogr Ser, online <http://www.archaeologicalplanningconsultancy.co.uk/mono/001/index.html>

Spall, C and Toop, N 2008. 'Before *Eoforwic*: new light on York in the 6th–7th centuries', *Medieval Archaeol*, **52** (1), 1–25, online <https://doi.org/10.1179/174581708x 335422> (accessed 17 December 2019)

Spratling, M 1979. 'The debris of metalworking', in G Wainwright and H Bowen (eds), *Gussage All Saints: an Iron Age settlement in Dorset*, 125–49, HMSO, London

Spratt, D (ed) 1993. *Prehistoric and Roman Archaeology of North-East Yorkshire*, CBA Res Rep 87, CBA, London

Stead, I 1980. *Rudston Roman Villa*, YAS, Leeds

Stead, I 1991. *Iron Age Cemeteries in East Yorkshire: excavations at Burton Fleming, Rudston, Garton-on-the Wolds and Kirkburn*, English Heritage, London

Stevens, C and Fuller, D 2012. 'Did Neolithic farming fail? The case for a Bronze Age agricultural revolution in the British Isles', *Antiquity*, **86**, 707–22

Stevens, C and Fuller, D 2015. 'Alternative strategies to agriculture: the evidence for climatic shocks and cereal declines during the British Neolithic and Bronze Age (a reply to Bishop)', *World Archaeol*, **47** (5), 856–75, online <https://doi.org/10.1080/00438243.2015.1087 330> (accessed 17 December 2019)

Stirk, D 2006. 'South Farm, Kexby: archaeological evaluation' unpublished On-Site Archaeology Rep OSA05EV14, On-Site Archaeology, York

Stoertz, C 1997. *Ancient Landscapes of the Yorkshire Wolds: aerial photographic transcription and analysis*, RCHME, Swindon

Stutz, L and Tarlow, S (eds) 2013. *The Oxford Handbook of the Archaeology of Death and Burial*, Oxford University Press, Oxford, online <https://doi.org/10.1093/oxfordhb/9780199569069.013.0001> (accessed 17 December 2019)

Swan, V 1992. 'Legio VI and its men: African legionaries in Britain', *J Roman Pottery Stud*, **5**, 1–33

Swan, V and Monaghan, J 1993. 'Head pots: a North African tradition in Roman York', *Yorkshire Archaeol J*, **65**, 21–38

Thurnham, J 1849. 'Description of an ancient tumular cemetery, probably of the Anglo-Saxon period, at Lamel Hill, near York', *Archaeol J*, **6**, 27–39

Tomlin, R 1988. 'The curse tablets', in B Cunliffe (ed), *The Temple of Sulis Minerva at Bath. Vol 2: the finds from the sacred spring*, 59–277, Oxford University Committee for Archaeology Monogr 16, Oxford University Press, Oxford

van der Veen, M 1989. 'Charred grain assemblages from Roman period corn dryers in Britain', *Archaeol J*, **146**, 302–19

van der Veen, M 1992. *Husbandry Regimes: an archaeobotanical study of farming in Northern England, 1000 BC–AD 500*, Collis Publications, Sheffield

van der Veen, M 1996. 'The plant macrofossils from Dragonby', in J May (ed), *Dragonby: report on excavations at an Iron Age and Romano-British settlement in North Lincolnshire*, 197–211, Oxbow Books, Oxford

van der Veen, M 2016. 'Arable farming, horticulture and food: expansion, innovation and diversity in Roman Britain', in M Millett, L Revell and A Moore (eds), *The Oxford Handbook of Roman Britain*, 807–33, Oxford University Press, Oxford

van der Veen, M and O'Connor, T 1998. 'The expansion of agricultural production in late Iron Age and Roman Britain', in J Bayley (ed), *Science in Archaeology*, 127–43, English Heritage, London

Vyner, B 2007. 'A great north route in Neolithic and Bronze Age Yorkshire', *Landscapes*, **8**, 69–84

Vyner, B 2013. 'Early Bronze Age pottery from Poppleton Bar, York', unpublished report OSA 12 EV17, On-Site Archaeology, York

Vyner, B 2018. 'The prehistory of York', *Yorkshire Archaeol J*, **90** (1), 13–28, online <https://doi.org/10.1080/00844 276.2018.1483060> (accessed 17 December 2019)

Walton Rogers, P 2007. *Cloth and Clothing in Early Anglo-Saxon England, AD 450–700*, CBA Res Rep 145, CBA, York

Webley, L, Bats, M, *et al* (eds) 2012. *Development-led Archaeology in Northwest Europe: proceedings of a* round table at the University of Leicester, 19–21 November 2009, Oxbow Books, Oxford

Weiss-Krejci, E 2013. 'The unburied dead', in Stutz and Tarlow 2013, online <https://www.oxfordhandbooks.com/view/10.1093/oxfordhb/9780199569069.001.0001/oxfordhb-9780199569069-e-16> (accessed 17 December 2019)

Wellbeloved, C 1842. *Eburacum, or York under the Romans*, Longmans, York

Westell, W 1931. 'A Romano-British cemetery at Baldock, Herts', *Archaeol J*, **88**, 247–301

Whittle, A, Healy, F and Bayliss, A 2011. *Gathering Time:*

dating the Early Neolithic enclosures of southern Britain and Ireland, Oxbow Books, Oxford

Whittaker, C 1995. 'Do theories of the ancient city matter?', in T Cornell and K Lomas (eds), *Urban Society in Roman Italy*, 9–26, UCL Press, London

Whyman, M and Howard, A 2005. *Archaeology and Landscape in the Vale of York*, YAT, York

Wood, I 2008. 'Barbarians, historians and the construction of national identities', *J Late Antiquity* **1** (1), 61–81

Wrathmell, S and Nicholson, D 1990. *Dalton Parlours: Iron Age settlement and Roman villa*, WYAS, Wakefield

Index